JOSEPH CONRAD'S TEXTS AND INTERTEXTS

IN HONOUR OF PROFESSOR WIESŁAW KRAJKA

CONRAD: EASTERN AND WESTERN PERSPECTIVES
Editor: Wiesław Krajka

VOLUME XXXII

JOSEPH CONRAD'S TEXTS AND INTERTEXTS

IN HONOUR OF PROFESSOR WIESŁAW KRAJKA

Edited with an Introduction by
EWA KUJAWSKA-LIS

MARIA CURIE-SKŁODOWSKA UNIVERSITY PRESS, LUBLIN
COLUMBIA UNIVERSITY PRESS, NEW YORK

2023

Cover Design
Marta and Zdzisław Kwiatkowscy
Agnieszka Muchowska

Typesetting
Idealit

ISBN 978-83-227-9677-1

Dofinansowano ze środków Ministerstwa Edukacji i Nauki
Publication financed by Ministry of Education and Science, Poland

Doskonała Nauka

MARIA CURIE-SKŁODOWSKA UNIVERSITY PRESS
ul. Idziego Radziszewskiego 11
20-031 Lublin, Poland
tel. (81) 537 53 04
www.wydawnictwo.umcs.eu
e-mail: sekretariat@wydawnictwo.umcs.lublin.pl

Sales Department: tel./fax 81 537 53 02
e-mail: wydawnictwo@umcs.eu

Printed by
Drukarnia “Akapit”, ul. Węglowa 3, 20-481 Lublin

TABLE OF CONTENTS

ABBREVIATIONS

I. Conrad's Works

AF	*Almayer's Folly*
AG	*The Arrow of Gold*
C	*Chance*
LE	*Last Essays*
LJ	*Lord Jim*
MS	*The Mirror of the Sea*
N	*Nostromo*
NLL	*Notes on Life and Letters*
NN	*The Nigger of the "Narcissus"*
OI	*An Outcast of the Islands*
PR	*A Personal Record*
Res	*The Rescue*
SA	*The Secret Agent*
SL	*The Shadow-Line*
TH	*Tales of Hearsay*
TLS	*'Twixt Land and Sea*
TS	*Typhoon and Other Stories*
TU	*Tales of Unrest*
UWE	*Under Western Eyes*
V	*Victory*
WT	*Within the Tides*
YS	*Youth: A Narrative, and Two Other Stories*

All references to Conrad's works are to the Dent Uniform Edition (1923–1928) or its reprints and other editions with identical pagination (e.g. Dent, 1946; Oxford University Press's World's Classics Edition).

II. Conrad's Letters

CL	*The Collected Letters of Joseph Conrad*. Gen. ed. Laurence Davies. 9 vols. Cambridge UP, 1983–2008.

ACKNOWLEDGEMENT

I would like to express my gratitude to Professors Chris Cairney, Peter Vernon, and David Schauffler for their invaluable suggestions for polishing the style of contributions by non-native speakers of English. Their diligent work was greatly appreciated by the authors; their comments extended beyond linguistic matters and their intellectual input contributed to the essays' final forms. They enthusiastically offered their time and availability to help in this project. On behalf of all the authors, I would also like to thank the Organizing Committee of the Seventh International Joseph Conrad Conference organized by the Institute of Modern Languages and Literatures, Maria Curie-Skłodowska University, Lublin, Poland, on 20–23 June 2022, particularly Anne Mydla and Jacek Mydla, who worked hard to make the event happen, and arranged the presentations of papers in absentia when necessary. Given the circumstances in which the conference was organized, in a post-pandemic time and while military conflict raged in a neighbouring country, their efforts in helping Conradians to gather were truly praiseworthy. Additionally, the authors are thankful to Professor Mark D. Larabee, the Executive Editor of *Joseph Conrad Today*, and Professor Wiesław Krajka, the Editor of *Conrad: Eastern and Western Perspectives* series, who generously made available critical resources on Conrad's fiction and thus helped to extend the analytical scope of the contributions. I personally would like to thank Professor Wiesław Krajka for his patient guidance in the publishing process. Finally, I am grateful to the authors for their constructive and harmonious collaboration, which has been indispensable to the preparation of this volume.

Ewa Kujawska-Lis

Ewa Kujawska-Lis,
University of Warmia and Mazury,
Olsztyn, Poland

Wiesław Krajka: An Appreciation

"Tom Lingard was a master, a lover, a servant of the sea. The sea took him young" (*OI* 13) – this description of one of Conrad's characters could be adapted to refer to a Conrad scholar: "Wiesław Krajka was a master, a lover, a servant of Conrad. Joseph Conrad took him young." If one Conradian word were to characterize Professor Krajka, it would definitely be *fidelity*: irrespective of his varied academic interests, including theory of literature and comparative literature, he remains faithful to his favourite author, continuously studying his life and oeuvre in various contexts; both closely examining the textual material, and placing Conrad's works in broader intertextual and intercultural perspectives. And the output of this life's adventure, if not a love affair, yet makes him one of the most eminent Polish Conradians.

The beginning of Professor Krajka's academic career in 1971 occurred when he earned an MA in English Studies and began to work at Maria Curie-Skłodowska University (UMCS) in Lublin, his *alma mater* which he has never left. This coincided with the publication of the first complete edition in Polish of Conrad's collected works, edited by Zdzisław Najder (1972–1974). This accidental synchronicity was fruitful for Conrad studies in Poland. For the first time Polish scholars could finally get hold of the entire oeuvre of the Polish-born writer in their native language, which resulted in many inspired analyses; while simultaneously there appeared a young scholar who could read Conrad both in Polish and English, and who could place him in the context of both Polish and world literature and culture. This possibility turned quickly into reality. Pursuing his academic work, Wiesław Krajka earned his PhD in English literature in 1975 and then, in 1981, obtained the post-doctoral degree of

Dr. habil. (*Doctor habilitatus*), and the title of Full Professor in 1995. This last distinction did not crown his career but ushered in a period of intense scholarship as the head of Conrad Studies Centre at UMCS from 1996 until his retirement in 2019. This place became the heart of Conrad studies in Poland and the cradle of new scholars.

Over his many decades of work, Wiesław Krajka has authored numerous publications, shedding ever more light on various aspects of Conrad's texts. Among his books, those dealing with the themes of isolation, identity, and ethos have uncovered new ground in Conradian scholarship: *Izolacja i etos. Studium o twórczości Josepha Conrada* (1988) in Polish, and its English version *Isolation and Ethos: A Study of Joseph Conrad* (1992). The latter appeared as part of East European Monographs series devoted to Eastern European history, politics, and culture. This collaboration was particularly fruitful as it led to the emergence of the series *Conrad: Eastern and Western Perspectives* initiated in 1992, which was published by East European Monographs/Social Science Monographs in Boulder and Maria Curie-Skłodowska University in Lublin until 2013, and by UMCS and Columbia University Press in New York since 2014, with world-wide distribution by Columbia University Press between 1992 and now. Wiesław Krajka is the editor of this outstanding series, which numbers 32 volumes thus far and serves as a publishing platform and a stimulating exchange of ideas for prominent Conradians from around the world. Their contributions to the series enrich the scholarly landscape, and along with academic journals such as *The Conradian*, *Conradiana*, or *L'Époque Conradienne*, are indispensable volumes for both novices and those well acquainted with Conrad's work. Professor Krajka has personally edited several volumes in this series.[1] Always working between Polish and English, between East and West, his interests extend far beyond the assessment of Conrad's Polishness. Historical, biographical, and literary affinities with Poland, although significant to his research, are just a fraction of his academic output, which embraces the explorations of colonial contexts, intertextual relations between

Conrad's works and those of other writers, including Polish authors, formal aspects of Conradian texts and, additionally, their adaptations in different media. Like every reader of Conrad, he seems to have a favourite text, which is "Amy Foster," one of the most disturbing and most universal of tales, which focuses on the topics most dear to him: isolation, loneliness, imperialism, and of the clash of cultures.

Professor Krajka has become internationally renowned as a Conrad scholar, and on five occasions served as visiting professor in the USA: at the University of Minnesota, Minneapolis (1989), University of Illinois, Chicago (1997–1998), and University of Rochester, New York (1997, 2002, 2007). He has published widely in international journals but this did not make him neglect Polish readers, both scholars and the general public. He has initiated the series *Joseph Conrad a Polska, Europa Środkowo-Wschodnia i świat* [Joseph Conrad and Poland, East-Central Europe and the world], published by UMCS in Lublin,[2] which aims at providing the essays of the most distinguished scholars in Polish translations (originally published in English in the series *Conrad: Eastern and Western Perspectives*) so that these might be available for a Polish readership. Such initiatives demonstrate his desire to offer valuable Conrad-related content to general and academic readers, and exemplifies his modesty and generosity: promoting others rather than himself.

His generosity is evident in the sheer number of projects involving cooperation with other scholars whom Wiesław Krajka invited on to his research teams, under the aegis of grants financed by the Polish Ministry of Science and Higher Education, but is even more clearly seen in his supervision of doctoral and master's degree dissertations. He has supervised nearly 250 MA theses, nearly 75 BA theses, and 17 PhD dissertations. Owing to his patient guidance and support, many of his mentees have themselves contributed greatly to Conradian studies, for instance his PhD students: Katarzyna Sokołowska, Monika Majewska, Wojciech Kozak, Brygida Pudełko, Lilia Omelan, Olga Binczyk, and Jarosław Giza, but also others who were aided at various stages of their academic development – Ewa

Kujawska-Lis, Agnieszka Adamowicz-Pośpiech, Grażyna Branny, to name just a few. He has served on the committees of numerous doctoral, habilitation, and professorial boards, both as head of such boards and a reviewer. His helpful and always professional approach has been conducive to the academic success of many younger scholars.[3] In 2006, he was the head of the committee that awarded Professor Stephen Fischer-Galati (University of Boulder, CO) with an honorary doctorate from Maria Curie-Skłodowska University in Lublin. In 2012 he was part of the committee that awarded an honorary doctorate from Adam Mickiewicz University in Poznań to J. M. Coetzee (South Africa/Australia).

For his devotion to Conrad and for his outstanding academic and organizational achievements (for many years he was an expert on the State Accreditation Committee responsible for ensuring the quality of education in Polish departments of English Studies) there were conferred on Professor Krajka numerous prestigious awards. These include: the Adam Gillon Book Award, II level, awarded by Joseph Conrad Society of America for *From Szlachta Culture to the 21st Century. Between East and West. New Essays on Joseph Conrad's Polishness* (2013); the Ministry of Science and Higher Education Award, I level, for the monograph *Joseph Conrad. Konteksty kulturowe* [Joseph Conrad. Cultural contexts] (1995); the Ministry of Science and Higher Education Award, II level, for the monograph *Izolacja i etos. Studium o twórczości Josepha Conrada* [Isolation and ethos. A study of Joseph Conrad] (1988); the Ministry of Science and Higher Education Award, III level, for the monograph *Angielska baśń literacka epoki wiktoriańskiej* [The English fairy-story of the Victorian epoch] (1981); numerous awards by UMCS; and the following Polish civil state decorations: the Silver Cross of Merit (1995), the Gold Cross of Merit (2001), and the Order of Polonia Restituta (2009).

But all these distinctions do not show the real face of Wiesław Krajka. Anyone who has attended any of the International Conferences entitled "Conrad's Footprints" and the accompanying study tours in Poland and Ukraine, over two decades from 1991 to 2022, will always remember their host: a man who was warm and welcoming, who looked after everyone and solved apparently unsolvable problems, who took pains to make everyone feel at home in a foreign country. He was always the first to arrive at the conference venue, and the last to leave. Conference members will also have appreciated his professional side: tactful comments always meant to extend the speaker's horizons and gain a better analytical, critical, and theoretical perspective; stimulating questions that generated insightful discussions which continued over coffee breaks and even over days. His criticism was always supportive and offered with a genuine belief in improvement. Is he a perfectionist? Yes, but with common sense. Demanding? Yes, but first of himself, then of others. Critical? Yes, but never for the sake of criticism as such.

Years of academic cooperation between Professor Krajka and scholars from different academic and ethnic backgrounds have not only generated excellent publications, but frequently turned into lasting friendships and appreciation. This can be evidenced by the three acknowledgments made by the authors of the essays included in the present volume and, at the same time participants of the conference that initiated it, which are illustrative of how Conradians feel about him: "I should like to take this opportunity to thank Professor Wiesław Krajka for his collaboration and friendship over many years. It has been a privilege to work with you Wiesław, and I'm proud to count you as a friend" (Peter Vernon); "I wish to sincerely thank Professor Wiesław Krajka for the opportunity to present at the 7th International Joseph Conrad Conference. I will also remain forever grateful for the opportunity to study under his patient guidance and for his trust and belief in me. The unique experience of the last International Conrad Conference has given me a new sense of purpose and new perspectives and ideas that I want to pursue. [...] I feel like I finally have topics worth pursuing, rather than veering into chaos of poeticised, abstract theories – that is my true gain from this experience" (Małgorzata Stanek), and "I remain ever indebted to my friends at UMCS for their academic support and feedback. This year the Conrad Conference was dedicated to the illuminating career of Professor Wiesław Krajka, and it has been my great privilege to find Professor Krajka as a continuous guide and source of inspiration. I express my sincere respect to and admiration for him, and I feel honoured to contribute to this volume" (Subhadeep Ray). For each author who offered their text to this project, a volume written in honour of Professor Wiesław Krajka, their contribution is more than a scholarly appreciation. It is an expression of gratitude for having crossed paths with a truly great man of letters.

NOTES

[1] *Conrad Eastern and Western Perspectives* volumes edited by Wiesław Krajka include: *Joseph Conrad: East European, Polish and Worldwide* (vol. 8, 1999), *A Return to the Roots: Conrad, Poland and East-Central Europe* (vol. 13, 2004), *Beyond the Roots: The Evolution of Conrad's Ideology and Art* (vol. 14, 2005), *Joseph Conrad: Between Literary Techniques and Their Messages* (vol. 18, 2009), *In the Realms of Biography, Literature, Politics and Reception: Polish and East-Central European Joseph Conrad* (vol. 19, 2010), *From Szlachta Culture to the 21st Century, Between East and West. New Essays on Joseph Conrad's Polishness* (vol. 22, 2013), *"Wine in Old and New Bottles": Critical Paradigms for Joseph Conrad* (vol. 23, 2014), *Joseph Conrad's Authorial Self: Polish and Other* (vol. 27, 2018), *Some Intertextual Chords of Joseph Conrad's Literary Art* (vol. 28, 2019), *Various Dimensions of the Other in Joseph Conrad's Fiction* (vol. 29, 2020). Volumes co-edited: *Conrad's Literary Career* (vol. 1, 1992), *Contexts for Conrad* (vol. 2, 1993), *Conrad at the Millennium: Modernism, Postmodernism, Postcolonialism* (vol. 10, 2001), and *Conrad in Africa: New Essays on "Heart of Darkness"* (vol. 11, 2002).

[2] Volumes that appeared in this series include: *Conrad a Polska* [Conrad and Poland] (vol. 1, 2011), *Polskość i europejskość w Josepha Conrada wizjach historii, polityki i etyki* [Poland and Europe in Joseph Conrad's visions of history, politics, and ethics] (vol. 2, 2013), *Styl Josepha Conrada a język polski i wielojęzyczność* [Joseph Conrad's style and the Polish language and multilingualism] (vol. 3, 2018), and *Joseph Conrad kresowy i uniwersalny: „Amy Foster"* [Borderland and universal Joseph Conrad: "Amy Foster"] (vol. 4, 2020).

[3] He has been a reviewer of 19 PhD dissertations at different Polish universities (University of Silesia, Nicolaus Copernicus University in Toruń, Jagiellonian University, University of Warsaw, University of Wrocław, and Adam Mickiewicz University in Poznań), and reviewed the academic output of scholars who were subsequently conferred the degree of Dr. habil. (12) and the title of Full Professor (10).

Ewa Kujawska-Lis,
University of Warmia and Mazury,
Olsztyn, Poland

Introduction

Joseph Conrad's Texts and Intertexts. In Honour of Professor Wiesław Krajka is a collection of essays which examine Conrad's oeuvre from various theoretical and analytical perspectives. Some of them offer a panoramic view of Conrad's works, focusing on particular thematic or formal aspects; others zoom in on one text and uncover its less frequently examined facets; still others set Conrad's texts against those of other writers. Thus what is common to all the contributions in this volume is the notions of textuality and intertextuality, both broadly understood. The essays present insightful interpretations of Joseph Conrad's novels, short fiction and autobiographical texts, and comparative readings with those of other writers from various cultural and ethnic backgrounds. They indicate what Conrad was influenced by, and how he influenced others.

The volume is organized according to the principle of chronology and thematic interests. The first set of essays looks at what was formative for Conrad and the parallels between his art and that of his predecessors, and/or reworking of motifs found in literature before he appeared on the scene. The opening text examines reading as a form of escapism and indicates the significance of books and of the reading experience in Miguel de Cervantes's *Don Quixote* and in *Lord Jim* (Stanek). It is followed by an analysis of female characters in selected Conradian works as influenced by John Milton's Eve and a post-Miltonian tradition that produced the *femme fatale* figure (Giza). The next paper moves to the realm of nostalgia, and compares Conrad's autobiographical accounts with those of Henry James (Wojciechowska), while the last chapter in this section presents Conrad as influenced by the opera and the philosophy of Arthur Schopenhauer (Szczepan-Wojnarska). This analysis of the operatic form as significant in the structure of *Almayer's Folly* serves as a bridge between the opening and the middle section of this volume, which is devoted to Conrad's literary art and focuses on the artistic organization of his texts (Richardson; Vernon; Arouimi) and the social, moral, and economic issues that he tackled in his early fiction and in his two political novels (Guarducci; Setecka; Unal). This set concludes with a panoramic overview of Conrad's interest in gunrunning (Davies), but is also thematically related to the terrorism and secrecy discussed in the previous essays. The next section of the volume suggests how Conrad may have influenced other writers and artists and contains comparative essays: with H. G. Wells (Pudełko), William Faulkner (Branny), Aksel Sandemose (Schauffler), and Premendra Mitra (Ray), as well as a comparison of *Victory* with its Hungarian stage adaptation (Csizmadia). The volume concludes with an essay that presents a cultural perception of the notion of social justice and deals with the reception of Conrad's political fiction in the contemporary world (Cairney). The volume, therefore, begins with the literary tradition preceding Conrad, continues with close readings of his oeuvre, and concludes with discussions of his impact on readers in the 21st century.

This volume is the first collection of studies that were presented at the Seventh International Joseph Conrad Conference organized by the Institute of Modern Languages and Literatures, Maria Curie-Skłodowska University, Lublin, Poland, on 20–23 June 2022, held under the Honorary Patronage of the European Parliament granted by its President David Maria Sassoli in 2020, and subsequently renewed by President Roberta Metsola in 2022, and dedicated to Wiesław Krajka in recognition of his superior achievements as a Conrad scholar. Organized during turbulent times, the conference brought together academics and enthusiasts of Conrad from around the world who were able to meet in person after a long time of isolation and online scholarly sessions. It was an intensive period of work, stimulating academic and personal discussions, and collaboration resulting in the present monograph, which is authored by scholars from Poland (8 papers), the United States of America (2), France (2), as well as the United Kingdom, Italy, Turkey, India, and Hungary (one contributor from each country), who thus represent the international community of Conrad researchers, exemplify a variety of approaches to this writer, and illuminate various aspects of his art.

Conrad was a voracious reader and so were his characters, as Małgorzata Stanek reminds us. Books were, after all, his first and best companions when he was a child. Books from his father's library shaped his sensibilities and sensitivity to literature and the creative employment of language, but also provided emotional and mental relief from the hardships of life. Using the concept of emotionscape as affective space, Stanek examines the functions of books and reading in Conrad's fiction, focusing on escape, in particular the escape into fiction as a way to cope with reality. Sketching briefly the trope of books, she argues that Conrad presents various dimensions of reading and meaning-making: both positive ("shelter-giving" escapism and self-isolation, as in the case of Kayerts and Carlier in "An Outpost of Progress") and destructive (negatively affecting the ability to function in social space, as in *Lord Jim*). Significant functions of books in Conrad's fiction are related to providing a sense of comfort and safety, and a link with civilization (*An Inquiry into Some Points of Seamanship* in "Heart of Darkness" is a token of civilization in the wilderness; Kurtz, despite being gifted in arts, "slides into madness in the wild wasteland"), but also offering a way to escape from what the characters find unbearable. As overviewed by Stanek, and exemplified by such characters as Yanko Goorall, Willems, Almayer, Karain, and some female characters, like Nina and Bessie, escapism (or the impossibility of escape) seems to be an ever-present motif in Conrad's works, whereas "[e]scaping into a fictional, imagined, fantasy world can lead to isolation as well as a loss of contact with the real world." This is particularly well illustrated in an intertextual reading of *Don Quixote* and *Lord Jim*, whereby in both works the eponymous characters are profoundly affected by books that stimulate their imagination and consequently their conduct. By comparing and contrasting Cervantes's masterpiece and *Lord Jim*, Stanek effectively argues that fiction can have a healing power (Quixote) and yet that it may be destructive when escaping into fiction leads to the denial of facts (Jim). This healing power is, however, also evident in Conrad's other works, particularly in the form of storytelling and writing, as characters and narrators are compelled to tell stories and to share their experiences with others. This seems to be a universal drive and basic need of human beings, and what Cervantes and Conrad addressed in their fiction is found today in the form of bookstagram, where users share what they read in an almost compulsive need to pass on what interests them.

Female characters, only briefly mentioned in the opening essay, are at the centre of attention in Jarosław Giza's analysis. His point of departure is the hypothesis that the presentation of wicked females by Conrad was influenced by the depiction of Eve by John Milton in *Paradise Lost* and the ensuing post-Miltonian tradition of shaping woman characters as evil and the concept of *femme fatale.* He places four Conradian women – Winnie Verloc (*The Secret Agent*), Freya ("Freya of the Seven Isles"), Flora de Barral's governess (*Chance*), and Susan Bacadou ("The Idiots") – in the context of that tradition and argues against the commonly held, too generalized and one-sided, view that female characters in Conrad "appear to be incapable of activity, depravity, and atrocious behaviour." On the contrary, he perceives some female characters as agential and "responsible for shaping the development of the stories" and "descendants of the Miltonian Eve," though noticeable differences between them may be found. Giza traces intertextual echoes between Eve, the archetypal evil, scheming and tempting woman, and Conradian female characters, attributing to them the Victorian concept of *femme fatale.* Thus he considers several intertextual parallels: suicide (contemplated by Eve, committed by Winnie and Susan), temptation and seduction as attributes of a post-Miltonian *femme fatale* (the governess, Freya, Winnie), criminality (Susan, Winnie), beauty (Freya), transformation (Winnie, Susan), and love and care (Winnie,

Susan). The intertextual reading, pointing to Conradian females' wickedness, is balanced by observations concerning the various social and individual motivations of these four females, leading to the conclusion that these are, indeed, complex characters who cannot be regarded solely through the prism of one trait, evil. On the contrary, their wicked, scheming, and even murderous conduct is motivated, to some extent, by the manner in which they were treated by others (men in particular) and by their personal and social circumstances. Hence, Giza rightly observes that "[t]he insurgency launched by Conradian *femmes fatales*, recognized as a defence of their own rights, legitimizes their struggle when they find themselves in an irrational situation since, in their heart of hearts, they sense that some things have gone absolutely awry." Consequently, these women are much more multifaceted than it might initially seem. Any reading of them as "ontologically unwavering in their wickedness" must be seen as superficial and ultimately misleading. In constructing these females, Conrad considered psycho-social constituents that give credibility to their behaviour.

Like Giza, Sylwia Janina Wojciechowska reads Conrad's work in relation to that of another author, Henry James, but unlike him she finds more differences than similarities. Her study offers a new perspective on the idea of nostalgia as employed by Conrad and James in their autobiographical works. As she stresses, it might appear surprising to discuss these two writers in the context of nostalgia, as both "were renowned for their disregard for sentimentalist sensibilities." Still, as Wojciechowska expertly demonstrates, what is commonly understood as nostalgia, that is, any intense longing for the past, and repudiated by both writers more or less explicitly, should be contrasted with the philosophical approach to this phenomenon as set forth by Jean-François Lyotard. The key to understanding nostalgic sentiments in Conrad's and James's writings, according to her, is to differentiate between the popular and the academic ideas associated with nostalgia. With a proper analytical and theoretical apparatus, Conrad's *The Mirror of the Sea: Memories and Impressions*, *A Personal Record*, and *Notes on Life and Letters* are evocative of *reflective* nostalgia as understood by Svetlana Boym, where what is missing and absent becomes significant and constitutes the conceptual frame. The notion of *reflective* nostalgia "explains the internal inconsistencies within the texts, the contradictions between various versions of certain events, as well as the unfilled *lacunae* in the recollections." Consequently, "the absent content," so frequently commented upon by other critics, in Conrad's reminiscences, but also their structure and coherence, are informed by this type of nostalgia and they can be read as expressions of a "nostalgic fascination with things past" and a "literary representation of Lyotard's modernist 'unpresentable'." Unlike Conrad's account of his past, which is marred by trauma but also actually often reflects the memories of others rather than his own, James's autobiographical writings, especially *A Small Boy and Others*, are very intimate and personal. This intimacy translates into formal differences between Conrad's and James's autobiographies, with the latter framing his memories via pastoral *topoi* and rhetoric, though only initially. Further in his *Autobiography*, James becomes ironical and plays with the pastoral convention. This, however, also corresponds with the understanding of *reflective* nostalgia which incorporates irony and humour. The application of the notion of nostalgia leads Wojciechowska to an innovative reading, by shedding new light on how *reflective* nostalgia is linked to thematic and formal aspects of autobiographical writing, especially the fragmentation and selectiveness of material.

Anna Szczepan-Wojnarska's essay closes the section devoted to various literary and personal influences upon Conrad. If the opening paper dealt with the impact of books on the future writer, this one focuses on music and explores the operatic mode in *Almayer's Folly*. It argues, again – as other critics have pointed out before – that Conrad's works demand an involved reader, one who will be able to identify links to the extra-textual reality, particularly the cultural and historical backgrounds. An erudite reader will be able to perceive *Almayer's Folly* as a mode of operatic performance that contains explicit references to Giuseppe Verdi and allusions to *Il Trovatore* ("Through the open shutter the notes of Verdi's music floated out on the great silence over the river and forest. [...] Nature slept in an exhausted repose after the fierce turmoil, while under the unsteady hand of the statesman of Sambir the Trovatore fitfully wept, wailed, and bade good-bye to his Leonore again and again in a mournful round of tearful and endless iteration" [*AF* 88-89]) which are meant to sensitize the reader to the operatic aesthetics. Stressing the role of music in Conrad's life and his acquaintance with the grand opera, Szczepan-Wojnarska asserts that he was not only influenced by opera, as were many other writers of his time, but also expected his readers to be familiar enough with this form of art to identify the references and thus interpret the novel through the prism of the tragic arias of *Il Trovatore*. Linking the novel with Verdi's opera enriches the interpretation of Conrad's characters and their fate. This, however, largely depends on the reader's active role in constructing the meaning of the text. Additionally, the essay explores the validity of the comparison of Almayer's long solo at the conclusion of the novel to *Tristan und Isolde* – a link Conrad made in a letter discussing the novel he was writing. Moreover, the essay stresses yet another link: that between Richard Wagner and Arthur Schopenhauer, whose philosophy inspired both the conception of *Tristan und Isolde* that Conrad alludes to and the writer himself. This can be seen in Conrad's characters who follow their desires, yet the realization of these desires leads to disaster. The comparative reading of the fates of Tristan and Isolde against those of Almayer and Nina reveals that for his artistic purposes "Conrad, without imitating Wagner's opera, transforms the myth of Tristan." Szczepan-Wojnarska's analysis illuminates both the way Conrad's novel may be read against and in parallel with two operas of his time, and also how his text is structured in an operatic manner with characters' arias and group scenes. Importantly, she draws attention to yet another facet of Conrad's art, "the Modernist dream of synaesthesia."

The notion of synaesthesia is at the heart of the following paper, which opens the set of texts devoted specifically to the interpretation and analysis of Conrad's literary output. Brian

Richardson explores how Conrad creates sense perceptions, with particular attention placed on the sense of sight which "often merges with, replaces, or is displaced by other senses." Multisensory descriptions are common stylistic traits in Conrad's works, and, as the author evidences, permeate his oeuvre from its very beginning with representations of sight, smell, and touch. Yet it is sight that predominates, and often depictions of touch and sound are represented visually, whereby "the aural is [...] consumed by the visual," while depictions of smell are quite rare and evoke either very positive or very negative sensory experience. Richardson also discusses the importance of sight in the context of characters who lose their sight, such as Diamelen in her dying moment and Arsat when he stares into the sun in "The Lagoon" and Captain Whalley in "The End of the Tether" and draws attention to the scenes that happen in the dark, in which scent, touch, and sounds become more prominent and eventually lead Conrad to develop synaesthetic representations. As the author emphasizes, Conrad's synaesthetic passages do not fall into the category of classical literary synaesthesia, where one sense impression is depicted in terms of another sense. Rather, he constructs realistic, though expressive, similes and/or metaphors in which one sense is substituted for or combined with another. With the development of his career, Conrad became bolder in his experimentation with sense perceptions and so, as illustrated by textual material from *The Rescue* and *The Arrow of Gold*, "later works reveal a more sustained interest in multisensory representations." As Richardson observes, such depictions, both evocative and powerful, are frequently related to love scenes, and undermine the claim that Conrad found it hard to represent love relationships and sensuousness.

Peter Vernon's essay explores Conrad's style further and considers other characteristic aspects of it, particularly narrative devices such as frames, theatrical images including stages, curtains, and reflective surfaces, which are operated rhetorically through *ekphrasis* and metonymy and grammatically through expressions that generate similes. The author notes that comparisons created with grammatical structures such as *as if*, *as though*, and *as of* are particularly frequent in critical moments, when characters are placed in extreme situations and circumstances. Examining Conrad's major works ("Heart of Darkness," *Lord Jim*, *Nostromo*, *Under Western Eyes*, and *Victory*), Vernon demonstrates how isolated, masculine protagonists found *in extremis* generate such depictions because in such moments some things cannot be expressed directly and require transformation for better representation. When transformed artistically, tragic scenes invite readers to play "the role of the protagonist's secret sharer." Yet, as Vernon argues, "although confronted with tragedy, the reader experiences joy through the intensity of engaging with Conrad's most 'writerly' texts." This close reading illuminates how Conrad exploits *ekphrasis* and metonymy effectively to transform characters and scenes into art images and in so doing forces the reader to focus attention on them, as they are foregrounded artistically. Grammatical structures also lead to specific transformations and Vernon distinguishes between them, demonstrating that they result in slightly different effects: *as if* moves the reader into a hypothetical realm, *as though* indicates a sense of concession and demurral, while *as of* is the most conceptual since an object predicts the subject itself. This is a truly subtle but extremely illuminating distinction that allows for a more informed interpretation of Conradian similes. Vernon uncovers interesting patterns in Conrad's style: for instance, he observes that "*as* clauses predominate at moments of highest tension when they combine with theatrical imagery," and discovers meaningful transitions from *as if* to *as though* phrases. Importantly, he exposes how Conrad consistently throughout his career linked his writing with the realm of art.

The art of writing is further explored by Michel Arouimi who traces textual echoes, repetitions, contrasts, and contradictions in *The Secret Agent*. Pointing to Arthur Rimbaud's understanding of contradiction as the "alchemy of word[s]," Arouimi focuses on this stylistic tool and offers a close reading of the novel, revealing ambiguity at various levels of the text which he interprets as a poetic expression of the conflicting relationships between the three main characters: Verloc, Winnie, and Stevie. By analysing the opening chapter of *The Secret Agent* in detail, Arouimi reveals how Conrad employs the setting to establish contradictions within characters (Verloc in particular), how characters are linked to each other as doubles (Winnie as a double of Verloc), and how the accumulation of material details is meant to contribute to the characterization. Verbal echoes in Conrad's work are not haphazard, as is illustrated by repetitions that appear in later chapters. The writer very carefully selected words and those that are repeated evoke specific images. Often such repetitions blur the differences between characters and between objects and people, as the same words are attributed to them. This is significant as, according to Arouimi, the monotony and lack of differences in the world evoked by such blurring indicate "a momentary triumph of Totality over Unity" and the blending of the past and the future. Verbal echoes, then, have metaphysical implications. The combination and arrangement of words that create mirror images and contradictions actually express "the ambiguity of the human condition": being torn between Totality and Unity. Each reading of Conrad's work enriches us; each reading reveals some new aspect. Arouimi's reading is yet another argument for the case that Conrad was the first stylist in English and challenges those critics who too easily dismiss repetitions as faulty or insignificant. On the contrary, it can be said that the significance of his art and its philosophical, moral, and social implications rest on the manner in which he selected and combined words.

Social and moral issues are addressed specifically in the following paper. Maria Paola Guarducci tackles the theme of family dissolution in texts set in Europe. By examining this topic in works from two periods in Conrad's career, the early short stories "The Idiots" (1896) and "The Return" (1898), and two texts from the middle period, "Amy Foster" (1901) and *The Secret Agent* (1907), she indicates how disturbing this problem was for Conrad since he kept returning to it. She also challenges the limiting approach of those critics who perceive Conrad as a pro-European who falsifies non-Western cultures, by revealing that he was not uncritical of Western Europeans and that, in fact, his portrayal of Europeans can be quite harsh. Guarducci asserts that Conrad was deeply concerned with the manner in which humankind is corrupted by power irrespective of the cultural background, seeing this as a universal human problem. Hence, Europeans are in no way unique in this respect. Referring to Conrad's biography (an exile from his homeland, a foreigner in his adopted country, a seaman who experienced non-Western cultures), she brings to the fore the fact that he developed a sense of relativism that made him aware of the complex nature of reality, which may accommodate more than one truth. This allowed him to perceive humankind critically and from the distanced perspective of an observer who himself experienced a clash of cultures. The four works selected for analysis present Europeans as humans with no flattery attached: they can be incompetent, unfeeling, violent, and cruel. The combinations of various factors, both individual faults and external pressures, in each story lead to the collapse of the family (or of relationships). In "The Idiots" this is effected partly because of the primitivism of Breton society. In "Amy Foster" Yanko's tragic situation and his complicated marriage have much to do with the limitations of English peasants who lack culture and openness to the Other, while being "trapped in the mechanisms of power, authority, and discrimination." In "The Return" the dissolution of the family is directly caused by the husband's personality (Alvan's tragic narcissism), but is also linked to the clash between the changeable cultural code followed by the British bourgeoisie and its late-Victorian Darwinian interpretation, according to which "any status quo is perceived as natural rather than cultural." In *The Secret Agent* the marriage is from its onset an economic transaction and here Conrad subverts the very idea of a happy marriage with the wife as a Victorian angel in the house. All these works deal with human psychology and present individuals in complex relationships in which injustice, anger, and frustration take their toll.

The theme of social relations is continued by Agnieszka Setecka, who looks specifically at how they are shaped in *The Secret Agent*, thus complementing the previous analysis, but from a different perspective. Taking Georg Simmel's essay "The Sociology of Secrecy and of Secret Societies" as a point of departure, she analyses the novel through the prism of its secrecy and the circulation of information as two major forces that impact upon the characters, their conduct, and mutual relationships. Secrets and information are seen as commodities of particular value that can be traded to obtain various benefits, be it economic (money) or social (power). Setecka offers a reading of the novel that concentrates on the flow and management of information: who keeps secrets from whom, who shares secrets with whom, who offers information to whom are all constitutive in establishing power relationships and gaining advantage over others. Social distinction is directly dependent on the possession of economic capital, but if information is treated in economic terms as a commodity, then the novel uncovers how deeply social relations (and human circumstances) are subject to transaction and how information follows the rules of the market. Thus, the novel reveals that different types of information have different values. In some cases the value of information depends on its unavailability (information provided by Verloc), in other cases it is exactly the opposite: it is the dissemination of information rather than limiting it that is profitable (sensational [mis]information expected by Mr. Vladimir). This can be clearly seen in the contemporary world in which the control of information, manipulation of information, and misinformation itself ensure power via control over public opinion. In his presentation of the power of information, Conrad was quite prophetic. As Setecka reminds us, "although they affect the public, newspapers in *The Secret Agent* never offer reliable information." This is a scenario implemented on a daily basis not only in the fictional reality created by Conrad, but in real politics.

Conrad's second political novel, *Under Western Eyes*, is scrutinized by Nergis Ünal who applies Mikhail Bakhtin's ethical architectonic, in particular the notion of "*answerability*," to examine the protagonist's circumstances and assess his conduct from a moral perspective. Beginning her discussion with the Conradian notion of fidelity, she argues that, depending on the critical perspective, Conrad can be perceived as both faithful and unfaithful in his life, similarly to the characters he created. This undecidability as regards the character's moral standing is demonstrated by the analysis of Razumov, who dramatizes the moral dilemma of fidelity and responsibility, the latter being the key notion in Bakhtinian ethics. Using Bakhtinian ethical framework, Ünal assesses Razumov as an active participant in his life: he takes action, and commits wrongdoing, but then takes responsibility for it. Following Bakhtin, who stresses the uniqueness of each individual and the need to consider the specific circumstances in which the individual finds himself or herself when evaluating personal conduct, which precludes universality as regards any correct way of acting, Ünal scrutinizes Razumov's particular situation to answer the question whether his act is one of betrayal and whether his conduct is moral. Her discussion is motivated by the fact that although frequently addressed in ethical discussions of the novel, this particular issue remains unresolved. Her interpretation leads her to conclude that the protagonist cannot be considered completely immoral. His apparent act of "betrayal" is motivated by his situation: his lack of family which means lack of support and his self-identificatory connection with Russia as a substitute for family, which makes him follow state policy. She argues that "his particularity of living under Russian autocracy is a kind of mischance for Razumov," and this, in a sense, explains why he acts the way he does: irrespective of what he did, he would still be viewed with suspicion by the authorities. This is the true tragedy of living under any autocratic regime. Additionally, Razumov, in line with the Bakhtinian idea of plurality, is assessed from the perspective of other centres of value judgment. He is torn between his own conception of himself and how he is perceived by others. This, in Ünal's interpretation, shows that by offering different perspectives, Conrad refrains from providing any specific judgment and makes the reader assess the protagonist's conduct. This is typically Conradian: ambiguity, plurality of judgments, and making the reader an active interpreter of the work. This, of course, invites ever new interpretations and evokes Bakhtin's idea of "great time": just as the world is everlasting, constantly expanding and changing, the character extends beyond the text and gains immortality through the possibility of novel interpretations offered by readers from different spaces, times, and backgrounds.

The moral issues addressed in the two previous papers (secrecy and betrayal) are presented by Laurence Davies from yet a different perspective. He considers the theme of gunrunning and emphasizes that like any other type of clandestine conduct in Conrad's fiction it is "neither morally neutral nor morally fixed," as "[e]verything depends on who does the running, where, when, and in whose name." Some characters get involved in smuggling weapons due to friendship, such as Lingard who assists Hassim and Immada. Others do it because they are convinced that this is the right thing to do, like Blunt and Doña Rita. Still others are interested in profit, like the narrator in "Karain: A Memory," or adventure, like Monsieur George. As Davies expertly demonstrates, the theme of gunrunning serves as a springboard for Conrad to explore a number of issues, including criminality, loyalty, legitimation, colonialism, and the making and breaking of nations, each requiring taking sides and making choices and judgments. In his essay, Davies provides an overview of Conrad's works that deal with gunrunning, evidencing that this was no fleeting and occasional matter but a fascination that was linked not only to the writer's personal experiences, but also to the historical contexts in which he placed his works as well as actual historical events and conflicts that he witnessed, which involved ethnicity, territoriality, and national identity. Living in turbulent times (though they were, as Davies stresses, in no way unique as regards the variety of conflicts), Conrad incorporated his fascination with clandestine behaviour into his work to an unusual extent for the literary output at that time and explored new vistas in which the topic could be treated figuratively to force readers to make judgments. As Davies concludes, Conrad "was himself a literary gunrunner. In short, he was explosive." He metaphorically blew readers' minds by not allowing them to remain indifferent.

Davies's essay indicates how Conrad was influenced by external political and historical circumstances and how different his writing was from that of his contemporaries with respect to the topics he tackled. The following paper, by Brygida Pudełko, opens the set of texts that trace how he influenced other writers and also how his works may be compared and contrasted to those of others. Conrad's personal relationship with H. G. Wells is well-known and well-documented, but Pudełko moves further and, having discussed both writers' approaches to writing, examines common themes and motifs in their works. In particular, she explores some affinities between "Heart of Darkness" and three novels by Wells: *The War of the Worlds* (1897), *When the Sleeper Wakes* (1899), and *Tono-Bungay* (1909). As she stresses, both writers were transitional figures: they were intermediaries between the old Victorian tradition of realism and the new ideas of Modernism, and combined the features of these two movements in their writing. Yet they differed in their approach to writing: while for Wells literature was a tool with which "to enlighten the world," for Conrad such "didacticism" was unacceptable. They were dissimilar in their approach to life, too, with Wells being a sort of revolutionary, and Conrad being a conservative. They differed in their stylistics, with Wells seeing himself as a journalist, and Conrad constantly searching for a better form of expression. And yet, despite their differences, and even the fact that Wells parodied both Conrad's style and Conrad himself as the Roumanian captain of the *Maud Mary* in *Tono-Bungay*, a close analysis of their works reveals many thematic affinities. As Pudełko observes, "[w]hat unites Wells and Conrad is their satirical and enlightened approach to the colonial politics of the imperialist powers. Both give a satirical picture of greedy colonial powers that carve up the planet." Both were deeply concerned with the violence of colonialism, and in his novel *When the Sleeper Wakes* (in which "Heart of Darkness" is mentioned), Wells dramatizes the situation of African soldiers attacking a European city, which is imagined by Marlow. Pudełko's essay evidences the intertextual links between Conrad's and Wells's works, with references and allusions by each to the other, that primarily point to both writers' preoccupation with colonialism.

Intertextual reading is also done by Grażyna Maria Teresa Branny, who exposes William Faulkner's unacknowledged debt to Conrad. By examining denegation in Conrad's short story "The Black Mate," she challenges the assertion that Faulkner, who frequently exploited this device, was its inventor. Denegation, defined by François Pitavy in relation to *Absalom, Absalom!* as the assertion of presence by absence, a phenomenon extending negation because it affirms what it negates, is traced in Conrad's story. Contrary to Conrad's own disparaging opinion of it and subsequent critical neglect, "The Black Mate" emerges as a text worthy of attention. Re-reading it through the prism of Bakhtinian and Lacanian contexts reveals its various ambivalences, especially the ambivalent moral judgment on the protagonist, thus yet again bringing to light this characteristic of Conrad's art. Branny reads the story as "an anticipation and ironic dismissal of *otherness* and its criminalization" and shows how Winston Bunter's distinctiveness is dramatized denegatively. Drawing on the Bakhtinian notion of a polyphony of voices, she argues that the allegations of otherness brought against the eponymous character are misguided, absurd, and false. Very close analysis of the textual material leads her to conclude that in his earliest short story Conrad was very much experimenting with the notion of denegation that Faulkner subsequently developed. By comparing passages from "The Black Mate" with Faulkner's *Absalom, Absalom!*, she indicates the differences in the writers' employment of this technique, with Conrad mainly introducing denegation in order to organize the plot and dialogue combined with the third person narration, and Faulkner offering more complex stream-of-consciousness narration, but she also – significantly – remarks on the similarities in the use of language, in the structuring of the flow of thoughts and of the texts, in the denegative construction of the characters. In both cases, "what is affirmed is immediately followed by its negation, to become again revoked, and then once more denied in the service of the truth of the matter." This essay not only uncovers how Conrad's short story enters into an intertextual relationship with Faulkner's novel, but also reveals a depth to "The Black Mate" that anticipates Conrad's subsequent experimentation with various modernist techniques.

As is evident from Branny's essay, textual affinities between Conrad and Faulkner are copious and include analogies of character, scene, phrasing, and imagery, as well as style and rhetoric. In the next paper, David Schauffler demonstrates how the same topic – that of immigration and alienation – can be developed quite differently. By reading Conrad's "Amy Foster" against Aksel Sandemose's novel *En sjømann går i land*, his essay again draws attention to the notion of otherness. This recurring theme in Conradian studies is given a fresh look since the essay focuses on how Sandemose analyses the relations of the stranger with the (non)receiving community in stark contrast to that of Conrad. Interestingly, the two writers and the two works share a lot. Both Conrad and Sandemose were seamen and both lived in adopted countries. Both drew heavily on their personal experiences in the respective works: Yanko Goorall is often linked to Conrad, while Espen Arnakke is perceived as Sandemose's alter ego. Both sketch a similar scenario for how the foreigner arrives in a foreign land: Yanko is washed ashore after the shipwreck, while Espen jumps from a ship and swims to a coastal village. But here the similarities end. The community rejects Yanko despite his efforts to assimilate. He poses no threat to the local villagers, though they perceive him as doing so. On the contrary, Espen is a source of disruption and commits murder. Schauffler's analysis probes much deeper than these similarities and contrasts. By adopting the concept of "*strangerness*," following the ideas of Georg Simmel set forth in his "The Stranger," he examines such essential qualities of the stranger as autonomy (both spatial and ontic: the stranger is not connected spatially with the new community, but is also not made of it, though gradually becoming its part), objectivity (while the stranger considers the receiving community objectively as a totality, he is looked at as an object), abstraction (this refers to various relations toward him), trade (the stranger trades on and profits from his difference in community), and the role of the stranger as a competitor. With these analytic tools, Schauffler traces the fates of Yanko and Espen, pinpointing oppositions between them while stressing that the mutual relationships between the stranger and the community are largely dependent on the type of the latter: whether human relationships are based in a given community on class structure or whether they are established competitively. In the first case, the stranger may be seen as representing "a direct competitor and potential threat, a curious foreign object, or a philosophical abstraction, an example of the human condition" – generally an object, thus lacking agency. In the second case, everyone is a stranger to everyone else, and the individual becomes a subject confronted by the "strangerness" of the society and this leads to agency. While Yanko becomes a victim of the community, which has agency, Espen is an agent: his own action leads to confrontation and conflict.

The pattern of comparing and contrasting two works is continued in the essay authored by Subhadeep Ray, who juxtaposes stories written by writers from two distinct linguistic, cultural, and literary backgrounds. Despite these differences, both Conrad and the Bengali writer Premendra Mitra share a modernist scepticism about representation and their works contain similar aspects of literary Modernism, hence affinities between them may be found in how they treat generic fixedness with a degree of fluidity. Ray compares Conrad's "The Tale" and Mitra's "The Discovery of Telenāpotā" with the application of Jacques Derrida's observations pertaining to the unsettlement of generic laws. As he suggests, both texts defy what might be expected of realistic fiction. Both writers construct stories within stories filled with speculations, suspicions, and ambiguity – this last feature appears often in the essays of the present volume, evidencing Conrad's preoccupation with what might be termed a plurality of truths. As Ray notes, the two stories that he compares "question even the identity and integrity of the subject-selves." His essay not only introduces a relatively little-known Bengali writer to Western readers, but also offers an informative analysis of "The Tale," in which he shows how Conrad's impressionist technique leads to the "resolution of nonresolution." As do other essays in the volume, his analysis examines the issue of *self* and *other* and their ethical responsibilities. As he observes, "[w]orks of Conrad and Mitra allow us to understand that illusion of laws is ethically bankrupt because it suggests the self's failure to be responsible for the 'other'."

Formal experimentation, which is explored by Ray in connection to Conrad, is applied to a Conradian text by Balázs Csizmadia in his study of a stage adaptation of Conrad's *Victory*. By moving it to a different medium, János Gosztonyi in his *Bűvölet* not only selected significant elements of *Victory* and combined them to create a new quality, as is typical of any adaptation when a new text endowed with an autonomous ontological status is created, but actually responded to Conrad's novel creatively and individually. Csizmadia enumerates changes to the plot and points to the much more active role attributed to Lena, who stabs Mr. Dodd (renamed Mr. Jones) to death before she dies, thus indicating the changed and more agential role of females in culture since Conrad's time. But one of the most significant features of this adaptation is the replacement of Captain Davidson, who does not feature in the play, by Conrad – named "Konrad," who is endowed with a double function: Konrad is both the autobiographical narrator and a participant in the events. This experimentation with Conrad's text is seen as consistent with Conradian narratives since it dramatizes the sense that we are perceiving the world through more than one reporting consciousness. This is, however, quite untypical of the dramatic mode, which is generally characterized by the immediacy of the here and now: with Konrad as narrator reporting the events in the past tense this immediacy is undermined from the opening scene. By focusing on the narrative levels in the play, Csizmadia discusses innovative aspects of this adaptation, in which mimesis mixes with diegesis: presenting (typical of the dramatic mode) is mixed with telling (typical of the epical mode). Though diegetic elements had been introduced into drama before and narration has become part of modern and postmodern plays, *Bűvölet* is atypical because, as argued by Csizmadia, Konrad is a homodiegetic narrator, a character in his own narrative, but he also has a generative function, whereby generative narrators are heterodiegetic. Thus, Konrad functions at different narrative levels and his narrative is actually a mixture of the homodiegetic and the heterodiegetic. Conradian narrative strategies have in this way been adapted for the stage, making the play very Conradian in the way the reality is mediated by the reporting consciousness.

The concluding essay of the volume recounts another experiment: that of introducing Conrad to students via a different text than that which is often chosen, namely "Heart of Darkness." Chris Cairney proposes to abandon an apologetic approach and the need to explain and justify Conrad's writing in the face of postcolonial criticism, and instead to focus on *The Secret Agent* as a text that can inspire discussions about personal liberty, social privilege, and equal opportunity, but also the situation of the individual in crisis – topics which are particularly relevant in the turbulent and unpredictable world of the 21st century, in which social unrest and violence are prominent. After the dramatic events of 9/11, American readers seem to have rediscovered *The Secret Agent* owing to its engagement with terrorist issues. But Cairney proposes to link this novel simultaneously to the concept of social justice, thus using it as a platform to discuss ethical dilemmas relating to terrorism and violence, on the one hand, and to equal rights and opportunities on the other, in the context of contemporary America. This essay illuminates how Conrad's novel fits into the modern cultural landscape and how it may inspire new generations of readers to consider issues of social justice: in particular how to demarcate (if possible) the border between what is justified and what is not; how to differentiate between terrorism and fighting for one's rights. Cairney offers a step-by-step analysis of *The Secret Agent*, pinpointing issues that may resonate with young Americans, and shows that Conrad's preoccupations will always be current.

The breadth and scope of the essays collected in this volume represent the scholarly interests of its authors. Conrad's major political novels, *The Secret Agent* and *Under Western Eyes*, are analysed, as are many works that are most critically acclaimed, such as *Lord Jim*, *Victory*, "Heart of Darkness," and "Amy Foster" – and yet each new reading unveils some interesting aspect, especially when these works are set in the intertextual context. But examinations of less often discussed texts, such as certain short stories ("The Black Mate," "The Lagoon," "The Idiots," "The Return," "Youth," "The End of the Tether," "Freya of the Seven Isles," "The Planter of Malata," "The Tale"), are prominent here because the authors in their re-evaluations challenge the prevailing, generally dismissive, opinions about them. Thematically, the essays tackle such diverse issues as escapism, femininity, the arts, illicit conduct, fidelity, secrecy, isolation, immigration, otherness, terrorism, and social equality. Yet from this collection, in which each contribution offers valuable insight into Conrad studies, there emerges one common trait discernible in all the works discussed: ambivalence. As the authors argue, no issue raised by Conrad is presented one-sidedly. Many interpretations are inscribed in his texts and the new contexts in which they are read will continue to open up new paths of interpretation.

Another facet that some of the collected essays draw attention to is how significant it was for Conrad to face life and bear the consequences of one's actions, and how continuously this theme emerges in his works. As Bakhtin, referred to in this volume in connection with his ethics, asserts, life requires the making of choices, and to live means to be an active participant in life. This contradicts passivity and indifference: an ethical human being cannot be indifferent, but needs to confront alternatives offered in life and take responsibility for his choices. This reminds one of a 2020 speech by Marian Turski, a Jewish-Polish Auschwitz survivor, in which he formulated his eleventh commandment, "thou shalt not be indifferent": "Thou shalt not be indifferent when you see historical lies. Thou shalt not be indifferent when the past is distorted for today's political needs. Thou shalt not be indifferent when any minority is discriminated against. Democracy hinges on the rights of minorities being protected. Thou shalt not be indifferent when any government infringes on the existing social contract."[1] Conrad and his works do not allow readers to remain indifferent. Present-day Ukraine, Conrad's birthplace, is being devastated by war to which one cannot be indifferent and his message, much like that of Turski's, resonates across the world powerfully.

NOTES

[1] The speech was delivered at the 75th anniversary of the liberation of Auschwitz-Birkenau, 27th January 2020; Accessed 23 Feb. 2023, <https://notesfrompoland.com/2020/01/28/do-not-be-indifferent-the-most-powerful-and-political-moments-from-auschwitz-commemoration/>.

Małgorzata Stanek,
Independent Scholar,
Lublin, Poland

Imagination and Inertness: Escapes and Fictional Spaces in Conrad

Introduction

Reading is a shelter that offers stability and takes the mind off of things that threaten to be overwhelming. It compensates for a certain emotional or psychological lack, it has the power of transporting us, it can reposition us spatially and temporarily, lead us into the realm of the imaginary, or allow us to live through a different sort of life (cf. Ablow 27). *The History of Reading, Volume 2: Evidence from the British Isles, c. 1750–1950* points out, for example, that during World War II, British readers more often reached for fiction, particularly light and escapist fiction (Halsey and Owens 6).[1] Such gratification resulted in a mixed feeling of pleasure and guilt. Reading, then, might be seen as an emotionscape.

Emotionscapes,[2] in my understanding, are "bubbles" into which individuals might escape, and their perception of time, space and other people becomes affected or clouded by the dominant mood of their "bubble." Their responses to the world become individualised. In "Disjuncture and Difference," Arjun Appadurai explains that the suffix *scape* connotes "deeply perspectival constructs" (296). In Conrad's fiction, as I understand it, emotions determine the response to the environment and sometimes become externalized in the object central to them, the ship being an example. Joyce Davidson and Christine Milligan observe in "Embodying Emotion Sensing Space" that "emotions *matter*. They have tangible effects on our surroundings and can shape the very nature and experience of our being-in-the-world. Emotions can clearly alter the way the world is for us, affecting our sense of time as well as space. Our sense of who and what we are is continually (re)shaped by how we feel" (524-25). Following this trail of thought, Romit Dasgupta defines emotionscape as a space "that has affect attached to it" (374). And that inspired my idea of emotionscape, i.e., affective space. In this paper, I am focusing on escape, that is, the employing of defensive mechanisms to cope with emotional strain and to remove oneself from the negative perception of the self, in order to look at how we flee and to what end. Of particular interest to me is escaping into fiction – understood as one's own idea of reality which might not necessarily have anything to do with how things are, and escaping into books; becoming trapped in one's own reeling mind, the healing power of a mental retreat but also how escaping into such mental spaces affects, even impedes, the ability to relate to others and function in the social space. Finally, I also consider the desire to tell a story – and like the ancient mariner, tell it until the heart stops burning – and show the power and possibility of social reading as Conrad, Miguel de Cervantes, and Ray Bradbury showed us before bookstagramming (sharing what you read on Instagram/social media as part of the book community) became a thing.

The Image of Books in Conrad's Fiction

Conrad's characters are often big and voracious readers and own impressive libraries. The following quotes provide a few examples: "He had asked for books it is true but there were but few in the cottage. He read them through in three days" (*C* 154); "One tall, broad bookcase, with glass doors, was full of books; but in the other, without shelves, and lined with red baize, were arranged firearms" (*N* 69); "A big bookcase (he was a great reader) occupied one side of his stateroom" ("The End of the Tether," *YS* 171). Although it is not entirely certain what reading material might have captivated Whalley quite so much (other than a reference to a poem), Helen Chambers (2018), discussing reading and reading spaces in Conrad and Conrad's work, points out that Whalley was able to precisely pinpoint a page reference from the Great Directory, which is indicative of Conrad's familiarity with the text, showing careful reading and great attention to bibliographic detail.

We know how important books were to Conrad and how they helped him in early childhood, influenced his life and shaped his work. He spent his early childhood burrowing in books. Tim Middleton, David Tutein, Hans van Marle, and Owen Knowles, discussing how extensive Conrad's reading was, offer lists of the works he read and owned – a library of nearly 900 books, providing a scholarly framework with which to investigate Conrad's reading. He read extensively in his youth. *A Personal Record* mentions "Victor Hugo and other romantics" (*PR* 70) along with "history, voyages, novels," "'Gil Blas' and 'Don Quixote' in abridged editions" (71), on top of poetry and his first introduction to English literature through his father's translations of William Shakespeare and enthusiasm for Charles Dickens. Furthermore, in the famous interview with Marian Dąbrowski for *Tygodnik Ilustrowany* in April 1914, Conrad discusses his extensive readings in Polish literature and the Polish Romantics that lent his work a quality English reviewers found *ungraspable*.[3] Studies of Conrad's work, apart from those mentioned, include discussions of genres, eras, and specific books. Some of his biographers (Frederick Karl, Zdzisław Najder, John Stape) also express interest in Conrad's reading, Karl focusing more on formative books and Stape examining Conrad's books and how he obtained them on various occasions.[4] Linda Dryden discusses Conrad and the imperial romance, and Stephen Donovan Conrad's attitude to magazine fiction. Susan Jones examines Conrad's reading of works by Marguerite Poradowska.

What you read is what you are, how you develop thought processes, therefore approaches to studying fiction through what their authors read are valid and may be informative. Scholars like Amar Acheraïou further point out that reading and interpretation transcend textuality to encompass the writer's background. The writer, especially in Conrad's conception, is the "secret sharer in the shaping of sense" and the reader is an active partner in this production of meaning (21). To read what the writer reads may foster and deepen this meaning-making process.[5] By engaging in this ongoing dialogue between reader and writer, a world of meaning and depth can be explored, creating a form of shared emotionscape. Aside from his extensively discussed literary influences, his stories include the trope of books, bookshelves, and avid readers of whom for me the most prominent and impactful example remains *Lord Jim*. Almost at the other end of the spectrum, we have Captain MacWhirr who, having derived all his know-how from the manual of seamanship, always attempts to do everything by literally following it, showing little flexibility, until a typhoon turns that procedure upside down. Conrad shows books, reading and meaning-making in both their positive, shelter-giving aspects, and their destructive dimensions. In Conrad, fiction – the stories we read or tell – can be destructive in several ways. First, it can prevent people from embracing something new, or unknown, and stop characters from getting to know something they fear (thus becoming limiting) and secondly, as in *Lord Jim*, it can affect the ability to function and relate to the world, social space, people, and even duties.

In "An Outpost of Progress," Kayerts and Carlier find a safe space in reading. However, it also serves to separate these characters from foreign cultures and embed them more strongly in what they know, preventing them from expanding beyond the borders of what is comfortable and safe:

> The two men understood nothing, cared for nothing but for the passage of days that separated them from the steamer's return. Their predecessor had left some torn books. They took up these wrecks of novels and, as they had never read anything of the kind before, they were surprised and amused. Then during long days there were interminable and silly discussions about plots and personages. In the centre of Africa they made acquaintance of Richelieu and of d'Artagnan, of Hawk's Eye and of Father Goriot, and of many other people. All these imaginary personages became subjects for gossip as if they had been living friends. They discounted their virtues, suspected their motives, decried their successes; were scandalised at their duplicity or were doubtful about their courage. The accounts of crimes filled

> them with indignation, while tender or pathetic passages moved them deeply. (*TU* 94)

Kayerts and Carlier are a great example of self-isolation through escape into fiction, as Wiesław Krajka points out in his comprehensive study of various aspects of isolation in Conrad's work, stating that this is their way of separating themselves from what is little-known to them and clinging to familiar values because, otherwise, the reality around them is hard to bear and mentally demanding (*Isolation and Ethos* 33). These books, classics, provide a safe way to deal with an unknown reality, and safety is important, but to feel safe we often need to feel comfortable. Being comfortable prevents the exploration of new territories. This is the reverse of the common, if not stereotyped, belief that books broaden the mind and expand mental horizons, leading us to learn more about foreign cultures. Conrad shows that it is possible to learn even less about foreign cultures and different ways of thinking by limiting ourselves to reading material that is familiar and comfortable. What follows is that a lack of familiarity with what is foreign leads to ignorance and greater fear of the unknown.

Another way books appear in Conrad's work is as perceived tokens of wickedness, specifically that of white men:

> And an old invalided jurumudi [...] explained to a small knot of unsophisticated citizens of Sambir that those books were books of magic – of magic that [...] gives them [white men] their wicked wisdom and their strength; of magic that makes them great, powerful and irresistible while they live, and – praise be to Allah! – the victims of Satan, the slaves of Jehannum when they die. (*OI* 299-300)

and a symbol and status of learning: "And, in truth, she was no longer girlish. It was said she often wrote State papers from her father's dictation, and was allowed to read all the books in his library" (*N* 150). The sense of the magic and appeal of books and what they offer is strong: "Captain Anthony was a great reader just about that time; and I, too, have a great liking for books. To this day I can't come near a book but I must know what it is about" (*C* 413); "'I am going back to my books,' he declared with a very serious face. 'My adventure is over!' 'Each one to his love,' she bantered us gently. 'Didn't I love books, too, at one time! They seemed to contain all wisdom and hold a magic power, too'" (*AG* 104). On the other hand, we also have characters like MacWhirr who may say: "These books are only good to muddle your head and make you jumpy" ("Typhoon," *TS* 87). But there is also much tenderness and respect for books, as in "Heart of Darkness": "by the door I picked up a book. It had lost its covers, and the pages had been thumbed into a state of extremely dirty softness; but the back had been lovingly stitched afresh with white cotton thread, which looked clean yet" (*YS* 99). And then: "I slipped the book into my pocket. I assure you to leave off reading was like tearing myself away from the shelter of an old and solid friendship" (99-100). In this instance, the book, belonging to the young Russian, is Townson's *An Inquiry into Some Points of Seamanship* which Marlow finds in the middle of the jungle. And suddenly, in this vast, hostile environment Marlow receives comfort. A book in the middle of the jungle and not just any book, but *The Manual of Seamanship* which is strongly relatable to him. It becomes like a glimpse of light, a doorway back to the world from which he comes. That brings comfort.

Alex Kurczaba notes this, stating that the book becomes more real than anything else in the Congo, even Kurtz (238). Further on, I discuss how stories told by characters create lingering memories, but these, by virtue of their transience, become more like distant dreams or fictions. This right here is a reversal: An object – a book – brings concreteness into a world that feels unreal, it really becomes "an emblem of sanity" (239).

Marlow examines the book and calls the author "a simple old sailor" with "a singleness of intention" and an honest concern for going about work. The book of seamanship is the focus of at least several interesting articles, such as by Jane Blanchard, and J. A. Arnold, which discuss its various implications as reflecting the sort of character the Company needs for achieving their purposes, but ultimately for Marlow it is more about serious intention with a moral purpose.

This description of leaving the "shelter of friendship" evokes the sensation of relating to someone who, through the pages, shares similar values, and the sense of reluctance in tearing oneself away lends itself to the idea that to read is to find a friend, a comfort zone to which one is happy to escape and which offers comfort when perhaps there is none to be found in the outside world or, indeed, if the world around us feels hostile and strange, as it does for so many of Conrad's characters and Conrad himself.

In his essay "Books," Conrad offers an explanation. They are "part and parcel of humanity" and "are worthy of regard, admiration, and compassion" (*NLL* 4). Books, writes Conrad, have their fate "and it's very much like the destiny of man." They share or, rather, contain and reflect, our values and our sins, our glories as well as our falls and failures. They are warnings and cautionary tales. Conrad asserts that: "[o]f all the inanimate objects, of all men's creations, books are the nearest to us, for they contain our very thought, our ambitions, our indignations, our illusions, our fidelity to truth, and our persistent leaning towards error" (5). Kurtz, who must be mentioned as he too owns a library, is something else entirely. He is a man who slides into madness in the wild wasteland. He has a gift for arts – poetry, music, arts, and speech/rhetoric. He is no one, appears fictional, barely there, a disembodied voice. A man larger than life, a worshipped god that commits atrocities. The interpretations veer towards the mythical. An interesting analysis is proposed by Nidesh Lawtoo, in conjunction with his reading of Lacoue-Labarthe and Conrad (87-143). The young Russian, Kurtz's admirer, claims the man has expanded his mind but wonders if it is even possible to see a "phenomenon" like Kurtz, a figure beyond the ordinary.

As noted by Acheraïou, reading is an active process of producing meaning and happens nearly all the time. Conrad's narrators and characters are also readers, some of them even detectives of the stories because they piece them together – Acheraïou proposes to divide them (94) into nominal (readers of texts) and metaphorical readers (active observers and interpreters of social contexts, cultural backgrounds, their own situations and those of others). Conrad's characters and narrators are often both at the same time. Marlow and the teacher of languages are both. The teacher reads Razumov's diary and Peter Ivanovitch's book on feminism and reads poetry together with Haldin. Marlow reads various documents and books, the unimaginative MacWhirr reads the manual on dealing with storms. Acheraïou agrees that in general, Conrad demonstrates an "obsession with readership and reading" (94-95).

Not all of the characters I am discussing are nominal readers because not all of them are moved by fictional pursuits. Nominal readers are of interest because of how fiction affects them (Jim, also Don Quixote, the enthusiast of chivalric romances). Metaphorical readers are interesting because, while their actions may not necessarily be inspired by what they read, most of them are still "secret sharers" of producing meaning and allay their fears and emotions through storytelling, sharing their stories. In doing so, they create a lingering memory that, while pervasive, feels like it was entirely fictional, but also permanently affecting (see the ending to "Karain," Jim's metafictional status, Yanko, or even Marlow's return from the Congo and memory of Kurtz). There are exceptions and interesting subversions like Captain Hagberd who creates his own fictional trap and is incapable of accepting or interacting with reality as it presents itself to him. The rhythmical pattern of his "to-morrow" initially lulls the reader into a dream, a hope, along with the anti-seaman. Therefore, to expand on the idea of emotionscapes and escape into mental, unreal spaces in which characters themselves are actively producing and receiving meaning, I find it productive to look at Conrad's characters who escape and how and where they escape.

Conrad's Characters and the Art of Escape

A desire to escape is a response to a sense of threat to the perception of self and stems from a desire to find shelter or relief. In 1990, Roy Baumeister proposed a psychological model of suicide called the "escape" theory. In this model, escape consists of six stages. Persons undergo experience. The experience leaves them aware that the outcomes fall below either the standards of society or those they have set for themselves. This awareness leads to an attempt to escape from the situation by actively striving to change the outcome, or by avoiding it altogether. They may blame these outcomes on their personality, and as a result, the self emerges as inadequate and incompetent. The individuals feel that their current situations do not meet their set of standards; they feel they have failed their own expectations. They seek to escape this negative psychological reaction by avoiding meaningful thoughts.[6] This avoidance of meaningful thought can lead to maladaptive coping strategies, such as denial, overthinking, and rumination. These strategies can interfere with problem-solving and lead to further negative emotions, undesirable behaviours, and a lack of meaningful action.

Conrad's characters largely escape in a manner that pushes them further into isolation and separation from the mundane world and the self, either because they cling too strongly to what they know or imagine, or because they have expectations and hopes for a better tomorrow. Yanko slips or escapes mentally into his language, and Leggatt becomes a part of someone else's life, like a moth drawn to light. Both cases are a kind of dream, a fiction. Yanko's country is far behind him and there is no one else in the area who would know it. Willems escapes humiliation, but it catches up with him in a confrontation between his wife and Aïssa. In *Almayer's Folly*, Almayer is caught up in escapist dreams, which, coupled with his lack of ability to empathize with characters, even his own daughter, outside his idealized European culture, make him not only isolated but also unpleasant and cantankerous and, like the protagonists of "An Outpost of Progress," he clings strongly to standards and values he thinks he knows. Karain's story is, at its core, a tale of betrayal and guilt, riddled with ghosts and nightmares. A guilty conscience makes escape impossible, though Karain considers the boat of the white men, the *unbelievers*, a place to hide which repels the stuff of fancy, a place of belief in the power of facts that does not lend itself to the supernatural or magic, or even more so, it has the sheer power of being a foreign element, something from outside.

> He looked round the little cabin [...]; he looked round as if appealing to all its shabby strangeness, to the disorderly jumble of unfamiliar things that belong to an inconceivable life of stress, of power, of endeavour, of unbelief – to the strong life of white men, which rolls on irresistible and hard on the edge of outer darkness. He stretched out his arms as if to embrace it and us. ("Karain: A Memory," *TU* 25-26)

Karain moves further inside it but is never quite able to escape. His entire venture is motivated by another person's escape, but in his quest, he can never quite escape from his own guilty conscience and one image, that of Pata Matara, replaces another, that of the woman. His hallucinations are as real to him as anger is to his friend. "My heart was torn with a strange fear, but could not die" (42). Karain cannot escape, even though he tries to find magic to do so – the sorcerer and sword-bearer, and then the narrator's schooner. The scene in the schooner resembles an exorcism. He is willing to follow the white men home until one of the narrator's friends presents him with the sixpence talisman. He subsequently disappears from their lives, but the memory, retold, lingers. The final sequences confront the reader with something that feels just like Karain's ghost – it is both permanent and ethereal, both something that changes one and something that feels unreal. The narrator and his associates have just returned from that fictional dream. Finishing a book often feels just like this, like returning from a long journey where reality feels strange for some time, and uncomfortable.

Karain's experience overall feels quite visceral and like the *opposite* of sheltering – as he cannot find shelter himself, neither can the reader, and he makes the reader feel the sense of discomfort. It is a madness that has no end. I find that mirrored to some extent in a French novel by David Diop – *At Night All Blood Is Black*. While the story grimly deals with the realities of World War I, Alfa, the Senegalese protagonist is also haunted by the death of his friend, "more-than-brother." But he goes mad at the fact that he has not killed his friend himself, launching into a murder spree to make up for it. The story shows how war brutalizes and destroys Alfa. The story has made me question my own sanity as a reader, considering how the narrative turns. Alfa is presented as a savage beast with a machete – a racial stereotype – and used in the war as a subhuman tool. His killing spree earns him the reputation of a sorcerer. I thought about this novella in relation to Conrad's stories for several reasons, but predominantly because of a reversal I found. Where Karain needed a sorcerer, Alfa became one himself, and more. Both ended up trying to escape and found no way to do so and no shelter. The writing reflects oral traditions and follows a mesmerising rhythm, marked by recurring phrases that highlight the madness and brutality of the experiences, making reading itself quite visceral and, therefore, the opposite of sheltering or protective. Not even the boat of white men can save Karain. For the reader, the experiences are depressing but also cathartic and thought-provoking.

Female Characters

Women who escape cause woe in Conrad's fiction, but what is their own situation? Women characters in Shirley Jackson's fiction – Merrikat and her sister, as well as Eleanor from *The Haunting of Hill House* – are presented as very vulnerable, with active imagination, living out a world of their own invention, with chilling consequences. They find a way to escape, but in both cases, it is an escape doomed to total failure. In another example, Jane Austen's Catherine Morland believes that the world around her is like the books she has read, leading her to make assumptions about the people she meets based on her knowledge of novels. As a result, she finds herself in situations that she is not prepared for and must find a way to navigate them using her own judgement. *Northanger Abbey* is integral to the article's theme and, while not discussed here, will be explored in the future. What about women in Conrad's work?

Female characters in Conrad are a very diverse group, some loyal, others cunning and relying on wit to gain advantage in not-always-perfect circumstances – Nina's mother comes to mind. Then there are characters like Amy who, while not unkind, are vulnerable and follow survival instincts.

Conrad's female characters are not deprived of imagination, which allows them to seek ways out of their predicaments or at least let them build resilience. My favourite character in this respect is Nina. Both Almayer and Nina are outside their own cultures, but Nina finds a way to escape. For Kaspar, there is no escape. He shows little imagination and compassion in dealing with his wife or daughter, and his dreams, while verging on love for Nina and a desire that they may lead better lives, are short-sighted, egotistic, and purely escapist. Dain, Nina's lover, escapes with his life, and Almayer pays with his life. Nina escapes to a new-old identity by escaping with Dain, though she becomes dead to Kaspar.

While Amy is described as having an "inertness" ("Amy Foster," *TS* 107) that makes her mind safe "from all the surprises of imagination" (though it is immediately followed up by "which of us is safe?"), her imagination is one which warns her of a possible threat. But she is limited in what she can understand and imagine beyond what is familiar to her. Her fear limits her understanding of Yanko's predicament in the final scenes. Her escape is one marked by a desire to protect her child but also one that discredits her as simple and unimaginative. "Does she ever think of the past?" (142), the story asks. Yanko's plight always awakens sympathy, but Amy, who is actually easy to resent, has to face the mundane, and there's no escape for her. In a sort of reversal, or perhaps parallel to Almayer, she is also trapped.

Escape is impossible for Bessie in "To-morrow." This often overlooked story with considerable interpretative potential introduces the conflict between father and son, drawing on the contrast between the two Hagberds. In his presentation on "The Social Archetypes of Identity" during the 7th International Conrad Conference, Wiesław Krajka points out that young Hagberd is sharply contrasted to his father, "a negative mariner," who "lived among a scheme of settled notions," suspicious of people, and who dreams of having his son home, married to Bessie, in an escapist fantasy that projects and tries to force his own personality on Harry. Young Hagberd is a spirit of wandering – a vagabond – and feels like a breath of fresh air because he represents a different mode of life to Bessie, whose only purpose in life is to slave for her blind father and Hagberd. Her general situation resembles a non-resolvable status quo. She is "stranded there after a storm and a shipwreck" ("To-morrow," *TS* 275). Harry's arrival and the escape he represents shows her what she does not have and, in this sense, build on the theme of coveting, that irreconcilable state of in-between, which leaves one yearning and incomplete.

What appealed to me in my reading of the story is that she demonstrates her imagination, the ability to imagine the possibility of a future different from her current situation. When Bessie talks to young Hagberd, as if in response, her ears become open "to the voices of the world, she heard beyond the rampart of the sea-wall the swell of yesterday's gale breaking on the beach with monotonous and solemn vibrations, as if all the earth had been a tolling bell" (268). While this evocative sonic storm attacks the senses and may indicate a kind of violation,[7] I read it as a means of escape, a possibility of imagining a different scenario: a seduction into a different mode of life that ultimately seems impossible. It is a moment of dreaming that, for a brief time, allows her to be transported somewhere else, into a wider, cosmic order, but dies away. In other words, in this reading Harry represents a fictional character that enters her life as a distant possibility but leaves like a whirlwind soon after. Harry is a disturbance to the captain's monotonous and comfortable flow of everyday life and a piece of fiction, because he does not conform to his father's set perceptions of what he should be. He emerges as "something wrong" (259, 277), a sort of a nightmare. Hagberd is focused on home, his attitude towards the sea is described as one of "profound and emotional animosity" (249), and he takes pride in staying close to the shore throughout his years of service. Hagberd's idea of home is encapsulated in the repeated futile refrain of "to-morrow" – it is Hagberd's own little world, a piece of fiction into which he escapes from something he does not confront, or rather confronts as one might a nasty dream – nods at it but tries to wave it away. Harry is something wrong that needs to go away for Hagberd's world to be okay. Hagberd insists that waiting for to-morrow is the "good home" that Bessie deserves, while the man he does not accept as his son "has no home" for he is "only a vagabond" (273). In this way, the story subverts the idea of home as a place of safety. Here it becomes a place of rotting and stagnation and unreal wishes, of waiting for the impossible. The wishful refrain is a trap and Harry will not let himself be caught in it. Harry's running away reads like a break from the mundane and the confinement of routine, "[b]ecause in a house you can at any time open the blamed door and walk away straight before you" (267). And he does, taking the reader with him. We leave Bessie without a sound – "no whisper of life" (276), where "all the hopeful madness of the world had broken out to bring terror upon her heart, with the voice of that old man shouting of his trust in an everlasting to-morrow" (277).

Escaping into a fictional, imagined, fantasy world can lead to isolation as well as a loss of contact with the real world. An overly active imagination and living a fictional life cause inertia and an inability to act in everyday life; it destroys social links to others and in some cases, causes an abandonment of duty.

Lord Jim and *Don Quixote*

I find this to be the core issue in both *Don Quixote* and *Lord Jim*. Like many readers, I have read Jim in various ways. The first read, when I was 17, brought a sense of identification – a lone figure struggling against a world that does not want to give him peace and let it go, and I thought he really was a unique individual. Reading inflated his ego and allowed him to create fantasy worlds that had little to do with reality. He focused on escaping from himself more than on the facts, showing a complete inability to accept himself as a human with failings and deal with the mundane. In turn, his life in the fictional world awarded him "utter insecurity for life and property" in a total reversal of the security of real life in which he sought danger and adventure in dreams (see, for instance, Hampson 130).

The basis for my wish to read these two novels consecutively, other than Conrad's familiarity with *Don Quixote*, were especially these two quotes, the first from *Don Quixote*:

> In short, our gentleman became so caught up in reading that he spent his nights reading from dusk till dawn and his days reading from sunrise to sunset, and so with too little sleep and too much reading his brains dried up, causing him to lose his mind. His fantasy filled with everything he had read in his books, enchantments as well as combats, battles, challenges, wounds, courtings, loves, torments, and other impossible foolishness, and he became so convinced in his imagination of the truth of all the countless grandiloquent and false inventions he read that for him no history in the world was truer. (Cervantes 21)

And this from *Lord Jim*:

> On the lower deck in the babel of two hundred voices he would forget himself, and beforehand live in his mind the sea-life of light literature. He saw himself saving people from sinking ships, cutting away masts in a hurricane, swimming through a surf with a line; or as a lonely castaway, barefooted and half naked, walking on uncovered reefs in search of shellfish to stave off starvation. He confronted savages on tropical shores, quelled mutinies on the high seas, and in a small boat upon the ocean kept up the hearts of despairing men – always an example of devotion to duty, and as unflinching as a hero in a book. (*LJ* 6)

In both cases, the characters become filled with fantasy and they are both set apart from "the babel of two hundred voices," with their spirited imagination and a longing for adventure and chivalry. Dreams are perhaps even more tangible for Jim than reality is for his fellow seamen, just as reality is instantly magical for Quixote.

It has become a truism to say that books let us live a thousand lives, and yet that feeling often accompanies the reading experience, and it is one truism I feel highlights Jim's experience. These two quotes are similar in the way they point out how books stimulate the imagination, whether for better or worse, except that I find Don Quixote a lot more sympathetic and genuine in the way he lives in his own version of the world and experiences it in his own way. He sees reality and things in a way that's truly magical and wondrous; this may be unhealthy imagination, and we could argue distortion, but it is also like colour being added to the otherwise mundane and helping me as a reader see that there can be magic in the most ordinary, little things if we choose to see it.

Jim's vision is also "enlarged." C. F. Burgess observed many years ago in *The Fellowship of the Craft* that Jim sees too much because "imagination is creative" (47), enlarges and distorts things and Jim "doesn't see things exactly as they are" (48). In this, he is very quixotic.

But Jim is mostly just escaping from himself. In a metafictional way, he escapes into Patusan, where he fills a vacancy for a larger-than-life hero, unable to deal with the immediate reality, and in a way, he realizes his dream of becoming an idealistic hero from a fictional story. When he talks to Marlow, he refers to Dain's parents as "people in a book." And their son, Dain, is the best friend he ever had – barring Marlow.

Jim becomes a metafictional figure, a protagonist returned to a book of stories, where as a character he rightfully fits, a realisation of his fantasies. Patusan is like a book of adventures he has read. It is where he wants to be. He becomes distant and unreal (also *unknowable*) to Marlow, who has cared about him. There is, however, that one scene towards the end of the book where they say farewell for the final time, which made me feel a lot of emotion. Marlow is a best kind of friend because, as Tadeusz Bobrowski did for Conrad, he tries to pull Jim out and set him in reality, even though he is doomed to fail, but the way he cares is precious; the text gives me the sense that Jim is very lucky to have a friend in Marlow. In turn, Don Quixote pulls his friend Sancho into his world and the two adventure together. Quixote sees the world in a different way: for him everything gains a sense of magic and wonder. He becomes almost a reality show star, to the entertainment of those who design adventures for him and Sancho. Quixote and Sancho are continuously metafictional; Jim moves towards metafictionality in the second part of the novel. These stories could be also interpreted as two different models of building resilience. Quixote strongly believes in reality the way he sees it and acts accordingly, ever chivalric; Jim has to atone and take responsibility for an act that was fuelled by his inability to act despite his imagined perception of himself, significantly doing so in the metafictional part of his adventures.

Two friendships, two characters dreaming of a book-like life, two different ways in which they realize that dream. However, Don Quixote feels a bit richer in experiences and adventures – including metafictional ones – and the way Quixote renders reality feels a lot more magical and wondrous, as if seen through rose-coloured glasses, making it seem appealing and worthwhile. The friendship theme is strong in both, but Marlow's practical but kind interest in his young protégé is gentler, while the characters surrounding Don Quixote, who try to lift him out of his fantasy, are unsympathetic and at times threatening in the way they try to pull him back from what they consider a dangerous affliction – and which they blame on the books.

Ivan Turgenev notes in his lecture on Hamlet and Quixote that we should not see Quixote just as a parody of chivalric romances, and in the second part of the novel, Quixote is no longer a buffoon but becomes a peer; he typifies "[f]aith, first of all, a belief in something eternal, indestructible? [...] Don Quixote is entirely permeated by an attachment to his ideal for which he is ready to endure untold misery, even to sacrifice his own life" (94). Unlike Jim, Don Quixote never betrays his beliefs. He perseveres in his commitment to live out the chivalric ideal no matter the cost. However, Jim's code is more complex (Hampson 116).

Cervantes deals with a lot of tropes common to chivalric romances, and he permits them to be seen within the narratives. These, in turn, give me as the reader a chance to explore various what-ifs. First, Don Quixote sees one thing. There are many fantastic adventures in this novel as a result, things that would make great fantasy. You meet windmills posed as giants, enchanted heads, enchanters, flying horses, and visions in caves. They are all amusing, and what's more, a lot of the adventures are devised by other characters for their own amusement, and they cover an amazing range of scenarios: from fights with windmills to sea adventures and sieges of towns. We explore a seemingly endless garden of possibilities: what if Sancho was a governor, for instance. These scenarios open up billions of fictional possibilities. Quixote and Sancho end up being protagonists within the story but also within stories/plots created for them by others, like protagonists of a reality show within the story.

While the episodes are parodies that allow us to laugh at Quixote and knights-errant, they are also a commentary on how fiction makes our lives more colourful. Quixote might be the subject of jokes, not all of them very nice, but he is still a sympathetic and lovable character, and his belief in the magical is lovely because instead of mundane reality he sees wonders. There are also stories upon stories of numerous characters, many of them love stories that end in various ways: some happily (much to my delight), others less so. Crucial among them is the story of the captive captain which transfers into fiction Cervantes's own experiences.

The book is amusing in its duality: it puts down what Cervantes considered to be the absurdities of chivalric romances, but at the same time gives life to them in the imagination of Don Quixote. The characters know they are the protagonists of a published book and the story deals with the process of writing, too. There are also some unsettling scenes about censorship and book burning, indicative of Cervantes's dislike of chivalric romances. Don Quixote is both sympathetic and lovable but he can also be read as a pompous madman: it depends on you, the reader, what you choose to see. His imagination drives him to see reality in a more wonderful way which can be healing, and this idea captured me in this quote:

> And your grace should believe me when I tell you [...] to read these books, and you will see how they drive away melancholy if you are so afflicted and improve your spirits if they happen to be low. For myself, I can say that since I became a knight errant I have been valiant, well-mannered, liberal, polite, generous, courteous, bold, gentle, patient, long-suffering in labors, imprisonments, and enchantments, and although only a short while ago I saw myself locked in a cage like a madman, I think that with the valor of my arm, and heaven favoring me, and fortune not opposing me, in a few days I shall find myself the king of some kingdom where I can display the gratitude and liberality of my heart. (Cervantes 430)

Quixote succeeds in building a strong case for fiction and its healing power, whereas Jim is a lot more destructive in the way he denies the facts. Yet rather than facts, what Jim tries to escape from is his own failure to be a perfect human and he insists on wanting to become a perfect hero. There are several scenes with Marlow which highlight this for me, one of them being their conversation about Jim's next steps, but what captures me in this scene is how kindly Marlow tries to pull him back:

> He was very far away from me who watched him across three feet of space. With every instant he was penetrating deeper into the impossible world of romantic achievements. He got to the heart of it at last! A strange look of beatitude overspread his features, his eyes sparkled in the light of the candle burning between us; he positively smiled! He had penetrated to the very heart – to the very heart. It was an ecstatic smile that your faces – or mine either – will never wear, my dear boys. I whisked him back by saying, "If you had stuck to the ship, you mean!" (*LJ* 83-84)

In the end, he fails; Jim realizes his dreams, and becomes completely consumed by them. But, as Marlow asks, "Is he satisfied – quite, now, I wonder?" (416).

Storytelling as Therapy.
Social Reading/Storytelling – Community Building

Writers of Conrad's and Cervantes's calibre are often marked by traumas that have left an indelible stamp on their work, and both of these had experiences that led them to hope for a change or liberation. Turning to books and writing was a way to heal. We know how deeply Conrad's early life marked him with the experience of events of broad, catastrophic proportions, both political and personal. Adam Mickiewicz's "Alas for us who fled in times of pest" (283), keenly endorsed by Apollo Korzeniowski, became his curse. Bobrowski's kind-hearted and diligent help, coupled with ideas inspired by books, opened the way to the response to Russian rule, so different from Apollo's. But Conrad was never truly free. Although Michael Greaney notes in *Conrad, Language and Narrative* that "regions of air and sky can be seen as an escape from suffocation of the drawing-room culture and its confining architecture" (51), as Conrad later commented, life at sea proved to have confines of its own, and there were moments it resembled the same sense of confinement he might have felt with Apollo. Looking at Conrad's life sometimes feels like observing one huge adventure in which the protagonist grows from error into solemn maturity. But he always seems to be dealing with some sort of sense of imprisonment, and I often imagine that books and writing greatly helped him through it. Cervantes too went through a harrowing experience when he was enslaved by pirates and imprisoned in Algiers, and he returned to this theme in *Don Quixote* and other works, telling the tale over and over in order to heal. "Since then, at an uncertain hour / That agony returns / And till my ghastly tale is told / This heart within me burns" ("The Rime of the Ancient Mariner"). The Ancient Mariner is compelled to tell his story. Telling his tale is part of his penance for killing the albatross. Cervantes included his experience of being a captive in his work; Quixote himself is a figure of mental imprisonment but one that also gives hope. Cervantes seemingly deals with his captivity over and over again. Conrad was a captive of bleak political circumstances from an early age; reading inspired his idea of getting into a marine school which in the end he could not do because he could not secure Austrian citizenship. And he had to get away for fear of being conscripted. "An old man's child, having lost his mother early, thrown out to sea out of the way while very young, he had not much experience of the tenderness of any kind" ("Freya of the Seven Isles," *TLS* 183). In every work, at every step, there is a part of Conrad and his experience reflected in the act of storytelling and oral storytelling shared among people of the same profession, mindset, or disposition or those acting as confidantes and protectors. In this respect, I also consider Marlow the seaman sharing his tales with fellow men of the sea.

Several Conradian characters illustrate the idea of storytelling as an act of healing, recalling and sharing as not least of all Marlow the narrator as well as the narrators in "Amy Foster" and *The Shadow-Line*. Kennedy tries to preserve Yanko's memory by the act of storytelling. The narrator in *The Shadow-Line* attempts to preserve his sanity in dealing with what appears to be the supernatural presence of a very villainous previous captain and a chain of events that weigh heavily on his first command, with echoes of "The Ancient Mariner," not least of which is his compulsion to tell this story. He experiences "a nightmare" when he finds out he has no quinine but only useless powder, and has to battle a pervasive, evil presence. It seems too much for his first command and he observes that he feels as if he is going mad and notes an overwhelming sense of guilt. His diary is a coping mechanism and a form of confession, as hinted at in the subtitle. This interesting theme with implications for potential further elaboration in the context of this paper is present in a lot of Conrad's works: Marlow could be said to be confessing his experiences in the Congo; the short story "The Tale" introduces the theme of a Captain who confesses how he sent a boat with her crew to their death. Falk also confesses to his gruesome crime, achieving a certain release. Razumov's diary is a complex set of confessions that also includes Haldin's. Razumov wants to be understood, but his stances lead us rather to question them and see their ambiguity. As the internal drama of doubt plays out, escape from guilt proves impossible, especially when he discovers feelings for Natalia Haldin. Like Jim, he ultimately delivers himself up to justice. The teacher of languages, expressing his surprise that Razumov would even want anyone to see his record, is compelled to say at the beginning of the novel that "mere words" must have "a wonderful soothing power" (*UWE* 5) as so many use them for "self-communion." Much like *Lord Jim*, the structure of *Under Western Eyes* is a fascinating interplay of accounts, with shifting temporal perspectives, but even then, emotions boil over; the palpable psychological tension resulting from Razumov's attempts to reconcile opposing allegiances is one of the strongest points of interest for me in this novel. Razumov is in his own emotionscape, trying to find comfort in writing and relief in confessing. Storytelling can save a life, as in *The Book of One Thousand and One Nights* that through its effective narrative demonstrates the impact a story can have on one's life.

Karain cannot escape, but his seeking out the white narrator and his companions provides testimony to the idea that storytelling offers a chance to find shelter. Karain wants to feel safe and protected. The narrator declares that the effect of Karain's story "is undying; it is but a memory and its vividness cannot be made clear to another mind any more than the vivid emotions of a dream" ("Karain: A Memory," *TU* 26), and "[h]is words sounded low, in a sad murmur as of running water; at times they rang loud like the clash of a war-gong – or trailed slowly like weary travellers – or rushed forward with the speed of fear" (27). A certain degree of hierarchy is implied; the person seeking shelter is dependent on the hospitality of the person in charge. However, Conrad states:

> No man will speak to his master; but to a wanderer and a friend, to him who does not come to teach or to rule, to him who asks for nothing and accepts all things, words are spoken by the camp-fires, in the shared solitude of the sea, in riverside villages, in resting-places surrounded by forests – words are spoken that take no account of race or colour. One heart speaks – another one listens; and the earth, the sea, the sky, the passing wind and the stirring leaf, hear also the futile tale of the burden of life. (26)

By telling his story, Karain finds a brief shelter. Marlow, by sharing his tales, creates a community of people who, regardless of race or background, unite in experiencing and sharing stories, and experiencing good and evil. Telling Jim's tale is therapeutic because Marlow can share his thoughts with others, assert the truth of Jim's existence, and give it shape and life through storytelling,[8] and test what he is saying against the experiences of like-minded people with similar experiences. But it also helps him to deal with loss, the loss of a dear protégé, a unique friend everyone has trouble figuring out, but perhaps even more so, with a sense of loss of a certain moment that can still linger and be recreated and captured through storytelling. Marlow seems to have felt it towards the end of the novel (the emotionality of the parting scene, for instance), however much he may have rationalized, feeling calm that Jim had finally mastered his fate.

Bookstagram works much the same way: it relies on sharing what we read and passing it on. And as Bradbury says in *Fahrenheit 451*: though people may burn it, let's keep it alive by memorising – sharing. The final moments when Montag meets up with a group of people who memorize books recall the ideas shown by Conrad through Marlow and even Cervantes, regardless of the tone he takes towards Quixote – the desire to keep stories and books alive, regardless of political circumstances, of banning, has to prevail. Conrad shows me the healing and liberating power of fiction in equal measure as Cervantes, the desire to keep sharing and keep stories alive that goes hand in hand with our desire to read, for so many different reasons. To escape, to heal, to forget. While escapes are dangerous (though then again, so is Hagberd's home with its rotting stagnancy), the "shelter of an old friend" with the tales they offer and the possibility of telling those tales, is irreplaceable.

NOTES

1 Of interest is also this site: https://www.open.ac.uk/Arts/reading/UK/, which provides further interesting insights and material for consideration in the future.

2 Unlike Ayu L. Saraswati, I develop emotionscapes as a concept that reflects individual, emotional reception of the world, rather than as

"a repository of culturally scripted and socially acceptable emotions that circulate transnationally" (11-12). Books and reading as a form of self-help put my understanding of emotionscapes closer to the idea developed by Alan Gartner and Frank Riessman, that emotionscapes put individuals in their own bubbles, separate and different from everyone else, like archipelagos (which Conradian characters are) but at the same time my focus is rather on how closing themselves in that bubble affects them, and more importantly, how it impacts their perception of the world, how objectivity and social relations may become muddled and lost, even further when fuelled by fiction and the experience of reading. The concept is important for me personally, and one could say that writing about it is a form of self-help. The definition of landscape on which Gartner and Riessman base their idea, however, applies because the emotionscape is an inner landscape (210-11).

[3] Marian Dąbrowski, "Rozmowa z Conradem" (1914), Polish version available online – see Works Cited. English translation in "An Interview with J. Conrad" in *Conrad Under Familial Eyes* (Najder) or in Jezierski. Significantly, Andrzej Busza wrote on the influence of Polish Romantic literature on Conrad, bringing the Polish sources to light in English-language studies.

[4] Research undeniably aided immensely by a thorough examination of all volumes of *CL*. This includes Conrad's correspondence with various writers, e.g. his letter to H. G. Wells of 25 May, 1986 and Hugh Clifford of 9 October, 1899, in which Conrad tells them how much he enjoys their work (*CL* 1: 282; 2: 199-200), letter to C. Graham dated 5 August, 1897, in which he discusses Kipling (1: 369), letter to Aniela Zagórska dated Christmas 1898, in which he reviews and recommends various books (2: 137), letter to Edward Garnett dated 20 January, 1900, where he mentions his father's translations (2: 243-47), and many others.

[5] Ruth Ozeki's *A Tale for the Time Being* depicts an intriguing reader-writer relationship between Ruth, a writer, and a Japanese teenage girl whose diary washes ashore Ruth's island after the tsunami of 2011.

[6] Thoughts themselves are a reaction and memories are powerful stimuli of those reactions, as they are for Jim, whose response continued to be filtered through the memory of his past experience. Perhaps moving to Patusan can even be viewed as a form of metaphorical suicide. Further interesting insights are addressed in Hardie-Bick.

[7] During the Conrad conference in June 2022, the participants were shown clips of an adaptation of the story and the play (Krajka, "Social Archetypes") which made me think of this part and the ending.

[8] "Now he is no more, there are days when the reality of his existence comes to me with an immense […] force; and yet […] there are moments, too, when he passes from my eyes like a disembodied spirit" (*LJ* 416).

WORKS CITED

Ablow, Rachel, ed. *The Feeling of Reading: Affective Experience and Victorian Literature.* U of Michigan P, 2010.

Acheraïou, Amar. *Joseph Conrad and the Reader: Questioning Modern Theories of Narrative and Readership.* Palgrave Macmillan, 2009.

Appadurai, Arjun. "Disjuncture and Difference in the Global Cultural Economy." *Theory, Culture and Society* 7 (1990): 295-310. Accessed 15 Nov. 2022. < https://doi.org/10.1177/026327690007002017>.

Arnold, J. A. "The Young Russian's Book in Conrad's 'Heart of Darkness'." *Conradiana* 8 (1976): 121-26. Accessed 5 Jan. 2023. Stable URL: <http://www.jstor.org/stable/24633901>.

Baumeister, Roy. F. "Suicide as Escape from Self." *Psychological Review* 97 (1990): 90-113. Accessed 14 Nov. 2022. <https://pubmed.ncbi.nlm.nih.gov/2408091>.

Blanchard, Jane. "The Book on Seamanship in 'Heart of Darkness'." *Pacific Coast Philology* 45 (2010): 42-52. Accessed 5 Jan. 2023. Stable URL: <http://www.jstor.org/stable/41413520>.

Bradbury, Ray. *Fahrenheit 451.* Harper, 2013.

Burgess, Chester Francis. *Fellowship of the Craft: Conrad on Ships and Seamen and the Sea.* Kennikat P, 1976.

Busza, Andrzej. "Conrad's Polish Literary Background and Some Illustrations of the Influence of Polish Literature on His Work." *Antemurale* 10 (1966): 109-255.

Cervantes, Miguel. *Don Quixote.* Trans. Edith Grossman. Harper, 2003.

Chambers, Helen. *Conrad's Reading: Space, Time, Networks.* Palgrave Macmillan, 2018. New Directions in Book History.

Coleridge, Samuel Taylor. "The Rime of the Ancient Mariner." 1834. Poetry Foundation. Accessed 20 May 2022. <https://www.poetryfoundation.org/poems/43997/the-rime-of-the-ancient-mariner-text-of-1834>.

Dąbrowski, Marian. "Rozmowa z Conradem." *Polskie zaplecze Josepha Conrada-Korzeniowskiego. Dokumenty rodzinne, listy, wspomnienia.* Ed. Zdzisław Najder and Joanna Skolik. Vol. 2. Gaudium, 2006. 217-23.

Digital Library of the University of Lodz. Accessed 12 Jan. 2023. <https://bcul.lib.uni.lodz.pl/dlibra/publication/211/edition/120/content>.

Dasgupta, Romit. "Emotional Spaces and Places of Salaryman Anxiety in Tokyo Sonata." *Japanese Studies* 31 (2011): 373-86. Accessed 11 May 2022. <https://www.tandfonline.com/doi/citedby/10.1080/10371397.2011.619169>.

Davidson, Joyce, and Christine Milligan. "Embodying Emotion Sensing Space: Introducing Emotional Geographies." *Social and Cultural Geography* 5 (2004): 523-32. Accessed 29 Dec. 2022. <http://dx.doi.org/10.1080/1464936042000317677>.

Diop, David. *At Night All Blood Is Black.* Trans. Anna Moschovakis. Farrar, 2020.

Donovan, Stephen. *Joseph Conrad and Popular Culture*. Palgrave Macmillan, 2005.

Dryden, Linda. *Joseph Conrad and the Imperial Romance*. Palgrave Macmillan; 2000. Perlego Ebook. <https://www.perlego.com/book/3502763/joseph-conrad-and-the-imperial-romance-pdf>.

Gartner, Alan, and Frank Riessman. *The Self-Help Revolution*. Human Sciences P, 1984.

Greaney, Michael. *Conrad, Language and Narrative*. Cambridge UP, 2009.

Hampson, Robert. *Joseph Conrad: Betrayal and Identity*. Macmillan, 1992.

Halsey, Katie, and W. R. Owens. *The History of Reading*. Vol. 2. *Evidence from the British Isles*. Palgrave Macmillan, 2011.

Hardie-Bick, James. "Escaping the Self: Identity, Group Identification and Violence." *Oñati Socio-Legal Series* 6 (2016): 1032-52. Accessed 1 Feb. 2023. <http://sro.sussex.ac.uk/id/eprint/62068/>.

Hervouet, Yves. *The French Face of Joseph Conrad*. Cambridge UP, 1990.

Jezierski, Bronislas A., et al. "An Interview with Joseph Conrad." *The American Scholar* 13 (1944): 371-75. Accessed 2 Feb. 2023. Stable URL: <http://www.jstor.org/stable/41204686>.

Jones, Susan. *Conrad and Women*. Clarendon P, 1999.

Karl, Frederick R. *Joseph Conrad: The Three Lives*. Faber, 1979.

Knowles, Owen. *A Conrad Chronology*. Hall, 1990. 2nd ed. Palgrave Macmillan, 2014.

Krajka, Wiesław. *Isolation and Ethos. A Study of Joseph Conrad*. East European Monographs, Columbia UP, 1992.

---. "The Social Archetypes of Identity in Joseph Conrad's 'To-morrow,' *One Day More*, and *Jutro* by Baird, Hussakowski and Sito." 7th International Joseph Conrad Conference. Lublin, June, 2022, Maria Curie-Skłodowska University, Lublin. Conference Presentation.

Kurczaba, Alex S., ed. *Conrad and Poland*. East European Monographs, Maria Curie-Skłodowska U, Columbia UP, 1996. Vol. 5 of Conrad: *Eastern and Western Perspectives*. Ed. Wiesław Krajka. 32 vols. to date. 1992- .

Lawtoo, Nidesh, ed. *Conrad's "Heart of Darkness" and Contemporary Thought: Revisiting the Horror with Lacoue-Labarthe*. Bloomsbury, 2012.

Mickiewicz, Adam. *Pan Tadeusz, or the Last Foray in Lithuania*. Trans. and Intro. Kenneth Mackenzie. Dent, 1966.

Middleton, Tim. *Joseph Conrad*. Routledge, 2013.

Najder, Zdzisław, ed. *Conrad under Familial Eyes*. Trans. Halina Caroll--Najder. Cambridge UP, 1983.

---, ed. *Conrad's Polish Background: Letters to and from Polish Friends*. Trans. Halina Carroll. Oxford UP, 1964.

Ozeki, Ruth. *A Tale for the Time Being: A Novel*. Penguin, 2013.

Saraswati, L. Ayu. *Seeing Beauty, Sensing Race in Transnational Indonesia*. U of Hawaii P, 2013.

Stape, John. *The Several Lives of Joseph Conrad*. Arrow, 2008.

Turgenev, Ivan, and Moshe Spiegel. "Hamlet and Don Quixote." Trans. Moshe Spiegel. *Chicago Review* 17.4 (1965): 92-109. Accessed 12 Dec. 2022. Stable URL: <https://doi.org/10.2307/25293952>.

Tutein, David W. *Joseph Conrad's Reading: An Annotated Bibliography.* Locust Hill P, 1990.

Van Marle, Hans. "A Novelist's Dukedom: From Joseph Conrad's Library." *The Conradian* 16.1 (1991): 55-78. Accessed 10 Nov. 2022. Stable URL: <http://www.jstor.org/stable/20873995>.

White, Andrea. *Joseph Conrad and the Adventure Tradition: Constructing and Deconstructing the Imperial Subject.* Cambridge UP, 1993.

Jarosław Giza,
University of Applied Sciences,
Nowy Sącz, Poland

Conradian *femmes fatales* – Winnie Verloc, Freya, the Governess, and Susan Bacadou: Utterly Evil?

> Conrad has drawn, at times, definitely offensive women [...]. It is in such figures that Conrad instills all the venom of his hatred of insincerity and vapid pose. (Curle 158)
> a belief in a supernatural source of evil is not necessary; men alone are quite capable of every wickedness. (*UWE* 151)

Joseph Conrad has undeniably been treated as a writer whose literary domain gyrated around a meticulous portrayal of the life of men and their adventures. Hence, there has always been an impression that the figure of woman could be less analysed, and would therefore be a less significant section of Conradian criticism. It seems enough to quote here a few scholars to get a glimpse at Conrad's approach to women in his literary fiction. For instance, Susan Jones in her article "Representing Women: Conrad, Marguerite Poradowska, and *Chance*" asserts that for many critics the explanation of Conrad's failure to portray women in a more active way is the fact that "in drawing on his experiences as a sailor Conrad had comparatively little experience of women" (59). Moreover, while referring to this aspect of Conrad's fiction, Bernard Meyer in his *Joseph Conrad. A Psychoanalytic Biography* maintains, as quoted by Monika Malessa-Drohomirecka,

> that the evident difficulties which the writer experienced in portraying the nature of relations between the sexes were caused by complexes which had arisen as a result of traumas and bitterness experienced in his youth and that the unconvincing nature of his literary portrayals of women was basically due to his ignorance and fear of them. (25)

A similar assumption is made by Neville Newhouse who acknowledges that Conrad's descriptions of women represent "a serious failure of communication" and adds that "Conrad invests femininity with an aura of sacred distance. His women, just because they are women, are set apart" (74), a statement functioning as an echo to Marlow's assertion about women in "Heart of Darkness": "It's queer how out of touch with truth women are. They live in a world of their own" (*YS* 59).

Women are therefore usually positioned in a fantasy domain of exquisiteness and, therefore, as indifferent to, and taken from, the ruthlessness of the mechanisms prevalent in the male world, being "protected and enshrined within the domestic sphere" on account of the fact that "the outside world of imperialist adventures is too harsh for [them] to survive and to understand" (Kao 118). The most straightforward assertions may be those expressed by Thomas Moser in *Joseph Conrad: Achievement and Decline,* who remarks on "Conrad's fear and hostility towards women in his female characters" (qtd. by Iwashimizu 147), and Malessa-Drohomirecka, who avers that Conrad's "attitude towards women was ambivalent and indecisive. On the one hand he sought their company, while on the other he was afraid of them. It was as if something was pulling him back and keeping him from fully committing himself" (38).

Therefore, there seems to be a sharp division between Conrad's portrayal of men and women. This partition is perceivable in the fact that the male protagonists, while taking a precise path between virtue and vice, good and iniquity, and while taking recourse to knowledge as the token of their powerfulness, are presented as overshadowing and overwhelming their female counterparts as far as proclivity towards action and evil is concerned. In Conrad, women very often function as being feeble and inert, displaying neither the bravery nor the moral commissions and failings of men, and seem to be "conceived of in terms of the roles they play vis-à-vis men," as suggested by Padmini Mongia (135). Therefore, it is held, even when Conrad does allow his female protagonists to be evil, cunning, depraved, and influential, their actions seem to be rather mean, one-dimensional, predictable, and insignificant. They appear to be incapable of activity, depravity, and atrocious behaviour. But

I cannot agree with the view that female characters in Conrad's literary world are invariably offered an inferior position in relation to male characters, occupying the background of the story at best. Female protagonists in Conrad's literary output are many a time responsible for shaping the development of the stories, appearing as equal to the male characters who, as argued by Heliéna Krenn, "achieve their deepest recognition of truths about themselves through the mediation and instrumentality of women" (105), who become "essential for the demarcation of masculinity" (Mongia 135).

However, in this paper I am not going to study all categories of women in Conrad's literary output but only a few examples whose powerfulness, influence over men, and iniquity are visible in their intensity. Since the notion of evil for Conrad stands for a diverse reality,[1] the ensuing analysis of wicked women will therefore be of multifaceted character. It will be achieved by juxtaposing women inclined to crime, deceit, pride, passion and a detrimental influence upon men (Winnie Verloc from *The Secret Agent*, the gorgeous and influential Freya ["Freya of the Seven Isles"], the criminal and mentally disturbed Susan Bacadou ["The Idiots"], and finally the malicious governess from *Chance*), and will thus defend the hypothesis that although "female characters emphasize the weaknesses of Conrad's heroes" (Turner 155), this less frequently analysed aspect of Conradian fiction discloses its potential to be considered one of the most significant.

A second hypothesis is that Conrad's portrayal of wicked and influential women is deeply embedded in previous literary depictions of evil female characters, drawing on, among others, John Milton's epic *Paradise Lost* and his portrayal of the first, gorgeous yet destructively influential woman, Eve. This premise is offered here as an extension of the assertion voiced by D. C. R. A. Goonetilleke, who claims that "Kurtz is a descendant from a tradition that features the hero-villains of Gothic tradition such as Ann Radcliff's Montoni in *The Mysteries of Udolpho* (1794) and Heathcliff in Emily Brontë's *Wuthering Heights* (1847) and goes back to Milton's Satan and

Faust" (12), an extension which presupposes that Conradian evil female characters can be perceived as descendants of the Miltonian Eve despite obvious discrepancies between them.

In my article "Sublimely Gifted but Destined to Fall: A Comparative Study of Conrad's Kurtz and Milton's Satan as the Archetype of Evil Genius," it has been suggested that "the publication of John Milton's *Paradise Lost* has effectively reopened the partly forsaken 'box' with archetypes so as to trigger novel philosophical, religious and literary reflection upon their indispensable value in constructing the narrative framework" (Giza 173). And in evidence of this affirmation, Eve – an archetype of the first woman capable of both good and evil – has succeeded in attracting unprecedented literary attention. This hypothesis is confirmed by the phenomenon that the reality of evil, assuming such shapes as powerful, albeit furtive force, a tempting influence, and a deceiving feeling of freedom from any established rules proves to be more charming than its opposite, the concept of good denoting truthfulness, honesty or humility. Besides, if we turn our attention to the literary ground and accentuate the narrative process of writing, "it is easier to draw a bad character than a good one" (Gardner 99). Thus, the figure of Eve has become ubiquitous and so often reshaped that one can justly assert that it is very deeply embedded as a literary archetype and has displayed the potential to inspire both those who create and those who read.

Even though Eve in Milton's *Paradise Lost* is presented as utterly evil and fallen after the Fall in Book 9, the first signs of her proneness to wickedness and transgression are already visible prior to Adam and Eve's sin of disobedience, when she is still in her unfallen state. This proclivity, in the form of vanity, is detectable in Book 4, where one can observe Eve admiring her own reflection in a pond. It is likewise detectable in her unusual request to Adam to separate their chores a few moments prior to Satan's temptation of them. But it is most visible in her being tempted by Devil, disguised as a toad, while she sleeps (the Foe chose Eve as the weaker vessel and inferior to Adam, who is very often presented as being full of knowledge and sensibility). She is therefore the one with whom Satan tries to initiate cooperation, and she progressively shows a readiness to respond to Satan's enticement.

However, Eve's full-blown proclivity for evil, cunning, hatred and harmful influence upon Adam is detectable a few moments prior to and, obviously, after the Fall. The most detectable influence of Satan's powerful temptation of Eve is her doubting in God (assuming Him to be a liar) and His caring love towards Adam and Eve while admiring the beauty of the forbidden fruit and entering into the intricate and cunning logic embedded in her by Satan.

It is just on account of those doubts that Eve willingly disobeys the behest of God and eats the forbidden fruit, believing Satan more than God. And after the sin of disobedience she assumes the multifaceted attire of evil. First of all, she is transformed into a feminine temptress, a "transgressor" (Milton 11.164) and Adam's "snare" (165) who exerts a harmful influence upon Adam, an influence that assumes several shapes. The most injurious one is obviously associated with her tricking Adam into eating the forbidden fruit. And a few lines later we observe that Adam "scrupled not to eat, / Against his better knowledge, not deceived, / But fondly overcome with female charm" (9.997-99). The ultimate form of this type of influence, however, is detectable in Eve's attempt to definitely reject God while offering suicide as a solution to their predicament, a resolution not realized by Adam and Eve. It is, however, the solution that is implemented by both Winnie in *The Secret Agent* and Susan Bacadou in "The Idiots," two women who are unable to cope successfully with the burden of the criminal acts that have been committed by them as a way of protecting them against atrocities of their spouses. Emotionally and psychologically shattered by their husbands, these two women resort to murder, and eventually to suicide, which is perceived by them as the only option.

Apart from the detrimental influence upon Adam, Eve – "Philistean Dalilah" (Milton 9.1061), "possessed" (1137), "perverted" (10.3) and "that bad Woman" (837) – is brimful with such negative emotions as anger, hate, obstinacy, and guile (the perfect visualization of the personality of the governess from *Chance*); she is a contemptible *femme fatale* and all those epithets function as attributes of the archetype of Eve as a wicked, scheming and tempting woman. Eve is likewise full of cunning greed, both firmly believing in Satan's lies more than in Adam's instructions and driving her futile attempt to overthrow the existing hierarchical order with Adam as her superior. Eve is also gloating in her sinful state. However, the most slanderous portrayal of the fallen Eve – subject to transformation through the course of the epic from a blameless, servile woman into a cunning agent of Devil – is offered by the furious Adam in Book 10, a portrait realized in the evil women in Conrad's literary work.

Therefore, establishing possible parallels between presentations of evil women in Conrad's literary output and Milton's Eve may introduce an exploration of further dimensions in studies of Conradian fiction, opening new fields for an interdisciplinary analysis, accentuating the fact that both the evil women in Conrad and the Miltonian Eve can be perceived as examples of *femmes fatales*.

The term *femme fatale* points to one of the archetypes one can find not only in the literary domain but also in the social context of the Victorian Era. This archetype indicates a not entirely predictable or controllable female character who is perceived as a menace or threat to a man on account of her not accepting restrictions imposed upon her by the male procedure of shifting her only to the domestic domain. Besides, although the *femme fatale* has generally been associated with a tempting, and therefore treacherous and powerful woman, exerting a seductive influence upon men (the governess/Freya/Winnie), she is also "vibrant and courageous, becoming somewhat intoxicating, and very different from her female counterparts such as the idealized domestic woman, or the shunned and ill-used fallen women" (Hedgecock xv). She is the one who blatantly rebels against conformist attitudes and while refusing to acknowledge and accept the domestic realm and its limitations, she is "regarded as unruly and dangerous" (Atkinson xxi). Moreover, as has been affirmed by Nina Auerbach, the *femme fatale* plays the part of a "magic woman, who breaks the boundaries of family within which her society restricts her" (1), and even that of a fallen woman who embodied "everything in womanhood that was dangerously, tragically, and triumphantly beyond social boundaries" (150), having its literary archetype in Milton's epic *Paradise Lost* where, as is claimed by Auerbach, "Milton's Eve gives powerful argumentative voice to her longing to reign rather than serve" (155).

Importantly, the *femme fatale* has been presented as capable of employing her charms in order to entice men into perilous situations and criminality, very often killing them in the process; but on the contrary, while defending her integrity and life against a tyrannous husband, she may likewise become the victim of her own devious scheming (Susan, Winnie). What is of importance here is that the portrayal of the *femme fatale* functions as "a clear indication of the extent of the fears and anxieties prompted by shifts in the understanding of sexual difference in the late nineteenth century" (Doane 1) and, on account of this type of presentation, such a beautiful and tempting woman can act as a herald of the threat of female sexuality and power over men. Significantly, the male characters who are tempted by the *femme fatale*'s exceptional beauty and charm tend to concentrate mostly on her sexual attributes (Freya, Winnie). It can therefore be suggested that it is the males' narrative that exposes *femmes fatales* as distinctly sexual and very often deadly, rather than their own deeds, thoughts or intentions. And finally, it is of importance to add that Conrad "was apparently drawn to *femmes fatales*, even sardonically and perhaps self-critically enjoying imperilling his male characters" (Turner 144).

Significantly, the depiction of iniquity and maliciousness (especially in the character of the governess), a powerful and calculating influence over a husband (Winnie) and other men (Freya and the governess), crime and murder (Winnie and Susan), and seductive temptation of these paragons of the *femme fatale* can be enhanced by a reference to Shakespeare, who, in Mark Antony's funeral oration in *Julius Caesar*, voices the truth that the "evil that men do lives after them; the good is oft interrèd with their bones" (3.2.76-77). Evil is more enthralling than its opposite, as Lady Macduff succinctly notes – "I am in this earthly world, where to do harm / Is often laudable, to do good sometime / Accounted dangerous folly" (Shakespeare, *The Tragedy of Macbeth* 4.2.76-78).

Giorgia Grilli in her *Myth, Symbol, and Meaning in Marry Poppins* declares that "Joseph Conrad's *Chance* is another example of the literary treatment of the governess depicted as monstrous [...] who delivers the coup the grace to [Flora's] innocence and devastates her faith in herself" (141). As a contrast to the Miltonian Eve, a dynamic and multi-dimensional character, the governess appears to be all the time acting as a one-dimensional woman endowed only with negativity, cunning, and evil. Grilli adds that the "governess is never named, and this anonymity and insistence on the impersonal intensifies the sinister aspect of this figure who evades specificity to become the universal agent of evil" (141).

The first reference to this mysterious character (Winnie is likewise marked with mysteriousness) is tinged with condemnation, since the reader is informed that Flora de Barral, a defenceless and neglected young girl, has been entrusted to the care of the governess who has straightforwardly despised and manipulated not only Flora but also her father. And this disparaging portrayal of the governess "who closely resembles a villain from a sensational novel" whose "actions are deliberately malicious" (Wright 82), cunningly playing the part of mother to Flora, is unfolded and reiterated many times, for example as follows:

> She didn't care for the child a bit, and [...], she bullied de Barral in a very lofty fashion. [....] she [Mrs. Fyne] told me however that even in the Priory days she had suspected her [the governess] of being an artificial, heartless, vulgar-minded woman with the lowest possible ideals. But de Barral did not know it. He literally did not know anything. (C 73)

Like the postlapsarian Eve, who proposes to Adam the sinister plan of mutual suicide so as to avoid the direct consequences of their sin of disobedience, the governess, referred to as "an intriguing person hatching a most sinister plot under her air of distant, fashionable exclusiveness" (90), is characterized as a woman prone to constant scheming and formulating iniquitous plans (one of those involves marrying her nephew to Flora de Barral). Both Eve and the governess readily resort to sneakiness, which they treat as an approach towards those around them in order to achieve some benefit for themselves. While taking recourse to her cunning, Eve desires to obtain a morsel of independence from the superior Adam, whereas the governess's approach is mostly dictated by greed and yearning for power. The stunned narrator – while remarking at the same time the governess's iniquitous influence upon men who are forced to deal with her: "I conclude she would have carried out whatever plan she might have formed. I can imagine de Barral accustomed for years to defer to her wishes" (91) – points out the unheard-of situation of the master being accustomed to heeding the whims of his servant! The depiction is further enhanced by the following assertion:

> It is evident to me that Mrs. What's-her-name would have had her atrocious way with very little trouble even if the excellent Fynes had been able to do something. She would simply have bullied de Barral in a lofty style. There's nothing more subservient than an arrogant man when his arrogance has once been broken in some particular instance. (92)

And similar depictions accentuating the governess's proclivity for methodical cunning and plotting abound later on in the story.

However, the inclination toward intrigues is not the only aspect of her wickedness. Like Eve, the governess is full of such negative traits as hatred and rage: "The woman was mad. 'Oh! Mrs. Fyne, don't tell me she wasn't mad. If you had only seen her face'" (139), and ungovernable passions that are graphically signified by her change in appearance: "Medusa's head with serpentine locks" (118) whose "teeth looked as though she wanted to bite [Flora]" and with "eyes [...], quite dry, hard and small in a lot of horrible wrinkles" (120). One of the first references to the sources of those menacing emotions is offered by Marlow in the following words:

> And that the secret of her envenomed rage, not against this miserable and attractive wretch, but against fate, accident and the whole course of human life, concentrating its venom on de Barral and including the innocent girl herself, was in the thought, in the fear crying within her. (103)

What follows immediately after this assertion is comprehensive analysis of the governess's personality and her abominable manner of conduct, which has always been focused upon hating all her charges, because she is seemingly incapable of experiencing positive emotions whatsoever. Significantly, she has been channelling wickedness and contempt not only towards those who have been under her charge, but towards herself as well, so that she appears in a similar light to the Miltonian Satan (and also partially to the Miltonian Eve and Conrad's Winnie), who shouts that he is forced to carry hell within him despite being in Paradise.

Nevertheless, it would be justified to propose the hypothesis that the governess is an even more advanced example of the evil female character than other Conradian wicked women. She discloses one trait that is not detectable in Winnie, namely hypocrisy. Therefore, the governess can be regarded as the most advanced incarnation of evil. While portraying Flora de Barral, Marlow clearly asserts that

> [s]he [Flora] stood, a frail and passive vessel into which the other [the governess] went on pouring all the accumulated dislike for all her pupils, her scorn of all her employers (the ducal one included), the accumulated resentment, the infinite hatred of all these unrelieved years of – I won't say hypocrisy. (119)

And, so as to enhance the sinister and even "insect-like" character of the governess, Marlow adds that she "revelled in the miserable revenge – pretty safe too – only regretting the unworthiness of the girlish figure which stood for so much she had longed to be able to spit venom at" (120). However, despite the meticulous analysis of the wickedness of the governess offered by Marlow, the most proper and succinct assessment of this sinister character, in my opinion, is suggested by Mrs. Fyne when she is explaining to Flora the intricacies of the surrounding world: "It is your former governess who is horrid and odious. She is a vile woman. I cannot tell you that she was mad, but I think she must have been beside herself with rage and full of evil thoughts. You must try not to think of these abominations, my dear child" (140).

Freya from the novella "Freya of the Seven Isles," a "siren seemingly controlling the waters" (Turner 154), who is portrayed as eroticism incarnate, "holding an explicit physical power over men" (143), is likewise endowed with an exceptional gift for manipulation and exerting influence upon the men who are within the range of her seductive and dominating activity. Moreover, similarly to Eve, Freya, "that infernal girl" ("Freya of the Seven Isles," *TLS* 221), the Lady of the Isles, is presented as possessed of physical beauty and overwhelming attractiveness. Both Milton's Eve and Freya are gorgeous and, being aware of this powerful attribute, they are not reluctant to use it in order to manipulate men who are within the reach of their influence. Eve employs her charm so as to convince Adam to her course of thinking and rejecting God's behest. Freya, on the other hand, uses her beauty in order to protect her father against a possible predicament instigated by Heemskirk.

Besides, emphasizing her extraordinary position in the male world, as the story unfolds Freya emerges as an unconstrained, resolute, fearless, vengeful, but sensible and proud woman. She is in fact a complicated and rounded character, determined to be the mistress of her own fate. Being aware of her dignity and significance, she is eventually powerful enough – despite her initial apprehension of the commander of the *Neptune* which results partly from her care towards her father – to exert influence upon two men who are closely associated with her life and activity, Jasper Allen and Heemskirk.

Her influence over Jasper is detectable from the very beginning of the story, in which the power of her sway is juxtaposed with her exceptional beauty, which many a time facilitates this process. Freya is a stunning temptress who can go to any lengths to exert influence and dominance over Jasper. She is so conscious of her power that she does not wish to be dependent on, and controlled by, Jasper or in fact by any other man. This is detectable not only in her body language but most importantly in her straightforward assertion to Jasper that she is, and will always be, a woman who is not to be restricted by anyone, an approach very similar to Eve's resolve to split up her and Adam's chores in the Garden of Eden, and thus to question her inferiority to Adam but also strive for independence and freedom in their relation. However, it is the type of influence that has been greatly stimulating Jasper during his enterprise focused upon making Freya his beloved spouse. Despite the fact that he has been under the powerful sway exerted by Freya, Jasper is presented as having willingly plunged into this net of subjugation because he took it for a challenge, the ultimate reward for which will be the possibility to call Freya his beloved wife. However, the dream is shattered when he loses his boat (regarded by him as a sacred haven or sanctuary where he could eventually hide and possess his beloved Freya) and when he is confronted with the truth that Freya never really loved him.

As far as the second man is concerned, Heemskirk is likewise entangled in a net of encounters and interactions with Freya. However, this relation is completely different from that between Freya and Jasper; it is marked by Freya's trepidation for her father's well-being which, in line with her father's own manner of reasoning, is dependent upon Heemskirk's favour. Nevertheless, despite initial apprehension (detectable, for instance, in her inexplicable laughter and tension), Freya becomes more and more powerful, gradually both increasing her influence over Heemskirk and diminishing his power over her, and eventually becoming a torture for him. Hence, the "desire-tormented Dutchman" (180) is dominated by Freya's bold approach towards him which is detectable in several aspects of her behaviour. Firstly, despite his high social position, she openly mocks him when talking to her father. Secondly, she verbally attacks Heemskirk, displaying "a fury of an atrocious character altogether incomprehensible to a girl like Freya" (187). Finally, she emotionally abuses and infuriates him by loudly playing the piano, the symbol of her emotional dominance over him. At the end of the story the narrator offers a precise portrayal of her power over Heemskirk and Jasper, claiming that "Freya haunted them both like an ubiquitous spirit, and as if she were the only woman in the world" (211).

Like Eve, Conrad's Winnie Verloc and Susan Bacadou are both female characters who are prone to changes and transformations from benevolence to iniquity. They are delineated through the prism of their inability to carry the heavy weight of the crime they have committed against their husbands in extremely dangerous moments instigated by the spouses. This powerlessness eventually leads to suicide, which in the case of Winnie functions as "the inexorable conclusion of the eruption of unthinking savagery which begins when she is forced to realize that all her self-sacrifice on her brother's behalf has been mistaken and in vain" (Sudbury 34). Like Eve prior to her fall, both Winnie and Susan, at the beginning of the two narratives, are described as taciturn, reserved, and rather quiet women trying to fulfil their familial, matrimonial, and social duties as dutifully as possible: Verloc's wife is "a woman of very few words" (*SA* 245), who very often "had no sufficient command over her voice" (246), and Susan Bacadou is simply a "quiet wife" ("The Idiots," *TU* 60) and a contented woman who does not like to be gossiped about, and tries to do her chores well.

Moreover, like the prelapsarian Eve, Winnie, up to the moment of her brother Stevie's demise, is characterized by the exceptional care, obedience and love she directs towards him, and conditionally towards her husband, Mr. Verloc. A similar character is detectable in Susan who is shown as a caring and loving mother who "watched with other eyes; listened with otherwise expectant ears" ("The Idiots," *TU* 63) staying constantly close to "the cradle, night and day on the watch, to hope and suffer" (64), spending "long days between her three idiot children and the childish grandfather" (64). Like Eve, who, at the start of her existence with Adam in the Garden of Eden, is presented through the prism of matrimonial attraction marked with surrender and obedience towards her husband, Winnie, as well as Susan, is portrayed as a caring and loving woman, "[Stevie's] only sister, guardian, and protector" (*SA* 262), who "glanced at him from time to time with maternal vigilance" (10), and who "used to come along, and carry him off to bed with her, as into a heaven of consoling peace" (167).

Similarly to the beautiful prelapsarian Eve, who is marked with blissful indifference, on account of her certainty that Adam will take care of everything, Winnie – likewise endowed with beauty – is depicted as being indifferent or even oblivious to the surrounding world as long as she is sure that she and her brother are safe and protected by the presence of Mr. Verloc. The reader is informed that Winnie has an air of lack of concern, and is not capable of any vehement protestation; she displays a self-reliant approach to life and her "philosophy consisted in not taking notice of the inside of facts" (154).

However, like the Miltonian Eve whose blissful existence is obliterated after her fall, both Winnie and Susan experience drastic events that overturn their tranquil existence and push them eventually into murder and evil. Winnie's façade of goodness, obedience, insouciance, love, and care is utterly shattered after Stevie's death, and Susan's peaceful existence is ruined by her husband's attempt at rape. Those are the moments during which the two women access their hidden reservoirs of frustration, madness, despair, hate, criminality, and yearning for suicide, but most importantly the capacity for action. Hence, the deeds and the manner of thinking of these beautiful and loving women change for the worse after the two critical incidents.

As with the Miltonian Eve, whose process of deterioration begins while she is sleeping, and is tempted by Satan disguised as a toad, both Winnie's and Susan's shattering moments are associated with evening and night. The attempted rape of Susan takes place in the evening ("The Idiots," *TU* 76) as does Winnie's premonition that something bad may actually happen in the near future (the incident happens just after her mother's departure): her "heart for the fraction of a second seemed to stand still too. That night she was 'not quite herself,' as the saying is, and it was borne upon her with some force that a simple sentence my hold several diverse meanings – mostly disagreeable" (*SA* 178). And from this moment on Winnie becomes apprehensive about Stevie's safety, and even more so after he and her husband depart to see Michaelis. And it is just this fancy (enhanced by the sense of apprehension and anxiety resulting from her brother's departure) that eventually explodes into a gigantic form of evil and crime after she hears about her beloved brother's death.

Significantly, it is not in the personality of Winnie but rather in her appearance, regressing "physically, Hyde-like, after Stevie's death" (Harrington 59) that the first detectable change is seen. After having eavesdropped upon Chief Inspector Heat's account about Stevie's atrocious death, the reader is offered a vision of Winnie's alteration: "her lips were blue, her hands cold as ice, and her pale face, in which the two eyes seemed like two black holes, felt to her as if it were enveloped in flames" (*SA* 209-10). Importantly, a change of appearance is likewise detected in Susan. She is described as a "deranged [...], mad, [...], miserable [...], accursed, [...], wicked, [...], horrible woman" ("The Idiots," *TU* 74-76) who, upon entering her mother's house after killing her husband, appears as a lunatic with "blazing eyes" (75). In *The Secret Agent*, the reader then observes the subsequent change in Winnie:

> [the] palms of her hands were pressed convulsively to her face, with the tips of her fingers contracted against the forehead, as though the skin had been a mask which she was ready to tear off violently. The perfect immobility of her pose expressed the agitation of rage and despair, all the potential violence of tragic passions. (*SA* 212)

Later we are even offered the vision of Winnie, a "savage woman" (285; this epithet is repeated one more time in Chapter 12 so as to enhance the impression), assuming a gothic deathlike appearance: "It was as if a corpse had spoken" (247), and the change peaks in her physical manifestation, stamped with ferocity, a few moments prior to killing her husband:

> A tinge of wildness in her aspect was derived from the black veil hanging like a rag against her cheek, and from the fixity of her black gaze where the light of the room was absorbed and lost without the trace of a single gleam. [...] Her face was no longer stony. Anybody could have noted the subtle change on her features, in the stare of her eyes, giving her a new and startling expression. (259-60)

She assumes a serpent-like form (functioning here as a clear reference to Milton's epic and the figure of Satan), as Ossipon observes while he is helping her after the murder:

> He felt her now clinging round his legs, and his terror reached its culminating point, became a sort of intoxication, entertained delusions, acquired the characteristics of delirium tremens. He positively saw snakes now. He saw the woman twined round him like a snake, not to be shaken off. She was not deadly. She was death itself. (291)

and eventually she assumes the form of utter nothingness at the end of the story, devolving "into a primitive past" (62), as is claimed by Ellen Burton Harrington.

Winnie's distorted appearance corresponds to the transformations in her thoughts and activities after she is informed about her brother's death, and the same happens to Eve after her sin of disobedience. Both women become marked with extraordinary activity and dynamism. While analysing the alteration that Winnie undergoes, Olga Binczyk asserts that

> Grief after her brother's death triggers in Winnie an outburst of psychological and physical strength [...]. Having stabbed her husband to death in cold blood, for the first time in her life she feels a "free woman" who can command "her wits, [...] her vocal organs," and be "in an almost preternaturally perfect control of every fibre of her body." (124)

And she immediately feels hatred towards her husband for murdering her brother:

> And there was the paralyzing atrocity of the thought which occupied her. [...] "This man took the boy away to murder him." [...] Mrs. Verloc's

> whole being was racked by that inconclusive and maddening thought. It was in her veins, in her bones, in the roots of her hair. [...] her teeth were violently clenched, [...] she was not a submissive creature. (*SA* 246)

She methodically assumes a habit of slyness so as to carry out the creeping thought of inflicting on her husband the same fate as he inflicted on her beloved brother. In the middle of her frenzy the reader is informed that Winnie was "clear-sighted," "cunning," "unhurried" and that her "brow was smooth" (261), in the manner of a professional killer who is capable of murdering in cold blood. As a resolute person she meticulously implements her sinister idea and becomes a murderess, like Susan Bacadou.

There is, however, a difference between those two murderesses. Winnie kills her husband with premeditation and careful planning, but Susan commits her crime impulsively and quickly, to protect her safety and integrity as a woman:

> And he would come. I begged him and Heaven for mercy. . . No! . . . Then we shall see. . . . He came this evening. I thought to myself: 'Ah! again!' . . . I had my long scissors. I heard him shouting . . . I saw him near. . . . I must – must I? . . . Then take! . . . And I struck him in the throat above the breast-bone. . . . I never heard him even sigh. . . . I left him standing. . . . It was a minute ago. How did I come here? ("The Idiots," *TU* 76)

However, the vehement emotions associated with these two criminal deeds are felt similarly by two women; both Winnie and Susan are theoretically capable of committing murder again if they were placed in similar situations: "I would tear you to pieces, I would kill you twenty times [...]. How many times must I kill you – you blasphemer! Satan sends you here. I am damned too!" (84), shouts Susan insanely at the vision of her dead husband. This testifies to their potential for evil and criminal tendencies that are very likely to be unearthed in dire straits.

But is it really possible that these Conradian examples of wicked women are ontologically unwavering in their wickedness? Are they really without thoughts, deeds, or circumstances that could, at least a little bit, extenuate the gravity of their crimes? Is it really credible that there is not a morsel of good in their psycho-moral constitution? Can they only be seen as stagnant constructs incapable of change? Are they then to be read as having been enchanted by the overwhelming lure of iniquity and their powerful influence over men? The answer to all these questions is negative.

The moment the reader is disposed to question the established views upon these literary characters as purely iniquitous, seductive, scheming, and prone to crime, one is certain to unearth some fresh lines of interpretation. Putting their iniquity aside for a moment, the reader can perceive them from a slightly different perspective.

Undeniably, the governess is generally presented as demonstrating malice, wickedness, and jealousy towards the children who have been entrusted to her care. She is iniquity and cunning incarnate, manipulative enough to steer and dominate not only the young inexperienced girl Flora but also her knowledgeable and experienced father. However, at one moment Marlow seems to extenuate the governess's conduct by asserting that, in part, her code of behaviour has been motivated by fear of losing her passing beauty and youth and, as is asserted by Leonard Orr, "thwarted desires and a sense of social entrapment" (261). Hence, the general assessment of her manner and life cannot be only one-dimensional. She is mostly evil and cunning, but the mitigating force of her suffering from self-repression and anxiety connected with the passing of time and her looks may therefore present her in a more sympathetic light.

Freya, with her seductive and tempting approach, is likewise motivated by trepidation: anxiety over her father's prosperity and well-being which is seemingly jeopardized by the presence and activity of the Dutch authorities. While being perceived in this light, it is possible to analyse Freya's dealing with Heemskirk as a means of protecting her father against possible outbursts of anger and fury from the Dutch captain. Therefore, it seems inaccurate to regard Freya only as a seductive and scheming *femme fatale* whose activity will inevitably lead to Jasper's ruin (taking the form of loss of his beloved ship). Accordingly, she may be seen as a loving daughter who vehemently fights for her father, who, on account of the terror inspired by Heemskirk, "let the beggar treat him with heavy contempt, devour his daughter with his eyes, and drink the best part of his little stock of wine" ("Freya of the Seven Isles," *TLS* 160).

Winnie Verloc's and Susan Bacadou's murders of their husbands cannot be treated as casual deeds at all; they are conducted in self-defence (Susan) and as the powerful reaction against the inexplicability of her beloved brother's suffering and pointless demise (Winnie). Their crimes are therefore not capricious acts but rather function as outcries against injustice and the suffering, pain, and anguish they experience on account of their husbands' brutality and iniquity. And, as Jetty de Vries has put it, "restricting ourselves to the evidence of the novel itself we might feel that she is only technically a criminal. Conrad certainly considers Winnie's crime as a crime passionnel, or in other words as a crime committed in extreme emotional duress" (13).

There is not any doubt that the dire straits and distressing episodes (the loss of a beloved member of the family, the fear of being raped by one's husband, social stigmata, the anxiety stemming from loss of attractiveness and winsomeness) that Conrad's *femmes fatales* are forced to go through make these women defiant, confirming in that way their innate dynamism and multifacetedness. Therefore, due to the effects of these challenging experiences, they cannot be merely perceived as utterly wicked. Rather, they are exposed as being trapped in dead-end situations (especially Winnie, Freya, and Susan). What is more, upon closer scrutiny the reader perceives them as being entrenched in the tragic triad of the vicious circle, as I have analysed in a previous article.[2] Nevertheless, they have recourse to revolt as portrayed by means of theoretical concepts framed by Albert Camus. Generally, their resistance against the tyranny they encounter causes them to discover autonomy outside the given discourse of power.

In his Foreword to Camus's *The Rebel*, Herbert Read sheds some light upon the concept of rebellion and it is crucial to grasp some of these theoretical points in order to comprehend *femmes fatales*' standards of behaviour more thoroughly. He draws the reader's attention to the fact that "revolt is one of the 'essential dimensions' of mankind" which is, in truth, "a principle of existence" (viii), and more importantly, it is "the basis of the struggle." In fact, mutiny is the "origin of form, source of real life" (x). These propositions classify those women who eagerly avail themselves of such an approach – manifesting its force in evil and commission of crime – as grasping an opportunity to unearth their own subjectivity. By doing so they condemn themselves "to a make-believe world in the desperate hope of achieving a more profound existence" (Camus 54), which cannot be found in the reality dominated by male authority and superiority. Camus writes that

> Rebellion is born of the spectacle of irrationality, confronted with an unjust and incomprehensible condition. But its blind impulse is to demand order in the midst of chaos, and unity in the very heart of the ephemeral. It protests, it demands, it insists that the outrage be brought to an end [...]. Its preoccupation is to transform. (10)

The insurgency launched by Conradian *femmes fatales*, recognized as a defence of their own rights, legitimizes their struggle when they find themselves in an irrational situation, since, in their heart of hearts, they sense that some things have gone absolutely awry (mostly Winnie and Susan).

To conclude, although, as is asserted by Jones in *Conrad and Women*, "the presence of women characters in Conrad's novels has caused the greatest difficulties for critics" (7), because he was a writer of sea stories centred on men, the effort to analyse women characters in Conrad's literary oeuvre and examine their hidden potential and possibilities is worthwhile. They are worth exploring not only because Conrad's later fiction puts distinctly more emphasis upon women and their importance in the world dominated by men. It is likewise significant on account of the fact that these women, especially the evil ones, function as realizations of "Conrad's 'metaphysics of darkness' which is to be traced in each [example] of Conrad's fiction," as is emphasized by Royal Roussel (qtd. by Binczyk 123).

The truth is that despite the fact that they "usually remain in an idealized and imaginary realm of subtlety and beauty, removed from harsh realities" (50), as is asserted by Wiesław Krajka in *Isolation and Ethos*, women, whose diverse portrayal "owes much of its profundity and uniqueness to the works of the Polish romantics, in particular to the ambivalent attitude toward female self-sacrifice and self-denial in the tradition of Polish romanticism" (Kao 127), do play fundamental roles in shaping male subjectivity. In line with Mongia, they function as "a medium of exchange within a world of masculine power" (145), playing a variety of roles and functions that allow readers "insight into the complicated negotiations of power that mark relations between the sexes and races" (147). They likewise are able to unearth their own subjectivity while taking recourse to both evil – perceived in the Conradian literary domain as a significant section of societal reality and a fundamental requirement of the development of human consciousness – and crime, which often appears as the only alternative for them on their way towards self-discovery, self-knowledge and freedom.

NOTES

[1] Evil as a significant constituent of existence for both Conrad and Milton is analysed by a wide number of critics. Milton's vision of iniquity is studied by, among others, such scholars as Eustace Tillyard in *Milton*, Arnold Stein in *The Art of Presence*, John Armstrong in *The Paradise Myth*, Stanley Fish in *Surprised by Sin* and Raphael Werblowsky in his *Lucifer and Prometheus: A Study of Milton's Satan*. As for Conrad's perception of evil, one can take recourse to such works as *Joseph Conrad: His Moral Vision* by George A. Panichas, *Joseph Conrad – The Major Phase* by Jacques Berthoud or lesser-known works of criticism such as *Out of Eden* by Paul Kahn, Part II of the book *A History of the Heart* by Ole Høystad, Chapter II of *Facing Evil* by John Kekes. All those works of criticism, generally, perceive iniquity not only as something heinous in its nature. It is likewise presented as an important reality, an integral part of life-time experiences enabling one to solve eternal dilemmas, as well as a fundamental phase of the development of human consciousness. What is more, the nature of iniquity is intrinsically associated with man's proud nature and ensuing rebellion as a symptom of the abuse of free will or betrayal of fellowship and rejection of social responsibility. Wickedness is often allied with the

concept of alienation – assuming many forms – designating a state of mind as well as of body.

[2] Even though my article entitled "Trapped in a Vicious Circle of the Tragic Triad... Miltonian Satan and Conradian Kurtz's Process of Unearthing Authentic Identity" focuses upon both Satan and Kurtz as being ensnared in the tragic triad, the premises of this phenomenon can likewise be applied to Conradian *femmes fatales*. The phenomenon is described by Viktor Frankl who holds that nobody is sure to be spared from coping with three commonly experienced realities in existence: the pain perceived as the reality of anguish, the death as the reality of our mortality (transitoriness of human life), and the guilt as the reality of our human imperfection. Those three polarities of the tragic triad comprise a great section of the life of man, and more importantly, they cannot be avoided. However, as well as being appalling, their significance arises from the fact that they are stimuli to steady development, to self-discovery.

WORKS CITED

Armstrong, John. *The Paradise Myth*. Oxford UP, 1969.

Atkinson, William. Introduction. *Joseph Conrad: The Lagoon and Other Stories*. Ed. William Atkinson. Oxford UP, 1997. vii-xxiii.

Auerbach, Nina. *Woman and the Demon: The Life of a Victorian Myth*. Harvard UP, 1984.

Berthoud, Jacques. *Joseph Conrad – The Major Phase*. Cambridge UP, 1978.

Binczyk, Olga. "Irony and Modern Entropy in Joseph Conrad's *The Secret Agent*." Krajka, *Between Literary Techniques and Their Messages* 113-29.

Camus, Albert. *The Rebel – An Essay on Man in Revolt*. Trans. Anthony Bower. Vintage, 1956.

Carabine, Keith, Owen Knowles, and Wiesław Krajka, eds. *Contexts for Conrad*. East European Monographs, Maria Curie-Skłodowska U, Columbia UP, 1993. Vol. 2 of *Conrad: Eastern and Western Perspectives*. Ed. Wiesław Krajka. 32 vols. to date. 1992- .

Curle, Richard. *Joseph Conrad: A Study*. Russell, 1968.

Doane, Mary. *Femmes Fatales: Feminism, Film Theory, Psychoanalysis*. Routledge, 1991.

Fish, Stanley. *Surprised by Sin: The Reader in* Paradise Lost. Harvard UP, 1998.

Gardner, Helen. *The Reading of* Paradise Lost. Clarendon P, 1965.

Giza, Jarosław. "Sublimely Gifted but Destined to Fall: A Comparative Study of Conrad's Kurtz and Milton's Satan as the Archetype of Evil Genius." Krajka, *Between Literary Techniques and Their Messages* 173-90.

---. "Trapped in a Vicious Circle of the Tragic Triad... Miltonian Satan and Conradian Kurtz's Process of Unearthing Authentic Identity." *The Self Industry: Therapy and Fiction*. Ed. Jarosław Szurman, Agnieszka

Woźniakowska and Krzysztof Kowalczyk-Twarowski. Uniwersytet Śląski, 2015. 285-95.

Goonetilleke, D. C. R. A. *Joseph Conrad's "Heart of Darkness."* Routledge, 2007.

Grilli, Giorgia. *Myth, Symbol, and Meaning in Marry Poppins*. Routledge, 2015.

Harrington, Ellen Burton. "The Female Offender, the New Woman, and Winnie Verloc in *The Secret Agent*." *The Conradian* 32.1 (2007): 57-69.

Hedgecock, Jennifer. *The Femme Fatale in Victorian Literature: The Danger and the Sexual Threat*. Cambria P, 2008.

Høystad, M. Ole. *A History of the Heart*. Reaktion Books, 2007.

Iwashimizu, Yumiko. "*Chance*. Conrad's A Portrait of a Feminist." *Centennial Essays on Joseph Conrad's* Chance. Ed. Allan H. Simmons and Susan Jones. Brill, 2016. 147-58.

Jones. Susan. *Conrad and Women*. Clarendon P, 1999.

---. "Representing Women: Conrad, Marguerite Poradowska, and *Chance*." *Conrad and Gender*. Ed. Andrew Roberts. Rodopi, 1993. 59-74.

Kahn, W. Paul. *Out of Eden: Adam and Eve and the Problem of Evil*. Princeton UP, 2010.

Kao, Pei-Wen Clio. "From Incapable 'Angel in the House' to Invincible 'New Woman' in Marlovian Narratives: Representing Womanhood in 'Heart of Darkness' and *Chance*." *The Conradian* 39.1 (2014): 116-29.

Kekes, John. *Facing Evil*. Princeton UP, 1990.

Krajka, Wiesław. *Isolation and Ethos. A Study of Joseph Conrad*. East European Monographs, Columbia UP, 1992.

---, ed. *Joseph Conrad: Between Literary Techniques and Their Messages*. East European Monographs, Maria Curie-Skłodowska UP, Columbia UP, 2009. Vol. 18 of *Conrad: Eastern and Western Perspectives*. Ed. Wiesław Krajka. 32 vols. to date. 1992- .

Krenn, Heliéna M. "The 'Beautiful' World of Women: Women as Reflections of Colonial Issues in Conrad's Malay Novels." Carabine, Knowles and Krajka 105-19.

Malessa-Drohomirecka, Monika. "The Influence of Conrad's Personal Experiences on the Modelling of Male and Female Characters in His Writing." *Yearbook of Conrad Studies (Poland)* 9 (2014): 23-43.

Milton, John. *Paradise Lost*. 1667. Penguin, 1996.

Mongia, Padmini. "Empire, Narrative, and the Feminine in *Lord Jim* and *Heart of Darkness*." Carabine, Knowles and Krajka 135-50.

Newhouse, Neville. *Joseph Conrad*. Evans, 1966.

Orr, Leonard. "The Later Novels." *A Joseph Conrad Companion*. Ed. Leonard Orr and Ted Billy. Greenwood, 1999. 251-78.

Panichas, A. George. *Joseph Conrad: His Moral Vision*. Mercer UP, 2005.

Read, Herbert. Foreword. *The Rebel – An Essay on Man in Revolt*. By Camus. Trans. Anthony Bower. Vintage, 1956. vii-x.

Shakespeare, William. *Julius Caesar*. 1599. *The Oxford Shakespeare* 601-26.

---. *The Oxford Shakespeare – The Complete Works*. Ed. Stanley Wells and Gary Taylor. Clarendon, 1998.

---. *The Tragedy of Macbeth*. 1606. *The Oxford Shakespeare* 975-99.

Stein, Arnold. *The Art of Presence: The Poet and* Paradise Lost. U of California P, 1977.

Sudbury, Rodie. "Anarchism and Suicide in *The Princess Casamassima* and *The Secret Agent*." *Conrad, James and Other Relations*. Ed. Keith Carabine, and Owen Knowles with Paul Armstrong. Social Science Monographs, Maria Curie-Skłodowska U, Columbia UP, 1998. 25-37. Vol. 6 of *Conrad: Eastern and Western Perspectives*. Ed. Wiesław Krajka. 32 vols. to date. 1992- .

Tillyard, Mandeville Wetenhall Eustace. *Milton*. Chatto, 1946.

Turner, Jennifer. "'Petticoats' and 'Sea Business': Women Characters in Conrad's Edwardian Short Stories." *The Conradian* 28.2 (2003): 142-56.

Vries, Jetty de. "The New Faces of Conrad's London and of Winnie Verloc." *The Conradian* 7.2 (1982): 4-19.

Werblowsky, Raphael. *Lucifer and Prometheus: A Study of Milton's Satan*. Routledge, 1952.

Wright, E. H. "The 'Girl-Novel': *Chance* and Woolf's *The Voyage Out*." *The Conradian* 39.1 (2014): 80-97.

Sylwia Janina Wojciechowska,
Jesuit University Ignatianum,
Cracow, Poland

Patterns of Nostalgia in the Autobiographical Reflections of Joseph Conrad and Henry James

The field of research delimited by the expression *patterns of nostalgia* seems somewhat outdated in contemporary academic discourse centred around such themes as, e.g., transhumanism, ecology, or apocalyptic visions towards which humanity is allegedly progressing. The juxtaposition of Joseph Conrad and Henry James is also fairly conventional: as both authors knew and admired one another, it is quite natural that academics examine their fiction for formal points of intersection (Carabine and Saunders; Maunsell; Simmons; Fothergill; Bell; Hampson). The position formulated below, however, re-approaches the ongoing discussion from a new perspective: the innovative approach involves the application of academic theories on nostalgia that appear to contribute to, and indeed enrich, the debate on autobiography since they help legitimize the idiosyncrasies in the narratives of both Conrad and James. Although *nostalgia* is viewed as being a classical Greek term, having existed from antiquity, as well as one suggesting sentimentality to the general public, I first intend to re-conceptualize the phenomenon, and then to re-consider the range of potentialities emerging from the deployment of nostalgia as a critical tool in the literary analysis of autobiographical (non)fiction.

It is perhaps rather surprising to invoke the names of Conrad and James in a discussion on nostalgia: both writers were renowned for their disregard for sentimentalist sensibilities, a concept repudiated in the first few paragraphs of Conrad's "Autocracy and War" as involving "pre-Victorian [...] arcadian tears, [enveloping] this facile emotion worthy of the golden age" (*NLL* 84-85). Out of context, these words only too readily underline the author's somewhat dismissive, and indeed perhaps even derisive, stance on nostalgia and over-sensibility. However, read against a broader context they still appear to criticize those who, while "shedding tears," yield to a nostalgia for pre-Victorian times (85). Steeped in pastoral rhetoric and undermined by ironic counter-statements, the paragraph first merely suggests, and then explicitly pleads, for emotions "of a sterner sort" (85). This is without doubt Conradian.

For James, simplified nostalgia is perceived through its association with European sentimental and pastoral literature, with his characteristically less than positive appraisal of simple nostalgia as the "widespread structure of feeling" (Tannock 453). This view is legitimized in the author's own work. Among the extremely few lengthy quotations included in *A Small Boy and Others*, there is a fragment from an adolescent poetic attempt[1] which, ironically, suggests pastoral readings infused with popular longing and oversentimentality. As is typical of the Jamesian manner of reasoning, the negative assessment may only be drawn through the literary associations that connote *simple* pastoralism[2] in the motifs of "th[e] lengthening shadow[s] o'er the plain," the *arcades ambo* topos, and the rhetorical formula of "rememberest thou" (James 234). The range of evocative phrases is dismissed as "European enough," with no explicit explanation apart from the provocative assertion that the few lines have, surprisingly, stuck "in [his] remembrance for reasons independent of [their] quality" (234). Ironically suggestive, the autobiographical *persona* merely implies his predilection for the sterner emotions to which Conrad openly exhorts in "Autocracy and War."

Having said that, the widespread understanding of nostalgia as an emotional state renders viewing the work of Conrad and James as nostalgic somewhat surprising. Nonetheless, it would seem that the crux of the matter is in the definition of the term, which, like the pastoral (Alpers 8), though familiar, proves misleading in the academic context. To the layman, nostalgia in all probability appears unexceptional, whereas experts have endeavoured – and, as yet, failed – to formulate a precise definition which would bespeak its significance as a mode of thought.[3] Thus, I wish to argue that there are at least two kinds of *nostalgia*, firstly that to which Conrad so powerfully objects in the quotation cited above, and secondly that which is described in, e.g., philosophy (Kant; Lyotard, *The Postmodern Explained*), sociology (Davis; Bauman, *Retrotopia* 7-25), and, amongst other, literary studies (Boym; Schweizer; Clewell). Whereas the former is an umbrella term for virtually any intense longing for the past – in fact, as broad as it is meaningless – the latter is a historical phenomenon with a distinct ontological record and a clear semantic charge (Dodman; Illbruck; Wojciechowska, "*Nostos*"). Hence, the common understanding of nostalgia indicates, albeit rather vaguely, an intensity of feeling with no clear content or message, and it thus fundamentally differs from the medical phenomenon first described as a life-threatening disease in Johannes Hofer's *Dissertatio medica de nostalgia, oder Heimwehe* [Medical dissertation on nostalgia].[4] As I have argued elsewhere, the paradox seems inherent in its historical record as even its name harks back to what prove to be misleadingly ancient roots: counterintuitively, the term was only coined in 1688 ("*Nostos*" 389-91). In the title page of the original treatise, the mixture of languages, fonts, and print sizes probably indicates the challenge the young medical student, Hofer, faced when trying to determine the nature of an obscure condition that, in his opinion, afflicted displaced Swiss militiamen.[5] The neo-Greek compound suggested a severe pain, an *algos*, triggered by the impossibility of a home-coming, a *nostos*. Over the years, Hoferian *nostalgia* has evolved and become a technical term applied in various fields ranging from medicine (Hofer; Zwinger qtd. in Illbruck), through psychology (Sedikides, Wildschut and Baden), history (Shaw and Chase; Illbruck; Dodman), and sociology (Davis), to cultural (Lowenthal) and literary studies (Boym; Clewell).

In the present paper, the essentializing of nostalgia formulated by Jean-Françoise Lyotard is considered the most compelling, notwithstanding the rather dismissive manner in which the philosopher applies the term in his research. In his famous essay, "Answering the Question: What Is Postmodernism?" Lyotard raises certain objections to the concept of *totality*, which, he argues, was preserved and consolidated in modernity with the help of nostalgia, a nostalgia for "the whole and the one, for the reconciliation of the concept and the sensible" (*The Postmodern Condition* 81-82). Though it may appear to the post-modern philosopher as a notion which restricts novel and innovative approaches, nostalgia thus defined is a founding concept of the modern, and modernist, mindset. Seen in this way, postmodern(ist) and modern(ist) sensibilities do not designate a sequential order nor a pre/post relation, but instead suggest divergent attitudes towards the past, tradition, and the currently questioned triumph of Western civilization: while modernity nostalgically invokes the visions of a lost unity, postmodernity bids valediction to the absent ideals, and in its stead focuses "on the power of the faculty [of the human mind] to conceive" (*The Postmodern Explained* 13).

My personal concern with regard to Lyotard's standpoint on nostalgia is governed by the wish to, on the one hand, clearly discriminate between the popular and the academic ideas generated by nostalgia, and on the other, to delineate the conceptual boundaries around modernist nostalgia. It seems that, for Lyotard, nostalgia's essential resonance is post-Kantian,[6] since the scholar links longing with the sublime. In *The Postmodern Explained: Correspondence*, Lyotard claims that "[T]he modern aesthetics is an aesthetics of the sublime. But it is nostalgic; it allows the unpresentable to be invoked only as absent content, while form, thanks to its recognisable consistency, continues to offer the reader or spectator material for consolation and pleasure" (14). I wish to argue that such an essentializing of the phenomenon provides an additional perspective when considering Conrad's prose, for example, the missing and the absent that constitute the conceptual frames of his works, particularly in the case of *The Mirror of the Sea: Memories and Impressions* (1906), *A Personal Record* (1912), and *Notes on Life and Letters* (1921).

As far as I am concerned, Lyotard's evocation of the "absent content" (*The Postmodern Explained* 14) is in line with what a famous Conradian scholar, Ian Watt, once observed regarding the inspiration behind Conrad's method of composition: the academic likened the writer to a "primitive nomad" who, in the process of creation, moves within "the landscape of memory" (93). Paradoxically, this holds for both his fiction and non-fiction. Anchored to the past, however, the "absent content" not only implies the recollection of certain events as recalled by the speaker, but also embraces a certain nostalgic fascination with things past, a fascination which deliberates upon both personal and communal concerns, with the latter embedded within the modernist "unpresentable": in the first autobiographical narrative, *The Mirror of the Sea*, the speaker appears to be searching for "consolation and pleasure," both symptomatic of modern nostalgia (Lyotard, *The Postmodern Explained* 14). Interestingly, the subject of the reminiscence remains vague enough and may primarily concern a loss recorded by the community, rather than the individual: although included within the general standpoint, the individual ranks as being of a lesser importance. I would claim that, while on occasion reminiscences about the past connote the popular understanding of nostalgia, Conrad's autobiographical narratives are framed through a nostalgic construct which helps essentialize the unpresentable "absent content" in recognizable, albeit vague, terms.

As suggested, the subject matter in Conrad's autobiographical reflections, and particularly in *The Mirror of the Sea*, is thus nostalgic *sensu* Lyotard, as it focuses on the chasm between the present and the absent, with the emphasis clearly placed on the latter, thus favouring the past as normative for the present; rhetorically, it is steeped in the elegiac mode, bringing consolation to both the speaker and the implied reader. Indeed, Conrad admits in a letter to J. B. Pinker, his publisher, the collection was meant to include "essays – impressions, descriptions, reminiscences, anecdotes and typical traits – of the old sailing fleet which passes away for good with the last century" (*CL* 3: 114). While the quotation connotes the "visible content" in its elegiac evocation of the experience of sailing, thus linking generations of sailors, it also contributes to the nostalgically conjured image of "the [once] whole and the one" envisioned as an organic union of the elements and sailors of all ages. Scholars have already addressed both issues, with Wiesław Ratajczak reading *The Mirror and the Sea* as a testimony to the turn-of-the-century breach in the intergenerational communication between sailors (80-85, 92). The implication suggested by a no-longer-present organic unity, in fact, contributes to a yet broader idea: I would read it as a literary representation of Lyotard's modernist "unpresentable" which, through the *pars pro toto* substitution, indicates the general breach noted by Conrad, a breach fundamentally transforming the human experience of living into a new phenomenon.[7] Apparently, *The Mirror of the Sea* is imbued with a nostalgia that, as far as I am concerned, acquires distinctly modernist features in its transfixed and critical stock-taking of what has irrevocably passed, with the loss both tangible and intangible. While the former means the broken bond reported during sailing expeditions, the latter highlights the more general nature of the rupture between man and the elements. In the context of nostalgia critiques, such a rupture has, indeed, been recorded by Stephen Spender who envisioned it as "a screen between nature and man [...] that [...] [prevents the establishment of a] harmonious relationship" (*The Struggle* 44).

It is perhaps significant that Spender – a poet, prose writer, literary critic, and an autobiographer himself[8] – endeavoured to rationalize the idiosyncrasies of the so-called moderns, i.e. his contemporaries who "distrust, or even detest, the idea of progress" (x), with the help of nostalgia (207-19). Nostalgia is, therefore, viewed as a solidifying[9] element of the modernist mindset by both Spender and Lyotard. Interestingly, Spender notes that, in contrast to that characterizing Victorian literature, modernist nostalgia disposed of the former "reformist passion [...] [and] social optimism," instead introducing an "utter hatred for the present, and contempt for progress" (211). This sounds familiar in the context of Conrad's autobiographical output since the content of the reflection is, indeed, markedly anti-progress and stimulated by images of the past which, while haunting the reminiscent *persona,* simultaneously deliver pleasure and consolation. Thus, *The Mirror of the Sea* may be viewed as a manifesto recorded by a member of a generation on the cusp of changes that would have far-reaching effects, a manifesto conveyed through the nostalgic tensions animating the static maritime descriptions in a manner that not only helps bestow an elegiac character on the narrative, but also enables the readers to recognize the "absent content" as familiar, albeit intangible and inexpressible.

The acute awareness of the past, "[t]he past as a prologue" (Watt 24), which characterizes Conrad's autobiographical writings, allows for a still more accurate categorization as regards its personal content: in my reading, the nostalgia-driven reminiscences acquire distinctively *reflective* traits *sensu* Boym. As the contemporary scholar asserts, various realizations of nostalgia across literature and culture have invited a formal divide between *restorative* and *reflective* nostalgia. While the former delivers fixed images of a ready-made version of the past,[10] the latter is concerned with

> historical and individual time, with the irrevocability of the past and human finitude [...]. *Re-flection* suggests new flexibility [...] [Reflective] nostalgia [...] is more oriented toward an individual narrative that savors details and memorial signs, perpetually deferring homecoming itself. (Boym 49)

It is within the category of *reflective* nostalgia that Conrad's autobiographical narratives may be classified; in fact, *reflective* nostalgia explains the internal inconsistencies within the texts, the contradictions between various versions of certain events, as well as the unfilled *lacunae* in the recollections and their episodic structure. The wavering and hesitative tone, while so characteristic of Conrad's prose in general (Watt 25, 31), is anchored in the patterns designed with the help of *reflective* nostalgia which Boym designates as a type of narrative that is "ironic, inconclusive and fragmentary" (50). Thus, the *reflec-*

tive nostalgia in Conrad's autobiographical narratives not only stimulates the internal tensions invigorating his recollections in terms of the content matter, but also shapes their formal side as far as the coherence and structure is concerned.

While also consistent with Boym's definition of the *reflective* nostalgic mode, James's application of modernist nostalgia in his trilogy, *Autobiographies* (Dupee), transfers the point of interest towards formal concerns: whereas the reminiscent Conrad favours the past over the present and is unwaveringly contemptuous of progress, James's involvement with the past is of a more intentionally artistic, and yet a less judgmental, awareness. Fascinating and consolatory, the past is re-enacted on the pages of his *Autobiographies* through a nostalgia marked in the form and the language, with the temporal tensions structuring the content in a manner favouring neither the past nor the present of the described community: though active, the tensions are unbiased in their exposure of the observed changes. The content is thus *reflectively* nostalgic in quite a different manner from that deployed by Conrad: the visible pleasure of reminiscing seems to be prolonged through the act of a creative re-staging of the recalled events in which Conrad's "time perpetually past"[11] (Olney 240) becomes present again in a series of vignettes portraying the remembered figures and places with the minutiae of a photographic camera. In the process of reminiscing, the lens of the camera repetitively embraces exposures of people, places, and objects – groups often consisting of the same members or elements – with further re-adjustments of the view and the focus, both changing over time. Thus, the subsequent, autobiographical snapshots can address the stories of several lives, with James's life centrestage, and the manner in which an individual, place or object features seems objective, however much such an assertion contradicts the subjective nature of autobiography.[12] Such a design agrees with the concept of the autobiographical *persona* acting as an impartial observer "dawdling and gaping" with unfeigned admiration at the progress of life (James 19). This is seen in the opening chapter of *Autobiographies,* when the speaker admits:

> My stronger rule, however, I confess, and the one by which I must here consistently be guided, is that, from the moment it is a question of projecting a picture, no particle that counts for memory or is appreciable to the spirit *can* be too tiny, and that experience, in the name of which one speaks, is all compact of them and shining with them. (18)

In addition to the appreciation of detail, the lines quoted above testify to yet another feature of James's attitude towards the autobiographical, namely that discerned by the so-called "topographical imagination," which presumes a distinct sensitivity to the visual in both real and imaginative landscapes (Czermińska 188). It is probably the rich visual sensitivity of the author that motivates a range of metaphorical assertions interlinking space and time in *Autobiographies*, which opens with an image of "knock[ing] at the door of the past [that] was open[ed] to me quite wide" (James 5). The translation of time into spatial categories – albeit quite common in fictionalized depictions of childhood (Grahame 1; Hartley 5) – also contributes to the re-enforcement of nostalgia, since nostalgic tensions embrace the interface of *then* and *there*: as I have argued elsewhere, the spatial and the temporal has been conceptually interrelated within the original and contemporary conceptions of nostalgia (Wojciechowska, "*Nostos*" 4-5). In James's *Autobiographies*, such linkings also betoken the photographic sensitivity to details in the sites of memory: the translations of time into space draw attention to the visual and the scenic. At this juncture, it is perhaps worth noting that, in contrast to the mechanism of the camera (Harker 319), while registering the visual particulars, the autobiographical consciousness chooses between elements intended to appear blurred and those emphasized in a given context; the subjects and the places thus "photographed" are filtered through the autobiographical mind, which may be interpreted in a variety of ways by different scholars. Apparently, the reminiscent *I* in James's *Autobiographies* is designed to be a detached observer who, if venturing critical statements, recedes behind the shield of irony: this renders the designed-as-objective featuring of the past idiosyncratic. It is in the detachment of the speaker that I would situate the major difference in the form of reflection between the two authors: in contrast to James, Conrad's involvement is intentional. Moreover, the dissimilarities in the formal design also include the use of conventions: whereas the Conradian elegiac tone attests to the superior quality of the no-longer-present wholeness, if expressed, the Jamesian elegiac valediction is narrowed in focus to embrace his deceased friends and family members, a rather more conventional approach. In other words, while Conrad declares his generation to have departed, together with the loss of intergenerational understanding, James searches for the remnants of a gone-yet-relevant past that is recognizable, and indeed retrievable, in the present moment; the lament is merely intended for the deceased. Such dissimilar deployments of "a constructed nostalgia" (Outka 256) result in divergent interpretative positions towards the present, namely indifferent and reconciliatory, respectively; as may be expected, they also impact on the form of reflection as they employ literary modes to differing extents.

Discernible in the impressions regarding community, the conceptual divide in the nostalgia-driven content of the autobiographical reflections is also displayed in the memories of the lives of both authors. The discrepancy may be explained by their divergent life experiences, on the one hand, and their dissimilar approaches to the process of writing, on the other. It hardly seems far-fetched to assume that the nostalgic yearning discernible in Conrad's later autobiographical narratives, *A Personal Record* and "Poland Revisited," both dedicated to personal matters, is partially motivated by his exilic experiences and by the loss of his parents at an early age. In such cases nostalgia, particularly the *reflective* kind, appears a natural emotion as it helps one "perform[…] a labor of grief both through pondering pain and through play that points to the future" (Boym 55). If compared to the Jamesian recollections of his early childhood in New York and Albany, as well as his Newport adolescence, Conrad's reminiscences of Berdichev, Ukraine, appear less detailed and individually marked; however, it is worth remembering that Conrad had little knowledge of his parents and, in consequence, in his narratives he retells the memories of his guardian, Tadeusz Bobrowski (Maunsell 23). As Jerome Boyd Maunsell notes, Conrad's "memories came from somebody else's self-portrait" (23). This sheds light on the lack of passages formally framed as pastoral vignettes that, however infrequent, do appear in the Jamesian *Autobiographies*. Apparently, the lack of emotional colouring in a child too small to appreciate his surroundings in a referential manner – a literal lack of content – prevented the formal sentimentalization of his earliest days through pastoral dressing and popular nostalgia. Conrad's childhood in *A Personal Record* is a childhood virtually *reflected* from another source, with the rendition thus somewhat devoid of individual colouring. On a personal level, the nostalgic tensions between past and present in *A Personal Record* thus stimulate acts of reconstruction with regard to identity by linking the unnamed, personal impressions of the reminiscent *persona* with national memory and history – forming parts of Lyotard's great metanarratives of modernity (*Kondycja* 69-77) – and also with the collective memories of several members of Conrad's social circle, his uncle Bobrowski included. In *A Personal Record*, Conrad's private memories overlap with a single-plot national tale, and also with the multiple plots of his friends and compatriots who share with him, and indeed give substance to, the common sites of a collective, cultural memory, against which his fragmented memories may evolve (Boym 53). In my view, this interlinking of various emplotments within a nostalgia-driven autobiographical narration not only renders any charges of referential inconsistencies irrelevant but, as Boym suggests, also feeds creativity, since the experimentation with time and the thematization of nomadic, and even exilic, experiences may be individually translated into "a survival strategy" (257).[13] This was, in fact, clear to Conrad who in one of his letters to H. G. Wells admitted that *A Personal Record* was "a unique opportunity to pull [himself] together" (*CL* 4: 149).

Multiple emplotments in the nostalgic interlinkings of past and present also characterize James's *Autobiographies*. Nonetheless, in contrast to Conrad,[14] James only permits other voices to explicitly enrich his story in its later parts: the numerous quotations from a series of letters add colour to the narrative of his adolescent and adult experiences. Supplemented by visuals in the form of an 1854 daguerreotype of himself and his father (James 773), the childhood phase is spared the verbalized opinions of the others that might intervene between the "gaping boy" and his life. On the one hand, this is certainly no coincidence in the case of a master of language (Veeder), since such additions might diminish the impression of the constant, childlike wonder that is revealed (James 773). On the other hand, however, this difference in the form of personal reflection, i.e. a reflection on intimate and private matters, may be accounted for through the divergent patterns of creation discernible in the so-called "autobiographical sites": as Małgorzata Czermińska asserts, if combined with biographical and topographical details, autobiographical narratives may represent several kinds of half-real/half-imagined memory sites; in this regard, I argue, Conrad and James fall into two distinct categories. As an exilic author recollecting his native country from a distance, Conrad sketches a homeland which embodies a "moved" site of autobiographical memory that is also informed with collective sites of the nation (Czermińska 200). By contrast, James, who elected to live outside his native land, features America as a "recollected site of memory" (200). In consequence, Conrad's dual commitments to his Polish and British *patris*[15] open his literarily remembered Ukrainian space[16] decidedly wider to the images preserved within the collective and diasporic memories (195); by the same token, the act of selecting Britain as where he intended to live allowed James to describe his native country with whatever particularity he chose, yet with the details able to be checked, a fact which, in effect, frames the portrayal as both intimate and personal.

The intimacy of representation becomes visible in the opening of *A Small Boy and Others*, which is both nostalgic and pastoral. The speaker first asserts that "to knock at the door of the past was in a word to see it open to me quite wide – to see the world within begin to 'compose' with a grace of its own round the primary figure, see it people itself vividly and insistently" (James 5); and a few lines further the *reflective* nostalgia is framed with the help of pastoral *topoi* and rhetoric:

> The "first" then – since I retrace our [William's and his own] steps to the start, for the pleasure, strangely mixed though it be, of feeling our small feet plant themselves afresh and artlessly stumble forward again – the first began long ago, far off, and yet glimmers at me there as out of a thin golden haze, with all the charm, for imagination and memory, of pressing pursuit rewarded, of distinctness in the dimness, of the flush of life in the grey, of the wonder of consciousness in everything; [...] It exhaled at any rate a simple freshness, and I catch its pure breath, at our infantile Albany, as the very air of long summer afternoons – occasions tasting of ample leisure, still bookless, yet beginning to be bedless, or cribless [...]. (6)

In a way which brings Lyotard to mind, the passage intimates the sweet-sour pleasure of reminiscence which, in James's case, seems to displace communal concerns: "the absent content" has acquired a distinctly personal dimension. However, the deployment of the pastoral mode – discernible in a range of evocative phrases and motifs, and given emphasis through binary oppositions and synaesthesia – interlinks *reflective* nostalgia with general speculations about the fleetingness of childhood and human transience. In consequence, it may be concluded that the pastoral form, consolidated within both literature and culture, compensates for "the absent content" by bestowing on it a recognizability which "continues to offer the reader or spectator material for consolation and pleasure" (Lyotard, *The Postmodern Explained* 14). Apparently, the pastoral *topoi* constitute the link between the individual and the collective, the absent and the present, and, finally, between form and content.

Nevertheless, at this juncture, it should be noted that "the pastoral of sentiment" (Marx 24) is exclusively invoked in the opening pages of James's *Autobiographies*. The subsequent chapters approach and deploy the pastoral convention with irony: like Conrad, James is renowned for his disdain for sentimentality, a sentimentality which connotes popular pastoral and popular nostalgia (Boym 338). While applying the formal elements of the pastoral convention in his intimations, in most cases James refrains from such sentimental tones as those quoted above, and instead re-assesses them with an ironic smile. Thus, he explodes the previously mentioned Arcadian sentiments in a somewhat challenging manner when asking "of what lost Arcadia, at that age, had I really had the least glimpse?" (James 27). The double referent of the *Autobiographies* thus negotiates the limits of sentimentality permissible within autobiographical reflection, with the resulting formal divide between the sentimental, childlike impressions filtered through the mind of the elderly reminiscent *persona* and steeped in pastoral clichés, and the unsentimental, mature observations in which the pastoral rhetoric is only introduced in a subversive, self-derisive manner. Through such assertions, the unfolding, changing content of reflection constantly re-considers the form it applies, and the nostalgic undercurrents correspond with, and indeed lay bare, the ready-made postures and clichés, which are seen to be ultimately empty and meaningless; this corresponds with the tone characteristic of *reflective* nostalgia since, as Boym asserts, nostalgia in its *reflective* version is open to irony and humour (49).

It may be concluded that the mode of nostalgia, and particularly that of *reflective* nostalgia, impacts on both the form and the subject matter of autobiographical reflection. Not only does it help account for the fragmentariness and apparent selective randomness discernible in the early-modernist texts under consideration, but, essentialized as a fundamental desire encouraging re-approaches towards "the absent," modernist nostalgia seems to be a multi-dimensional phenomenon that can be employed in both idealizing and critical stances. According to Tammy Clewell:

> [O]ne of nostalgia's tendencies may be intent on returning to the imaginative terrain of an idealized past, another tendency, much more future-oriented in its aims, consists of exploiting the capacity of nostalgia to expose the mechanized brutalities, social iniquities,

> dizzying effects of technological change, the spiritual emptiness of the age. (Introduction 3)

From my perspective, although both Conrad and James may be described as *reflectively* nostalgic, their deployments of nostalgia in the selected narratives under consideration are, in some ways, if not in every way, dissimilar: while Conrad exposes the deficiencies of his age through nostalgia-driven irony, James purposefully plays with conventions, as well as with stylistic and rhetorical devices. Both authors thus re-design autobiography and render the modern sense of self.

NOTES

[1] It is included in a passage dedicated to a friend, Vernon King, who died in the American Civil War – see Rowe and Haralson 21. The elegiac character of the fragment accords well with the pastoral reminiscences. More on the pastoral and elegy in Wojciechowska *(Re)Visions* 35.

[2] On the distinction between *simple* and *complex* pastoral, see Marx 24; Wojciechowska *(Re)Visions* 15-16.

[3] Consider, for example, Kant's (69) initial attempt to make the term more accessible, with *nostalgia* renamed *homesickness*, and his ensuing rejection of the emotion, together with the post-Kantian stance by Lyotard, to be discussed further in this article. On the positive appraisals of nostalgia, see Spender, *The Struggle*; Boym; Illbruck; Clewell; Dodman.

[4] Hereafter, a copy of Hofer's manuscript stored at the Jagiellonian Library in Cracow, Poland, is the reference used in this article: Hofer, *Dissertatio Medica de Nostalgia, oder Heimwehe.* [Medical dissertation on nostalgia]. Basileae: Jacobi Bertschii. It is misdated to 1678.

[5] Hofer indicated, however, that the disease could affect anyone – more in Dodman 16-42.

[6] Kant belittles nostalgia due to its "inventive," and not entirely "recollective" character. For a negative Kantian appraisal of "the *homesickness* of the Swiss" – as the philosopher terms nostalgia – see Kant 286-91.

[7] See Maya Jasanoff's seminal *The Dawn Watch: Joseph Conrad in a Global World* on the extent of the continued transformation at the cusp of the twentieth century.

[8] Consider *World Within World. The Autobiography of Stephen Spender* which thematizes the experience of living in Britain in the 1930s.

[9] The adjective is applied to inspire reflection on Bauman's liquid modernity, as opposed to solid modernity (*Liquid* 25-26).

[10] In *The Future of Nostalgia*, Boym explains the mechanisms governing *restorative*, or *unreflective*, nostalgia when used in propaganda discourse (41-43). On the methods of countering them, see 61-71.

[11] In his study on autobiography, James Olney differentiates between the traditional autobiographical accounts, in which time is perpetually past, and works of high modernism in which time is perpetually present (240-53). In the former, the autobiographical speaker moves backwards and forwards between past and present, whereas in the latter he dismisses memory and his past as the organizing principles and instead traces the "atemporal consciousness, or awareness or active sensibility" of the mind (252). Though different from the Conradian volumes, James's *Autobiographies* still fall within the first category.

[12] For the interlinking of literature, art, and photography in James's recollections, see Buchholtz.

[13] As Boym explains, nostalgia helps describe intimacy, and also what she calls "diasphoric intimacy": see 251-54.

[14] Consider the citations from *Almayer's Folly* on page 3 in *A Personal Record*, the letter cited on page 20, and the uncle's description of Conrad's mother in Chapter II on pages 27-28. See also Peacock 151-56.

[15] On the conceptualization of *patris* as distinct from *patria*, see Wojciechowska *"Nostos"* 391-94.

[16] Interestingly, as an example of the type, Czermińska mentions Jerzy Stempowski's "Esej berdyczowski" [The Essay on Berdichev], which literally connotes Conradian narratives (196).

WORKS CITED

Alpers, Paul. *What Is Pastoral?* U of Chicago P, 1996.

Bauman, Zygmunt. *Liquid Modernity*. Polity P, 2017.

---. *Retrotopia. Jak rządzi nami przeszłość.* Trans. K. Lebek. Państwowe Wydawnictwo Naukowe, 2018.

Bell, Millicent. "James and Conrad: The Fictions of Autobiography." Carabine and Knowles with Armstrong 81-96.

Boym, Svetlana. *The Future of Nostalgia*. Basic, 2001.

Buchholtz, Mirosława. *Henry James i sztuka auto/biografii*. Wydawnictwo Naukowe Uniwersytetu im. Mikołaja Kopernika, 2011.

Carabine, Keith, and Owen Knowles, with Paul Armstrong, eds. *Conrad, James and Other Relations*. East European Monographs, Maria Curie-Skłodowska U, Columbia UP, 1998. Vol. 6 of *Conrad: Eastern and Western Perspectives*. Ed. Wiesław Krajka. 32 vols. to date. 1992- .

Carabine, Keith, and Max Saunders, eds. *Interrelations: Conrad, James, Ford and Others*. East European Monographs, Maria Curie-Skłodowska U, Columbia UP, 2003. Vol. 12 of *Conrad: Eastern and Western Perspectives*. Ed. Wiesław Krajka. 32 vols. to date. 1992- .

Cichoń, Anna Izabela. "Autobiography and Supplementarity: Joseph Conrad's *A Personal Record*." *"Wine in Old and New Bottles": Critical Paradigms for Joseph Conrad*. Ed. Wiesław Krajka. Maria Curie-Skłodowska UP, Columbia UP, 2014. 29-44. Vol. 23 of *Conrad: Eastern and Western Perspectives*. Ed. Wiesław Krajka. 32 vols. to date. 1992- .

Clewell, Tammy. "Introduction. Past 'Perfect' and 'Present' Tense: The Abuses and Uses of Modernist Nostalgia." Clewell 1-24.

---. ed. *Modernism and Nostalgia. Bodies, Locations, Aesthetics*. Palgrave Macmillan, 2013.

Czermińska, Małgorzata. "Miejsca autobiograficzne: propozycja w ramach geopolityki." *Teksty drugie: teoria literatury, krytyka, interpretacja* 5 (2011): 183-200.

Davis, Fred. *Yearning for Yesterday. A Sociology of Nostalgia*. Free P, 1979.

De Man, Paul. "Autobiography as De-facement." *Comparative Literature* 94 (1979): 919-30. Accessed 31 Jan. 2023. Stable URL: <https://www.jstor.org/stable/2906560>.

Derrida, Jacques. *Pozycje. Rozmowy z Henri Ronsem, Julią Kristevą, Jean-Louis Houdebinem i Guy Scarpettą*. Trans. Adam Dziadek. FA-art, 1997.

Dodman, Thomas. *What Nostalgia Was. War, Empire, and the Time of a Deadly Emotion*. U of Chicago P, 2018.

Dupee, Frederick. *Henry James: Autobiography*. Princeton UP, 2014.

Fothergill, Anthony. "Memory and Experience Lost: Conrad's 'Karain: A Memory' and James's 'The Beast in the Jungle'." Carabine and Knowles with Armstrong 113-22.

Fowler, Alastair. *Kinds of Literature: An Introduction to the Theory of Genres and Modes*. Clarendon P, 1982.

Grahame, Kenneth. *The Golden Age*. Dover, 2005.

Guyer, Paul, Allen W. Wood, and Robert B. Louden eds. *Immanuel Kant. Lectures on Anthropology*. Cambridge UP, 2012.

Hampson, Robert. "Gossip in Conrad, James, and Ford." Carabine and Saunders 69-92.

Harker, Margaret. "The Eye of the Camera." *Journal of the Royal Society of Arts* 121 (1973): 319-24.

Hartley, Leslie Poles. *The Go-Between*. Penguin, 2000.

Hofer, Johannes. *Dissertatio medica de nostalgia oder Heimwehe*. Jacobi Bertschii, 1688.

Illbruck, Helmut. *Nostalgia. Origins and Ends of an Unenlightened Disease*. Northwestern UP, 2012.

James, Henry. *Henry James. Autobiographies. A Small Boy and Others. Notes of a Son and a Brother. The Middle Years. Other Autobiographical Writings*. Ed. Phillip Horne. Library of America, 2016.

Jasanoff, Maya. *Joseph Conrad i narodziny globalnego świata*. Trans. Krzysztof Cieślik and Maciej Miłkowski. Wydawnictwo Poznańskie, 2018.

Jenkins, Keith. *Why History? Ethics and Postmodernity*. Routledge, 1999.

Kant, Immanuel. *Anthropology from a Pragmatic Point of View*. Ed. Hans H. Rudnick. Trans. V. L. Dowdell. Braun, 1996.

Lowenthal, David. *The Past Is a Foreign Country Revisited*. Cambridge UP, 2015.

Lyotard, Jean-Françoise. *Kondycja ponowoczesna*. Trans. Małgorzata Kowalska and Jacek Migasiński. Aletheia, 1997.

---. *The Postmodern Condition. A Report on Knowledge*. Trans. Geoff Bennington and Brian Massumi. U of Minnesota P, 1984.

---. *The Postmodern Explained: Correspondence*, 1982-1985. Afterword Wlad Godzich. Trans. Barry Don, Bernadette Maher, Julian Pefanis, Virginia Spate, and Morgan Thomas. U of Minnesota P, 1992.

Marx, Leo. *The Machine in the Garden. Technology and the Pastoral Ideal in America*. Oxford UP, 1964.

Maunsell, Jerome Boyd. *Portraits from Life: Modernist Novelists and Autobiography*. Oxford UP, 2018.

Olney, James. "Some Versions of Memory/Some Versions of *Bios*: The Ontology of Autobiography." *Autobiography: Essays Theoretical and Critical*. Ed. James Olney. Princeton UP, 1980. 236-67.

Outka, Elisabeth. "Afterward. Nostalgia and Modernist Anxiety." Clewell, *Modernism and Nostalgia* 252-61.

Peacock, Noel. "'Undefaced Image': Autobiography and Vision in *A Personal Record*." *Conrad's Century. The Past and Future Splendour*. Ed. Laura L. Davis. East European Monographs, Maria Curie-Skłodowska U, Columbia UP, 1998. 151-66. Vol. 7 of *Conrad: Eastern and Western Perspectives*. Ed. Wiesław Krajka. 32 vols. to date. 1992- .

Ratajczak, Wiesław. *Conrad i koniec epoki żaglowców*. Wydawnictwo Naukowe Uniwersytetu im. Adama Mickiewicza, 2010.

Rowe, John Carlos, and Eric Haralson eds. *A Historical Guide to Henry James*. Oxford UP, 2012.

Said, Edward W. *Joseph Conrad and The Fiction of Autobiography*. Harvard UP, 1966.

Saunders, Max. "Reflections on Impressionist Autobiography: James, Conrad and Ford." Carabine and Saunders 7-42.

Schweizer, Bernard. "Modernism and the Referendum on Nostalgia in Rebecca West's 'The Return of the Soldier'." Clewell, *Modernism and Nostalgia* 25-35.

Sedikides, Constantine, Tim Wildschut, and Denise Baden. "Nostalgia: Conceptual Issues and Existential Functions." *Handbook of Experimental Existential Psychology*. Ed. Jeff Greenberg, Sander L. Koole, and Tom Pyszczynski. Guilford P, 2004. 200-14.

Simmons, Allan. "Conrad on James: Open-endedness and Artistic Affiliation." Carabine and Knowles with Armstrong 97-112.

Shaw, Christopher, Malcolm Chase. *The Imagined Past: History and Nostalgia*. Manchester UP, 1989.

Spender, Stephen. *The Struggle of the Modern*. Hamilton, 1963.

---. *World Within World. The Autobiography of Stephen Spender.* U of California P, 1966.

Tannock, Stuart. "Nostalgia Critique." *Cultural Studies* 9 (1995): 453-64.

Veeder, William. *Henry James – The Lessons of the Master.* U of Chicago P, 1975.

Watt, Ian. *Conrad in the Nineteenth Century.* U of California P, 1979.

Wojciechowska, Sylwia. "*Nostos,* Nostalgia, and Pastoral in 20th-century British Prose Fiction." *Papers on Language and Literature* 57 (2021): 388-409.

---. *(Re)Visions of the Pastoral in Selected British and American post-Romantic Fiction.* Wydawnictwo "WAM," 2017.

Anna Szczepan-Wojnarska,
Cardinal Stefan Wyszyński University,
Warsaw, Poland

Almayer's Aria

The importance of music for Joseph Conrad manifests itself in his personal relationships and narrative techniques analysed by various researchers, i.e. E. C. Bufkin, Jeffrey Meyers, Lawrence Davies, Wiesław Krajka. This article refers to *Almayer's Folly. A Story of an Eastern River* and concerns Conrad's remark expressed in a letter to his aunt, Madame Marguerite Poradowska, in which Conrad comments on the operatic form, reminiscent of the final scenes of his first novel. Discussing *Almayer's Folly. A Story of an Eastern River*, which he was writing at the time, Conrad tells Poradowska that the last chapter "begins with a trio . . . and ends with a long solo for Almayer which is almost as long [as] Tristan's in Wagner" (2 May 1894; *CL* 1: 155-56). Following this remark, the present article will consider the role of the reader in the construction of the text, the role of music in Conrad's life, and the reference to the meaning of Conrad's *aria*.

The Role of the Reader

The reader's perspective inscribed in the text and projected by the author allows us to believe that the reader can detect the slightest traces left by the author which refer to the non-novelistic world. Krajka explains this aspect of Conrad's narrative technique in the light of Roman Ingarden's theory of literary art, rooted in phenomenology. "According to Ingarden, a literary work of art lives multiple lives through its readings. And reader-response theory claims that the ultimate meaning of a literary work of art is created through its interactions with the readers' literary and cultural selves" ("Crossing over Media" 267). In addition, I would like to draw attention to the fact that this multiplication begins not only with the methods of individual reception, but also with the information contained in the text, although at first glance this may seem to be of negligible importance.

Amar Acheraïou's discussion of the ideal Conrad reader seems to be constructed on a similar presumption:

> My belief is that the evoked ambivalent process testifies to Conrad's perception of the ideal reader as both a discerning consumer of textual truths and a responsible producer of literary meaning. For all its ambivalence and elitism, Conrad's theory of reader response in the end seeks to make the reader a dynamic partner and active collaborator in the construction of textual meaning. (7)

The Conrad reader, being both a consumer and a producer of meanings, becomes a dynamic partner of the author like in Laurence Sterne's novel *The Life and Opinions of Tristram Shandy, Gentleman*. Sterne's novel announced a new, modern notion of the reader as an active participant in the production of textual meaning and has therefore become a point of reference in contemporary discussions of literary criticism.

Conrad creates a space to interact with readers – but not to the extent that Sterne did by placing in the book Tristram's drawings, plain blank sheets, or notation for Uncle Toby's song. I argue that Conrad expects the reader to identify the various facts and details belonging to the external cultural and historical framework in which he situates his fictional worlds. Moreover, it demands readers to accompany the author not only at the linear level of following the plot, but also at the interpretive one. In comparison to Sterne, Conrad does not give the score of *Il Trovatore*, which is mentioned at the very beginning, but evokes its operatic aesthetics to prepare the reader for the final scene of Almayer's personal drama and his final monologue in the mode of Richard Wagner. In my opinion, such a requirement of close knowledge of operas and their context appears as the author's direction to read the novel as a mode of operatic performance.

The Role of Music

Conrad's love of music is associated with sensuality, sensitivity, and some of the most important moments of his life, such as his first memory of his mother:

> My earliest memory is of my mother at the piano; of being let into a room which to this day seems to me the very largest room which I was ever in, of the music suddenly stopping, and my mother, with her hands on the keyboard, turning her head to look at me. ("The First Thing I Remember" 98)

It is also related to his first months in Marseille (Najder 41), France, his courtship of Émilie Briquel, to whom he gave the score of *Carmen*, the Chopin piano concerts played by the pianist composer John Powell in Conrad's house and Conrad's fondness of Jane Anderson, who sang the melodies of the American South to him. Two of Conrad's friends, Richard Curle and Joseph T. Rettinger, questioned Conrad's taste for music, but Gérard Jean-Aubry testified that Conrad had a deep love of music. Various references to music have been explored in detail by Jeffrey Meyers who puts an emphasis on biographical aspects of music in Conrad's writings and identified numerous allusions to operas. Also Bufkin, analysing *Nostromo*, noted that, in its vastness, this novel uses a wide range of genres, just like grand opera. Highly inspirational articles by Laurence Davies, Pamela Bickley, and Robert Hampson provide an in-depth examination of operatic mode used by Conrad.

First of all, music lies at the heart of Conrad's most important statement about his art, Preface to *The Nigger of the "Narcissus,"* in which Conrad emphasizes the importance of appealing to the senses and calls music the art of arts, which recalls Arthur Schopenhauer's thought about the highest status of music among the arts. The philosopher, whose works Conrad was familiar with, appreciated the influence of music on human feelings and praised it for strengthening the meaning of art and reality.

Various sources confirm Conrad's acquaintance with opera, its techniques and repertoire. Boris Conrad (32, 49) recorded in his memoirs his father's love of opera (in particular *Cavalleria Rusticana* and *Carmen*), which was confirmed by John Galsworthy and Jean-Aubry. Undoubtedly, Conrad's operatic predilections were shaped by his stay in France, that was the heart of grand opera at that time. The leading composer of the grand opera was Giacomo Meyerbeer, whose works Conrad appreciated despite the disregard of popular opinion. Frank Baldanza lists the operas performed in Marseilles during the relevant period: among Meyerbeer's were performances of *Les Huguenots*, *L'Africaine*, *Le prophète*, and *Robert-le-diable*.

The art of opera with its romantic concepts, violent and passionate characters appealed to emotions and therefore influenced many writers and their work, especially the grand opera, which used sudden actions, grotesque contrasts, and spectacular shows.[1]

Undeniably, Conrad was a music lover who knew different musical forms and was accustomed to music from early childhood, moreover, his concept of art was modern and synaesthetic, which is why he referred to music in many aspects of his novels.

Recorded Aria

The features of the humanistic vision of culture and civilization are imitated by Conrad in the spirit of scepticism towards the nature of knowledge, as Hampson pointed out, and perhaps that is why the initial allusion to Giuseppe Verdi's opera may surprise readers even more as it is performed as a recording, and furthermore – a deformed one. The popular form of performance recorded on a barrel organ breaks the exclusivity of opera art, which, in my opinion, testifies to Conrad's modern and discursive approach to art in general.

Lakamba was hardly an opera admirer, but he had a taste in music. After he tells his advisor Babalatchi that Almayer must not reveal the secret of gold to the Dutch and suggests that Babalatchi poison him, Lakamba demands music. Babalatchi reluctantly fulfils Lakamba's demand to bring a box of music given to him by the white captain, Lingard. The question arises whether at this particular moment Lakamba wanted to listen to music, or rather, through this modern mechanical noise, he wanted to demonstrate his friendly relationship with Rajah Laut.

Babalatchi used a gift from Lingard to appease Lakamba, but his use of the box is described in grotesque terms. During the "performance" Babalatchi constantly falls asleep and moves the organ barrel more slowly than expected, or suddenly makes breaks and abruptly rotates the movement faster than the singers could sing, as if he could catch the time that passed. The original musical score is deformed by the recording itself and by Babalatchi's lack of skill in using a modern mechanical invention to perform the recording, as well as by his lack of musical competence and knowledge of how that piece of music is to be performed properly and heard pleasurably. As a result, Babalatchi fills the unresponsive jungle with alien but soothing sounds. Lakamba slumbers comfortably in an armchair, and the music box plays arias from *Il Trovatore*, a four-act opera by Verdi, one of the most recognizable and famous composers of that time.

The Italian libretto, written in large part by Salvadore Cammarano, is based on the play *El Trovador* by Antonio García Gutierrez (1836). The libretto of *Il Trovatore* is considered the most absurd and complicated of Verdi's operas, but after the premiere at the Theatro Apollo in Rome on January 19, 1853, *Il Trovatore* began an international career, attracting audiences around the world, and Conrad, realizing this fame, expects readers to decipher the context of the opera despite Babalatchi's incompetence. The aria recorded on the barrel organ comes from the first scene of the last act of the opera. This is the aria of Manrico, who has already been captured in a battle and sings his farewell to life and his beloved Leonora while waiting for death. Their love is tragic and overshadowed by the tragedies of the past. The most tragic arias taken out of context seem to be devoid of original pathos, but, in the end, they sound as if they have gained universal pathos of unquestionable tragedy. Pathos resulting not only from the plot and score, but also from the tragedy of being heard but misunderstood. This lack of understanding unexpectedly combines literary and musical tools for expressing tragedy in their collective failure to embody the realm of tragedy and discrepancy between language and reality.

Traces of Schopenhauer and Wagner

It can be argued that operatic poetics has a general kind of influence on Conrad's prose, one that flows from the bottom of inspiration. Geoffrey Meyers noted that "Conrad was particularly fond of opera – especially Meyerbeer, Verdi and Bizet – and used operatic gestures, language, themes and plots throughout his career" (179).

Conrad, writing to a distant relative of Poradowska, described the last chapter of his first novel in musical terms and compared it to Wagner's *Tristan und Isolde* (1865). This allusion may have been caused by the situation of participating in Wagner's opera together with Poradowska, as Davies (129) noted, but Mario Curreli[2] also pays attention to the presence of Wagner in another novel by Conrad – *Nostromo*. Given Conrad's preference for Meyerbeer, who had been heavily criticized by Wagner for his aesthetic, for his art and simply for being Jewish, it would be doubtful to assume that he knew Wagner's important ideas and theoretical works, but this is not impossible. In addition, Conrad referred to experimenters in other plays:

> I am long in my development. What of that? [...] And G. Elliot [sic] – is she as swift as the present public (incapable of fixing its attention for five consecutive minutes) requires us to be at the cost of all honesty, of all truth, and even the most elementary conception of art? But these are great names. I don't compare myself with them. I am *modern*, and I would rather recall Wagner the musician and Rodin the Sculptor who both had to starve a little in their day – and Whistler the painter who made Ruskin the critic foam at the mouth with scorn and indignation. (31 May 1902; *CL* 2: 418)

Conrad clearly expressed his modernist alliances, which allow us to take a closer look at Wagner's opera. The inspiration for the opera *Tristan und Isolde* was not only Wagner's love for Matilda Wassendonck, but a very important factor for the German romantic movement, such as the rediscovery of medieval Germanic poetry in general, but in particular the version of Gottfried von Strassburg's *Tristan*. There are several versions of this quintessence of medieval romance, but Wagner decided to dramatize the Strassburg version after his friend Karl Ritter tried to do so, as he wrote in his autobiography: "He had, in fact, made a point of giving prominence to the lighter phases of the romance, whereas it was its all-pervading tragedy that impressed me so deeply that I felt convinced it should stand out in bold relief, regardless of minor details" (617). Almost at the same time, Wagner became acquainted with the philosophy of Schopenhauer through another of his friends, the poet Georg Herhweg, impressed by the work *The World as Will and Representation*. Wagner admitted that Schopenhauer influenced his opera: "This must have been partly due to the serious mood created by Schopenhauer, which was trying to find ecstatic expression. It was some such mood that inspired the conception of *Tristan und Isolde*" (617). Wagner also shared his interests in Schopenhauer and *Tristan* in a letter to Franz Liszt (December 16, 1854):

> Never in my life having enjoyed the true happiness of love I shall erect a memorial to this loveliest of all dreams in which, from the first to the last, love shall, for once, find utter repletion. I have devised in my mind a *Tristan und Isolde*, the simplest, yet most full-blooded musical conception imaginable, and with the "black flag" that waves at the end I shall cover myself over – to die. (Gutman 103)

Schopenhauer's influence on Joseph Conrad has been written about by various Conradian scholars, such as Owen Knowles and Gene Moore,[3] Martin Ray,[4] or Nick Panagopoulos,[5] beginning with Galsworthy's famous sentence about Conrad that "Schopenhauer gave him satisfaction" (91). While Knowles and Moore provide a brilliant summary of secondary literature examining Conrad's relations with Schopenhauer, Ray (42) explores how both Conrad and Schopenhauer looked with anxiety at tension between language and reality, and he argues that a variety of ambiguities and conscious paradoxes encountered in the works of Schopenhauer corresponded to Conrad's "own inquiring and hesitant philosophy of language." Ray claims that it is more appropriate to see Schopenhauer as a corroborator than a mentor to Conrad. The opposite view is presented by Wiliam Bonney[6] who, by attributing transmission of Oriental philosophy to Schopenhauer, argues that Conrad's understanding of Orient was shaped by Schopenhauer. Examining a few of Conrad's works (*Lord Jim*, "Heart of Darkness," *The Secret Agent*, *Under Western Eyes*, *Victory*), Nick Panagopoulos suggests that knowledge of Schopenhauer's and Nietzsche's philosophy illuminates the central concerns of Conrad's fiction like the basic assumption that the world of senses is devoid of substance, that reason is limited and subservient to feeling. The author argues that the novelist was often grappling with the same problems as Schopenhauer and Nietzsche, and responding to some of the key issues of the Idealistic movement in the history of ideas. In conclusion, Panagopoulos states that Conrad rejects some of Schopenhauerian ideas, such as his prescription of detachment, as an escape from the snares of the world, but incorporates the Schopenhauerian ontology. Despite the differences in the adopted perspectives, they all emphasize that Conrad's characters are guided by unattainable desires, the realization of which leads to disaster. That is why I am convinced that Conrad's comparison between Tristan's solo and Almayer's farewell to Nina has a very strong justification.

Like Tristan, Almayer asks to be released from the feelings and dreams that tormented him and turned his life into ruins. Both Almayer and Tristan ask the question of the meaning of existence and are divided between the world of Day and the world of Night. In the kingdom of Day, Almayer must have been false to the powers of the Spirit, but in the kingdom of Night, he waged his own conspiracy with Dain and Lakamba. He lives in the realm of the unreality in possessing gold, of golden future in Europe, of his own marriage and, finally, of strong relationship with Nina. Despite the fact that her true feelings are feelings of love for her father, but in the sphere of representation she was simply the obedient daughter of Almayer, in the kingdom of the will – she was a proud woman who, once neglected and humbled, decided to find her place and love regardless of her father's expectations. Hampson insightfully argued, referring to Homi Bhabha's findings, that readers witness "Nina's continuous performance of identity through a constant negotiation of her own hybridity" (85). The word *performance* appears crucial to my interpretation because Nina seems to be well aware of different cultural codes which demand her to behave according to their patterns.[7] She is ready to die at the moment of the confrontation between Almayer and Dain (who also fits the Wagnerian paradigm): in the kingdom of representation, Dain is a merchant who serves Almayer and supports his plans, in the kingdom of the will, Dain is the powerful son of the Bali's rajah and takes Almayer's most prestigious jewel – his daughter, and thus destroys the white man's illusions. Almayer seems to be aware that the final moment of his love for his daughter marks the moment of his death, as all his dreams and vital forces were focused on Nina. Nonetheless, his death is neither immediate nor spectacular, which is consistent with the Day's logic. Without Nina, Almayer's life becomes purposeless and, at the same time, he realizes that he cannot enter her new world. The most tragic moment of this scene is the moment when Almayer realizes that his dream of being with her as a loving father and protector is unrealistic and cannot be part of the reality of the Day and the kingdom of representation. Therefore, he repeats that he will not forgive Nina, he repeats this phrase to himself rather than to her. He must follow the daytime realm of representation – the Schopenhauerian Phenomenon, he cannot be a white father from a very good Dutch family approving the choice and fate of his daughter. Hampson highlights that Almayer fails to accept his daughter's hybridity and "at the moment of crisis" (in chapter 11), when he has the option of accepting the identity that Nina has found for herself, he asserts instead his identity as "the only white man on the east coast" and sacrifices his daughter to this pride in racial origins.

Parental love, that natural and pure relation between father and daughter are banned in the perspective of representation.

Almayer and Nina, just like Tristan and Isolde, can only be united in the realm of Night, that is, the realm of unity, truth, and reality that can be achieved after the death of lovers. Almayer can express and prove his love for Nina by sacrificing himself for her in the kingdom of Night, which is signified by Schopenhauer's Noumenon. Almayer allowed Nina to escape with Dain, whereas he stayed on the island and, metaphorically, buried Nina's footsteps. The small graves on each of her traces signify that she died to him, just as he died to her. Her departure freed him from his unattainable thirst for gold and wealth, his vow never to forgive her, paradoxically facilitated her decision to leave him. However, at the same time, they expressed mutual love beyond a mode of representation. Nina is not discouraged by Almayer's words, his tone assures her that her father really loves her. The sound effect of his voice pervades her heart and means more than the meaning of pronounced words. She correctly deciphers his feelings, regardless of his identity's performance, which confirm Schopenhauer's thoughts about will and representation. In other words, the kingdom of Night means freedom and, simultaneously, death. Conrad, without imitating Wagner's opera, transforms the myth of Tristan in his individual way not only because it refers to parental love, which is expected, not forbidden, but also because it refers to the universal character of human relationships that seem to be an art of losing rather than excess of sin, or revolt breaking norms. Almayer, on the other hand, unlike Tristan awaiting Isolde's ship to arrive, is envisaging the disappearance of Nina's boat and, at this very moment, he proves to be the most loving father. This leads to the conclusion that only renunciation of desire brings inner peace in accordance with the Schopenhauerian ideas.

Audience

The conclusion suggested above may visualize the wish of empathetic readers, but is it really the case that the renunciation of desire brings Almayer inner peace? After the climax of his meeting with Nina, Almayer decided to forget about her, and because of this, he burned down his office and the house where he lived with her. Yet nothing helped him to forget and he was gradually recognized by Ali as haunted by ghosts, however, this version of events is challenged by the narrator, revealing Ali's naivety to readers. Nevertheless, Ali's interpretation of Almayer's deeds (The Phenomenon) reveals the truth (Noumenon) of his constant suffering and naivety in making decisions about aspects of life that cannot be managed by the decision-making process, such as remembering or forgetting. In the last period of his life, Almayer was deprived even of his enemies and accompanied only by a Chinese opium addict and a monkey. The protagonist dies when his grandson is born, which can be seen as an achievement of inner peace based on the fact that when Nina became the mother of Dain's firstborn son, her position is secured. The birth of Nina's son is also the time of Taminah's death, which endangered many lives. Readers or spectators of the tragedy receive detailed information about the events that took place after the climactic scene, however, without reliable narrative's authority all details lose their credibility.

In my opinion, Conrad takes into account another factor in his elaboration of Schopenhauerian and operatic ideas: the time to recognize one's own desires and the time to renounce them. In the key scene of the conversation with Nina, Almayer discovers that he knew nothing about his beloved child and recognizes that he lived in the realm of the Day, the Phenomenon, the rules and shared expectations that he followed. It is at this moment of discernment that he must renounce his newly discovered true desires for love and family. He must immediately renounce his acknowledged desires, unlike Tristan, who has time to think. Nina's tear falling on his face unites them as the only sign of love, because for her it is also the only moment in which she experiences the love of her father. Their tragedy is heightened by the realization that they both lived in error, relying on Phenomena, but both loved each other throughout their lives in the kingdom of Noumenon. Nina has the chance to express herself for the first time in the novel as she does not respond to anyone's expectations. Dain has his voice too, briefly but long enough to express that he can only guess Nina's feelings and actually misunderstands them or rather comes to the point when he realizes that he does not understand her, or the white woman within her.

Manrico's cry, Tristan's despair, Almayer's monologue of loss prove the repetitive character of human experience. Each of them lived immersed in illusions, dreams, lies and only at certain moment of life came to true cognition, to true life. The deformed recording of Manrico's aria at the beginning of the novel leads to disillusionment about the main protagonist, his plans and moral qualities, as well as about the narrative mode that cannot prevent de-contextualization of the emotional burden of plot. The operatic mode of arias (as equivalents of emotions) and music (as equivalents of action) saves their authenticity and enables the audience to keep faith in protagonists' confessions. At the same time, it separates emotions from plots, intrigues, mistakes, and politics as different modes of being. While emotions can be true but mistaken, the plots and intrigues are compound of mistakes and mistaken impressions – they never reveal their true schemes.

John Lester asked a very important question in reference to Conrad and music: "Does the master of words automatically appreciate the master of notes?" (247). Without pretending to answer this question, I assume that Conrad did appreciate mastery of music not only as a listener but also as a creator, constructor who knew the craft of sound and wanted his readers not only *to see* but to hear as well. Neither words nor notes can articulate the real existence; neither literature nor music can bring remedy to human pain, but they both resonate with the vibrant tone of philosophy without which they could hardly find path to each other. The Modernist dream of synaesthesia is broadened in Conrad's prose by inclusion of the recording as a figure of technical repetition.

As in some opera performances, the last scene of the novel is a group scene: all the Arabs of Sambir come to see Almayer's body, Abdulla confirms Almayer's death but he does not enjoy his victory, Lingard's plot appears only to be a surface illusion of an eastern romance, Ali creates the narration that suites him and builds illusion about his competence and courage. Abdulla recognizes that his own death is approaching not as a danger or Almayer's revenge on him but as a natural order of things. His victory seems diminished without Almayer's presence. As the faithful Muslim Abdulla praises Allah. Such an ending scene with a profound prayer of the former enemy on the occasion of death of "the unfaithful," the only white man on the coast contrasts with the first scene in the novel, with initial calling for a meal by Mrs. Almayer. These two scenes are constructed in counterpoint mode that confirms Conrad's sense of irony: not common meal but community of death evokes some sense of unity or at least interdependence.

Almayer's aria is the last expression of the only white man on the East Coast who is compared to a broken instrument that can no longer serve any art when his tragedy ends.

NOTES

[1] This topic is widely analysed in Peter Conrad's *Romantic Opera and Literary Form*.

[2] See Curreli.

[3] See Knowles and Moore.

[4] See Ray.

[5] See Panagopoulos.

[6] See Bonney.

[7] See Hampson.

WORKS CITED

Acheraïou, Amar. *Joseph Conrad and the Reader. Questioning Contemporary Theories of Narrative and Reading*. Palgrave Macmillan, 2009.

Baldanza, Frank. "Opera in Conrad: 'More real than anything in life'." *Studies in Literary Imagination* 13 (1980): 1-16.

Baxter, Katherine Isobel, and Richard J. Hand, eds. *Joseph Conrad and the Performing Arts*. Ashgate, 2009.

Bickley, Pamela, and Robert Hampson, "'Lips That Have Been Kissed': Boccaccio, Verdi, and *The Arrow of Gold*." *L'Epoque Conradienne* (1988): 75-91.

Bonney, Wiliam. *Thorns and Arabesques: Contexts for Conrad's Fiction.* Johns Hopkins UP, 1980.

Brooks, Peter. *The Melodramatic Imagination: Balzac, James, Melodrama and Excess Mode.* Yale UP, 1976.

Bufkin, E. C. "Conrad, Grand Opera, and *Nostromo.*" *Nineteenth-Century Fiction* 30 (1975): 206-14. Accessed 20 June 2022. Stable URL: <https://doi.org/10.2307/2932953>.

Conrad, Joseph. "The First Thing I Remember." 1921. *Congo Diary and Other Uncollected Pieces.* By Conrad. Ed. Zdzisław Najder. Doubleday, 1978.

Conrad, Peter. *Romantic Opera and Literary Form.* U of California P, 1977.

Curreli, Mario. "The Leitmotifs from Coleridge and Wagner in *Nostromo* and Beyond." Nostromo. *The Centennial Essays.* Ed. Allan H. Simmons and John Henry Stape. Rodopi, 2004. 96-109.

Gutman, Robert W. *Wagner – The Man, His Mind and His Music.* Harcourt, 1990.

Hampson, Robert. *Intercultural Encounters in Joseph Conrad's Malay Fiction.* Palgrave Macmillan, 2001.

Hand, Richard J. "Conrad's Drama in a World Theatrical Context." *Beyond the Roots: The Evolution of Conrad's Ideology and Art.* Ed. Wiesław Krajka. East European Monographs, Maria Curie-Skłodowska U, Columbia UP, 2005. 385-99. Vol. 14 of *Conrad: Eastern and Western Perspectives.* Ed. Wiesław Krajka. 32 vols. to date. 1992- .

Kerman, Joseph. *The Opera as a Drama.* Vintage, 1956.

Knowles, Owen, and Gene M. Moore. *Oxford Reader's Companion to Conrad.* Oxford UP, 2001.

Krajka, Wiesław. "Crossing Over Media Prose Narrative ('To-morrow') into Drama (*One Day More*) into Filmic Opera/Musical Drama (Baird, Hussakowski, and Sito's *Jutro*)." *Conradiana* 48 (2016): 257-70. Accessed 13 Jan. 2023. Stable URL: <https://www.jstor.org/stable/26920953>.

Lester, John. "Conrad and Music." *Conrad's Literary Career.* Ed. Keith Carabine, Owen Knowles and Wiesław Krajka. East European Monographs, Maria Curie-Skłodowska U, Columbia UP, 1992. 247-61. Vol. 1 of *Conrad: Eastern and Western Perspectives.* Ed. Wiesław Krajka. 32 vols. to date. 1992- .

Meyers, Jeffrey. "Conrad and Music." *Conradiana* 23 (1991): 179- 95. Accessed 13 Jan. 2023. Stable URL: <http://www.jstor.org/stable/24634730>.

Najder, Zdzisław. *Joseph Conrad: A Chronicle.* Trans. Halina Caroll-Najder. Rutgers UP, 1983.

Panagopoulos, Nick. *The Fiction of Joseph Conrad: The Influence of Schopenhauer and Nietzsche.* Lang, 1998.

Ray, Martin. "Conrad, Schopenhauer, and 'Le Mot Juste'." *The Conradian* 33.1 (2008): 31-42. Accessed 13 Jan 2023. Stable URL: <http://www.jstor.org/stable/20873624>.

Wagner, Richard. *My Life.* Vol 2. (authorized English translation). Dodd, 1911.

Brian Richardson,
University of Maryland,
College Park, MD, USA

Sense Perception and Synaesthesia in Conrad's Fiction

Joseph Conrad is rightly celebrated for his fascination with sight, and equally for the compelling depictions of visual effects that he created. We see this, for example, in subjective depictions of a character's visual field that can take on the intensity of the late work of an impressionist painter like Monet or Degas. The captain's first view from sixty miles away of the beautiful island in the Indian Ocean at the beginning of "A Smile of Fortune" states: "I became entranced by this blue, pinnacled apparition, almost transparent against the light of the sky, a mere emanation, the astral body of an island risen to greet me from afar" (*TLS* 3).[1] In Conrad's fiction, however, sight often merges with, replaces, or is displaced by other senses, as I will attempt to explore in this essay.

Precisely because sight is the preeminent sense in Conrad's narratives and his theory of fiction, obscurity and sightlessness are invariably possible, lingering threats, dangerous and frequently deadly. We think of the ominous fog on the river "more blinding than the night" ("Heart of Darkness," *YS* 101) just before the attack in "Heart of Darkness," the dangerous London fog in *The Secret Agent,* and the fateful "dense night" in the Golfo Placido in *Nostromo* where Decoud's "hand held before his face did not exist for his eyes" (*N* 262). There is also the surprise-filled darkness that begins the central events in *Lord Jim* and "The Secret Sharer" and the setting of the attempted mutiny in *The Nigger of the "Narcissus"*: "In the shadows of the fore rigging a dark mass stamped, eddied, advanced, retreated" (*NN* 122). In some cases, sight is supplemented or replaced by other senses. In "The End of the Tether," as we will shortly see, vision yields to touch, as the hands of the visually impaired Captain Whalley "see" what his eyes cannot perceive. Hugh Epstein notes that in "Heart of Darkness," in the many nocturnal scenes "the orientation provided by sound becomes a means of a specifically human definition amid a fecund natural world" (Epstein 163).[2] Other sensory perceptions are also evoked here: "the white fog" on the river is described as "very warm and clammy" ("Heart of Darkness," *YS* 101) and "choking, warm, stifling" (107). Hearing the cry of desolation from the invisible natives on the shore "it seemed as though the mist itself had screamed" (102), as a synaesthetic simile is offered (see Ambrosini 90).

Conrad was interested in creating multisensory descriptions from the beginning of his career. Near the end of his first novel, *Almayer's Folly* (1895), Nina arrives to rejoin Dain. Watching her approach, Dain "stood still, fighting with his breath, as if bereft of his senses" (*AF* 171). She immediately throws her arms around him and in the firelight they look into each other's eyes; she gives him

> one of those long looks that are a woman's most terrible weapon; a look that is more stirring than the closest touch, and more dangerous than the thrust of a dagger, because it also whips the soul out of the body [...]; a look that enwraps the whole body, and that penetrates into the innermost recesses of the being. (171)

Conrad goes on to discuss "[m]en that have felt in their breasts the awful exultation such a look awakens" (172). Here, the actual physical embrace being experienced is displaced by the look that Dain perceives, which is then invested with bodily attributes; that is, touch yields to vision which then is imaged as an inner haptic experience.

As this example illustrates, sight typically predominates and often seems to displace the other senses: Conrad's lush tropical forests and jungles are often strangely silent, and his infrequent depictions of touch and kissing are often presented in visual descriptions rather than as tactile sensations, as I will discuss shortly.[3] It is especially interesting to examine the ways that Conrad represents blindness in his work. His early work features three characters who lose their sight, some quickly (Diamelen and Arsat in "The Lagoon"), and the other, more gradually (Captain Whalley). Near the beginning of "The Lagoon" (1896), we are given a visual description of the setting: "At the end of the straight avenue of forests cut by the intense glitter of the river, the sun appeared unclouded and dazzling, poised low over the water that shone smoothly like a band of metal" (*TU* 187). This is immediately followed by a line that stresses the purely visual nature of the perception: "The forests, sombre and dull, stood motionless and silent on each side of the broad stream" (187). Conrad further emphasizes the absence of other sensory stimuli as he continues: "In the stillness of the air every tree, every leaf, every bough, every tendril of creeper and every petal of minute blossoms seemed to have been bewitched into an immobility perfect and final" (187). There is no sound, there is no breeze to feel, and no scents are mentioned.[4] Even the paddling of the canoers is depicted primarily visually: the eight paddles "rose flashing regularly, dipped together with a single splash" (187): here, we finally get a modest sound, but it is one that is marked as alien to the profoundly immobile setting, "a land from which" it seemed "the very memory of motion had forever departed" (188). Soon, a sound does come from the jungle, "the repeated call of some bird" (188), though it is "a cry dissonant and feeble"; significantly, the call soon "lost itself, before it could reach the other shore, in the breathless silence of the [tropical] world" (188); the aural is thus consumed by the visual.

Arsat equates truth with sight; he is thus dubious about written words: "A writing may be lost; a lie may be written; but what the eye has seen is truth and remains in the mind" (194). Arsat knows his wife's illness is critical because of sensory failures: first she heard voices, then she lost her hearing, next she was unable to see: "She sees nothing. She sees not me – me!" Arsat laments (191). She no longer speaks, and "she burns as if with a great fire" (192). As she lies dying, Arsat recounts the story of their union. Diamelen was serving their ruler's wife, and thus was forbidden to marry. Nevertheless, they grow increasingly enamoured of each other. Arsat recounts the multisensory nature of their courtship:

> when the sun had fallen behind the forest I crept along the jasmine hedges of the women's courtyard. Unseeing, we spoke to one another through the scent of flowers, through the veil of leaves, through the blades of long grass that stood between our lips; so great was our prudence, so faint was the murmur of our great longing. (196)

This supreme moment of endearment, which evokes several senses, is done in the dark, as sight yields to scent and touch to words, a foretaste of the synaesthetic representations that Conrad would develop in subsequent works. With his brother, he forms a plan to elope with her. During the escape, Arsat abandons his brother to a certain death but escapes with Diamelen. Now, many years later, Diamelen dies. In the morning, as a final penance, Arsat stares into the sun until he is blind. Thematically, this is a most appropriate ending for a tale of the senses that focuses on sight.

"The End of the Tether" (1902) is another of Conrad's examinations of sight and opacity; it is simultaneously another of his studies of the act of interpretation; its central drama is to determine the correct explanation for the unusual behaviour of Captain Whalley. An early passage suggests something is wrong concerning the visual. The narrative's second sentence offers a vivid ocular description: "The sunrays fell violently upon the calm sea – seemed to shatter themselves upon an adamantine surface into sparkling dust, into a dazzling vapour of light that blinded the eye and wearied the brain with its unsteady brightness" ("The End of the Tether," *YS* 165). After this panoramic vision, we get the odd information that "Captain Whalley did not look at it" (165). This is an odd disjunction: when we get the first visual image and the first character is presented, it is normal to assume that that figure is the focalizer who perceives the view. But Conrad keeps the protagonist and the sight apart. As such it is an apposite introduction to this tale of non-seeing and meshes nicely with the image of blindness that the intense light can produce. We soon learn that

Whalley does not always need sight to determine his location in the water: "At any moment, as he sat on the bridge without looking up, or lay sleepless on his bed, simply by reckoning the days and the hours he could tell where he was – the precise spot of the beat" (166).

In this work, Conrad plays with the reader's comprehension of such images as we observe the Captain searching for the image of two distant mountains to establish his precise location: they

> had to be searched for within the great unclouded glare that seemed to shift and float like a dry fiery mist, filling the air, ascending from the water, shrouding the distances, scorching to the eye. In this veil of light the near edge of the shore alone stood out almost coal-black with an opaque and motionless solidity. Thirty miles away the serrated range of the interior stretched across the horizon, its outlines and shades of blue, faint and tremulous like a background painted on airy gossamer on the quivering fabric of an impalpable curtain let down to the plain of alluvial soil [...]. (219-20)

This passage, which reads like another powerful impressionistic description (or even expressionistic considering the "veil of light") is in fact much more realistic as it accurately depicts the visual field of Captain Whalley near the beginning of "The End of the Tether" – and this description is presented before the reader learns that the Captain is going blind. What has seemed metaphorical turns out to be unusually literal.[5] The blindness leads, at the end of the work, to a moving synaesthetic depiction, almost more literal than figurative: Whalley "fell on his knees, with groping hands extended in a frank gesture of blindness. They trembled, these hands feeling for the truth. He saw it. Iron near the compass" (329).

Before continuing it will be useful to indicate the historical and cultural discourse on the senses at this period. Nineteenth-century Britain had a thoroughly hierarchical ordering of the various senses. In his *Analysis of the Phenomena of the Human Mind*, James Mill made the argument that "[t]he pleasures and pains of Hearing and Sight are best remembered of any. This gives them higher value in life; the addition made by the actual, by the ideal, is, in their case, the greatest of all" (8). Constance Classen explains that nineteenth-century evolutionary theory declared that attending to visual over tactile or olfactory sensations

> was a defining trait of the human species, which at some point in its long transition from animality had learned to take its hands and nose away from the ground and stand up and look around. Aping the evolutionists, social theorists claimed that the most evolved people – namely Europeans – manifested a similar interest in sight as the most evolved and rational sense.
>
> So-called primitive races – namely indigenous peoples – by contrast, were assumed to remain mired in an irrational tactile world. (182)

It is in this cultural – and imperial – context that we can situate Conrad's depiction of the "lower" senses, and the power such descriptions therefore could assume.[6] Smell is fairly rare in Conrad, and is usually marked by strongly positive or strongly negative valence. We occasionally get a salient scent, such as Marlow's first encounter with the Far East in "Youth": "suddenly a puff of wind, a puff faint and tepid and laden with strange odours of blossoms, of aromatic wood, comes out of the still night – the first sigh of the East on my face" (*YS* 37). Smell is here blended with the touch of the wind on his cheek and immediately given an Orientalist colouring, as Marlow states he can never forget that smell, which "was impalpable and enslaving, like a charm, like a whispered promise of mysterious delight" (37). It is perhaps the rarity of depictions of scent that make them particularly resonant. In "Heart of Darkness," Marlow undergoes the opposite odiferous experience, this one produced by the horrid odour of rotting hippo meat. The narrator of "A Smile of Fortune" also has an unpleasant experience with the "most awful smell" of the potatoes his ship is carrying: "Whiffs from decaying potatoes pursued me on the poop, they mingled with my thoughts, with my food, poisoned my very dreams" (*TLS* 82). In this case the foul smell also carries the allegorical weight of the captain's dubious experience on the island. Such descriptions of odours are fairly rare both in Conrad and in Modernism in general.

Nevertheless, we will see that Conrad frequently invokes it when depicting amorous desire.

There is another, unfamiliar sense that Conrad represents. In a vertiginous account of being blown off the deck of a ship, Marlow mixes sensory descriptions on board the *Judea* in "Youth." He thinks he sees the ship's carpenter trying to tilt the bench; he

> immediately became aware of a queer sensation, of an absurd delusion, – I seemed somehow to be in the air. I heard all round me like a pent-up breath released [...] and felt a dull concussion which made my ribs ache suddenly. No doubt about it – I was in the air, and my body was describing a short parabola. (*YS* 22-23)

This description includes sight, sound, touch, and proprioception, or the body's perception of its orientation in space.

Multiple senses are brought together in Conrad's synaesthetic depictions. It should be noted that Conrad generally avoids what could be called classical literary synaesthesia, where one sense impression is depicted in terms of another sense, as in Keats' line: "And taste the music of that vision pale" ("Isabella" xlix). Though literally impossible, such statements can have an evocative, poetic power (see Tsur 283-94). Conrad's constructions are typically more realistic, though still suggestive, often qualified by the use of a simile. In his depictions, one sense is often displaced by or combined with another. Nostromo's tactile desire for Giselle Viola is framed in terms of sound, sight, scent, and metaphors of touch: "Her voice enveloped him like a caress. She bemoaned her fate, spreading unconsciously, like a flower its perfume in the coolness of the evening" (*N* 535). That is, the sound of her voice was like the touch of an embrace, and her (visually perceived?) lamenting is compared to the scent of a flower in a space that is both cool and semi-dark. Though her lips are described as "shaped for love and kisses," the depiction of those kisses are entirely visual rather than tactile: once they do embrace, Nostromo "showered rapid kisses upon the upturned face that gleamed in the purple dusk" (538).

Early in "The Planter of Malata" (1915), Geoffrey Renouard recalls his first meeting with Felicia Moorsom. He remembers

> the sway of her figure in a movement of grace and strength – felt the pressure of her hand – heard the last accents of the deep murmur that came from her throat so white in the light of the window, and remembered the black rays of her steady eyes passing off his face when she turned away. He *remembered all this visually.* (*WT* 12; emphasis added)

Oddly, though characteristic of Conrad's sensory descriptions, both the memory of the sound and the emphasized touch of her hand are reduced to a visual impression. It is as if, in these earlier works, Conrad is shying away from direct descriptions of touch, and presenting them primarily through the other senses – usually sight. Nevertheless, the effect of the description is quite evocative.

Later that night, however, visual images vanish and other sensory imaginings return:

> In the evening, on board his schooner, sitting on the rail, his arms folded on his breast and his eyes fixed on the deck, he let the darkness catch him unawares in the midst of a meditation on the mechanism of sentiment and the springs of passion. And all the time he had an abiding consciousness of her bodily presence. The effect on his senses had been so penetrating that in the middle of the night, rousing up suddenly, wide-eyed in the darkness of his cabin, he did not create a faint mental vision of her person for himself, but, more intimately affected, he scented distinctly the faint perfume she used, and could almost have sworn that he had been awakened by the soft rustle of her dress. He even sat up listening in the dark for a time, then sighed and lay down again, not agitated but, on the contrary, oppressed by the sensation of something that had happened to him and could not be undone. (23)

Here, in the absence of nearly all sensory effects, Renouard imagines her bodily presence, and even feels the scent of her perfume and the sound of her dress. Intriguingly, touch – the sense one would normally expect to be best represented in such a vision – is curiously absent, though it had been powerfully present at their first meeting. The sense of touch, we may observe, is quite rare in Conrad after its exoticized presence in *An Outcast of the Islands*; as Conrad continues to write, however, touch becomes increasingly prominent.[7]

These later works reveal a more sustained interest in multisensory representations. In the description of Edith Travers in *The Rescue*, Conrad pushes the visual until it yields a kind of tactility:

> Her complexion was so dazzling in the shade that it seemed to throw out a halo round her head. Upon a smooth and wide brow an abundance of pale fair hair, fine as silk, undulating like the sea, heavy like a helmet, descended low without a trace of gloss, without a gleam in its coils, as though it had never been touched by a ray of light; and a throat white, smooth, palpitating with life, a round neck modelled with strength and delicacy, supported gloriously that radiant face and that pale mass of hair unkissed by sunshine. (139)

This could almost be a description of a painting, one which, however, reproduces the heaviness of the mass of hair, its silken texture, and its regular undulations. The sense of sight predominates, and the use of similes modifies the intensity of the depiction, though the seeming heaviness of the hair and the actual throbbing of the blood are prominent, thus helping to produce a powerful, sensual effect.

We may also note that on one occasion Monsieur George, who has been pursuing Rita throughout *The Arrow of Gold*, finally rests his hand heavily on her shoulder, and it "did not give way, did not flinch at all" (*AG* 218). He slips lower and holds her around the waist; then, "[he] had a distinct impression of being in contact with an infinity that had the slightest possible rise and fall, was pervaded by a warm, delicate scent of violets and through which came a hand from somewhere to rest lightly on my head" (219). The experience, though brief, is intoxicating. Here, the visual sense is sublimated and smell and touch, including the perception of warmth, predominate. This cluster of sensations provides a sense of the infinite, an extremely pleasant grouping of undifferentiated feelings that seems to negate and rewrite the dangerous, shocking, and ominous sensations felt by Dain in a similar situation in

Almayer's Folly. Conrad has turned the panic of the visual into the pleasure of tactility.

Overall, we observe that multisensory descriptions are usually devoted to representing amorous desire, usually a shared desire. The ages of the enamoured may vary but the intensity of the passion is similar in each case, whether the principals are Malay, Italian, French, or even English, who are very rarely mentioned in such contexts, despite their ubiquity in Conrad's works. The writing is typically evocative, powerful, and often beautiful; as such, it tends to problematize claims of Conrad's supposed difficulty in representing love relations. It is clear that he can at times represent erotic desire very effectively.

We also see a development among these depictions. Conrad starts with the impressively literal evocation of whispering through the jasmine hedges, "through the blades of long grass that stood still before our lips" ("The Lagoon," *TU* 196). Later synaesthetic images stress the visual, at times seeming to reduce the other senses to that of sight. The emphasis on sight makes a space for its negation: Conrad magisterially explores the sensory world where vision is occluded or absent. By the time we come to "The Planter of Malata" (1915), touch becomes more central in multisensorial descriptions, and once we reach *The Arrow of Gold* (1919), it is the foundation for the depiction, the tenor rather than the vehicle of a metaphor. Altogether, it is an impressive and enjoyable journey.

NOTES

[1] For a brief overview of Conrad and impressionism, see Watt 171-76; Peters; Ferguson.

[2] On the interaction between sight and sound in "Heart of Darkness," see Free; Ambrosini.

[3] See Lindskog, and see Hooper on the unusual silences in "Heart of Darkness"; for a more general account, see Ray.

[4] At the end of the story's fifth paragraph, once the group has landed, we are informed of "the darkness scented and poisonous of impenetrable forests" ("The Lagoon," *TU* 189).

[5] See Volpicelli for additional discussion of limited vision in this work and others.

[6] Some theorists, it should be added, have argued for a distinction among the senses based on their relative complexity. Tsur writes that the "sensory domains [of] touch, heat and weight can make fewer kind of distinctions than, say, the senses of sight and hearing. They can also less reliably discriminate among the various degrees of the sensory attributes present in their respective domains" (285).

[7] For an account of the changing role of touch in Conrad's work, see my article, "'All His Life Seemed to Rush into That Hand'."

WORKS CITED

Ambrosini, Richard. "The Politics of Observing: *Heart of Darkness* as a Visual, Aural and Conceptual Polyptych." *The Conradian* 46.1 (2021): 81-96.

Classen, Constance. *The Deepest Sense: A Cultural History of Touch.* U of Illinois P, 2012.

Epstein, Hugh. *Hardy, Conrad and the Senses.* Edinburgh UP, 2019.

Ferguson, Rex. "Personal Impressions: Fingerprints, Freud, and Conrad." *New Formations* 79 (2013): 43-62.

Free, Melissa. "Frustrated Listening: The Aural Landscape of *Heart of Darkness*." *Conradiana* 47 (2015): 1-16.

Hooper, Myrtle J. "The Heart of Light: Silence in Conrad's *Heart of Darkness*." *Conradiana* 25 (1993): 69-76.

Lindskog, Annika J. "'It was very quiet there': The Contaminating Soundscapes of 'Heart of Darkness'." *The Conradian* 39.2 (2014): 44-59.

Mill, James. *Analysis of the Phenomena of the Human Mind.* 1829. Longmans, 1869.

Peters, John G. *Conrad and Impressionism.* Cambridge UP, 2001.

Ray, Martin. "Language and Silence in the Fiction of Joseph Conrad." *Critical Essays on Joseph Conrad.* Ed. Ted Billy. Hall, 1987. 46-67.

Richardson, Brian. "'All His Life Seemed to Rush into That Hand': The Poetics and Erotics of Touch in Conrad's Fiction." *Conradiana* 50 (2018): 159-74.

Tsur, Reuven. *Toward a Theory of Cognitive Poetics.* 2nd ed. Sussex Academic P, 2008.

Volpicelli, Robert. "Modernist Low Vision: Visual Impairment and Weak Narrative in Conrad and Joyce." *Novel: A Forum on Fiction* 51.1 (2018): 60-78.

Watt, Ian. *Conrad in the Nineteenth Century.* U of California P, 1979.

Peter Vernon,
Université de Tours,
Tours, France

"The Gaiety of Language is Our Seigneur"[1]: On the Function of Art in Some of Conrad's Major Works

This paper examines aspects of Conrad's language concerning transformations as they occur when a description moves abruptly from a narrative level of verisimilitude into another figurative level of art and art objects. Some of Conrad's major works will be analysed to see that this phenomenon appears when the invariably isolated protagonist is found *in extremis*. The transformations occur by means of a number of narrative devices such as frames and reflective surfaces, theatrical and cinematic images of stages, curtains, close-ups etc., which are operated rhetorically through *ekphrasis* and metonymy, and syntactically through *as if, as though, as of, as from* expressions. (The frame in art of course also has implications for narrative frames.) Analysis of how the rhetorical terms function will concentrate on examples from "Heart of Darkness" and *Lord Jim*, while an examination of the syntax seen in *as* clauses will range more widely in Conrad's work, where the novels will be discussed chronologically in order to determine whether one technique predominates more than another as his work progresses, or conversely whether his narrative techniques remain unchanged. The paper ends with an examination of why Conrad resorts so frequently to these narrative moves and concludes that there are certain things that cannot be said directly; the reader's empathetic share is therefore solicited and brought into the tragedy to share in the guilt of the human condition; in short, the reader plays the role of the protagonist's secret sharer. But, although confronted with tragedy, the reader experiences joy through the intensity of engaging with Conrad's most "writerly" texts.[2]

It need not be repeated that Conrad's imagination is visual, for that is evident in almost every line he wrote, and the famous apologia to his readers merely reinforces that claim, it is "before all," a desire to make the reader "*see*" (*NN* x). And in order to make the reader see, his images are often theatrical and cinematographic, with flashbacks, close-ups, fade-outs, pan shots, iris shots, etc.; these cinematic techniques cast in prose, show the new medium's influence, and also predict the numerous film versions that have been made of his novels. Stephen Donovan writes that Conrad's patrician attitude meant that he despised early cinema, which was mostly frequented by the working classes, but nevertheless: "such was the power of early cinematic spectacle that it could even affect a writer like Conrad who formulated his literary project in opposition to the increasingly visual nature of nineteenth-century culture" (238).[3] Conrad frequently includes theatrical or cinematic light and sound effects, typically employing thunder and lightning at critical moments in the plot. Initially this might be regarded as a crude application of the Pathetic Fallacy, but given Conrad's super-subtle ironic stance, it might more correctly be interpreted as his expression that the natural world does not so much sympathize, as comment ironically on absurd humanity.

Conrad was interested in the visual arts, he knew artists personally, and sat for some like Rothenstein, and Epstein.[4] Throughout his life and manifest in very many letters there are references to painters such as Correggio, Velasquez, Millais, the Pre-Raphaelites, and also to Turner who seems to have influenced Conrad's impressionistic descriptions. For example his description of the *Judea* might well be an *ekphrasis* of one of Turner's paintings of ships on fire: "Between the darkness of earth and heaven she was burning fiercely upon a disc of purple sea shot by the blood-red play of gleams; upon a disc of water glittering and sinister" ("Youth," *YS* 34-35). The dramatic contrasts of texture and palette found in Conrad's virtuoso impression of the *Judea* bear a striking similarity to Turner's *Fire at Sea* or *The Fighting Temeraire*.[5] Donald R. Benson gives a useful survey of scholarship on Impressionism and Conrad, then concentrates on atmosphere in his work: "so frequently evoked in Impressionistic painting [... focusing] on two crucial aspects of the concept, the visual and through it the ontological" (30). Benson points to evocations of atmosphere in the 1890s, drawing on Mallarmé, Laforgue, and Pater.[6] However, Impressionism is but one aspect of the vast subject that connects Conrad and the visual arts, and this paper attempts to answer but a single question which has two facets: *how* linguistically does Conrad achieve his visual images, and *why* does he have recourse to them at crucial moments in his novels.

A visual imagination such as Conrad's has implication for his entire artistic endeavour whose aims, as expressed through Marlow in *Lord Jim*, are twofold: to present "a meticulous precision of statement" (*LJ* 30), and "to make an intelligible *picture*" (343; emphasis added), in an image which reveals his conscious pictorial ambitions. Even more definitively, in the Pater-inspired Preface to *The Nigger of the "Narcissus,"* we find that his ambition is defined as "a single-minded attempt to render the highest kind of justice to the visible universe, by bringing to light the truth, manifold and one, underlying its every aspect" (*NN* vii). In attempting to render the highest kind of justice through art to individuals caught in extreme situations, Conrad may be said to join Nietzsche in reflecting a modernist zeitgeist[7] whose cultural expression will necessarily be complex and difficult to recuperate[8]; thus, to engage with the modern work of art will demand work from the reader/perceiver of the art objects. Conrad's impressionist descriptions must be seen alongside his desire for realist verisimilitude in terms of human experience and ethics, and much of the excitement and joy generated by reading him emerges from the tensions engendered by these diverse ambitions.

Initially it seems as though Conrad does not do *sfumato*, his descriptions are rendered in a Caravaggesque chiaroscuro, where characters and objects are strongly delineated. These characters are often seen as either black or white[9]; good or bad; characters are classified as "us" or "them," and they are discovered in positions of claustrophobia or else a vertiginous aporia; we are in the frame, to adopt a term from cinema, or we are out of it. Frames are a limit, and Conrad's interest is to discriminate, as finely as it is possible to do, between reality and image, between light and darkness. But, as though to subvert classification, Conrad filters all through a heavily ironic tone, which is exemplified by the term *in the frame* referring to suspicions of guilt in the context of crime and crime fiction: if one is *in the frame*, one is a suspect, and that seems to have particular application to Conrad's fiction, where the guilt of protagonist and reader alike is manifest. As noted earlier, the reader plays the role of a secret sharer to the protagonist, and Conrad through Marlow addresses reader and interlocutor alike in terms of bitter irony: we are all "under a cloud" (*LJ* 339, 342) or "[a]ren't we all in the same boat?" (125), or "[w]e exist only in so far as we hang together" (223), these common, clichéd expressions make an evident ironic comment on our mutual human guilt.

Examples of black and white strongly lit and strongly shadowed chiaroscuro aesthetics are seen throughout "Heart of Darkness," straightforward examples may be found in descriptions of the natives, especially the witch doctor, represented silhouetted black against the glow of a fire (*YS* 143).[10] The technique allows Conrad to train a spotlight on his characters so that the reader is put in the position of a spectator in a cinema or theatre – the illuminated figure inevitably emerges from obscurity before fading out again into shadow; Kurtz's Intended, Jim, Stein, etc., are all portrayed in this manner. Philosophically, Conrad's chiaroscuro black and white must be seen as a reflection of the dichotomy that makes up human existence: black and white are both necessary to express the truth of the human condition, and in attempting to bring forward truth into the visible universe, Conrad understands with Spinoza, that "[a]s the light makes both itself and the darkness plain, so truth is the standard both of itself and of the false" ("Postulate 43," Spinoza 58).

As Spinoza suggests, the truth emerges only when Black and White are seen in a dynamic dialectic,[11] and this is the point to be made regarding Conrad's frames which create boundaries so that an image may be seen as petrified in its perspective and separated from everything that it is not. However, he only *seems* to create boundaries because *in extremis* Conrad's boundaries (like his value systems) collapse. The point here is *in extremis*, for Conrad discovers his protagonists in extreme situations of solitude, and there he tests, anatomises, judges, and leaves the reader with an ethical question: would we, *could* we, have done any better? What would the reader do if found in the same situation as Kurtz, Jim, Decoud, Razumov, Heyst, etc.? These men (for almost all his protagonists are men) are isolated; they are notably without family, cut off from social ties; Jim may be seen as representative of their situations when Marlow reports: "I can't with mere words convey to you the impression of his total and utter isolation" (*LJ* 272). In *Nostromo* Decoud "died from solitude" (*N* 496),[12] Razumov is similarly isolated "there is no one anywhere in the whole great world [he] could go to" (*UWE* 354), while in *Victory* Heyst "had always had a taste for solitude" (*V* 28). Frank Kermode does not mention Conrad in his essay "Solitary Confinement"[13] but I think it germane to this argument, and so do not hesitate to bring forward his notion of the condition of man as being alone and poor, this is figurative in the case of most readers, but in the case of Conrad's protagonists the condition is not figurative at all.

The human condition, when discovered in extremity, demands strategies for survival: what then can the protagonist do in his extreme situation? Why, create fictions of course; he invents stories to enable himself to achieve a semblance of control and authenticity in life. As Joan Didion wrote in *The White Album*, "[w]e tell ourselves stories in order to live" (11). Conrad predicts Didion when Marlow comments, in an aside in *Lord Jim*, of "some fable of strife" that enable men to get through life (*LJ* 35), and later in the novel Marlow will be even more specific about the necessity of creating fictions in order to survive the horrors of life by the unwearied efforts we make "it is as sunny an arrangement of small conveniences," which enable him to finesse what he had earlier called the "irremediable horror of the scene" (313).[14] Further, throughout his narratives, Marlow frequently breaks off to comment on the necessity of a belief, such as a code of work for example, but the narrative then explodes these codes when under extreme conditions, and thus they may be regarded as yet more fictions.

Classified by Stein as a romantic, Jim has been brought up on light, romantic literature (6 and *passim*).[15] He is an example of the protagonist creating visions and fictions of himself, which in the end become more powerful than life or love itself as he knowingly goes to his death, sacrificing himself and his love for Jewel in order "to fulfil a shadowy ideal of conduct" (416). While Razumov's "story," demanded by Natalia, will simultaneously bring about his downfall and his salvation (*UWE* 354). Conrad is supremely aware of how and why men create fictions, and this is exemplified when Jim himself becomes the subject of stories in order to explain how he is transformed from a banal merchant seaman into becoming "Tuan Jim," as the natives of Patusan know him. From one perspective Jim is a blunderer, a stutterer, a poor sinner etc., but from the natives' perspective he seems semi-divine: "he *ascended* the Patusan river" (*LJ* 229; emphasis added), and god-like he falls from the clouds, as "a being who *descended* upon them" (243; emphasis added).[16] The Christic echoes seen in the parallel structures of ascended/descended, are one with the miraculous natural events concerning him: "[t]here was already a story that the tide had turned two hours before its time to help him on his journey up the river" (242-43), though *this* fiction is totally undercut when we remember his absurd fallibilities. The truth of the situation is only to be found in the unstated ambiguities of language (where the reader is unaided by narrative authority), and must lie in between, or in a dual existence. Jim is *more* than a poor sinner, but *less* than a god, or else he is both simultaneously. It is impossible to choose because of the relative viewpoint adopted by Conrad, as William T. Bonney writes: "perceivers of Conrad's art are rendered even more powerless to achieve a definitive orientation than are his most sensitive characters" (127). In contrast to Jim, it is conspicuously his *in*ability to create fictions that destroys Decoud in *Nostromo*: he "was not fit to grapple with himself single-handed" (*N* 497). Decoud's appalling isolation and sensory deprivation causes him to lose all sense of self and self-belief, creating a "disillusioned weariness which is the retribution meted out to intellectual audacity" (501).[17] The human condition in Conrad's work is thus seen to be a choice of nightmares, and it matters not which choice is made, for both will inevitably betray the protagonist: should one adopt a stoic distance, casting a cold eye on life, on death; or rather throw oneself into life and follow the dream? If like Heyst one chooses detachment then one is betrayed by life; if one chooses to act from idealism like Kurtz, Jim, or Decoud, then equally one is betrayed by the act. Either choice brings one to failure and death, or else to fulfilment and death, depending on the reader's viewpoint. Conrad perceives the human condition as tragic, but it is a tragedy which is always alleviated by grim, sardonic humour.

Many critics of Conrad's fiction have commented on his complex systems of analogy and symbolism, and Donald C. Yelton's two chapters on "The Demon of Analogy" (151-209), are exemplary. However, Yelton stays on the metaphoric and analogic level, and here I want to examine two further methods of recuperating Conrad's texts. He frequently employs *ekphrasis* and metonymy to bring the reader before the extremity of the human condition. These rhetorical figures may be found together in one description, which is inevitably represented in chiaroscuro. *Ekphrasis* is defined as the representation of an object or a scene described in terms of another medium, for example an art object (a painting, or sculpture) described in words, or a description from one plane of reality transformed into a plane of art. As many theorists have pointed out, *ekphrasis* does not simply operate on the level of "autonomous descriptive pieces," but rather the figure functions to slow down the narrative, which therefore allows for a better exploration of the narrative's "fundamental heterogeneity," it is a figure that is both "interruptive and constitutive of narrativity" (Bal 342, 345). In other words, while the figure created by *ekphrasis* operates on another plane of reality, it also signifies (and powerfully) in the comprehension and recuperation of the text, and the reader thus encounters it at crucial moments in the narrative. While *ekphrasis* moves the reader into the plane of art imagery, the other transforming figure is metonymy (Gr. name change), which rests on the same plane of reality, it is specifically *not* metaphoric. A special case of this is synecdoche (part for whole) where only one part of an entity is described (for example a woman's head rather than her whole body in Kurtz's painting, or the description of the Intended's disembodied head in "Heart of Darkness"). One may also perceive metonymy operating when an attribute is substituted for the thing itself (the crown always represents the monarchy and the monarch), and in "Heart of Darkness" Kurtz's sinister painting may be seen as metonymic of the darkness which overtakes him.[18]

An analysis of this painting may stand as an exemplum of Conrad's utilisation of art imagery on the rhetorical level. Kurtz's painting exemplifies both of Conrad's rhetorical techniques: it is simultaneously a description of a painting, and the painting signifies the physical and moral darkness into which he has fallen. Marlow discovers the picture when he is about to leave the "papier-maché [sic] Mephistopheles" ("Heart of Darkness," YS 81), whose forked beard and hooked nose, perhaps signify a Jewish[19] Mephistopheles: "Then I noticed a small sketch in oils, on a panel, representing a woman, draped and blindfolded, carrying a lighted torch. The background was sombre – almost black. The movement of the woman was stately, and the effect of the torch-light on the face was sinister" (79).[20] As so often in Conrad's writing, we are considering images of light and darkness, and the penumbra that accompanies them. At one level the painting is easy to decipher: Astrea and Libertas, the goddesses of Justice and Liberty, represented with their respective emblems of a blindfold for impartial Justice, and a torch for freedom and Liberty. But within the context of "Heart of Darkness" the significance of the painting is much less clear and rather more disturbing. From out the sombre, almost black background, the figure is described in terms of "stately movement," as though it had magically come to life. Upon re-reading the novella, the figure becomes even more disconcerting, in that its imagery predicts Kurtz's Intended, when Marlow finally encounters her, also emerging out of darkness. The painting is evidently metonymic of Kurtz's magnificent peroration in the report he wrote for the "International Society for the Suppression of Savage Customs,"[21] on which he had scrawled "Exterminate all the brutes!" (118). One can almost hear the bitter irony in Marlow's voice stating the name of the organisation which had suppressed "savages," even more savagely than their customs, in an irony reinforced by the description of the power of Kurtz's voice: "This was the unbounded power of eloquence – of words – of burning noble words" (118). Kurtz's eloquence is shown to be as empty and hollow as the Society itself. Within the context of "Heart of Darkness," images of light and darkness, of torch-bearing Liberty and blindfolded Justice are both seen as deeply suspect. Marlow reports that explorers and adventurers, like the Romans two thousand years earlier, are "going at it blind" (50), the irony engendered by "blind" is evident, and the exploitation of the African continent by these "pilgrims" cannot be regarded as anything other than rapine. Conrad's continued disgust at colonial exploitation is repeated when, much later, he writes of the malicious pleasure he felt at the fate of the Conquistadores: "those pertinacious searchers for El Dorado who [...] [endured great toil and suffering, and emerged with] empty pockets in the end" (*LE* 4, cited incorrectly by Hampson 135n79).

The *ekphrasis* of Kurtz's painting predicts the final act of the narrative, when Marlow encounters the Intended, and when Kurtz's face again haunts Marlow: "while I waited he seemed to stare at me out of the glassy panel" ("Heart of Darkness," *YS* 157). Yet again we come across the key notion of frames. The glassy panel of the mahogany door functions as a mirror, Marlow should be looking – he is looking – at a reflected image of himself, but what he recalls is an image of Kurtz, and this vision powerfully reinforces a concept of doubles so prevalent in Conrad's work, with its implication of identity, and shared guilt (cf. "The Secret Sharer," *TLS* 104).[22] The shared guilt of the doubles leads to the reader's realisation that he could never have done any better than the protagonist if found in a similar situation; as Marlow reports, we are all part of society, and simultaneously we are all condemned. As noted previously "[w]e exist only in so far as we hang together" (*LJ* 223), and we live "under a cloud" (336, 339).[24] The description of Kurtz's own ambiguous painting gives no detail of any frame, but at the crucial moment of the story when Marlow encounters the Intended, he sees Kurtz's frozen image framed in the door panel. Marlow has inherited her portrait and her letters (his first view of her then is perceived through the medium of art), and before Conrad brings her on stage into the dusky light through the medium of Marlow's focalisation, the reader is reminded of two significant preceding episodes: Kurtz's claim that all he wants is Justice; and subsequently a vision of the wild forest enveloped and enveloping Kurtz's empty rhetoric. At this culminating moment, Marlow summons up his memory of Kurtz: "[h]e lived then before me; he lived as much as he had ever lived – a shadow insatiable of splendid appearances, of frightful realities; a shadow darker than the shadow of the night, and draped nobly in the folds of a gorgeous eloquence" ("Heart of Darkness," *YS* 155). The contrasts and connections between surface appearance and horrid reality are reinforced in the prosody by the anapaestic rhythm of these lines, combined with the repetitions of "lived" and "shadow," and the bi-syllabic adjectives "splendid" and "frightful," which qualify the tetra-syllabic nouns "appearances" and "realities." The reader is powerfully reminded of Kurtz's devouring shade and the invasive wilderness rhetorically juxtaposed with the painting and Kurtz's eloquence. It is within these contexts that the Intended comes on stage: "A high door opened – closed. I rose" (156), the empty sign of the dash succinctly represents her entrance (though empty, the sign is full of potential signification), but the reader must wait for her description until she takes centre stage, where she seems to personify Justice and Liberty in herself, for Conrad embeds a subtle reminder of Kurtz's picture in the language register of both scenes. The painting, as we have noted, is seen in terms of "stately movement," while Kurtz's shadow is "draped nobly" in his eloquence. More evidently her description, in the swiftly darkening room, strongly resembles that of Kurtz's picture: "She came forward, all in black, with a pale head, floating towards me in the dusk" (156-57) and, in a characteristic move, Conrad then gives a close-up camera shot of the girl's head emerging from the darkness, like a Madonna or icon from a Memling or Grünewald altarpiece the only part of her that is visible is her face, Conrad gives no detail of her body other than that she is dressed in mourning.[24]

Cinematographic images like this are seen throughout his work:[25] "The room seemed to have grown darker, as if all the sad light of the cloudy evening had taken refuge on her forehead. This fair hair, this pale visage, this pure brow, seemed surrounded by an ashy halo from which the dark eyes looked out at me" (157). The triple use of the determiner "this" combined with the simple, general, monosyllabic, almost abstract qualifiers: "fair," "pale," "pure," and the simple, general, nouns: "hair," "visage," "brow" certainly bring an *impression* of her face powerfully before us, but it is as a *donnée*, something given, an image in the common domain. It is not an individualized image, but rather one that we can recuperate immediately, for we have seen it many times before. The image is evidently associated with death; Marlow has "seen" them together (of course he has not, but he has imagined them in a powerful empathetic identification of doubles); he has seen "his death and her sorrow" (157), and Kurtz lives but as a shadow for Marlow, as much as he had ever lived in reality, and for the woman too his shadow, his *shade*, is symbolized by the "ashy halo." The ironies rebound one upon another: Kurtz *intended* to bring light to the wilderness, but instead falls into its darkness; his *Intended* is pale with blond hair, but she is seen at dusk, with an ashy halo, and her head floats towards Marlow like a ghost. The very environment seems to emerge from a gothic ghost story or borrowed from a somewhat more hygienic Miss Havisham's "Satis House." The Intended lives in marmoreal time and space: "The bent gilt legs and backs of the furniture shone in indistinct curves. The tall marble fireplace had a cold and monumental whiteness. A grand piano stood massively in a corner; with dark gleams on the flat surfaces like a sombre and polished sarcophagus" (156). Death, grief, and the death of love are evidently signified in this metonymic description, which is remarkable for both impressionism and abstraction. On this stage-set, surfaces are all hard and all reflect light, they are of gilt, marble, and highly polished wood, and they are very generalized; the reader must imagine for himself the ormolu baroque chairs and furniture (we are not told precisely what furniture, nor the disposition nor number of chairs, and there is a conspicuous absence of colour, things being either black or white). The fireplace is qualified as tall (like the door from which Marlow entered, and the door through which she came on stage), and it is as cold and monumental as a grand tomb; finally the piano is not some domestic upright tucked into a corner, it is a massive grand piano, it gleams darkly and, in the single simile in this passage, it is "like a sombre and polished sarcophagus." And how much more powerful is the description with the single conjunction, *and* functioning as a hendiadys, splitting the qualifiers, and thus generating even more unease; a sarcophagus which is sombre *and* polished is so much more sinister than a merely sombre, polished one (one could make the same point about the fireplace or the "high and ponderous" front door through which Marlow entered the house, 155). Objects in this passage are large, imposing, glittering, and dead – perfect metonyms for Kurtz, for the "Society," and finally for the lost, wasting life of the Intended.

The two figures *ekphrasis* and metonymy both transform characters and scenes into art images, and combine to render objects and characters more significant in thus focusing the reader upon the human condition in extremity. Conrad's chief story teller, Marlow, who spins his artistic yarns through many volumes, is yet another aspect of art, for he is himself described as an art object. He is seen in terms of three-dimensional sculpture with sunken cheeks, a straight back, and an ascetic aspect, and with "the palms of hands outwards, [he] resemble[s] an idol" (46), shortly afterwards the pose becomes more specific "he ha[s] the pose of a Buddha preaching in European clothes and without a lotus flower" (50), an image repeated in the final paragraph of the novella, where he is qualified as being "in the pose of a meditating Buddha" (162). The repeated images of idol, pose, and Buddha, running throughout the tale, draw the reader's attention to the fictionality of the story, and in this way the tale reinforces its own artistry.[26] The two rhetorical figures, as we have seen, interrupt the plot, which cannot move forward whilst a description is occurring, however they are essential to a deeper understanding of the novel for Kurtz's painting, or the description of Jim's farewell to Marlow, for example, contribute essentially to the reader's necessary confrontation with Conrad's ambivalent stance.

Thus far this paper has analysed certain transformations of art objects into words, or descriptions of reality into images of art, and as we have seen, these rhetorical moves permit the reader to recuperate certain important aspects of the text. However, these transformations may also be analysed logically through an examination of grammatical structures: *as if*, *as though*, *as of*, *as from*, etc., which also move an image from one frame of reality to another. These transformations (they are so much more than devices) have enormous implications for Modernism. As will be seen, there is a subtle distinction to be made between these terms: *as if* operates to move the reader into a hypothetical realm, whereas *as though* carries with it a sense of concession and demurral, while *as of* is the most conceptual of all, whereby the notion of an object predicts the subject itself. In *Nostromo* for example, Decoud imagines his life as appended to a taut cord of solitude and silence, and he imagines it "snapping with a report *as of* a pistol – a sharp, full crack" (*N* 498-99; emphasis added), and this *as of* clause predicts the manner in which he will end his life just one page later. Conrad's prose eventually encourages the reader to consider the subtleties of representations of art and reality in what Wallace Stevens states concisely: "As it is, in the intricate evasions of as" ("An Ordinary Evening in New Haven," *Collected Poetry and Prose* 415). The evasions of *as* are almost always associated with those moments in the novels when Conrad is writing at the limit probing the ethical and existential situations of his protagonists.

As clauses predominate at moments of highest tension when they combine with theatrical imagery; such moments as Marlow's farewell to Jim, the privileged man's understanding of Jim's death, Decoud's suicide, Razumov's confession, Heyst's recognition of Lena's achievement and sacrifice, etc. These key moments will be analysed chronologically looking first at two parallel encounters from "Heart of Darkness" (1899). The first occurs after Marlow's continuous digression, when he first catches sight of Kurtz, and resenting "the absurd danger of our situation, *as if* to be at the mercy of that atrocious phantom had been a dishonouring necessity" ("Heart of Darkness," *YS* 133; emphasis added). The second comes from the description of the Intended who carries "her sorrowful head *as though* she were proud of that sorrow, *as though* she would say, I – I alone know how to mourn for him as he deserves" (157; emphasis added). Dusk has fallen, the room grows darker, and all the light takes refuge on her forehead. These two *as though* constructs subtly link Kurtz and his Intended, for in a sense their egoism is shared. She does not say, but the "*as though she would say*" combined with the superfluous, repetitive "*I*" along with the description of her dead, wasting life, in her dead, wasted environment signifies their joint "life-in-death" existence. Kurtz, when the reader finally confronts him at the culmination of Marlow's quest, is also seen in terms of sculpture, petrified in the image of a funereal monument, an animated memento mori:

> his body emerged from it [his covering] pitiful and appalling *as from* a winding-sheet. I could see the cage of his ribs all astir, the bones of his arm waving. It was *as though* an animated image of death carved out of old ivory had been shaking its hand with menaces. (34; emphasis added)

Here *as though* operates to move the reader into a vision of Kurtz as an art object, while *as from* may be seen in terms of time and space, he is as good as dead yet still in life, though he will soon be dead in fact. The description of this "Nightmare Life in Death," which is in the same isotopy of the "stately movement" seen in Kurtz's painting, could have been borrowed from Coleridge. Kurtz is still just living, but the hand of death is so far upon him that his covering becomes a winding-sheet, his rib-cage is "all astir," and the archaic construction of the *a*-prefix, is then reinforced by the gothic horror of an animated corpse shaking its hand with menaces.[27]

In *Lord Jim* (1902) the climax of Marlow's farewell to Jim is described in now familiar chiaroscuro: the sun is half-submerged, the forest seems the stronghold of night, while the Western horizon is "one great blaze of gold and crimson," the black natives merge into the black background, while Jim's white "otherness" catches all "the light of the world" (*LJ* 335-36). They float down stream towards the sea, which will carry Marlow away forever leaving Jim behind, far from the world he had renounced, exiled in "the very heart of untouched wilderness" (331). The scene is expressed in theatrical terms, linguistically operated through variations of *as* clauses:

> till suddenly at a bend it was *as if* a great hand far away had lifted a heavy *curtain*, had flung open an immense *portal*. The light itself seemed to stir, the sky above our heads widened, a far-off murmur reached our ears, a freshness enveloped us, filled our lungs, quickened our thoughts, our blood, our regrets – and, straight ahead, the forest sank down against the dark blue ridge of the sea. (331; emphasis added)

The theatrical elements in this extract are extraordinary, and they are extraordinarily perverse. The reader is faced with the supremely dramatic situation of Marlow's farewell to Jim, which is announced by the word "suddenly" catching the reader's attention, and immediately a *deus ex machina* raises the heavy theatre curtain, and flings open an "immense portal" (the drama is reinforced by the violent verb "flung" and the elevated register of "portal"), and so the play can begin. We enter the realm of art, announced through *as if* which moves the reader into a different, heightened reality; suddenly the claustrophobia of the situation, with the enclosure of the forest, metonymic of Jim's enclosed, circumscribed world, is swept away: light "stirs," the sky "widens," "murmurs" are heard, there is "freshness" in the air, thought "quickens," and everything breathes life and freedom, while the forest "sinks down," subjugated by the liberating element of the sea. The dramatic liberation of the situation for Marlow is made even more pertinent when one remembers the contrasting, parallel description of Jim's laborious voyage upstream to Patusan for the first time: "At the first bend he lost sight of the sea with its labouring waves for ever rising, sinking, and vanishing to rise again – the very image of struggling mankind – and faced the immovable forests rooted deep in the soil, soaring towards the sunshine" (243). This passage, detailing Jim's journey upstream, describes precisely the same bend that Marlow and he navigate while floating downstream. While in the earlier passage, rowing upstream, Jim lost sight of the sea, perceived as a monotonous image of struggling mankind, captured in the image of "labouring waves." He is then faced with the immoveable, claustrophobic, triumphant forest, overwhelming the sea: "soaring towards the sunlight, everlasting in the shadowy might of their tradition" (243). Thus in returning to the sea, Marlow's journey reverses Jim's, and freedom replaces claustrophobia. A superficial reading would perceive Jim's journey into the forest as a heroic effort, but the heroism is constantly undercut by the absurd situation in which he is presented: for he is sitting on a tin box, with an empty revolver, being hooted at by monkeys (243-44). Readers of *Lord Jim* are of course aware of characteristic narrative echoes, parallelism, and repetitions; another evident example may be found in the ring – that talisman of entry into Patusan – given by the old Scottish trader to Stein, given by Stein to Jim, then given by Jim to Dain Waris; and it is this ring that comes full circle when finally it rolls to Jim's feet just as he is shot dead.

Stein's cavernous study provides another example in *Lord Jim* of a critical moment in the text articulated through *as* clauses, and seen theatrically, when the stage is set for Marlow to "consult" Stein as a patient consulting a doctor as to what ails Jim, and what might be done for him. Once again the reader is placed in a chiaroscuro environment where Stein disappears and then reappears before delivering his famous analysis of following the dream, and submitting to the destructive element, he moves out of the lamp-light and

> It had an odd effect – *as if* these few steps had carried him out of this concrete and perplexed world. His tall form, *as though* robbed of its substance, hovered noiselessly over invisible things with stooping and indefinite movements; his voice, […] was no longer incisive, seemed to roll voluminous and grave – mellowed by distance. (213; emphasis added)

The *as if* clause, segueing into *as though* is particularly subtle: *as if* triggers the now familiar transition from reality into that of a stage set, which places Stein in the role of a consultant, and then abstracts him into a consulting "form." *As though* even more abstractly removes all matter from his substance, and effectively transforms him into a ghost.

Later in some of the darkest lines of the novel Marlow, having reminded the reader repeatedly that what he is narrating is a love story, comes across the grave of Jewel's mother in the moonlight:

> For a moment it looked *as though* the smooth disc, falling from its place in the sky upon the earth, had rolled to the bottom of that precipice […]. It threw its level rays afar *as if* from a cavern, and in this mournful eclipse-like light the stumps of felled trees uprose very dark, the heavy shadows fell at my feet on all sides, my own moving shadow, and across my path the shadow of the solitary grave perpetually garlanded with flowers. (322; emphasis added)

Here the syntactic sequence (from *as though* to *as if*) reverses the sequence set in Stein's study (where *as if* progressed to *as though*). There are further repetitions detailing how and why Western men always leave their native women. This has happened to Jewel's mother and it predicts what will happen to Jewel.[28] In the passage above, the concession seen in *as though* signifies that although we know that the moon cannot in reality have fallen into the precipice, it merely appears that way, but when it throws its rays *as if* from a cavern, the reader has been transported into the realm of myth.[29] Earlier in his narrative Marlow pauses again to foreshadow events that predict Jim's transformation into "Lord Jim," "*as though* he had been the stuff of a hero" (175; emphasis added), this concession evidently reflects his troubled, unheroic past.

A very similar narrative move occurs when Marlow terminates his monologue, and the focus switches to the otherwise unnamed "privileged man" who receives Marlow's package, opens it, looks within, and then walks to the window, whose clear panes enable him to look afar "*as though* he were looking out of the lantern of a lighthouse" (337; emphasis added), and here again the hesitation is marked, and his clear vision undercut by the confused weather without "driving rain," "falling dusk," "austere bursts of sound," etc. (337). A slightly different and even more hesitant figure is introduced when Marlow attempts to believe in Stein's following the dream: "The whisper of his conviction seemed to open before [him] a vast and uncertain expanse, *as of* a crepuscular horizon on a plain at dawn – or was it perchance, at the coming of the night" (215; emphasis added).[30] The hesitations are even more marked in the context by the absurd "swish swish" of Stein's slippers, and his "twitching lips" (214) in trying to make explicit his dream, and even more from the oxymoronic image of a crepuscular horizon seen at dawn. *As if* clauses inform the art images in *Lord Jim*; Marlow apprehends the unreality and total otherness of Patusan, which is perceived "like a *picture* created by fancy on a *canvas*" (emphasis added), the images engraved on his memory are fixed in art; all the emotions, hates, fears, "remain in my mind," he says, "just as I had seen them – intense and *as if* for ever suspended in their expression" and so he turns away from the picture returning to the sea and the West, and therefore to the rational world of verisimilitude (330; emphasis added).

In *Nostromo* (1906) published just four years after *Lord Jim*, the reader encounters Decoud in a small boat, carrying the silver, the monstrously egotistic Capataz and, as yet unknown to them, the coward Hirsch. Decoud is faced with an experience that resembles a peaceful death: "In this foretaste of eternal peace they [images of passions and dangers] floated vivid and light, like unearthly clear dreams of earthly things that may haunt the souls freed by death from the misty atmosphere of regrets and hopes" (*N* 262). This is as far from the reality of agitations, passions and dangers experienced on shore as it is possible to get. The scene is so vivid, so visual, that it could well translate onto the screen in the hands of a great director (though it would be virtually impossible to stage).[31] The waters are "strangely smooth, *as if* their restlessness had been crushed by the weight of that dense night" (261; emphasis added), and the whole episode is marked by synaesthesia of a solitude that "could almost be felt," and "the blackness [that] seemed to weigh upon Decoud like a stone" (262-63). The unreality of the scene is narrated in terms of negatives: there is no light, no sound, the sea is as black as the sky above, and there is an overwhelming, obscure nothingness (261-62). Decoud cannot even see Nostromo sitting next to him and he experiences the unreality palpably: "[Decoud] had the strangest sensation of his soul having just returned into his body from the circumambient darkness in which land, sea, sky, the mountains, and the rocks were *as if* they had not been" (262; emphasis added).

The gulf under its poncho of clouds "remained breathless, *as if* dead rather than asleep" (265; emphasis added) – the personified gulf obviously cannot be either breathless or asleep, but its animation is wonderfully paradoxical given the absence of sensory stimulation experienced by the characters. The Capataz snuffs the candle and to Decoud it was "*as if* his companion had destroyed with a single touch the world of affairs, of loves, of revolutions" (275). His suicide is marked with two *as if* clauses, which underline the bathos and waste in confronting the indifference of nature, and reveals Decoud's lack of moral compass, which will have disastrous consequences for Nostromo. Decoud's suicide and disappearance, weighed down by the silver ingots, violates the integrity of the silver hoard which in turn would cause Nostromo to be accused of theft, and would be intolerable to his monstrous self-esteem. Decoud rows out from the cliff "that stood behind him warm with sunshine, *as if* with the heat of life, bathed in a rich light from head to foot *as if* in a radiance of hope and joy. He pulled straight towards the setting sun" (500; emphasis added). Here we really are in a land of fantasy where the cliff is anthropomorphized, and hope, joy, radiance, etc., all emanate from it. However, that optimism is rudely shattered when the reader perceives that he is rowing in a westerly direction towards the setting sun, always associated with death.

In comparison the construction *as though* operates slightly differently in *Nostromo*: when Nostromo announces that he could not kill Hirsch after witnessing Decoud giving him water "*as though* he were [his] brother" (284; emphasis added), a concession visualized in an art image, which recognises Hirsch's humanity, while also recognising his cowardice, and therefore he cannot be Decoud's "brother." When the narrative of Decoud's isolation is resumed after a gap of some hundred pages, he will determine to commit suicide, by rowing out into the gulf, shooting himself, and sinking with the weight of four silver ingots. The decision made on the tenth day of his despairing isolation is announced by a succession of brief declarative sentences with none of Conrad's usual subordination. In Decoud's mind: "Nostromo was dead [...]. She [Antonia] had not survived [...]. And all exertion seemed senseless" (498). The play between *as if* and *as though* in *Nostromo* is subtle to a degree, but it has the effect of bringing the reader visually as close as possible towards the appalling nothingness experienced by Decoud, who cannot believe the cord of silence snapping, and when it does snap, only the reader can hear the pistol shot, for Decoud is already dead (499-501).

Under Western Eyes (1911), once again rehearses theatrical imagery, combined with thunder and lightening effects, experienced at a critical moment in the narrative just prior to Razumov's confession: "the real drama of autocracy," the narrator tells us, "is not played on the great *stage* of politics"; the narrator has a "glimpse *behind the scenes*" which reveals something "more profound than the words and gestures of the *public play*" (*UWE* 338-39; emphasis added). While Razumov hovers off-stage, he attempts to brave out his guilt, but is unable to rid himself of his secret, seen in the ghost of his double Haldin, whom he has betrayed. At this supreme moment the narrator gives the reader a glimpse of the latter's grieving mother:

> I had the certitude that this mother refused in her heart to give her son up after all. It was more than Rachel's inconsolable mourning, it was something deeper, more inaccessible in its frightful tranquillity. Lost in the ill-defined mass of the high-backed chair, her white, inclined profile suggested the contemplation of something in her lap, *as though* a beloved head were resting there. (339; emphasis added)

The reader and, of course, Razumov know that Haldin is dead, and that he died horribly under torture; we also know that Razumov is the betrayer, and the characters not privy to the secret are those closest to him: his mother and sister. Conrad drags out the confessional truth ever so slowly, thus the *as though* clause here does not move the reader into a flight of fancy, but rather into the concession that though Mrs. Haldin still has hope, the pietà described above, is the metonymy of her grief and predicts the revelation of the fact of his death. She and her dead son are seen *as though* they are carved on a marble sarcophagus as marked by her complete immobility, her pallid face, which is undefined except as it is seen in profile, her dead son rests his head in her lap, the semi-transparent gloom and shadow giving perspective to the sculpture and the pale hand (seen earlier, 338) resting on the shadowy chair. At this point Razumov is in the clear, no one suspects, nor can suspect his guilt (the only witness has committed suicide), it is the guilt itself that drags the confession out of him: "I can't shake him off" (341) he says of his double Haldin, and then unexpectedly he encounters Haldin's sister Natalia, whom he loves, and he is lost. The scene of his confession is spot-lit by "[t]he light of an electric bulb high up under the ceiling searched that clear square box into its four bare corners, crudely, without shadows – a strange *stage* for an obscure *drama*" (342; emphasis added). He is framed in the opened door, "in the searching glare of the white ante-room [...] *as if* rooted for ever to the spot of his atrocious confession" (355; emphasis added). The confession is silent and made to Natalia by the gesture of pointing a denunciatory finger to his breast. He stands stock still, Natalia, equally silently points "mournfully at the tragic immobility of her mother," who has "the stillness of a sombre painting" (355). The lack of dialogue and repetitive gestures, combined with the art image, underline the tremendous theatricality of the scene. Finally Razumov flees the apartment and makes his second confession into his journal. The third confession is made to the revolutionaries, by evoking his double: "Thus he saves me," he says of Haldin, which brings closure to this aspect of the narrative, with his mutilation and predicted death (362, ff).

Our final examples are taken from *Victory* (1915), which once again rehearses themes of isolation and exile, but this time from choice rather than necessity. Heyst's choice of nightmares is based on an intellectual and emotional refusal to engage with life. But, as stated earlier, it does not matter whether one acts, or refrains from action: in Conrad's world both lead to tragic destinies. The culminating act of *Victory* dramatizes Lena's short-lived triumph in obtaining Ricardo's knife, thus rendering him harmless. As usual in Conrad's fiction, the climactic scenes are punctuated by ominous, rumbling thunder. Lena's triumph is temporary, because when Jones shoots at Ricardo he merely wounds him, but the shot kills her. It remains for Heyst, finally realising that he has neglected life, to immolate himself with his dead lover: "woe to the man," he says to Davidson, "whose heart has not learned while young to hope, to love – and to put its trust in life!" (*V* 410). Conrad constructs the last act of his drama around two dialogues – one between Ricardo and Lena, the other between Jones and Heyst – which are parallel in the total misapprehensions of the characters, and are exemplary of dramatic irony. Ricardo believes that he has found his soul mate in Lena; Jones believes that Heyst has cunningly hidden treasure on the island, but he is completely unaware that Heyst has brought Lena to Samburan. Meanwhile, Heyst is unaware of Lena's plot to obtain the knife, while her last thought is that she has triumphed over death and will be united with Heyst. In a way these scenes could be classified as comedy, and Heyst actually points to the "politely grim raillery" of his dialogue, while outside the thunder mutters "fatuously." However, this is comedy of a particularly grim and nauseous kind. Jones has a horror of women – his homosexuality is evident although unstated – and his betrayal by Ricardo, his right-hand man, together with his misunderstanding of the situation between Lena and Heyst, may be said to raise a wry grimace. Meanwhile, Ricardo's incoherent slobbering over Lena's shoe is more farce than tragedy; though from another point of view the scene cannot be seen as pure farce, because her achievement in obtaining Ricardo's knife is heroic, though her death is tragic. The human condition, as we have seen in Conrad's work, is simultaneously tragic and a pitiful comedy.

The scene is set then: Ricardo leads Heyst to meet the etiolated, gentlemanly monster that is Jones, as a thunderstorm rumbles in the background, with "[t]he great cloud covering half the sky hung right against one, like an enormous *curtain* hiding menacing preparations of violence" (374; emphasis added). Jones (a character who is prefigured by Gentleman Brown in *Lord Jim*)[32] has a spectral quality, he is "gruesomely malevolent, *as of* a wicked and pitiless corpse" (382; emphasis added). He is fleshless, encased in a blue dressing gown, with a shrill, screaming, infantile voice, and is sick with fever. He even takes on the role of a pantomime doll in his fury at the discovery of Ricardo's treachery, executing a dance of rage in the middle of the floor, and Heyst is "fascinated by this skeleton in a gay dressing-gown, jerkily agitated like a grotesque toy on the end of an invisible string" (389). And so the reader is confronted with the final act of this comical-tragedy, with thunder rumbling "as of a naval action somewhere on the horizon," and with lightning garishly flashing illuminating the scene as Heyst and Jones leave to confront Ricardo and Lena. The scene is narrated from Heyst's focalisation: "[b]ut in the brilliant square of the door he saw the girl – the woman he had longed to see once more – *as if* enthroned, with her hands on the arms of the chair. She was in black; her face was white, her head dreamily inclined on her breast" (391; emphasis added).

The scene epitomizes the whole argument of this paper. It is supremely dramatic: the door frame, the chiaroscuro black and white, brilliantly lit by candles with lightning flashing, and thunder rumbling outside, together with Lena's description, regally enthroned, and empowered with Ricardo's knife. The scene is also marked by a displaced sexuality: everything "trembles incessantly," "the earth, the sky itself, shivered all the time," the entire universe is "shuddering" and the only still point is "the woman in black sitting in the light of the eight candle-flames," a sight which seers "his very brain with the radiation of infernal heat" (392), a flame which literally predicts their immolation at the end. The scene now shifts into Lena's focalisation, as she now lifts "the curtain" in the opening of chapter 12, to describe how she managed to obtain the knife, and thereupon the language becomes enriched with an elevated, biblical resonance[33]: "She had done it! The very sting of death was in her hands; the venom of the viper in her paradise, extracted, safe in her possession – and the viper's head all but lying under her heel" (399). This elevated language register, enriched with biblical echoes, is immediately undercut by the bathos of Ricardo crawling on the floor, slobbering over her feet. Jones shoots, Ricardo escapes temporarily, Lena is mortally wounded, Heyst learns at last what she has done for him, and simultaneously learns what he has lost. Heyst literally pulls down the curtain, as Davidson comes on stage to act the role of frame narrator of Lena's death, and tie up the plot line with Heyst's self-immolation. Like all the major characters in this novel, Lena is deceived until the last – she believes that she has triumphed over death, and that Heyst will take her to his heart for ever (406-07), but she is dying, and all he is capable of is a realisation of loss. In his inability to express love, his only act can be that of suicide and, like Jim before him, he can only achieve victory with the sacrifice of his own life. The pattern established in earlier works is maintained in the catastrophe of *Victory*, where Conrad once more shifts the language into art, as Lena is transformed into a marble sculpture: "The faint smile on her deep-cut lips waned, and her head sank deep into the pillow, taking on the majestic pallor and immobility of marble" (406). The culminating act of *Victory* epitomizes the way Conrad throughout his work adopts theatrical images via *ekphrasis* and metonymy to shift the frame of reference from verisimilitude to that of art, and almost invariably he has recourse to *as of*, *as though*, *as if*, *as from* constructions which have the effect of confronting the reader with an unsayable truth.

This paper has demonstrated that Conrad has recourse to art images, particularly theatrical and cinematic images, when his protagonists are discovered *in extremis*. Five major works representative of his early, middle, and late periods have been examined chronologically to try to establish whether one technique predominates over another as his work progresses. Tentatively one might conclude that Conrad's plotting may be said to be tighter towards the end of his career, but as yet I can find no evidence for a similar process in his literary technique – on the contrary Conrad's voice seems to have sprung full-grown from out his head. From early works like "Heart of Darkness" (1899) through to a late work such as *Victory* (1915) he remained consistent, and consistently inventive in transforming the human experience under pressure into the realms of art through the subtle ambiguities of *as*, and through his master images from theatre and cinema. Conrad has continual recourse to these strategies since they solicit the reader's share and promote what Barthes has called the "*jouissance*" of the reading experience in these most "writerly" texts. In a very real sense Conrad's novels read their readers who are found "hanging together" with the protagonists in a mutual guilt of human existence, though they are rewarded with the joy of reading his texts.

NOTES

[1] "Natives of poverty, children of malheur, / The gaiety of language is our seigneur" (Stevens, "Esthétique du Mal," *Collected Poetry and Prose* 284).

[2] I am drawing on Barthes's formulation of the "text of pleasure" contrasted with the "text of bliss" (13-14). To paraphrase and inevitably simplify Barthes's subtle argument, the text of pleasure is found in most nineteenth-century novels, which the reader consumes pleasurably; whereas the text of bliss discomforts the reader, and breaks with cultural norms. Barthes's interest is in the abrasions of language, in its cutting, in the language's ability to face the reader with aporia; an aporia which is evident throughout Conrad's fiction (11-13).

[3] Donovan points out Conrad's fascination with, and knowledge of, moving pictures; he even planned an early film-play with Stephen Crane (251).

[4] Rothenstein's pastel portrait (1903) was donated to The National Gallery by Emile Mond (NPG, 2097), along with a fine preliminary sketch donated by Lady Gosse, Epstein's bust was purchased by the same gallery in 1960 (NPG, 4159). The connection with Emile came about when his cousin Alfred Mond purchased *The English Review*, edited by Ford, in 1909. Conrad published several articles with the journal between 1909 and 1917, and serialised *Under Western Eyes*, and *The Shadow-Line* there (see Najder, *A Life* 400-01; Harding, 221-43).

[5] Turner's paintings were deposited with The National Gallery from 1856 onwards; they were transferred to the Tate in 1897. Conrad wrote to Galsworthy that his son Borys had become "Turnerite" (*CL* 4: 12). Conrad had easy access to Turner's paintings, since from 1880-1886 he lodged at N° 6, Dynevor Road, Stoke Newington (Najder, *A Life*, illus. 360-61; Jasanoff 62).

[6] Mallarmé "celebrates Manet for his air" which dominates everything, Laforgue for the "Impressionist's [...] light bathing everything," and Pater's "integrating physical reality and consciousness into a diffused spatial order [...] informing the whole with an ultimately spiritual energy" (Benson 31).

[7] Conrad repudiated Nietzsche in terms of "mad individualism" (*CL* 2: 108), but it cannot be avoided that Nietzsche's thought on Modernism is similar to Conrad's. By moving the frame of reference, as Kofman has shown with regard to Nietzsche, metaphor becomes the concept which thus attempts to free society from one-dimensional thinking (Kofman 14-16); in short it ushers in the polyvalence and ambiguities of the Modern, the complexities of which are exemplified in Conrad's work.

[8] In referring to "recuperation" of a text, I am drawing on the French term *récupération* as employed by Derrida, et al. The term is elaborated by Culler in *Structural Poetics* (137), where he defines structuralist criticism as being "recuperation, naturalization or *vraisemblablisation* as the reading process which brings the text 'within modes of order which

culture makes available'" (cited in Makaryk 617). In short, an attempt to close the text which, in the case of Conrad, is doomed to failure, for his polysemy resists closure.

[9] Bonney has pertinently remarked of chapter 6, Part 3 of *Nostromo* (394), that "the narrative opens with a citation of descending shadows, a chiaroscuro landscape, and ends clinging to chromatic glories which lend futilely and anachronistically 'an air of rosy youth' as the evening sun declines" (132-33).

[10] William J. Cook Jr., drawing on previous research, states that in "Heart of Darkness" the central image is found in the contrast between light and darkness (4).

[11] For example, the very first sentence of *Victory* points to the connection between coal and diamonds – black and white allotropic manifestations of carbon – an example that may stand for Conrad's enduring interest in this dichotomy (*V* 3).

[12] While the 10 days of his total isolation are interminable for Decoud, within the text they pass in two pages, as narrative time ironically speeds up for the reader (*N* 496-98).

[13] Kermode is writing about a British spy, imprisoned and interrogated by the Gestapo, who keeps sane, and is eventually saved, by creating fictions: one fiction created for the Germans as coherently, plausibly real as possible; another fiction for himself, whereby he populates his world, and invents time in the shape of a clock to anchor himself in reality, and to "apprehend the increasing pressure of an approaching end" (160), a concept which is not unlike Stevens' mental construct in "Notes Towards a Supreme Fiction" (329 ff.).

[14] This notion also seems to be part of the modern zeitgeist, for Ibsen expresses it in *The Wild Duck* [1884, trans. 1890 by Clara Bell, and also in 1890 trans. by William Archer]: "Take the saving lie from the average man and you take his happiness away, too" (Act V). Conrad was evidently influenced by Ibsen's world view, noted by Cedric Watts who has analysed the strong connection between *The Secret Agent* and Ibsen (47).

[15] In fact, as John Gillies has perceptively noted, the so-called pure characters (he is referring to Miranda, Ferdinand, and Kurtz, but Jim also fits this pattern), identify the impure characters, what Julia Kristeva calls the "abject" or "outcast." Kristeva has an important *aperçu* in perceiving that this is situated in laughter since laughing is a way of placing or displacing abjection (Gillies 144; Kristeva 8, the abject or deject is not at all unaware of his situation). If Miranda's purity identifies impure Caliban, so Jim's purity may be said to identify Cornelius and Brown.

[16] A similar view of Western intruders perceived by natives is remarked when the harlequin figure in "Heart of Darkness" describes Kurtz as a Jove--like figure to the natives: "he came to them with thunder and lightning, you know – and they had never seen anything like it – and very terrible" (*YS* 128).

[17] Decoud's failure of "intellectual audacity" is paralleled and contrasted on the same page with Nostromo's failure of "audacious action" (*N* 501). These contrasting narrative patterns reflect the same mode of thought as the duality of Black and White analysed previously.

[18] *Ekphrasis* and metonymy are defined in Cuddon (252, 510, respectively), but I will also be drawing on Rimmon-Kenan (67, ff.) and Wolf (63-82).

[19] Conrad's stereotypical portrayal of Jews, with attributes of cowardice, and commerce, is an unfortunate cliché of the times; see also his depiction of Hirsch as a "little hook-nosed man," with a "hooked beak," and who "speaks in a strange anxious whine," he has thick lips and moves by slinking and crawling along the ground (*N* 201-03, 270-73), on whom Daleski has an excellent two-page discussion (121-22).

[20] The dark palette of paintings seems to be endemic in Conrad: in "The End of the Tether" Captain Whalley's late wife is portrayed in "a flat bituminous oil painting representing the profile and one black ringlet" (*YS* 171). Whereas the portrait of Heyst's father glooms above Heyst's head, in profile, and otherwise the painting is colourless apart from the white paper on the crimson table-cloth (*V* 189, 219).

[21] It is evident that Conrad has borrowed this notion, along with other gothic elements, from his close reading of Dickens (whom his father translated), particularly from *Bleak House*, with its notions of "Telescopic Philanthropy" and "the Brotherhood of Humanity" (Dickens 82, 90). Hampson correctly suggests King Leopold's "Association for the Exploration and Civilizing of Africa" (137n), but though the facts are taken from history, the tone comes directly from Dickens's fiction.

[22] "The Secret Sharer," emphasizes the isolated position of the captain (*TLS* 91-92), and his double (104), and fundamentally this is an expression of empathy. Here Marlow identifies with Kurtz through the powerful empathetic movement of his search, although he has never been in the latter's extreme position of being overtaken by the wilderness, Kurtz had stepped over the edge, whilst Marlow "had been permitted to draw back [his] hesitating foot" ("Heart of Darkness," *YS* 151). Marlow remains faithful, since Kurtz had summed up the horror of existence, which he felt incapable of doing himself.

[23] I have analysed some of these concepts in an earlier article on *Lord Jim* (Vernon 28-29).

[24] Madonnas emerging from a dark background seem to be found more frequently in Northern Iconography than in the Italian Primitives where the faces tend to emerge from light. The contrast between any Fra Angelico, and the Isenheim Altarpiece will make the point.

[25] The chiaroscuro image with its detail of fair hair, as though lit with a spotlight focused on her face is powerfully reprised in *Lord Jim* when Marlow says farewell to the protagonist, and it is worth noting how cinematographic these images are, particularly the fade-out when Jim vanishes

from sight (*LJ* 336), and one can almost see the "iris shot" from a scene change or time shift in a silent movie. In contrast to Kurtz's Intended, Jim as ever is dressed all in white, and as with the scene of the Intended, darkness is falling. As Marlow heads out to sea, Jim's figure recedes, first to the size of a child, and then but "a tiny white speck, that seemed to catch all the light left in a darkened world," and suddenly he vanishes (336). Conrad wrote to Pinker before giving his lecture on literary art and reading from *Victory* that he thought "the imaginative literary art [is] based fundamentally on scenic motion, like a camera" (Schwab 342).

[26] Hampson's list of articles on the subject of Marlow's pose is useful (126n). His note remarks that the pose is partly ironic and partly straight, but although Conrad's irony is ubiquitous, it is difficult to see any irony in the Buddha pose.

[27] *The Rime of the Ancient Mariner* (1834 text) is written in archaic English, though less archaic than the original text of 1798: "Eftsoons, I wist, agape" for example (Coleridge). Coleridge writes that the sun peers through the ribs of the ship, while the Nightmare Life-in-Death is dicing with the skeleton of Death itself for the souls of the mariners. The Ancient Mariner also predicts Conrad's protagonists in terms of his total isolation: "Alone, alone, all, all alone, / Alone on a wide wide sea!".

[28] This is almost a trope of the time: Pierre Loti's *Madame Chrysanthème* (1887), John Luther Long's "Madame Butterfly" (1898) which inspired Puccini, and most pertinent of all, Kipling's "Without Benefit of Clergy" (1890): "He will go back to his people in time, said the mother" (21). That this might be regarded as colonial hegemony is the subject of another paper, but it is worth noting that these views are all expressed by white writers about native women.

[29] Plato's cavern from *The Republic* (514a 520a, 278-86), as reprised in 1 Cor.13, 12, "For now we see through a glass darkly; but then face to face."

[30] The words "perchance" and "horizon" (he will later employ "bourne" and "undiscovered country," [*LJ* 337-38]) at this critical moment of hesitation, when just a page earlier he had referred to Shakespeare, are part of the mostly implicit references to *Hamlet,* which inform *Lord Jim* on the theme of existence, non-existence, and above all *how* to exist (see Vernon 14-20).

[31] It is a tragedy that David Lean died before he could complete his film of *Nostromo*, in which Marlon Brando had been asked to star. However, the script is extant, as well as detailed set designs, and a history of the complex negotiations involved (see Pelan).

[32] The banal names given to Conrad's villains: Jones (*V*), Brown (*LJ*), and Smith from "Amy Foster" seem to predict Arendt's comments on the banality of evil.

[33] Which recalls the tone of *Nostromo* at the moment of Decoud's suicide: "It is done, he stammered out in a sudden flow of blood" (*N* 501),

in a pattern already established by *Lord Jim*, "He hath taken it upon his own head" (*LJ* 415).

WORKS CITED

Bal, Mieke. "Over-Writing as Un-Writing: Descriptions, World-Making and Novelistic Time." *Narrative Theory: Critical Concepts in Literary and Cultural Studies*. Ed. Mieke Bal. Vol 1. Routledge, 2004. 341-88.

Barthes, Roland. *The Pleasure of the Text*. Trans. Richard Miller. Hill, 1975.

Benson, Donald R. "Impressionist Painting and the Problem of Conrad's Atmosphere." *Mosaic: An Interdisciplinary Critical Journal* 22.1 (1989): 29-40. Accessed 21 Nov. 2022. Stable URL: <https://www.jstor.org/stable/24780451>.

Bonney, William T. "Joseph Conrad and the Betrayal of Language." *Nineteenth-Century Fiction* 34 (1979): 127-53. Accessed 14 Oct. 2021. Stable URL: <https://www.jstor.org/stable/2932905>.

Coleridge, Samuel Taylor. "The Rime of the Ancient Mariner." 1834. Poetry Foundation. Accessed 25 May 2023. <https://www.poetryfoundation.org/poems/43997/the-rime-of-the-ancient-mariner-text-of-1834>.

Cook, William J., Jr. "More Light on 'Heart of Darkness'." *Conradiana* 3 (1971-72): 4-14. Accessed 21 Nov. 2022. Stable URL: <https://www.jstor.org/stable/24641661>.

Cuddon, J. A. *The Penguin Dictionary of Literary Terms and Literary Theory*. Penguin, 1998.

Daleski, H. M. *Joseph Conrad: The Way of Disposession*. Faber, 1977.

Dickens, Charles. *Bleak House*. 1853. Ed. Norman Page. Introd. J. Hillis Miller. Penguin, 1971.

Didion, Joan. *The White Album*. 1979. Harper, 2017.

Donovan, Stephen. "Sunshine and Shadows: Conrad and Early Cinema." *Conradiana* 35 (2003): 237-56. Accessed 21 Nov. 2022. Stable URL: <https://www.jstor.org/stable/24635126>.

Gillies, John. *Shakespeare and the Geography of Difference*. Cambridge UP, 1994.

Hampson, Robert, ed. *Heart of Darkness with The Congo Diary*. Penguin, 1995.

Harding, Jason. "The Right Accent Conrad and the 'English Review'." *Conradiana* 41 (2009): 221-43. Accessed 3 Jan. 2022. Stable URL: <https://www.jstor.org/stable/24635293>.

Houston, Gail. "Fictions to Live By: Honourable Intentions, Authorial Intentions, and the Intended in 'Heart of Darkness'." *Conradiana* 28 (1996): 34-47. Accessed 21 Jan. 2022. Stable URL: <http://www.jstor.org/stable/24634901>.

Ibsen, Henryk. *Three Plays*. Trans. Una Ellis-Fermor. Penguin, 1959.

Jasanoff, Maya. *The Dawn Watch: Joseph Conrad in a Global World*. Collins, 2017.

Kermode, Frank. "Solitary Confinement." *Sense of An Ending*. By Kermode. 1966. Oxford UP, 2000. 155-97.

Kipling, Rudyard. "Without Benefit of Clergy." *The Mark of the Beast and Other Tales*. By Kipling. Ed. Roger Burlingame. New American Library, 1964. 19-42.

Kofman, Sarah. *Nietzsche and Metaphor*. 1972. Trans. Duncan Large. Athlone P, 1993.

Kristeva, Julia. *Powers of Horror: An Essay on Abjection*. Trans. Leon S. Roudiez. Columbia UP, 1982.

Lindquist, Sven. *"Exterminate All the Brutes": One Man's Odyssey into The Heart of Darkness*. Granta, 1997.

Makaryk, Irena R., ed. *Encyclopedia of Contemporary Literary Theory: Approaches, Scholars, Terms*. U Toronto P, 1993.

Najder, Zdzisław. "Fidelity and Art: Joseph Conrad's Cultural Heritage and Literary Programme." *Conrad in Perspective: Essays on Art and Fidelity*. By Najder. Cambridge UP, 1997. 199-212.

---. *Joseph Conrad: A Life*. Camden, 2007.

Pelan, Tim. "David Lean's *Nostromo*: The Old Man and the Untold Tale of the Seaboard," *Cinephilia and Beyond*. Accessed 4 Dec. 2022. <https://cinephiliabeyond.org/david-leans-nostromo-old-man-untold-tale-seaboard/>.

Peters, John G. "Point of View in Conrad's 'Heart of Darkness' and the Ultimate Uncertainty of Knowledge." *Yearbook of Conrad Studies (Poland)* 2 (2006): 23–29. Accessed 24 Aug. 2021. Stable URL: <https://www.jstor.org/stable/26414163>.

Plato. *The Republic*. Trans. and Introd. H. D. P. Lee. Penguin, 1959.

Rimmon-Kenan, Shlomith. *Narrative Fiction: Contemporary Poetics*. Methuen, 1983.

Schwab, Arnold T. "Conrad's American Speeches and His Reading from *Victory*." *Modern Philology* 62 (1965): 342-47. Accessed 20 Feb. 2020. Stable URL: <https://www.jstor.org/stable/436369>.

Spinoza, Benedict De. *Ethics*. Ed. and trans. Edwin Curley, Introd. Stuart Hampshire. Penguin, 1996.

Stevens, Wallace. *Collected Poetry and Prose*. Ed. Frank Kermode and Joan Richardson. Library of America, 1997.

Vernon, Peter. "Hanging Together, Not the How but the Why: *Lord Jim* and the Function of Intertextuality." *Yearbook of Conrad Studies (Poland)* 8 (2013): 7-30.

Watts, Cedric. "*The Wild Duck* and *The Secret Agent*." *Conradiana* 25 (1993): 47-52. Accessed 28 Oct. 2021. Stable URL: <http://www.jstor.org/stable/24634798>.

Wolf, Werner. "*Mise en cadre* – A Neglected Counterpart to *Mise en abyme*: A Frame-Theoretical and Intermedial Complement to Classical Narratology." *Postclassical Narratology: Approaches and Analyses*. Ed. Jan Alber and Monika Fludernik. Ohio State UP, 2010. 58–82.

Yelton, Donald C. *Mimesis and Metaphor: An Inquiry into the Genesis and Scope of Conrad's Symbolic Imagery*. Mouton, 1967. Studies in English Literature 39.

Michel Arouimi,
Université du Littoral,
Dunkirk, France

Poetics of Contradiction in *The Secret Agent*

Many critics have already observed the "interplay between technique and message" (Krajka, Introduction 2) in some of Conrad's works, with the word *message* referring to an insight "into the human condition." Conrad himself suggests the phenomenon of interplay in the Preface to *The Nigger of the "Narcissus"* when he speaks of his "devotion to the perfect blending of form and substance" (*NN* xiii), with the word *devotion* lending a religious connotation to this crucial definition, and the word *form* implying the literary techniques used to depict the events related in the novel: "It is to show [...] its form; and through [...] its form [...] reveal the substance of [...] truth" (xiv). Previous critical works have examined Conrad as a literary technician by exploring contradictions in his work related to the contrast or accord of human races, of feminine and masculine characters, or more generally of a "mixture" of positive and negative traits on many levels of the text.

The objective of my analysis is to show the stylistic means used by Conrad, especially in *The Secret Agent*, "to reach the secret spring of responsive emotions" with the objective of making the reader *see* or feel, in a sensitive manner, the hidden "Truth [or secret]" lying in the depth of our souls. I quote here the Preface to *The Nigger of the "Narcissus,"* in which the following words express the nature of such a secret: our sense of pity, and beauty, and pain, "the presented vision of regret or pity, of terror or mirth" (xiv).

Conrad's chief stylistic tool in this quest is *contradiction.* Even the appearance of the artist ("We watch the movements of his body, the waving of his arms, we see him bend down" xv) reveals the contradiction, a word used in "Heart of Darkness," which lies in our souls: a contradiction revealed by words, or by the report of words, or images. One might consider this conception of *contradiction* as a sort of the "alchemy of word[s]" in the sense that Arthur Rimbaud gave to this expression. Conrad of course knew Rimbaud's works and life, for example through his exposure to the essay by Charles Whibley which Conrad quoted in 1899 in a letter to his editor.

Certain words and phrases in *The Secret Agent* reveal this hidden "Truth" (or "secret") that the poet Conrad found "within himself, and in that lonely region of stress and strife, [...] a gift and not an acquisition" (*NN* xii). The word *gift* is maybe too nice for the darkness of such a region, a region that inspires the contrasting effects of sense in the very first pages of *The Secret Agent*. The same may be said of the whole structure of the novel, a structure symbolized by the circles drawn by the young brother-in-law of the "secret agent," such agent being an incarnation of the contradiction we're speaking of. Some critics underline the ironical meaning of such art. But we could give it another sense if we interpret some of Conrad's works through René Girard's theory. Wojciech Kozak, in his reading of *The Nigger of the "Narcissus,"* has shown the importance of the purgation of violence by a scapegoat. Perhaps that could also define the structure of *The Secret Agent*. More precisely, the "double bind" (that is to say the main cause of this violence: the contradiction emanating from the "father figure") could give deeper meaning to the "mixture of positive and negative traits" in Conrad's writings.

But this explanation finds its end in some thoughts from Conrad himself, for example in a letter to Edward Garnett written in 1898, quoted by Alex Houen in his essay on "terrorism and literature": "The secret of the universe is the existence of horizontal waves whose varied vibrations are at the bottom of all states of consciousness [...]. Therefore it follows that two universes may exist in the same place and in the same time" (49). This metaphysical vision *contradicts* the Girardian one. This ambiguity takes its higher form in the very first pages of *The Secret Agent*: a poetical expression of the dark "region" of our souls – or a representation of an artistic research into the secret of life, if "politically motivated characters," as suggested by Thomas Jackson Rice in his reading of *The Secret Agent*, can be seen as "figurative writers and artists" (Krajka, Introduction 7).

Such an ambiguity has been felt by Arthur Rimbaud (I have written elsewhere on the haunting power of ideas, a topic pursued by Rimbaud which also appears in the imagination of the author of "Heart of Darkness"). A chapter of Rimbaud's *Season in Hell* is titled "Delirium II" or "Alchemy of the Word." Such an "alchemy" – a poetical way to conciliate contraries – cannot be seen by Rimbaud himself (for reasons that remain obscure) as a celebration of the Unity or sacred One (or Word). Conrad's state of mind on this issue seems to have been similar.[1]

The theme of religion is not wholly absent[2] within the questioning of the fundamental meaning of Harmony, whose power of fascination can be considered proportional to the antagonistic forces that structure our psyche and determine the harmful forms of duality, the "dual forces" discussed by Conrad in some letters.[3]

In *The Secret Agent*, chapter IX, a reference to the Book of Revelation makes us recognize an echo of the "sharp two-edged sword," symbolizing the Word, in the fatal knife seen by the still-innocent eyes of Mrs. Verloc "examining the sharp edge of the carving knife" (*SA* 193). Indeed, these words appear in a long passage in which the smallest details (movements, mere objects: "two knives and two forks") are manifestations of the dual violence of which the mythical Unity would be the sublimated expression.

A Secret Contradiction

Now the critical point of view of Rimbaud on his own art takes another form, beyond any influence, in *The Secret Agent*. The text of the first chapter, on any level of the text, is saturated by an ambiguity which can be seen as a poetical expression of the conflictive relation of characters (Verloc and Winnie, and Stevie). To be more precise, this ambiguous way of writing, an "alchemic" way to conciliate contraries, instead of celebrating a divine Unity, is adapted to the psychology of Verloc, a sort of benevolent father who turns into a murderer. We can think of Abraham, of course, but in terms far removed from the biblical lesson. The Unity we're speaking of is in fact divided, through many details we could see as devilish corruptions of this Unity.

The very first sentences of the novel are redolent of this fact. Verloc's official work is not a job, according to the contradictions incarnated by this character. The same is true of the customers of his shop, and with Winnie herself, who appears to be a "double" of Verloc in the first chapter. Many repeated details suggest the link between different characters in a sort of mirror effect. This phenomenon is not so surprising, but I shall focus my reading on a strange aspect of Conrad's writing. In the first chapter of *The Secret Agent* many material details seem to express contradiction within characters' brains (or destinies). Moreover, the succession of these details is connected with the poetical instinct of Conrad, something like the "instinctive rhythms" alluded by Rimbaud in his "Delirium II."

A Mixture of Characters

The first chapter of the novel can be divided into three parts: first the setting; and then the introduction of the main characters, with a progressive insight into the brains of Verloc, Winnie, Winnie's mother, and Stevie. But the soul of these characters is also highly expressed in the setting of the shop. The equilibrium of this chapter is established by its first (and very short) paragraph, in which the words "in the morning," and, in another sentence, "all before the evening" (3), suggest the cosmic undertones of this discreet *incipit*. But the very first sentences are relevant of the ambiguity of Harmony: "Mr. Verloc, going out in the morning, left his shop *nominally* in charge of his brother-in-law" (3). I emphasize the word *nominally*: perhaps an allusion to the different *names* of these brothers-in-law, who are certainly not brothers. This first paragraph ends with these sentences: "Mr. Verloc cared but little about his ostensible business. And, moreover, his wife was in charge of his brother-in-law" (3). Such a business does not merit this name, even if it is one. Verloc's official work is not a job, according to the contradictions incarnated by this character. Moreover, the quoted sentences, at the beginning and at the end of this paragraph, suggest a sort of identification of the shop ("in charge") and the brother-in-law ("his wife was in charge of his brother-in-law" 3). The identity of these characters seems to vanish in the "evening."

The same with the difference between the customers: predominantly "very young men" without much money, and even the older ones "looking generally as if they were not in funds" (4) (as is generally more often the case of young men). This contradiction takes a more sophisticated and more visual form in the older men's description: "the collars of their overcoats turned right up to their moustaches" (4). Moustaches seems to be a French word – like the "French comic publications hung across a string" in the shop (in the previous paragraph, 3). French comic publications contrast with the seriousness of old moustaches. The antagonism of languages reinforces the tension between these moustaches and, in the following words of the same sentence, the feet: "traces of mud on the bottom of their nether garments" (4). A little later in this chapter, the "dark smooth moustache" of Verloc (7) has probably a different aspect than the older men's moustaches.

Another detail of note is the customers' legs: "the legs inside them [garments] did not, as a general rule, seem of much account either" (4). In the next part of the same chapter, some detail about Winnie's mother grabs our attention: "Her swollen legs rendered her inactive" (6). This sort of mirror effect is typical of Conrad's writing, especially in "Heart of Darkness" and in *The Secret Agent*. In this chapter, the textual link between the customers' legs and those of Winnie's mother, with her "black wig under a white cap" (6), anticipates the mannish attitude of Winnie when she kills Verloc. Black and white are the obvious symbols of such ambiguities. Conrad seems to give us a bitter lesson that could be helpful in the meaning of our "gender studies."

Winnie's mother "considered herself to be of French descent" (6). The expression "French descent," repeated in the same paragraph ("Traces of the French descent which the widow boasted") echoes the "French comic publications hung across a string" (3). Beyond the snobbery of this old woman, the humour of Conrad must not hide his extraordinary sense of the link between men and the objects that surround them. Everything in our world is an aspect of a hidden "Truth" (or Unity). But this metaphysical insight is shadowed by the devaluation of this feminine character, not so different from a comic publication.

The black wig echoes the "casket of black wood" evoked in the third paragraph, after another black detail: "two-and-six in heavy black figures" marked on "yellow paper envelopes" (3). All these black details are linked to form a greater black enigma, reinforced in this chapter by Stevie's work, the blacking of shoes ("Stevie was put [...] to black the boots of the gentlemen" 10). From the "black wood" to this blacking, the irony of Conrad could concern, beyond a certain idea of Unity symbolized by blackness, his own work: Blackwood was the name of one of his editors (for the first publication of "Heart of Darkness"). The idea of writing is suggested by the "paper envelopes."

These "yellow paper envelopes" are followed by the photographs of "the faded, yellow dancing girls" (5). These details suggest that there is no difference between paper and girls, even if they dance. In the Preface to *The Nigger of the "Narcissus"* Conrad writes: "All art [...] appeals primarily to the senses, and the artistic aim when expressing itself in written words must also make its appeal through the senses, if its highest desire is to reach the secret spring of responsive emotions" (*NN* xiii). The "plasticity" and the "colour" of words, in the same passage, could very well have in Conrad's mind the colour and aspect of the "faded, yellow dancing girls," a ridiculous incarnation of Harmony. But what sense must we give to such an irony?

In the same way, the sound of the shop's bell could recall the "music [...] ring of sentences" (xiii) in the Preface to *The Nigger of the "Narcissus,"* but this bell "clattered [...] with impudent virulence" (*SA* 4). The word *impudent* is echoed, in the following paragraph, by some words about Mr. Verloc himself: "With a firm, *steady-eyed* impudence [...] he would proceed to sell over the counter some object looking obviously and scandalously not worth the money which passed in the transaction" (4-5; emphasis added). No less remarkable is the third allusion to the "hopelessly cracked" bell, also rendered here simply as the "cracked bell," when Winnie Verloc appears, "[s]teady-eyed *like her husband*" (5; emphasis added): this bell is the perfect symbol of their cracked relationship.

Different characters, and moreover objects and men, do not really differ. This blurring of differences can be interpreted as a result of mimicry[4] in society. This phenomenon finds its most negative symbol in the second paragraph of *The Secret Agent*, with a descriptive allusion to the house whose ground floor is occupied by Verloc's shop in London: "one of those grimy brick houses which existed in large quantities before the era of reconstruction" (3). Conrad suggests here the lack of differences in our world, be it ancient ("brick houses") or modern. In a sense, this monotony indicates a momentary triumph of Totality over Unity (of course, as we know today, the "era of reconstruction" is not the end of the monotony of "large quantities"). In such a sentence, the past and the future seem to embrace.

A Perverted Unity

The contradiction I was speaking of is not only in Verloc's mind, nor in London: it pervades our culture. But I shall be modest with this inquiry, limiting it to the "objects." Despite the seeming realism of the first paragraphs of the novel, they are also full of highly symbolic details. First, the "brick houses." The brick in itself, even if it is not really described, and the bricks with their lines, heaping, and contrasting with the clear coat of clay, are material symbols of totality: the *same*, with its negative meaning. Meanwhile, this meaning takes a positive form in the drawings of Stevie.

Let us consider first an example from the end of chapter I: "His spare time he occupied by drawing circles with compass and pencil on a piece of paper" (18). Here the "innocent" Stevie (the "artist") appears like an allegory of the writer himself. The same in chapter III:

> seated very good and quiet at a deal table, drawing circles, circles, circles; innumerable circles, concentric, eccentric; a coruscating whirl of circles that by their tangled multitude of repeated curves, uniformity of form, and confusion of intersecting lines suggested a rendering of cosmic chaos, the symbolism of a mad art attempting the inconceivable. (45)

But this cosmic symbolism loses its higher sense with Stevie's disintegration when the bomb explodes: so many pieces of cloth, of blood; another "chaos" whose violence is vaguely exorcised by Stevie's circles. The artistic activity of Stevie is an answer to the human violence which surrounds him.

Later in the novel, when Winnie understands what happened to her poor sacrificed brother, chapter IX ends with these details: "the gold circlet of the wedding ring [...] glittered exceedingly with the untarnished glory of a piece of some splendid treasure of jewels, dropped in a dust-bin" (213). From Stevie's circles to this circlet, Conrad renews the myth of the Androgyne (whose main symbols are gold and the circle), without forgetting the ageless violence probably conjured up by this myth.

Jacob Lothe in *Conrad's Narrative Method* (1991), and Douglas Kerr in "Joseph Conrad's Magic Circles" (2003), both suggest a link between Stevie's circles and Conrad's art of writing.[5] These circles can also be seen as a symbol of the internal balance of such a narrative.[6] The "Observatory" is nothing less than a profanation or at least a derision of these cultural foundations.[7] The poetical instinct of Conrad reaches its highest level in the passage in chapter V that depicts the discovery of Stevie's remains by the Chief Inspector:

> He had seen something like a heavy flash of lightning in the fog. [...] He ran between the trees towards the Observatory. [...] The Chief Inspector's eyes searched the gruesome details of that heap of mixed things [...] his reason told him the effect must have been as swift as a flash of lighting. (87)

The theme of vision in such a description ("seen [...] a flash of lighting [...] towards the Observatory") suggests the luminous (and ironic) meaning of that Observatory, among the Conradian variants of the *Fiat Lux*, more obvious in "Heart of Darkness."

Kurtz in "Heart of Darkness" has been named by some critics a "diabolic Christ." No less diabolic is Verloc's shop in *The Secret Agent*: "a square box of a place, with the front glazed in small panes" (3). This makes me think of a study by Michel Pastoureau, *L'Etoffe du diable* (The devil's cloth); in ancient times, these sorts of shapes were used in representations of the devil. A square is sometimes seen as a symbol of the devil – the devil considered as an incarnation of duality. And Conrad knew that his art, in its topics and its forms, was linked, as a catharsis, with duality.

The Girardian "double bind" takes its most discreet materialization in the door of the shop, in the second paragraph: "In the daytime the door remained closed; in the evening it stood discreetly but suspiciously ajar" (3). Closed and open, discreetly but suspiciously. The contradiction takes a very refined form in these words. The same in the following paragraph, where "the two gas-jets inside the panes were always turned low, either for economy's sake or for the sake of the customers" (3-4). The humour of this sentence will be very soon obvious in the next paragraph, in which Conrad evokes the customers who "were not in funds"; an economic problem – that is to say, a mirror effect between the gas-jets and the customers.

I have already noted the bell; despite its sounding power, "[i]t was hopelessly cracked" (4). Moreover, this bell is "hung on the door by means of a curved ribbon of steel" (3). We would be wrong to smile; such a "ribbon of steel" is a subtle anticipation of the "innumerable circles suggesting chaos and eternity" (237) which, under Stevie's pencil, are no less than an exorcism or duality.

Despite all this, the faded unity seems to relive with some other (unique) details. For example, in the window of the shop, there is "a dingy blue china bowl" (3). I shall not make of this china bowl an equivalent of the Buddha at the beginning of "Heart of Darkness" (Conrad, in "Heart of Darkness," manipulates several Buddhist symbols: William Bysshe Stein had the idea of "a bottisattva scenario"[8]). But we note the contrast between the delicacy of china and its dingy aspect. The china bowl is made of a respectable material, but this is not the case when we consider, a little later in this chapter, "the dusty glass door behind the painted deal counter" (*SA* 4). From dingy china to dusty glass, the difference is not even so sure. Dust everywhere, with its poetical power of uniformity.

The objects on sale in the shop, as they are described, merit the same attention, especially "a small cardboard box with apparently nothing inside, for instance, or one of those carefully closed yellow flimsy envelopes" (5). The adverbs "apparently" and "carefully" suggest the misleading appearance or the uncertain value of these goods. And the "small cardboard box" echoes the significance of the already-emphasized "square box of a place," that is to say, the shop itself, represented by this cardboard box, like a Chinese bonsai.

The Secret Measures

This art of writing, in 1907, is reminiscent of the art of Braque, one of the great cubist painters. For example, just before the murder of Verloc by Winnie, her image, and in particular her facial features, are linked with pieces of furniture, etc. (I could illustrate this idea with other passages of *The Secret Agent*). Conrad considered himself to be a painter (see the Preface to *The Nigger of the "Narcissus"*), but the idea of literature haunts his writings. In the third paragraph of *The Secret Agent*, the "china bowl" takes its place in a sentence surrounded by literary motifs: "paper envelopes," "French comic publications," and before the end of the same paragraph, an allusion to "old copies of obscure newspapers, badly printed, with titles like *The Torch, The Gong*" (3). The words *"Torch"* and *"Gong"* evoke Light and Sound, the association of which has a metaphysical symbolism in China and some other Eastern cultures. Beyond the literary value of these motifs lies the Unity which is its hidden source, and in a certain way its hidden goal.

I shall emphasize the "closed yellow paper envelopes, very flimsy" (3), repeated a little later as "carefully closed yellow flimsy envelopes" (5). Here the word "yellow" finds an echo in the next sentence: "Now and then it happened that one of the faded, yellow dancing girls would get sold to an amateur, as though she had been alive and young" (5). This marvellous sentence dominates all those enigmas concerning duality. The ambiguity of time, "[n]ow and then," and of dreamy desires and reality expresses a human truth, maybe *the* Truth, in which the "double bind" has no place. Here Conrad gives a sort of humoresque sense (or colour) to the mystery which lies in Stevie's drawings, despite the violence of his inspiration. And another (and major) aspect of Conrad's art is shown by the long sentence making up the entirety of the third paragraph, with the enumeration of objects; this enumeration gives an impression of perfect symmetry, despite the poverty of these objects. There are no small things in the ordered world Stevie seems to dream of, which is perhaps the real world:

> The window contained photographs of more or less undressed dancing girls; nondescript packages in wrappers like patent medicines; closed yellow paper envelopes, very flimsy, and marked two-and-six in heavy black figures; a few numbers of ancient French comic publications hung across a string as if to dry; a dingy blue china bowl, a casket of black wood, bottles of marking ink, and rubber stamps; a few books, with titles hinting at impropriety; a few apparently old copies of obscure newspapers, badly printed, with the titles like *The Torch*, *The Gong* – rousing titles. (3)

In the next sentence, "the two gas-jets," just like the "two-and-six," can be read like a clue about the writing of this sentence. The "china bowl" and the "casket of black wood" define the middle of the enumeration; the other objects, four in succession before the bowl, express different aspects of an ambiguity which could be a perverted expression of the "Truth" ("more or less undressed girls," etc). After this bowl and this casket, four other objects, more simply described, are only made of printed paper. We note the symmetrical and contrastive position in the two halves of this long sentence of "a few apparently old copies": "*The Torch*" and "*The Gong*," and "French comic publications."

More sophisticated is the counterbalance between the three expressions at the beginning of the long sentence quoted above: "more or less [...] nondescript [...] few *numbers*" (emphasis added), and, at the end of the sentence, the three repetitions of the word "titles." This is a rhythm of writing whose measure is revealed by the words: "marked two-and-six." Perhaps the number 3 expresses, in itself, the meaning of such alchemic expressions ("more or less [...] nondescript")? Here, Conrad follows his poetical instincts, renewing the ancient knowledge of "China" (or Asia) concerning the primal Unity, or the One, whose link with Two and Three defines the root of Creation. I have spoken of the "poetical instinct" of Conrad, but many studies have been published about the probable influence of Buddhist culture in "Heart of Darkness." Could such an instinct be animated by this knowledge? Regardless, the humour of Conrad reveals the corruption of this knowledge, and violence and dualism find a sort of remedy in such a myth (or truth?).

The word "marked" is the twenty-sixth word of the sentence, followed by the words "two-and-six." And the words "marking ink," echoing the word "marked," are followed by twenty-six words till the end of the sentence – excepting the names or "*The Torch*, *The Gong*." This phenomenon can be found in other great writers, but I do not pretend to give its definitive explanation.[9]

The same with the black details: the "black [figures]" is the thirty-first word of the sentence (if we separate two and six), and the words "black wood" are followed by thirty-one words, excepting the two names. This is the way the author of the Preface to *The Nigger of the "Narcissus"* renews the "old words," with the magic of words. Such a sentence can be compared to the "circles" sketched by Stevie, a representation of Conrad himself as a writer. Even if the "cracked bell," echoing the words "[t]he bell [...] cracked," can be heard like another symbol, if not as brilliant, of this art of writing.

Father and Brother

The "symmetry of form" could have a dark origin, first suggested in the eighth paragraph of the first chapter. Mr. Verloc, with "his business of a seller of shady wares, [but] exercis[ing] his vocation of a protector of society" (5), is an incarnation of the "double bind." The same, more surprisingly, is true of Winnie, in the seventh paragraph: "Steady-eyed like her husband, she preserved an air of unfathomable indifference behind the rampart of the counter" (5).[10]

In the middle of this chapter, Winnie's appearance, and in particular "the extremely neat and artistic arrangement of her glossy dark hair" (6), has a self-critical meaning for Conrad's art, and Winnie's destiny itself is shown through these words. In the next sequence, "her unfathomable reserve, which never went so far as to prevent conversation" (6), echoes her "unfathomable indifference"; such an "artistic arrangement" of hair (or poem?) would be nothing but a way to domesticate a sleeping violence as old as humanity, one that will never die.

Another divided soul, later in this chapter, is Stevie, with his two main necessary occupations: "[to] wash the dishes in the basement kitchen, and to black the boots of the gentlemen patronizing the Belgravian mansion" (10). Not less remarkable, "he was easily diverted from the straight path of duty by the attractions of stray cats and dogs, which he followed down narrow alleys" (8). The word "diverted" sounds like *divided*. Here Stevie incarnates the effect of the paternal *double bind* in a human brain. This diversion is an illusion, with the fight of cats and dogs equalling the tension of nervous relationships surrounding Stevie. Moreover, this fight reveals an underlying concern of *The Secret Agent*, a novel that relives the myth of the enemy brothers, associated here with the sacrifice of Isaac (and perhaps even more present in Melville's mind in his inquiry on "The symmetry of form" in *Billy Budd*).

I could show that the Father figure, seen as a source of the contradiction called the "double bind," is reflected in many passages and in many ways in this novel. Before the death of

Stevie, no less than an infanticide, Conrad suggests, in this first chapter, the parricidal desires so darkly linked to the infanticide, a universal and timeless problem:

> When he had reached the age of fourteen a friend of his late father, an agent for a foreign preserved milk firm, having given him an opening as office-boy, he was discovered one foggy afternoon, in his chief's absence, busy letting off fireworks on the staircase. [...] Wild-eyed, choking clerks stampeded through the passages full of smoke, silk hats and elderly business men could be seen rolling independently down the stairs. (9)

The words "late father," "agent," "chief's absence," are highly suggestive. The contrast between "a foreign preserved milk" and the work of "elderly business men," needs no comment.

No less contrastive are Stevie's features:

> He was delicate and, in a frail way, good-looking, too, except for the vacant droop of his lower lip. [...] When startled by anything perplexing he used to squint horribly. However, he never had any fits (which was encouraging); [...] before the natural outbursts of impatience on the part of his father. (8-9)

Stevie does not imitate this father, but the "natural outbursts" are inscribed in his own flesh.

This enigma is completed by some highly refined details in the last paragraph of this chapter: "By this time a growth of thin fluffy hair had to come to blur, like a golden mist, the sharp line of his small lower jaw" (10). And yet this is the time when Stevie is "occupied by drawing circles with compass and pencil on a piece of paper" (10). Here we see the blurring of youth and maturity, and even the association of "compass and pencil" (that is to say circle and straight line: two associated symbols of unity), or, less obviously, the link between these simple drawings and "the sharp line of his [...] jaw." Conrad is probably trying, in a poetical way, to sidestep the effects and origin of the "double bind" in a non-explicit metaphysical insight into the origin of creation; at least in Stevie's intuition, now in the third chapter, "a coruscating whirl of circles that by their tangled multitude of repeated curves, uniformity of form, and confusion of intersecting lines suggested a rendering of cosmic chaos; the symbolism of a mad art attempting the inconceivable" (45).

This same paragraph in chapter III ends with this sentence: "The artist never turned his head; and in all his soul's application to the task his back quivered, his thin neck, sunk into a deep hollow at the base of the skull, seemed ready to snap" (45-46). We can appreciate a self-portrait of Conrad in these lines, with the "deep hollow," in its allegorical sense, representing the ambiguity of Conrad's artistic responsibility.

One thing we can be sure of concerning the cosmic comparison between his art and the origin of creation is the deep significance of the material details underlined in the first chapter. In a previously quoted passage depicting Stevie's fireworks, we encounter a Big Bang of words, yet not so chaotic: "He touched off in quick succession a set of fierce rockets, angry catherine wheels, loudly exploding squibs – and the matter might have turned very serious" (9). Catherine, in French culture, is a perfect name for witches; these "wheels" reveal the darker meaning of Stevie's circles: a "very serious" problem, which guides the pen of Conrad. We go back to black.

In the Middle of the Book

The Big Bang metaphor could be adapted to the first paragraph of *The Secret Agent*, a valuable *incipit* of the whole novel. Numerous other mirror effects would need a long discussion. In chapter IV, the detail of Stevie's loose lower lip is echoed by an evocation of Ossipon's lips: "the assertion caused the robust Ossipon to bite his lower lip" (67-68). This passage relates a stormy conversation about the recourse to bombs in terrorist attempts, but the dread felt by Ossipon does not reveal the horror of his character, to which Winnie is going to fall victim. Similarly, in chapter VI, another character, Michaelis, suspected of having committed the attempt, offers features which are Stevie's: "mild-voiced and quiet, with no more self-consciousness than a very small child, and with something of a child's charm – the appealing charm of trustfulness" (107). But, not so surprisingly, in the previous chapter, the words "an appealing sweetness" (94) express the sensibility of the Chief Inspector Heat, a man we can trust and rely on.

These mirror effects take place, significantly, at the very middle of the novel of thirteen chapters, a novel whose construction can be qualified by the word *alchemic*. The sophisticated construction of *The Secret Agent* is centred on chapter VI, although that chapter is devoted to characters exterior to the drama. Now, the end of chapter VII, which coincides roughly with the middle of the narrative, offers us a complex vision evoking the reconciliation of contraries in the mythical Unity under the form of an association between oranges and lemons.

The triangular form of the setting (we could interpret in this way the "Δ" which is the secret mark of the "secret agent"), and of course the word "temples," confirm this mythical dimension: "an open triangular space surrounded by dark and mysterious houses, temples of petty commerce emptied of traders for the night. Only a fruiterer's stall at the corner made a violent blaze of light and colour" (150). The following sentence is lighted by coloured fruit: "Beyond all was black, [...] the glowing heaps of oranges and lemons." Such a splendour is worth the repetition at the beginning of the following paragraph, but the seductiveness of these colours is now qualified by the presence of a policeman: "The policeman on the beat projected his sombre and moving form against the luminous glory of oranges and lemons."

In chapter XII we find an echo of the vision of the same fruit, whose "triangle shape" is again noted: "The fruiterer at the corner had put out the blazing glory of his oranges and lemons, and Brett Street was all darkness, interspersed with [...] the few lamps defining its triangular shape" (273). A little later, this image is in turn followed by the metaphor, "a triangular well of asphalt and bricks" (276), symbolizing the relation of Mrs. Verloc, the murderer of her husband, with the latter's false friend, who will bring poor Winnie to her loss – a strange *triangle*, more bitter than sweet. This double echo to the "open triangular space" in chapter VII, suggests a triangle of words.

Moreover, the "triangle shape" and the "triangular well" in chapter XII counterbalance two key details in chapter V: "a larger triangular piece of dark blue cloth [...] the triangular piece of broadcloth" (89-90) found by Chief Inspector Heat among Stevie's remains. The haunting power of these remains contaminates the space of the town itself. Conrad suggests the illusion of limits between extreme opposites (men and town, death and life, darkness and colours, etc.).

The counterbalancing of these details in chapters V and XII is a sort of frame for the link between the "triangular space" in chapter VII and the "overcoat" of Mr. Verloc, "hanging in a triangle on each side of the chair" (183) in chapter IX. This "triangle" could be the most perfect and terrifying symbol of this writing process. And in chapters VII and XII, the name of "Breet Street," with its triangular space, has probably been chosen by Conrad for the suggestiveness of its letters, the repetition of "reet" figuring the two sides of a triangle, crowned by three letters: Br/S.

In chapters VII and XII ("The fruiterer at the corner had put out the blazing glory of [...] orange and lemons" [273]), a simple assortment of colours (or of fruit) could be the poetical expression of the conflict between the avatars of mythical Father and Son. This enigma, which involves all the aspects of "the symmetry of form," is centred on the figure of the victim, embodied by Stevie. If Verloc has let the innocent Stevie carry the fatal bomb, he himself is animated by an unconscious drive at parricide, which probably is *the* key to the calamities in our civilization. This desire of parricide is wonderfully conveyed by the secret link (but apart from Stevie), in chapters VIII and XI, of the "orange" cheeks of Winnie's mother, and of Verloc's feelings about the trouble caused by "Stevie's violent disintegration," seen by Verloc as a slip on an orange peel! In chapter VIII: "her big cheeks glowed with an orange hue under a black and mauve bonnet. [...] It was a complexion that under the influence of a blush would take on an orange tint" (159). And in chapter XI: "It was like slipping on a bit of orange peel in the dark and breaking your leg" (236). Slipping on Mrs. Verloc's face? From the word “cheek” to the word “peel,” and from the word “blush” to the word “breaking,” a link is established, a link which reveals the effects of the “founding murder” in our culture.

I shall end with Winnie, when her tragic posture in chapter IX reflects symmetrically the “violent” sitting motion of the Assistant Commissioner of Police in chapter VI. Conrad is abrupt in this phallic image of Winnie paralysed by the horror of Verloc’s conduct and its consequences:

> She sat rigidly erect *in the chair* [...]. The palms of *her hands* were pressed convulsively [...] against the forehead, as though the skin had been a mask which she was ready to tear off *violently*. The perfect immobility of her pose expressed the agitation of rage and despair, all the potential *violence* of tragic passions, better than any shallow display of shrieks, with the beating of a distracted head against the walls, could have done. (212; emphasis added)

Winnie, here, embodies all the effects of the contradiction, whose role in the foundation of the sacred might well be very nicely suggested by the word “palms” (of her hands), or by the mention of the “temples” against which, later, Winnie is going to press her hands.

This situation in chapter IX can remind us of a few sentences in chapter VI, where the image of the Assistant Commissioner of Police worried by his rival, the Chief Inspector, seems to express the agony of the creator at grips with the urgent necessity of exorcizing the contradiction in his art:

> he sat down violently. “Here I am stuck in a litter of paper,” he reflected, with unreasonable resentment, “supposed to hold all the threads in my hands, and yet I can but hold what is put in my hand, and nothing else. And they can fasten the other ends of the threads where they please.” (115)

The androgynous implication created by the association of the phrases “he sat down” and “she sat rigidly” (chapters VI and IX), is too obvious to be commented on. More interesting, the words concerning Winnie’s temper: “violently,” “all the potential violence,” are a repeated echo of the words: “he sat down violently.” This is another reason for the taste of the author of such a novel for triangular symbols. The mention of the "hands" of Winnie echoes the inner thoughts of the Assistant Commissioner of Police: "in my hands [...] in my hands." But we must add that chapter IX ends with a second mention of "Mrs. Verloc's left hand," adorned by her golden wedding ring (213). I could insist on the shifting of singular and plural ("hand[s]"), expressing the power of "Number and Harmony," alluded to by Rimbaud in his most famous letter (15 May 1871). The sense of this textual wedding of Winnie and the Assistant Commissioner is shadowed by the "agitation of rage and despair" which makes of Winnie a *reflection* of the Assistant Commissioner: "he reflected, with unreasonable resentment." The "unreasonable resentment" of this reasonable man resonates with the justified rage of this feminine dementia crisis.

We, the readers, have some doubt about the difference, or even the existence, of these characters. In the same paragraph in chapter VI, the second sentence is highly relevant: "Suddenly his suspicion was awakened" (115). The "threads in my hands," in the sixth sentence, could represent the perplexity of Conrad himself, the artist, marvellously gifted for measured forms, but made anxious or at least suspicious by the darker meaning of Harmony. These literary preoccupations are vaguely suggested in the next sentence (or paragraph): "He raised his head, and turned towards his subordinate a long, meagre face with the accentuated features of an energetic Don Quixote. 'Now what is it you've got up your sleeve?" (89). *Don Quixote* has been quoted by René Girard as an example of our corrupted desires, whose power and effects are deeply questioned by Conrad in his own literary field.

I have tried to show that the plot in *The Secret Agent* achieves an acute reflection on the meaning of art, and especially on the meaning of literature. Many critics perceive the interest of the "structure" of the novel in two parts, expressing as a whole a "metaphysical analysis of evil."[11] But the historical or sociological issues of such readings tend to obscure the metaphysical meaning of the structure itself, considered (in my own pages) in its most subtle forms. In *The Secret Agent*, perhaps more deeply than in any other of Conrad's works, a game of words, at many levels of the text, gives form to the ambiguity of the human condition: we are either condemned to the violence of Totality (symbolized by Stevie's remains), or we are trying to find a path for Unity (ironically symbolized by the Observatory). For us, with our perplexed eyes, the difference between Totality and Unity is not easy to see. Conrad's writing seems to provoke in our minds an awareness of this unresolved problem.

NOTES

[1] "The artist, then, like the thinker or the scientist, seeks the truth and makes his appeal. [...] the thinker plunges into ideas, the scientist into facts" (*NN* xi). These words from the Preface to *The Nigger of the "Narcissus"* can remind us of the ideas expressed by Rimbaud in his most famous letter, written in 1871 – but Conrad, in 1897, could not have read this letter, published in 1912.

[2] The "alchemic" way to celebrate this Unity could be the hidden stake of "Heart of Darkness" with the Buddha, at the beginning and at the end of the novel. But in the first chapter of "Heart of Darkness," the most remarkable, and most repulsive, symbol of the conciliation of contraries, is the coast: "smiling, frowning, [...] grand, mean, insipid, or savage" (*YS* 60).

[3] See his letter to Ford, 23 April 1902 (*CL* 2: 409), or the pages published by Conrad in the *New York Times "Saturday Review,"* 2 Aug. 1902 (*CL* 2: 348-49).

[4] In "Heart of Darkness," the Harlequin, obsessed with Kurtz, is an incarnation of this dangerous mimicry.

[5] Earlier, Avrom Fleishman considered Stevie's circles as an "emblem of moral freedom" (205); Leon Guilhamet underlines their "too-obvious" symbolism of perfection (145).

[6] For example, we might think of the diagrams in Towson's book in "Heart of Darkness." "Heart of Darkness" is exemplary too for its staging of the problems attached to literary creation and its questioning of the foundations of religious tradition, not so obvious in *The Secret Agent* (see note 5).

[7] The presence of the Bible in Conrad has been shown by Dwight Hilliard Purdy. "Ironic New Testament parallels" can be found in many novels of Conrad (Steiner 75). Conrad's irony toward the Bible can be more discreet in *The Secret Agent*: see the remarks by Sylvère Monod (192).

[8] See Stein 1969-70; Brashers 1969; Lombard 1971.

[9] See Arouimi 2007; 2018.

[10] Here we can think of the coast in "Heart of Darkness"; a mixture of yes and no, that could inspire a certain need of symmetry.

[11] See Kilroy 2018.

WORKS CITED

Arouimi, Michel. *Anticipations littéraires du terrorisme: Rimbaud, Melville, Conrad, Tchékhov, Troyat, Kafka, Camus et Ramuz*. Hermann, 2018.

---. *Les Apocalypses secrètes: Shakespeare, Eichendorff, Rimbaud, Conrad, Claudel, Tchékhov, Ramus, Bosco, Carlo Levi*. L'Harmattan, 2007.

---. *Poétique du récit et mythe du Verbe. Le "Verbe" de Conrad*. Diss. U of Paris XII, 2001.

---. "Rimbaud: une hantise de Conrad." *Joseph Conrad*. Ed. Josiane Paccaud-Huguet and Claude Maisonnat. L'Herne, 2014. 187-89.

Brashers, H. C. "Conrad, Marlow, and Gautama Buddha: on Structure and Theme in 'Heart of Darkness'." *Conradiana* 1 (1969): 63-71.

Dobrinsky, Jean. "From Whisper to Voice: Marlow's Accused Inheritance." *Cahiers Victoriens et Edouardiens* 16 (1982): 77-104.

Fleishman, Avrom. "The Symbolic World of *The Secret Agent*." *English Literary History* 32 (1965): 196-219.

Guilhamet, Leon. "*The Secret Agent* as the Imitation of an Action." *The Polish Review* 20.2/3 (1975): 145-53.

Houen, Alex. *Terrorism and Modern Literature: from Joseph Conrad to Ciaran Carson*. Oxford UP, 2002.

Kerr, Douglas. "Joseph Conrad's Magic Circles." *Essays in Criticism* 53 (2003): 345-63.

Kilroy, Gerard. "*The Secret Agent*: A Far from Simple Tale." *Yearbook of Conrad Studies (Poland)* 13 (2018): 56-64.

Kozak, Wojciech. "Ambivalence in *The Nigger of the 'Narcissus'*." Krajka, *Between Literary Techniques* 215-37.

Krajka. Wiesław. Introduction. Krajka, *Between Literary Techniques* 1-15.

, ed. *Joseph Conrad: Between Literary Techniques and their Messages*. East European Monographs, Maria Curie-Skłodowska UP and Columbia UP, 2010. Vol. 18 of *Conrad: Eastern and Western Perspectives*. Ed. Wiesław Krajka. 32 vols. to date. 1992- .

Lombard, François. "Conrad and Buddhism." *Centre d'Études et de Recherches Victoriennes et Edouardiennes 2: Studies in Joseph Conrad*. Ed. Claude Thomas (1971): 103-12.

Lothe, Jacob. *Conrad's Narrative Method*. 1989. Clarendon, 1991.

Monod, Sylvère, ed. *Conrad: Œuvres III*. Bibliothèque de la Pléiade, 1987.

Pastoureau, Michel. *L'Étoffe du diable, une histoire des rayures et des tissus rayés*. Seuil, 1991. Point Essais.

Purdy, Dwight Hilliard. *Joseph Conrad's Bible*. U of Oklahoma P, 1964.

Rice, Thomas Jackson. "Politics and Prophylactics: *The Secret Agent* and *Under Western Eyes*." Krajka, *Between Literary Techniques* 93-112.

Stein, William Bysshe. "*The Heart of Darkness*: A Bodhisattva Scenario." *Conradiana* 2 (1969-70): 39-52.

Steiner, Joan E. "Modern Pharisees and False Apostles: Ironic New Testament Parallels in Conrad's 'Heart of Darkness'." *Nineteenth-Century Fiction* 37 (1982): 75-90.

Todorov, Tzvetan. "Connaissance du vide." *Poétique de la Prose*. By Todorov. Seuil, 1980. 161-88.

Whibley, Charles. "A Vagabond Poet." *Blackwood's Edinburgh Magazine* 165.1000 (1899): 402-12.

Maria Paola Guarducci,
Roma Tre University,
Rome, Italy

(Un)Familiar Ground. European Domestic Dramas in the Fiction of Joseph Conrad

When dealing with Joseph Conrad's representation of cultures and peoples in his works it is very common to find extensive analyses of how he portrays the Other, this being an extra-European subject. Since Chinua Achebe's provocative 1974 attack on "Heart of Darkness,"[1] Conrad's negative representation of non-Western subjects has become a critical cliché in postcolonial studies; taken for granted, it has often steered the readings of this topic in his works in forced directions. As a matter of fact, since the author's scepticism and implicit disapproval of the European colonial enterprise are also undeniable and acknowledged, the two aspects provide a contradictory critical breeding ground: on the one hand Conrad would seem to be a "thoroughgoing racist" (Achebe 11), while on the other he could be considered one of the first critics of imperialism.[2] As Edward Said pointed out with crystal clarity in his *Culture and Imperialism*, Conrad was indeed among the first to recognize European colonialism's violence and rapacity and to write about them (20-35). While we could to a certain extent agree with Achebe that *his* Africa (or any of the many non-European countries Conrad wrote about) is portrayed as "the other world" (2), we are also entitled to disagree with the Nigerian writer's following assumption according to which this other world equals "the antithesis of Europe and therefore of civilization" (2). On the contrary, Conrad caught Europe in its crisis and was sharp enough to see the failure of its humanism *vis-à-vis* colonialism (Collits 34). Although Achebe admits that "Conrad saw and condemned the evil of colonial exploitation" (19), he also claims that he was unaware of its deep racism. The fact that Conrad's supposed falsification of non-Western cultures may be considered a *fait accompli* in literary criticism has little to do with Conrad himself: it is rather the outcome of a selective and detrimental reading of his works which stems from Manichean interpretations that still haunt the Anglo-Polish writer's output, such as we/they, here/there, black/white, men/women, culture/nature, civilization/wilderness, Europe/rest of the world, centre/periphery, etc. If we broaden the context and complicate our reading of his oeuvre, leaving fixed oppositions aside, we can see that the writer's depiction of, generically speaking, Western Europeans is by no means more edifying than that of his inscrutable when not unreliable, generically speaking, Africans (to limit ourselves to Achebe's remarks).

In this essay I will concentrate my analysis on some works Conrad set in Europe and whose characters are European. I will discuss how in these texts the author provides an uncompassionate portrayal of one of European culture's strongholds: the family, that is the microcosm on which Western society (and Victorian Britain) was built. The topic of family dissolution will be explored as it appears in "The Idiots" (1896) and "The Return" (1898),[3] included in his first collection of short stories, *Tales of Unrest* (1898), and in two works of his middle period, namely "Amy Foster" (1901)[4] and *The Secret Agent*, his novel of 1907. In the Author's Note (1919) he added to the 1920 edition of *Tales of Unrest*, Conrad notoriously dismissed "The Idiots" as "an obviously derivative piece of work" (*TU* vii) and "The Return" as "a left-handed production" (viii). However, these two works are particularly relevant to my analysis because they provide the textual space where Conrad started training his literary skills and comprise a precocious ground for the representation of his world, a geography that in *Tales of Unrest* already spanned three of the continents he had experienced at first hand before becoming a professional writer.[5] "Amy Foster" and *The Secret Agent* show, on the other hand, how the author's reflection on the family, a little domain in itself whose efficiency was so important for the late Victorian world he took as his own on becoming a British subject in 1886, still depicts it as constituting the litmus test for society at large and shows how its dissolution produces, as in his previous texts, the same tragic outcomes.

While for the collective imagination of his times Conrad's works fell into the categories of adventure literature and travel writing, especially because he made his literary debut with *Almayer's Folly* (1895) and *An Outcast of the Islands* (1896), it became soon clear that his project was much more ambitious than this made it seem.[6] Conrad's reflections about the mystifying and hypocritical rhetoric of the philanthropic mission by which Europe spoiled the rest of the world, the ideologically fabricated nature of power and the way it corrupts humankind at all latitudes are harboured in his writings, explicitly or implicitly, from the very beginning of his career. It seems to me that in Conrad's oeuvre nothing about Europe and its natives can be read in terms of celebration and that his portrayal of Europe/Europeans as it comes forth in the texts I have selected is deeply troubling. In the works I will discuss, in spite of some scattered and minor references to extra-European countries, nothing speaks of the *exotic*,[7] while everything closely relates to Conrad's biography. "The Idiots" is set in Brittany, where Conrad spent his honeymoon in April/May 1896, "The Return" and *The Secret Agent* in London, a city that always attracted him, and "Amy Foster" in Kent, the area where he lived his last years together with his family. One must also remark that the protagonist of "Amy Foster," Yanko Goorall, is a Polish Carpathian migrant and the story itself relies very much on Conrad's Eastern European background, to the point of being defined by Nico Israel "a precise register of Conrad's private grief" (*Outlandish* 29).[8] Said, in his seminal *Joseph Conrad and the Fiction of Autobiography*, has also underlined some common traits the Anglo-Polish author shares not only with Yanko but also with the second internal narrator of the story, a Marlow-like figure, a former adventurer called Kennedy. We can therefore say with Olha Bandrovska that by merging France, Britain, and Poland in his writings Conrad managed "to create a holistic picture of diversified civilizational interactions" (121), and somehow succeeded in representing "the spiritual experience of all Western civilization" (111) – a spiritual experience, as we will see, that glorifies neither the place nor its autochthonous peoples.

Before proceeding, it is useful to underline again that Conrad's depiction of non-Western characters is historically informed by the late Victorian ethos that objectified and vilified first nations in order to control, manipulate, and exploit them, and, last but not least, justify colonialism and its misconduct. In *Culture and Imperialism* Said himself allows that the implicit imperialism of "Heart of Darkness" is related to the "inevitable and unavoidable" (26) epistemology at work in the final years of the nineteenth century. On the contrary, most of Conrad's unsparing descriptions of Europeans, based on his deep concerns about notions of class, race, and gender (Schneider 4), were countertrend in his time and do not demand a similar explanatory context. A permanent exile, Conrad soon developed a relativism that made him an unaware pioneer in a discourse whose implications were to branch out only much later on. As John Peters has observed, it was because of this relativism that the author distanced himself from late Victorian realism in favour of a linguistic, stylistic, and theoretical search that could accommodate more than one truth at a time to account for reality, achieving that kind of writing from which Modernism, soon to became prominent in the British literary scene, developed (9).

Conrad's (and his family's) sufferings under the Russian Empire, his first-hand knowledge of non-Western cultures as a seaman, and his own experience as a foreigner wherever he settled played a significant part in the shaping of his perspectives on peoples, cultures, and places and also in his own sense of estrangement. It is not surprising to read how he describes himself in a letter to his friend John Galsworthy dated August 22, 1903:

> I feel myself strangely growing into a sort of outcast. A mental and moral outcast. I hear of nothing – I think of nothing – I reflect upon nothing – I cut myself off – and with all that I can just only keep going or rather keep on logging from one wretched story to another – and always deeper in the mire. (*CL* 3: 54)

Significantly, "mire" recurs in the works here discussed: as metaphor (the stalemate at the heart of "The Return" as well as at the end of *The Secret Agent*, when Winnie's anxiety leads her to commit suicide), and as a mass of natural, sticky matter (Ploumar's muddy roads, the mix of sand, water and seaweed that makes Susan's final escape difficult in "The Idiots," the mud that often covers Yanko in "Amy Foster," etc.).

"The Idiots" and "The Return" belong to Conrad's first attempts at short fiction (undertaken partly, it seems, for financial reasons) which he made in a literary style inspired by his masters. As Yves Hervouet has successfully shown, "The Idiots" in particular works as a *pastiche* wherein Gustave Flaubert, Guy de Maupassant, and Emile Zola merge,[9] while "The Return," for which many critics point to Henry James and Henrik Ibsen, is equally indebted to *Bel-Ami* and *Une soir* (32, 52). "Amy Foster" as well has, among others, French sources: in particular Flaubert's *Madame Bovary* and *Un cœur simple* (76), and *The Secret Agent* is generally acknowledged to be the most Dickensian among Conrad's novels, though also indebted to Zola, James, Ivan Turgenev, and Fyodor Dostoevsky (97).

"The Idiots" deals with a couple of rich but unlucky French farmers, the Bacadous. The natural landscape plays a crucial role in this story, anticipating the tragic outcome from its very first lines, where we read of the sun shining violently over meagre trees that point their dry branches at the sky, an image which brings to mind Dante's forest of suicides. The plot focuses on the farmers' preoccupation with the land and plays on the concept of its fertility as the cause of human anxiety about the need to ensure a lineage to take care of it.[10] In this story, the wife's final rebellion against her husband's obsession over patrilineal hierarchy results in the violent deaths of both of them. No one dies, although death is a central metaphor, in "The Return," a novella about the urban upper middle class claustrophobically set in a London house where Alvan Hervey and his nameless wife live and where their *ménage* disintegrates. Here the author explores the Victorian urban bourgeoisie's conformism, which is defended by passive aggressiveness and rests upon compromises and severe rules about behaviour, belonging, and reputation. "Amy Foster" goes back to the countryside setting of "The Idiots" with its tragic atmosphere, although this time the places and characters, with the exception of its protagonist, are English. In this story too the landscape is relevant and the English coastal villages are depicted in their "defensive" (Carabine 189) isolation which turns out to be also the main metaphor of the tale. As in the other stories, the couple is doomed to a catastrophic albeit predictable failure, due to the local people's rooted lack of trust and empathy towards a foreigner. In spite of its subtitle – *A Simple Tale* – *The Secret Agent* stages a complicated political storyline involving a number of immigrants living in London, at the time an indulgent asylum for radicals from all over Europe, and leading to a bomb explosion whose side-effect, the accidental killing of the protagonist's mentally disabled brother-in-law, provokes the sudden collapse of the Verloc couple/family. Both the streets of the intricate metropolis and the different internal settings with their multiple secrets (largely Verloc's home and shop) play a crucial role in this sophisticated and multi-layered novel.

At first sight the four plots seem to share only, in very general terms and in very different ways, the topic of the dissolution of a couple/family in a European context. This dissolution is due to peculiar dysfunctions and events respectively associated with the specificities of the characters depicted, which also bring to light, in all four cases, a criticism of the social classes and the cultures/societies to which the characters/couples belong: environments whose mechanisms work in favour of their own preservation at the expense of the individuals. All the stories hide Darwinian subtexts: a struggle for the survival of the fittest whereby the society with its rules and hypocrisy seems to take the place of the harsh and merciless nature described by science (Niland 60; White 15).

In "The Idiots," Conrad's meticulous lens focuses on the world of French farmers, outlining how their visceral relationship with the land is totally unromantic and, if anything, based upon money, the real driving force behind what was once idealized, in art and literature, as the rural way of life. Here, an abusive husband, the anticlerical republican Jean-Pierre Bacadou, ends up being killed by his wife Susan when he tries to rape her in a selfish attempt to father a fit and vigorous male heir after they have had four mentally disabled children who are unable to take care of the land, which has been owned by his family for generations. As Ellen Burton Harrington has observed, the Bacadous are both parents of unsuitable children and unsuitable children themselves, because they got married and removed the patriarch who was too old to do the job, according to Jean-Pierre, without waiting for his natural death as the local customs prescribe (18). A creepy setting, where "[t]he heavens above the house seemed to be draped in black rags, held up here and there by pins of fire" ("The Idiots," *TU* 72), hosts the tragedy of the Bacadou couple. After submitting to Jean-Pierre's will for a long time, Susan rebels against her social/marital role as child bearer and kills her husband with a pair of scissors in a fit of fear and desperation. She then runs away, finding no support from anyone including her cynical mother, Madame Levaille, an influential businesswoman in that conservative, almost feudal area. In the end the young woman falls (or throws herself) from a cliff and dies while running away from a man, significantly "an old African soldier" (83) named Millot, who apparently was trying to help her. If it is true that Susan is hallucinating in mistaking Millot for her dead husband, it is also worth emphasizing that Millot's attempted rescue is in fact a chauvinist challenge that he accepts "laughing, swearing meaninglessly out of pure satisfaction, pleased with himself for having run down that fly-by-night" (83). A chase more than an attempt to help, as Daniel R. Schwarz has remarked (114), this act, which is performed by Millot with no empathy, and in which Susan still plays the part of a potential prey/victim of another benign colonizer, could not realistically lead to a happy ending. In Conrad's fiction the portrayal of women as sexual prey trying to reject the marriage plot and patriarchal values is not infrequent and these women all, more or less, succumb to the unchanging structure of the Victorian system, like Winnie

Verloc in *The Secret Agent* but also like Mrs. Hervey in "The Return," who is unable to leave her husband and eventually returns to resume a domestic *ménage* where, she knows very well, she has no power, no initiative, no freedom whatsoever.[11]

Although death seems to be the inevitable epilogue to this French domestic drama where there is no trace of hope, it is plausible that when Conrad wrote "The Idiots" he did not have in mind a tragedy *tout court*, as the story has a caustic coda which contradicts the idea that its ending is incomplete and does not offer any retrospective illumination (Erdinast-Vulcan 186). The last scene of the story portrays the idiots' grandmother, the plot's *éminence grise*, feigning compunction at the idea that her only daughter, because she committed suicide, will not be buried in consecrated ground. Her friend and ally, the Marquis de Chavanes, though, is ready to help her out by providing a different version of Susan's death as long as his Breton *tribe* is not further disturbed by the Bacadous, political troublemakers:

> "It is very sad. You have all my sympathy. I shall speak to the Curé. She was unquestionably insane, and the fall was accidental. Millot says so distinctly. Good-day, Madame."
>
> And he trotted off, thinking to himself: "I must get this old woman appointed guardian of those idiots, and administrator of the farm. It would be much better than having here one of those other Bacadous, probably a red republican, corrupting my commune." ("The Idiots," *TU* 85)

Laurence Davies has underlined the double ending of "The Idiots," pointing out that Susan's mother has the final say, although not the final judgment (26). The epilogue portrays, though, a clash of the titans in which none of the survivors is innocent: not Susan's mother (and family values), not the Marquis (and politics), not even the priest (and the Catholic Church), in that they will all be involved in the *editing* of the young woman's death for posterity. "All's well that ends well" seems to be the highly ironical epilogue of "The Idiots," expressed by Conrad through the Marquis' indirect point of view. The peasants can keep on being superstitious, the workmen can keep on wasting their salaries getting drunk at their employer's shop (ironically, again, Madame Levaille's) where they burst out in gross performances of male aggressiveness, and the idiot children can continue to hang around the fields where the anonymous internal narrator first spotted them as a sarcastic visual comment on this parody of the survival of the fittest. There is no justice, no God, no transcendent meaning, as Hugh Epstein has remarked (220). In all honesty, this collapse of a couple/family under the pressure of a rather primitive Breton society does not look like a flattering portrayal of European natives or European civilization.

The combination of social and personal incompetence, collective responsibility, individual faults and fatalities in "The Idiots" brings to mind "Amy Foster," which shares with "The Idiots" not only its tragic aspects but also an ironic touch. The eponymous (anti-)heroine, although she is not the protagonist of the story, is described in the first scenes by the local doctor, Kennedy, who remarks how "[i]t's enough to look at the red hands hanging at the end of those short arms, at those slow, prominent brown eyes, to know the inertness of her mind" ("Amy Foster," *TS* 107). Kennedy later admits, as Marlow does of the African people in "Heart of Darkness," that she represents "an inscrutable mystery" (109) to him. According to Kennedy's report, Amy looks very shy, has a light stammer when she speaks, is short sighted and even though she is tender with everyone, she seems to be more comfortable with animals than with human beings; locals consider her stupid. Harrington underlines how the doctor's description suggests some traits of degeneration, which might indicate that she does not deserve the exceptional Yanko (16), that is, the actual protagonist of the story. If the depiction of this local girl relies upon the scientific remarks of a doctor, which are yet insufficient to account for her mystery, Yanko, a foreigner, is described at the beginning through the point of view of the locals who, Kennedy relates, reject him right away, classifying his body and manners according to stereotypes. A Polish migrant who finds himself in England after the German ship that was to take him to America sinks off the coast of Kent, Yanko is left at the mercy of the inhospitable Kentish communities whose coarse members consider him an alien. They define him "a 'horrid-looking man' […] a hairy sort of gipsy fellow […] a funny tramp [...] an unfortunate dirty tramp […] some nondescript and miry creature […] one mass of mud and filth from head to foot" ("Amy Foster," *TS* 118-20). We will later learn, from Kennedy's enlightened perspective, that Yanko was actually very good looking. If the locals describe him as "babbling aloud in a voice that was enough to make one die of fright" (119), producing "burst of rapid, senseless speech" and "jabbering in a most discomposing manner" (120), the doctor informs us he addressed the people politely in his mother tongue, could sing very well and after a relatively short time became fluent in English. As Wiesław Krajka has pointed out, Yanko is superior to his English hosts from all points of view, but he is "different" ("Between Mental Spaces" 155-58). Difference implies an excess of identity rather than a lack of it; therefore Yanko is always visible among the uniform mass of locals and his attention-getting presence disturbs the English community which reacts with different degrees of violence towards him. This violence they justify as defensive, as if they were dealing with a threatening monster.[12] No matter how helpless and harmless Yanko is when he lands in Kent, the locals feel entitled to lock him up "like a bear in a cage" ("Amy Foster," *TS* 120) and comically call for alleged experts to scrutinize him and guess his origins. Only Amy *fosters* Yanko, to the point of falling in love with and marrying him. His union with an indigenous woman, though, does not make him accepted by the other locals who keep on linking him to either fauna or flora, that is, to wildlife. The mother of his child, Amy, also eventually fails him and by running away during a feverish attack in which he asks for water in his mother tongue, leaves him to die alone in their isolated and cold home.[13] Scared, incapable of even guessing the mysterious word – language can indeed be an unbridgeable gap – Amy conforms at last to the pattern of her fellow villagers. On the other hand, she had already started detaching herself from her man, once again according to Kennedy's report, when he was trying to establish a bond with their baby singing and talking to him in his mother tongue.

Amy is substantially silent for most of the story and this allows us to think, following Myrtle Hooper's analysis of "Amy Foster," that there is an inarticulate suffering on her part that neither Kennedy nor the first narrator are interested in exploring (64). It is true, though, that whatever the case, England is Yanko's *heart of darkness*, because although he has tried to absorb the way of life from the people and the place (including their language), he is not ready to give up his culture, a culture the English are not interested in knowing and sharing with him, as Nathalie Martinière has observed (72). Some details about the composition of "Amy Foster" are, I think, of help here. The work was written and published ten years after Conrad's crucial trip to Congo (1890), from which he had come back traumatized, carrying the material for his most controversial short novel on Otherness. "Heart of Darkness" marks the end of the time when the empire could be naively seen and philanthropically justified, but it is also a text where Africans (the Others *par excellence* in Conrad's canon) stand out as an unfathomable mass. A lot can be said, instead, about the English portrayed in "Amy Foster," written in the same years and also dealing with Otherness. The story apparently has nothing to do, strictly speaking, with colonization, but it ends up being a parody of a colonial text, "a colonial story in disguise" (Ruppel 130) which sheds a disturbing light on the British culture that ruled the waves. If "Heart of Darkness" does not depict Europeans outside the Belgian and British middle- and lower-middle classes, "Amy Foster" ventures into the peripheral world of English peasants: not enlightened, not equipped with culture, yet equally trapped in the mechanisms of power, authority, and discrimination.

The plot of "The Idiots" unrolls in the open air of the Northern French countryside while that of "Amy Foster" takes place in a secluded part of Kent; both stories suggest the moral bankruptcy of the equally selfish environments where they are set (Schwarz 113). The setting of "The Return" is quite the opposite, but the novella's epilogue, as we will see, has similar pessimistic implications. Although the first scene takes place in a London West End train station from which a mass of people flows, heading home at the end of a working day, the great part of the story is set in the (disputably) elegant rooms of Mr. and Mrs. Hervey's dwelling. From the crowded metropolitan open space, packed with anonymous rushing individuals who all look alike, Conrad progressively narrows the focus to Alvan Hervey, following his mechanical walk back home. Once the door of his house is shut behind him we will never leave this oppressive and cold location of dark wood, red carpets, marble statues, and heavy curtains reminiscent of a funeral parlour. Indeed the house acts as the grave in which Alvan and his wife bury their dead relationship (although one is legitimately allowed to ask whether it was ever alive), after she had unsuccessfully tried to leave him with a letter and he, to the reader's surprise, moves out at last, unable to come to terms with the mystery his wife in particular and women in general have come to represent.

Alvan is depicted as a member of the British middle class, conforming blindly to a code of behaviour deemed proper only because it is perceived as *natural*, that is, a set of inherited rules that because of their endurance through time (their survival) no one is allowed to discuss. Needless to say, Darwin's end-of-the-century vulgate is heard again:

> "Life is a serious matter. If you don't conform to the highest standards you are no one – it's a kind of death. [...] From a child you had examples before your eyes – you could see daily the beauty, the blessings of morality, of principles...." [...]
>
> "Rigid principles – adherence to what is right," he finished after a pause.
>
> "What is right?" she said, distinctly, without uncovering her face. "Your mind is diseased!" he cried, upright and austere. "Such a question is rot – utter rot. Look round you – there's your answer, if you only care to see. Nothing that outrages the received beliefs can be right. Your conscience tells you that. They are the received beliefs because they are the best, the noblest, the only possible. They survive...." ("The Return," *TU* 157)

Conrad seems to emphasize here a confusion on the part of this austere representative of the British bourgeoisie between a cultural code, which is changeable and disputable, and its interpretation according to the late-Victorian reading of Darwin, whereby any status quo is perceived as natural rather than cultural, which means it produces the best of possible worlds, in this case also the most correct from a moral point of view: "the received beliefs." As in "The Idiots" Pierre Bacadou was haunted by his own anxiety, thinking he had to behave as his male predecessors had done and ensure patrilineal ownership of the land (Maisonnat, "The Venomous Sibillation" 56-57), Alvan too is a victim of his own tragic narcissism, due to which he is also pathologically unable even to relate to himself, let alone to face a marital crisis as an adult would. "The Return" is indeed not so much about the Herveys' crisis as about the tension it generates in a man's mind, a tension he does not know how to deal with (Bonney 85). It is telling to remark how Alvan's perceptions of time and space suddenly alter when he notices – reflected in one of the mirrors – the letter his wife has left him on the dressing table. The mere sight of what he perceives as an anomaly hitting, unannounced, his stable surroundings shakes him; without needing to read its content "he experienced suddenly a staggering sense of insecurity, an absurd and bizarre flash of a notion that the house had moved a little under his feet" ("The Return," *TU* 125). The letter is an ominous item (Birdseye 173). It is the eccentric unexpected, breaking through the irreproachable life of this aspiring Victorian gentleman. Once the truths of a loveless marriage, of a woman who has fallen for someone else and has left have entered Alvan's so far well-ordered life, he is no longer in charge. His wife's behaviour opens up a stream of emotions he does not know how to process. He is overwhelmed by a new set of feelings that subverts his inner being and his relationship with himself: "He was disgusted with himself, with the loathsome rush of emotion breaking through all the reserves that guarded his manhood" ("The Return," *TU* 130). There is no way back for Alvan; even when his wife comes back and the marriage could be resumed, he is the one who cannot return to his old, unaware self. For a narcissist, a repenting wife is not really an issue.

There are no authorial comments on Alvan's puzzling final departure, but Conrad provides many instances of his schizophrenic nature throughout the text. Victorian novels and culture may well encourage Alvan's deep concern about women as double beings – he thinks "[t]he woman's a monster" (129) – whose enigma is impossible to decode, but duplicity, in a Jekyll/Hyde fashion (R. L. Stevenson's novel had come out twelve years before "The Return"), is definitely embodied by Alvan Hervey himself. At the beginning of the story, when he has just entered the dressing room, we are told of a myriad of mirrors multiplying his image in a series of (so far) reassuring doubles:

> The room was empty, of course; but, as he stepped in, it became filled all at once with a stir of many people; because the strips of glass on the doors of wardrobes and his wife's large pier-glass reflected him from head to foot, and multiplied his image into a crowd of gentlemanly and slavish imitators, who were dressed exactly like himself; had the same restrained and rare gestures; who moved when he moved, stood still with him in an obsequious immobility, and had just such appearances of life and feeling as he thought it dignified and safe for any man to manifest. (124)

In one way or the other, Alvan is used to being among his peers: uniformity reassures him. The passage above follows the preamble of the story, where Conrad pictures him walking among the commuters: an army of men whose "backs appeared alike – almost as if they had been wearing a uniform; their indifferent faces were varied but somehow suggested kinship, like the faces of a band of brothers" (118). Celia M. Kingsbury has pointed out how conformity, good behaviour, and the suppression of truth were the principles characterizing life in late Victorian London (32), a code Alvan never questioned and always complied with. The trauma represented by his wife's letter brings his split self to the surface. The letter, as an individual, original, startling, unforeseen, and improper item, breaks the delusive integrity of this man and the security of his home. It changes the nature of his reflected images from a group of obliging and well-behaved gentlemen, similar to the commuters in the first scene, into a horde of maddening intruders he does not acknowledge as his own projections. It is the beginning, as Benedetta Bini has observed (177n18), of Alvan Hervey's process of dissociation: "In the shock of that startling thought he looked up, and saw to the left, to the right, in front, men sitting far off in chairs and looking at him with wild eyes – emissaries of a distracted mankind intruding to spy upon his pain and his humiliation" ("The Return," *TU* 129).

As in *The Strange Case of Dr Jekyll and Mr Hyde*, Alvan's dissociation from himself cannot happen without affecting the body: "Something unknown, withering and poisonous, had entered his life, passed near him, touched him, and he was deteriorating" (130). Not even when his wife is back is Alvan capable of recovering his integrity; on the contrary, in the dialogue that follows the scene of Mrs. Hervey's return, Alvan's split self surfaces: "he heard his own voice with the excited and sceptical curiosity with which one listens to actors' voices speaking on the stage in the strain of a poignant situation" (144). If the wife is at last ready to go back to their previous routine in spite of the manifest breakage in their relationship, Alvan cannot.

Since Victorian couples and families represented a microcosm whose propriety and high standards stood for the well-being of the macrocosm (by extension the British nation and its empire), the Herveys and the way Conrad describes their collapse jeopardize the idea of a functional society made of functional people. Once again, in "The Return," with its prototypical characters and their failure as emotional human beings, European natives can hardly provide upstanding models.

If an unexpected event brings to light the Herveys' double nature, if women can regress as Susan does in "The Idiots," if foreignness can be such an issue in England as it is in "Amy Foster," *The Secret Agent*, initially a short story titled "Verloc," is the novel where duplicity, regression, and isolation are most evident. As in the other texts discussed, home is not a safe haven in *The Secret Agent*, either. Wendy Moffat has rightly remarked how in Conrad's fiction marriage and home are always sites of violence (467). It is a latent violence, at work beneath the apparently quiet surface of things: it can (or cannot) occur any time without warning.

Falsehood dwells in London's heart: from its macrosystem to its smallest cell, home. Adolf Verloc's identity as a secret agent working for the (possibly) Russian government is ignored by his wife as well as by his comrades. In this novel the *ménage* of the Verloc couple works as a financial transaction, similar, if seen from the outside, to the one keeping together Alvan Hervey and his wife: an impersonal agreement established on a well calculated balance between costs and advantages, functional for everyone's individual needs, liable to go to pieces if one of its contractors, knowingly or unknowingly, withdraws. In this text, too, Conrad subverted and rejected the Victorian happy marriage plot. Adolf has found in Winnie a young and pleasing wife who, without asking too many questions, unknowingly provides him the appropriate cover for his secret activity as an agent, is available for sex in the measure he desires and is responsible for his home and official business, a stationary shop which is in fact a pornography shop where a group of anarchists gather. For her part, in order to ensure a livelihood for her sick mother and her disabled brother, Winnie has accepted this loveless but economically secure marriage and assumed the role of a Victorian domestic angel. Conrad makes clear that Winnie, like many women with no means at that time, had no choice if she wanted to provide shelter to the members of her own family, who had survived, as she had, the harassment and abuse of an alcoholic father and were not, nor would ever be, autonomous and self-sufficient. Women, like foreigners, are lonely beings often exposed to the pervasive violence of the system and Conrad does not use his customary irony when describing Winnie's sufferings both as a child and, later on, as an adult (Nadelhaft 78, 100). According to Harrington, the author sympathizes with women characters such as Susan and Winnie, whose ultimate suicides underline the hopelessness of their rebellion against the patriarchal figures that have betrayed them (32). In both texts, according to her, there is a comic twist in the way the uxoricide is presented, as the two women kill their husbands in an "exaggerated refusal to consent to marital sex" (33), although an aggravating factor for Winnie is the discovery of Adolf's involvement in her brother's death. Both Susan and Winnie use household utensils to get rid of their men, thus manifesting the uneasiness of their position within the domestic sphere: "there are things no woman can bear" ("The Idiots," *TU* 81) is Susan's thought and self-justification when running away. By stabbing Adolf with the carving knife she is supposed to use to cut the roast, Winnie in particular, as Anne Luyat has pointed out (108), acts as one who "[i]nto that plunging blow [...] had put all the inheritance of her immemorial and obscure descent, the simple ferocity of the age of caverns, and the unbalanced nervous fury of the age of bar-rooms" (*SA* 263).

Susan and Winnie also fail to find new protectors and are left with no options but to take their own life, an epilogue always at hand in Conrad's times for fictional women who could not adapt.[14] As in "The Idiots," idiocy is also found in *The Secret Agent* as both a pathological condition and as a figurative representation of the madness characterizing society at the turn of the century. Foreshadowing chaos in an apparently well-organized system such as British society, the target of anarchist and revolutionary plots, *The Secret Agent*, Conrad's only novel to take place entirely in London and set in the year the author became a British subject (1886), is also a *domestic* drama in the sense that it portrays the society Conrad chose for his own in crisis.[15] It is also a cosmopolitan novel where the Western world is caught at an impasse. *The Secret Agent* portrays, with sharp irony, the total incompetence of both the individuals who wish to subvert the system and of those who should prevent this. No revolution is possible where there are no ideas or values and where people ignore each other's identities and objectives. No truth will ever surface from an alleged mystery investigators fail to clarify. Martin Halliwell goes so far as to say that the figure of the idiot Stevie is the symbolic centre of the political intrigue, underlining how unusual it is to see such a fellow living in a proper home rather than being interned, as happened in Victorian and Edwardian London, in a workhouse for poor people or in a psychiatric asylum (315). Although Conrad wrote in a letter to J. B. Pinker dated June 1, 1907, "I don't want the story to be misunderstood as having any sort of social or polemical intention" (*CL* 3: 446), *The Secret Agent* does work as an indirect comment on contemporary Britain both in its international and local dimensions. The centrality of Stevie, the only human being incapable of lies and duplicity, makes him the ironical emblem of a general imbecility affecting the institutions, including the Russian embassy, and their opponents. It is not surprising that the novel was not warmly received by English readers and reviewers and even so that recurring criticism, as Conrad himself remarked in a letter dated October 4, 1907 to Edward Garnett, deals with the author's foreignness: "I've been so cried up of late as a sort of freak, an amazing bloody foreigner writing in English (every blessed review of S.A. had it so – and even yours)" (488).

"The Idiots," "The Return," "Amy Foster," and *The Secret Agent* engage with families and contexts that bring to the fore the upsetting, albeit at times ironical, representation of a varied human landscape filled with ambiguities, injustice, incompetence, anger, resentment, frustration. All set in what was supposed to be the most enlightened and civilized part of the world, these stories, read together, help us putting Conrad's complex and much discussed geography in perspective. It is thanks to his extraordinary way of observing the world from an insider/outsider's perspective that we can gain an unsettling sight of that familiar ground called *home* that one feels more comfortable in not judging.

NOTES

[1] Achebe's talk at the University of Massachusetts became an influential essay included in the 1989 collection entitled *Hopes and Impediments*, from which I quote.

[2] The bibliography on this topic is extensive; therefore, for the purpose of this article, I limited myself to Begam and Valdez Moses; Billy; Collits; Fincham and Hooper; Hamner; Kaplan et al.; Kestner; Peters; Said.

[3] "The Idiots," written in April and May 1896, had come out in October 1896 in *The Savoy*, while "The Return," composed in September 1897, appeared for the first time in *Tales of Unrest*, having earlier been rejected by more than one publisher, Conrad always having refused to publish it in instalments.

[4] Published in instalments in *The Illustrated London News*, "Amy Foster" was included in *Typhoon and Other Stories* in 1903.

[5] This is the contents of *Tales of Unrest*: "Karain: A Memory," "The Idiots," "An Outpost of Progress," "The Return," "The Lagoon." The specular arrangement according to the stories' settings (Asia, Europe, Africa, Europe, Asia) turns out to be very suggestive: Africa is positioned at the "heart" of the collection, framed between settings of its oppressor, Europe, while Malaysia, the setting of Conrad's debut as a writer but also, according to his own words about "The Lagoon" in the Author's Note of 1919, "the end of my first phase, the Malayan phase" (*TU* v), opens and closes the collection.

[6] Richard Ambrosini has retraced this coherent, albeit solitary and at times frustrating path, in *Le storie di Conrad.*

[7] Some have successfully argued that Brittany was considered exotic when Conrad visited it and wrote "The Idiots" (White 7). Although Conrad seemed not to bond easily with the Bretons (Rivoallan 18), France was very much part of his European past and present experiences, as he had lived in Marseilles and was fluent in French. As for "Amy Foster," it is true that Yanko Goorall is considered exotic by the Kentish people but the whole story is about the possibility of his rooting/becoming British in Colebrook through a class upgrading and marriage (that is, through the opportunity of creating a family).

[8] Many critics have discussed Yanko Goorall's origins, which Conrad never explicitly mentions in the story although in his letter of April 2, 1902 to H. D. Davray he defines Yanko "an Austro-Polish highlander" (*CL* 2: 399). For an exhaustive analysis on this subject, see Krajka; Brzozowska-Krajka.

[9] Claude Maisonnat has gone even further by exploring the way in which Conrad's English in this story is hybrid, since French is supposed to be the language of all the verbal exchanges in the tale ("Le français dans l'écriture conradienne").

[10] Hervouet recalls Milton Chaikin's early observations about the relationship between this tale and *La Terre* (1886) by Zola, where the wealth represented by the land provokes a domestic tragedy unveiling the clash between the immortality of the land and the mortality/instability of the humans (34-35).

[11] The only successful exception is Flora de Barral in *Chance* (1913). Both Susan Jones and Harrington explore this issue in their works.

[12] Nico Israel successfully compares Yanko to Dracula, partly because of his Eastern European origins ("Exile, Conrad" 371).

[13] For some interesting analogies between Conrad's biography (including the language switch during a fever) and "Amy Foster" see Herndon.

[14] It is useful to remark again how Flora de Barral in *Chance* is an exception. Sharing the same lack of choices Winnie Verloc suffers from, Flora tries to commit suicide but is saved by Marlow's arrival. Even though everyone fears, with reason, that she might eventually take her own life, she survives and heads for one of the few happy endings in Conrad's novels.

[15] For a historical examination of the social and political turmoil in London at the time of *The Secret Agent*'s setting and publication see Jasanoff.

WORKS CITED

Achebe, Chinua. "An Image of Africa: Racism in Conrad's *Heart of Darkness*." *Hopes and Impediments. Selected Essays*. By Achebe. Doubleday, 1989. 1-20.

Ambrosini, Richard. *Le storie di Conrad. Biografia intellettuale di un romanziere*. Carocci, 2019.

Bandrovska, Olha. "The Civilizational Other in Joseph Conrad's Œeuvre." *Various Dimensions of the Other in Joseph Conrad's Fiction*. Ed. Wiesław Krajka. Maria Curie-Skłodowska UP, Columbia UP, 2020. 109-23. Vol. 29 of *Conrad: Eastern and Western Perspectives*. Ed. Wiesław Krajka. 32 vols. to date. 1992- .

Begam, Richard, and Michael Valdez Moses, eds. *Modernism and Colonialism: British and Irish Literature 1899-1939*. Duke UP, 2007.

Billy, Ted. *A Wildeness of Words. Closure and Disclosure in Conrad's Short Fiction*. Texas Tech UP, 1997.

Bini, Benedetta. "La moglie senza nome" and "Note." Joseph Conrad. *Il ritorno*. Marsilio, 2016. 9-29, 175-80.

Birdseye, Lewis E. "The Curse of Consciousness: A Study of Conrad's 'The Return'." *Conradiana* 9 (1977): 171-78.

Bonney, William. "Contextualizing and Comprehending Joseph Conrad's 'The Return'." *Studies in Short Fiction* 33 (1996): 77-90.

Brzozowska-Krajka, Anna. "Korzeniowski vs Korzeniowski, or a 'Colloquy of Texts': an Instance of Active Intertextuality." Trans. Wiesław Krajka. *A Return to the Roots: Conrad, Poland and East Central Europe*. Ed. Wiesław Krajka. East European Monographs, Maria Curie-Skłodowska U, Columbia UP, 2004. 159-71. Vol. 13 of *Conrad: Eastern and Western Perspectives*. Ed. Wiesław Krajka. 32 vols. to date. 1992- .

---. "Yanko Goorall: a Waxwork from the Wax Museum of Polish Romanticism." Trans. Wiesław Krajka. Krajka, *Joseph Conrad: East European* 165-82.

Carabine, Keith. "'Irreconcilable differences': England as an 'Undiscovered Country' in Conrad's 'Amy Foster'." *The Ends of the Earth. 1876-1918*. Ed. Simon Gatrell. Ashfield P, 1992. 187-204.

Collits, Terry. *Postcolonial Conrad. Paradoxes of Empire.* Routledge, 2005.
Davies, Laurence. "'Don't you think I'm a lost soul?' Conrad's Early Stories in the Magazines." *Conradiana* 41 (2009): 7-28.
Epstein, Hugh. "'Where he is not wanted': Impression and Articulation in 'The Idiots' and 'Amy Foster'." *Conradiana* 23 (1991): 217-32.
Erdinast-Vulcan, Daphna. "'Signifying Nothing': Conrad's Idiots and the Anxiety of Modernism." *Studies in Short Fiction* 33 (1996): 185-96.
Fincham, Gail, and Myrtle Hooper, eds. *Under Postcolonial Eyes: Joseph Conrad after Empire.* U of Cape Town P, 1996.
Halliwell, Martin. *Images of Idiocy. The Idiotic Figure in Modern Fiction and Film.* Ashgate, 2004.
Hamner, Robert D., ed. *Joseph Conrad: Third World Perspectives.* Three Continents P, 1990.
Harrington, Ellen Burton. *Conrad's Sensational Heroines. Gender and Representation in the Late Fiction of Joseph Conrad.* Palgrave Macmillan, 2017.
Herndon, Richard. "The Genesis of Conrad's *Amy Foster.*" *Studies in Philology* 57 (1960): 549-66.
Hervouet, Yves. *The French Face of Joseph Conrad.* Cambridge UP, 1990.
Hooper, Myrtle. "'Oh, I hope he won't talk': Narrative and Silence in 'Amy Foster'." *The Conradian* 21.2 (1996): 51-64.
Israel, Nico. "Exile, Conrad and 'La Différence Essentielle des Races'." *Novel: a Forum on Fiction* 30 (1997): 361-80.
---. *Outlandish: Writing between Exile and Diaspora.* Stanford UP, 2000.
Jasanoff, Maja. *The Dawn Watch. Joseph Conrad in a Global World.* Harper, 2017.
Jones, Susan. *Conrad and Women.* Clarendon P, 1999.
Kaplan, Carola, Peter Lancelot Mallios, and Andrea White, eds. *Conrad in the Twenty-First Century.* Routledge, 2005.
Kestner, Joseph A. *Masculinities in British Adventure Fiction. 1880-1915.* Ashgate, 2010.
Kingsbury, Celia M. "'The novelty of real feelings': Restraint and Duty in Conrad's 'The Return'." *Conradiana* 32 (2000): 31-40.
Krajka, Wiesław. "The Alien in Joseph Conrad's 'Amy Foster' and Jerzy Kosiński's *The Painted Bird.*" *Conrad and Poland.* Ed. Alex S. Kurczaba. East European Monographs, Maria Curie-Skłodowska U, Columbia UP, 1996. 195-215. Vol. 5 of *Conrad: Eastern and Western Perspectives.* Ed. Wiesław Krajka. 32 vols. to date. 1992- .
---. "Between Mental Spaces of the Self and the Other in 'Amy Foster': Dialogue of Culture and Values? Alterity? Hospitality?". *Joseph Conrad's Authorial Self. Polish and Other.* Ed. Wiesław Krajka. East European Monographs, Maria Curie-Skłodowska UP, Columbia UP, 2018. 151-74. Vol. 27 of *Conrad: Eastern and Western Perspectives.* Ed. Wiesław Krajka. 32 vols. to date. 1992- .

---, ed. *Joseph Conrad: East European, Polish and Worldwide*. East European Mognographs, Maria Curie-Skłodowska U, Columbia UP, 1999. Vol. 8 of *Conrad: Eastern and Western Perspectives*. Ed. Wiesław Krajka. 32 vols. to date. 1992- .

---. "The Multiple Identities of Yanko Goorall." Krajka. *Joseph Conrad: East European* 131-64.

Luyat, Anne. "The Wretched Gang: Conrad's Grotesque as a Mirror of European Political Evolution." *Conrad's Europe. Conference Proceedings*. Ed. Andrzej Ciuk and Marcin Piechota. Opole UP, 2005. 105-15.

Maisonnat, Claude. "Le français dans l'écriture conradienne." *Cahiers victoriens et édouardiens* 78 automne. 2013. 1 Sept. 2013. Accessed 11 Aug. 2022. <http://journals.openedition.org/cve/959>.

---. "The Venomous Sibillation of Subdued Words: Literary Heterosis and Generic Crossbreeding in 'The Idiots'." *L'Epoque Conradienne* 28 (2002): 43-59.

Martinière, Nathalie. "Amy Foster ou l'impossible hybridation." *L'Epoque Conradienne* 35 (2009): 67-81.

Moffat, Wendy. "Domestic Violence: the Simple Tale within *The Secret Agent*." *English Literature in Transition. 1880-1920* 37 (1994): 465-89.

Nadelhaft, Ruth L. *Joseph Conrad*. Harvester, 1991.

Niland, Richard. *Conrad and History*. Oxford UP, 2009.

Peters, John G. "'A Voice Crying in the Wilderness': Joseph Conrad's Lasting Legacy." *Yearbook of Conrad Studies (Poland)* 13 (2018): 7-15.

Rivoallan, Anatole. "Joseph Conrad and Brittany." *The Conradian* 8.2 (1983): 14-18.

Ruppel, Richard, "Yanko Goorall in the Heart of Darkness: 'Amy Foster' as Colonialist Text." *Conradiana* 28 (1996): 126-32.

Said, Edward W. *Culture and Imperialism*. Chatto, 1993.

---. *Joseph Conrad and the Fiction of Autobiography*. Harvard UP, 1966.

Schreiner, Lissa. *Conrad's Narrative of Difference. Not Exactly Tales for Boys*. Routledge, 2003.

Schwarz, Daniel R., "Moral Bankruptcy in Ploumar Parish: A Study of Conrad's 'The Idiots'." *Conradiana* 1 (1969): 113-17.

White, Andrea. "'The Idiots': 'A Story of Brittany' under Metropolitan Eyes." *Conradiana* 32 (2000): 4-19.

Agnieszka Setecka,
Adam Mickiewicz University,
Poznań, Poland

The Sociology of Information in Joseph Conrad's *The Secret Agent*

In his essay "The Sociology of Secrecy and of Secret Societies" (1906), Georg Simmel analyses secrecy as "a universal sociological form" (463), which determines human social relations and constitutes the private and the public domain by managing the flow of information. He believes that the play between concealment and revelation, or between desire for knowledge and discretion, shapes "shadings and fortunes of human reciprocities throughout their whole range" (466). As a "sociological technique," secrecy draws a line between those who have access to information and those who are excluded from "the circle of secrecy" (464). Consequently, information acquires a particular value, especially when withheld from others, and a possessor of secrets gains an exceptional powerful position. Private information or "spiritual private property" (454) becomes a commodity which bears on the social standing of the owner and which, like other commodities, can be exchanged for money or power (Marx and Muschert 225). Simmel's essay thus lays (often unacknowledged) grounds for sociology of information, which constitutes the broad framework for the following analysis of *The Secret Agent* (1907) by Joseph Conrad.

This article concentrates on the role of secret information in forming social alliances and on the management of information as a particular form of commodity in *The Secret Agent*. The flow of information in the novel, like the circulation of money, shapes and defines the whole web of dependencies between the characters and, much like the possession of economic capital, it is a source of social distinctions. While the group of anarchists in the novel are brought together by their common secret and vaguely illicit activity, Mr. Verloc, the eponymous secret agent, by selling the information about their activities, does not only betray the group but he also forms an alliance with the unnamed Embassy, where he was, at one time, thought to be a particularly valuable agent. Fearing exposure, he also agrees to become a police informer and passes information to Inspector Heat, thus securing for himself the protection of the police. Since the Inspector is obliged to report to his superiors, and they report further along hierarchical lines, Verloc becomes a node in a web of relations and dependencies. At the same time, the information they possess, invest characters with a form of power that, according to Simmel, can "modify fortunes, to produce surprises, joys, and calamities" and are thus analogous to the power associated with the possession of money (465-66).

The idea of secret information as a commodity and its exchange as "a form of commerce" (Simmel 467) is enhanced in the novel by the fact that Mr. Verloc's activity as an informer appears to be merely an extension of or a variation on his job as a shopkeeper. He starts his cooperation with the Embassy by selling information on French gun design and, when he settles in England, he continues his employment as an informer on the anarchist groups in London. Although he opens a shop merely in order to gain credibility in the circles he is expected to spy on or, as he puts it, "[h]e had gone into trade for no commercial reasons" (*SA* 54), his business proves in many ways analogous to his actual employment. Mr. Verloc tells Mr. Vladimir that he sells "[s]tationery, newspapers" (36), but it is the description of his shop window that is more revealing:

> [it] contained photographs of more or less undressed dancing girls; nondescript packages in wrappers like patent medicines; closed yellow paper envelopes, very flimsy, and marked two-and-six in heavy black figures; a few numbers of ancient French comic publications hung across a string as if to dry; a dingy blue china bowl, a casket of black wood, bottles of marking ink, and rubber stamps; a few books, with titles hinting at impropriety; a few apparently old copies of obscure newspapers, badly printed, with titles like *The Torch*, *The Gong* – rousing titles. (3)

Brian W. Schaffer notes that the "sordid, decaying, and 'secret' pornographic materials" juxtaposed in Verloc's shop window with the "equally secret, decaying, and morally dubious revolutionary tracts" (444), embody "late-Victorian England's pervasive twin-anxieties over uncontrolled sex and politics" as well as satirically represent "the very connection between the pornographic and the revolutionary threat" (443). The semi-pornographic, semi-legal and vaguely improper objects Verloc trades suggest commodified human desires and thus become an example of the "subordination of human life to the imperatives of the commodity system" John Lutz (1) sees as ubiquitous in *The Secret Agent*. Significantly, these objects represent and cater to Verloc's customers' secret inclinations, not to be shared with the larger public, which only emboldens him to demand a "scandalously" high price for them. His clients pay not just for the goods he sells but also for a vague and unspoken promise of keeping their secrets.

Indeed, Verloc's business promises a degree of discretion, which seems to reconcile Winnie to the fact that her private quarters are adjacent to it. She views her parlour as "[e]nsconced cosily behind the shop of doubtful wares, with the mysteriously dim window, and its door suspiciously ajar in the obscure and narrow street" (*SA* 194-95). The "dim windows" convey the impression of constant semi-darkness in the shop, which is further enhanced rather than dispelled by "two gas-jets inside the panes [which] were always turned low, either for economy's sake of for the sake of the customers" (3-4). In addition, Mr. Verloc's reticence, and his wife's "air of unfathomable indifference" (5) and "her unfathomable reserve" (6) imply their ability to keep secrets, which would be much appreciated by the customers frequenting the shop, whose appearance and behaviour suggest their wish to remain anonymous. They were described as "slipping" into the shop or "dodg[ing] in sideways" with "their hands plunged deep in the side pockets of their coats" and having "the collars of their overcoats turned right up to their moustaches" (4), as if not wanting to be noticed or recognized.

Although Verloc seems to be "the anti-model of an anarchist" (Lee 2), and Mr. Vladimir, the First Secretary in the Embassy, finds both Mr. Verloc's "ostensible occupation" (*SA* 36) and his marriage to be a particularly unfitting cover for an agent, it does not prevent Mr. Verloc from believing himself quite successful, especially that he was much appreciated by Mr. Vladimir's predecessor. In fact, selling anarchists' secrets is much more profitable than selling anarchists journals, or, in other words, information is a commodity of much higher value than whatever goods Verloc can sell in the shop. It explains why he "cared but little about his ostensible business" (3), as the reader is informed at the beginning of the novel, and why he continues his work for the Embassy when asked to provoke a bomb outrage. He fears that the termination of his employment as an informer might mark an end to his comfortable life to which he was accustomed. Indeed, when he is finally exposed and realizes he might be forced to depend for his livelihood on his shop, he does not seem very optimistic. Looking at the counter he "ascertain[s] at a glance the number of silver coins in the till. These were but few; and for the first time since he opened his shop he took a commercial survey of its value. This survey was unfavourable" (54). And yet his occupation as a shopkeeper, which he chose "for no commercial reasons" (54), functions very well as a cover for his real business. As the narrator points out, Verloc "had been guided in the selection of this peculiar line of business by an instinctive leaning towards shady transactions, where money is picked up easily" and, even more importantly,

> it did not take him out of his own sphere – the sphere which is watched by the police. On the contrary, it gave him a publicly confessed standing in that sphere, and as Mr. Verloc had unconfessed relations which made him familiar with yet careless of the police, there was a distinct advantage in such a situation. (54)

In addition, his work in the shop and his activity as a secret agent are mutually dependent, since, as Cord-Christian Casper indicates, the trade in pornographic material allows Verloc to maintain the seemingly bourgeois household and "to keep up his semblance of bourgeois respectability" while "[Inspector] Heat enables the continued flow of wares to receive information" so that "the cycle of transgressive wares and confidential information is shown to form a closed system of 'shady transactions' [...] guiding Verloc's very choice of profession" (277).

Mr. Verloc, both in his capacity as the secret agent of the Embassy and in his capacity as a shopkeeper and an anarchist, is thus caught in a complex network of secrets, further complicated by his marriage and his private domestic life. If, as Simmel observes, "[s]ecrecy secures [...] the possibility of a second world alongside of the obvious world, and the latter is most strenuously affected by the former" (462), Mr. Verloc lives simultaneously several lives, the relation between them determined by the interplay of secrecy and openness, or what he considers private and public in each of his roles. Simmel indicates that in the nineteenth century "publicity takes possession of national affairs" so that "the government themselves publish the official data without concealing" (468), while "the individual has gained possibility of more complete privacy" (469). In *The Secret Agent*, however, the boundary between the public affairs and the private lives is blurred: Mark Conroy points to "the effacement of the border between public and private realms" (203), and Cristina Mathews notices that "Conrad collapses the domestic space of the home and the domestic space of the Empire at home" (22). Indeed, "Verloc's shop and home are intimately related" (20), and although the shop seems to be drawn "more toward the home, women, and family than toward the public sphere of commerce" (20), it is the domestic life which might be seen as an extension of Verloc's ostensible business. Lutz claims that *The Secret Agent* exposes the idea of private life as "providing a refuge from the public sphere" since it is "completely subordinated to the laws of consumption and political expediency that dominate the social world" with a "structure [that] remains internal to [the political and economic sphere]" (6) and that "the overlapping reality of commercial exchange and of marriage suggests not two *separate* spheres colliding, but a single space dominated by the imperatives of the market" (5).

Paradoxically, then, it is Verloc's occupation that is shrouded in secrecy which remains the most private aspect of his life unknown even to his wife. Mr. Verloc is very well aware of the significance of secrecy in his line of work, and, as a trader, he knows the worth of the goods he sells, be they pornographic pictures or information on the anarchist circles in London. He also seems to be well enough acquainted with the laws of the market to realize that the value of information depends on its unavailability. Just like the possession of economic capital, the possession of information unavailable to others bestows on the owner with a degree of power. Mr. Verloc himself acquires so high a position as an agent in Baron Stott-Wartenheim's eyes that Mr. Vladimir, seeing him for the first time, is surprised to realize that this "fat" and "lazy" (*SA* 21, 22) commonplace looking man was

> the famous and trusty secret agent, so secret that he was never designated otherwise but by the symbol Δ in the late Baron Stott-Wartenheim's official, semi-official, and confidential correspondence; the celebrated agent Δ, whose warnings had the power to change the schemes and the dates of royal, imperial, or grand-ducal journeys, and sometimes cause them to be put off altogether! (27)

The secret information Verloc provides, therefore, gives him not just a financial remuneration but also a sense of power, even if it is only indirect and cannot be publicly recognized, as well as promotes his feeling of self-importance.

For Verloc secret information has measurable value, which can be reduced when it becomes too widely known. In other words, he is aware of what Simmel described as "a scarcity value" of information (491). Information as commodity thus follows the rules of the market, where the price of an item depends on its availability. While the late Baron Stott-Wartenheim, Mr. Vladimir's predecessor in the Embassy, shared these views on information and appreciated the secrets reported to him by Mr. Verloc, Mr. Vladimir himself abides by a different philosophy on the value of secret information. He claims that Verloc "form[ed] a false conception of the nature of a secret service fund" (*SA* 22) and rather than rely on Verloc's information, he fabricates his own. He wants his informant to confirm his own false ideas, which he can use for his own political benefit:

> And Mr. Vladimir developed his idea from on high, with scorn and condescension, displaying at the same time an amount of ignorance as to the real aims, thoughts, and methods of the revolutionary world which filled the silent Mr. Verloc with inward consternation. He confounded causes with effects more than was excusable; the most distinguished propagandists with impulsive bomb throwers; assumed organisation where in the nature of things it could not exist; spoke of the social revolutionary party one moment as of a perfectly disciplined army, where the word of chiefs was supreme, and at another as if it had been the loosest association of desperate brigands that ever camped in a mountain gorge. (29-30)

Rather than keep secrets away from the public, to act on them judiciously, Mr. Vladimir wants to manipulate public opinion, or, to be more accurate, to "influenc[e] the public opinion here in favour of a universal repressive legislation" (30). He requires the kind of information – or misinformation – that boosts newspaper sales. The value of information as understood by Mr. Vladimir does not then depend on its reliability but lies in its political potential. The two ways of understanding the role of information reflect Simmel's and Goffman's approaches respectively. Simmel claims that "the commodity value of information lies in its scarcity and the ability of secret holders to restrict access. A secret that becomes public loses its value to the initial holder" (Marx and Muschert 225). In other words,

> secrets accrue a special value, even if their content would in itself be valueless. They hide the real value of the content by keeping it hidden. Blacked-out spaces in texts, empty spaces on maps or even neurotic symptoms indicate that something has been intentionally hidden, and spark speculation about its extraordinary value or meaning. (Vermeir and Margócsy 161)

Goffman, on the other hand, indicates that information, which he understands in terms of publicity, is the only property not diminished in value by being shared: "In public relations, advertising and propaganda, the more widely known the information, the greater its value to its source" (Marx and Muschert 225). In fact, Benjamin J. Bates describes information as a unique commodity, because of its "infinite reproducibility" and due to the fact that "the transfer of information goods to another does not diminish the stock of information held by the initial holder" (4).

Mr. Vladimir depends on newspapers to spread information and making it publicly available, thus giving him political leverage. The role of the press is, in fact, crucial in the novel, constituting the most significant and easily accessible – although not necessarily the most accurate – source of information for the general public. Most importantly, newspapers become "a vital political instrumentation of engaging, administering, and manipulating public opinion on matters foreign and domestic" (Mallios 160). The control over information, as both the Assistant Commissioner and Mr. Vladimir well understand, by steering the public opinion, can ensure a degree of power, and the press itself, as Peter Mallios puts it, has "exceptional facility as an instrumentation of political or state authority" (54). If the press contributes to the control over the public opinion, it is, at the same time, "a unique kind of commodity" which "is exchanged and circulated like any other commodity but which simultaneously poses as an effective source of knowledge concerning the nature of social reality" (Lutz 10-11). Newspapers sell information and claim to disclose secrets, but if they profess "to serve the ideals of enlightenment, order, respectability, and disinterested knowledge" they are also "a profit-motivated enterprise" and thus might be "contaminated by interests that have nothing to do with the common good, interests that are more properly understood in relations to the laws of commerce" (10-11). Indeed, although they affect the public, newspapers in *The Secret Agent* never offer reliable information: neither do they fully disclose the truth about the bombing, nor do they manage to explain Mrs. Verloc's death, the latter remaining "an impenetrable mystery" (*SA* 307) known only to Comrade Ossipon and the reader.

The relation between information and capital well illustrated by the circulation of the press is manifest also in the fate of Verloc's money. When Verloc realizes that his part in the Greenwich bombing as well as his role as an agent will be revealed to the anarchists, he draws the money he got for selling their secrets from the bank and gives it all to his wife for safekeeping. Significantly, this scene shortly precedes the moment when "[f]or the first time in his life [Verloc] was taking that incurious woman into his confidence" (239). In other words, both the money and the knowledge of her husband's secrets come to Winnie almost simultaneously. After his death, she almost immediately offers herself, the money that she got from her husband, and the secret of Verloc's death to Comrade Ossipon. The capital thus transferred to Comrade Ossipon comes together with "the cursed knowledge" (307) of Winnie Verloc's sad fate. Indeed, the narrator indicates that Comrade Ossipon was "well informed" (308) as regards Winnie's death, which was described by the papers as "an impenetrable mystery" (307).

Before Verloc entrusts Winnie with his secret and his money, their relationship is presented as a transaction based only on very limited information about each other. Although "[a]ll relationships of people to each other rest, as a matter of course, upon the precondition that they know something about each other" (Simmel 441), both characters evidently deem it sufficient to know only "that degree of truth which is essential for the life and progress of our species," as Simmel (441) put it. Winnie is concerned merely with her husband's capability to support herself and her family, while no other aspects of his life interest her much. In fact, on marrying Verloc, Winnie seems to have renounced her power and freedom, which manifested in her "almost disdainful incuriosity" (*SA* 237) and her claim that "things do not stand much looking into" (177), as if she did not participate in the circulation of information. Indeed, she "wasted no portion of this transient life in seeking for fundamental information. This is a sort of economy having all the appearances and some of the advantages of prudence. Obviously it may be good for one not to know too much" (169). Winnie herself constitutes a secret never uncovered by her husband, since "a systematically incurious person remains always partly mysterious" (237), and Verloc seems unaware of her motivation in marrying him. For her the marriage is evidently one of convenience since she exchanged "her own love-match for the marriage that will ensure a home for Stevie" (Harrington 52), or, as Lutz indicates, it is a form of prostitution (8). Therefore, like information, Winnie becomes a commodity.

If the flow of information corresponds, then, with the flow of money, "the control of information, like money, acts as a stratification resource" (Ragnedda and Muschert 4). *The Secret Agent* shows that the access to information reflects class relations and defines the vertical and horizontal relations between characters. Indeed, if information is treated as a commodity having particular economic value, then the position of the characters in the society depends not just on their economic capital but also on their knowledge – often unavailable to others. This is particularly striking in the relationship between Chief Inspector Heat, and the Assistant Commissioner, which is described by Robert Hampson as showing a "nuanced account of class dynamics" (83), and where each is expected to report to his superior on the findings concerning the Greenwich explosion.

Chief Inspector Heat is not quite ready, however, to share all he knows about the affair with the Assistant Commissioner, and he is particularly unwilling to reveal his acquaintance with Verloc or the agent's true occupation. Heat believes, not without reason, that his own position in the police hierarchy rests on his knowledge of or access to other people's secrets. This is why he considers his reaction to the news of the bombing, which reveals his ignorance of the matter, as harmful to his reputation. He also believes that "confession of ignorance" (*SA* 98) to the public might affect the credibility of the police:

> First of all, the fact of the outrage being attempted less than a week after he had assured a high official that no outbreak of anarchist activity was to be apprehended was sufficiently annoying. If he ever thought himself safe in making a statement, it was then. [...] He had affirmed that nothing of the sort could even be thought of without

> the department being aware of it within twenty-four hours; and he had spoken thus in his consciousness of being the great expert of his department. [...]
>
> "There isn't one of them, sir, that we couldn't lay our hands on at any time of night and day. We know what each of them is doing hour by hour," he had declared. And the high official had deigned to smile. This was so obviously the right thing to say for an officer of Chief Inspector Heat's reputation that it was perfectly delightful. (84)

Heat's boast of his knowledge of all the movements of the anarchists and their plans is thus rather overstated. This is humiliating for him since it puts into question his expertise and the reliability of his information. He is desperate to discover the secret of the bombing, while at the same time he is unwilling to divulge any information he obtains. When he finds a label with the address amongst "heap of rags, scorched and bloodstained" (86) brought from the place of the explosion, he only mentions it to the Assistant Commissioner when pressed. Much like Verloc, Heat is obliged to convey information to his superiors, although he does it only when "driven down to the ground by unfair artifices" he "elected to walk the path of unreserved openness" believing that "to know too much was not good for the department, the judicious holding back of knowledge was as far as his loyalty dared to go for the good of the service" (126-27). The unwillingness to share information reflects the tug for power between Chief Inspector Heat and the Assistant Commissioner, and "shows the Special Crimes Department to be an arena of conflict between two differing conceptions of professional ethics" (Glazzard 72). It also exposes controversy about illicitly obtained information, which, as the Assistant Commissioner confesses to Sir Ethelred, might be fabricated in order to profit from it.

Interestingly enough, just like Verloc, Chief Inspector Heat does not draw a clear line between his public and his private person. He finds out Verloc's secret because, as he explains, "A personal friend of [his] in the French police gave [him] the hint that the fellow was an Embassy spy. Private friendship, private information, private use of it – that's how [he] look[s] upon it" and he indicates that the information he thus obtained was "a private affair of [his] own" (*SA* 128) although he uses it for a professional purpose. His refusal to share this "private information" with his superiors stems from his desire to "do [his] work in [his] own way" since "[t]here are things not fit for everybody to know" (132). This is a view the Assistant Commissioner does not approve: "Your idea of secrecy seems to consist in keeping the chief of your department in the dark. That's stretching it perhaps a little too far, isn't it?" (132). Heat, like any spymaster, is unwilling to reveal Verloc as his source, especially that he believes in the value of the information Verloc presents, to the point that the Assistant Commissioner begins to suspect that "the reputation of Chief Inspector Heat might possibly have been made in a great part by the Secret Agent Verloc" (131). Indeed, when Verloc decides to make "full confession" (210), and reveal the story of the Greenwich bombing and his part in it, Heat is mostly worried that "[t]he turn this affair was taking meant the disclosure of many things – the laying waste of fields of knowledge, which, cultivated by a capable man, had a distinct value for the individual and for the society. It was sorry, sorry meddling" (210). Ostensibly concerned with exposure of the secret, the Chief Inspector wants to control just as how much would be revealed to the public and how much he would keep to himself thus securing the smooth operation of "the whole system of supervision" (211).

The Assistant Commissioner himself obtains information not only from his employees and along official lines but also through his – or rather his wife's – connections in the superior social spheres. The circulation of information to and from the drawing room of "the great lady" who befriended the Assistant Commissioner further compromises the border between the private and the public. The great lady, concerned with the fate of her protégé Michealis, is ready to use her influence to ensure no suspicion is attached to him in relation to the Greenwich bombing. The Assistant Commissioner, in turn, concerned as he is about his own social position, is very happy to inform the lady of Michaelis's innocence, and thus ensure her friendship.

It is also in the lady's drawing room that he meets Mr. Vladimir and can confirm his theory concerning the course of events leading to the bombing. Interestingly enough, the great lady's drawing room is divided in two parts by a screen so that a more private space is created; it is "a cosy nook for a couch and a few arm-chairs in the great drawing-room, with its hum of voices and the groups of people seated or standing in the light of six tall windows" (105-06). This "private side of the screen" (109) is evidently intended for the more privileged guests who either constitute the great lady's close circle, or who are prominent figures who can share information on current affairs.

Paradoxically, the anarchists, whose position in the social hierarchy is low, seem to be the least informed as to the Greenwich bombing. Simmel indicates that members of secret societies "form groups through their association with others around knowledge they share" (226), but in *The Secret Agent* they do not have any secret of value. If their meetings and plans are of any interest to the police and the Embassy, it is only as a result of the paradoxical logic of a secret:

> since exclusion of others from a possession may occur especially in the case of high values, the reverse is psychologically very natural, viz., that what is withheld from the many appears to have a special value. Accordingly, subjective possessions of the most various sorts acquire a decisive accentuation of value through the form of secrecy, in which the substantial significance of the facts concealed often enough falls into a significance entirely subordinate to the fact that others are excluded from knowing them. (Simmel 464)

The anarchists themselves constitute a bunch hardly evoking fear, they are presented as "a group of incurable dreamers whose views are in no way translated into action" (Juszczyk 44) or as "fearful grotesques" (Mulry 105), and as the novel progresses it becomes clear that they could hardly offer any real threat to the society: Michaelis, "the ticket-of-leave apostle" (*SA* 35), is evidently incapable of any action and he is not quite aware of what is going on around him. Karl Yundt is described as "toothless," which refers to the real state of things but it is also an indication of his harmlessness, especially that his passion is "worn-out," his fierceness is "impotent" (42). Comrade Ossipon, the youngest and therefore theoretically the ablest of the anarchists meeting in Mr. Verloc's place is, in fact, mostly interested in women and his efforts are directed at making at least one of them support him. Indeed, Mr. Verloc himself is quite aware of the inefficiency and, in fact, powerlessness of the anarchists: he sees them as "hopelessly futile" and "asked himself scornfully what else could have been expected from such a lot, this Karl Yundt, this Michaelis – this Ossipon" (52). Perhaps only the Professor, who keeps himself apart from other anarchists in the novel, is capable of any such action. But both the Professor and the remaining anarchists learn about the bombing from a newspaper, which constitutes for them the only source of information.

The lives and actions of the anarchists, in turn, including their apparently secret meetings and plans, are not, in fact, secret to the police. When Comrade Ossipon worries that he will be detained in relation to the bombing, the Professor tells him: "You might ask the police for a testimonial of good conduct. They know where every one of you slept last night. Perhaps if you asked them they would consent to publish some sort of official statement" (77). At the same time the anarchists' ignorance of Verloc and his role in the bombing, or about his spying on them for the benefit of the foreign Embassy is revealed. Verloc himself boasts to Winnie that "[t]here isn't a murdering plot for the last eleven years that I hadn't my finger in at the risk of my life. There's scores of these revolutionists I've sent off, with their bombs in their blamed pockets, to get themselves caught on the frontier" (238), thus trying to impress Winnie by his own initiation into the secrets and expressing the feeling of power it seems to give him. So the relation between the anarchists and Verloc are by no means symmetrical.

By introducing the figure of a secret agent and presenting the anarchist circles in London, Conrad's novel clearly refers to the popular genres of a spy thriller or detective fiction whose plots concentrate on the discovery of secrets. *The Secret Agent*, however, moves beyond the common conventions of the two genres, revealing the ways the circulation of secrets corresponds with the circulation of money, shaping the social life and social relations. In the novel, the knowledge of secret information establishes characters' position in social hierarchy and constitutes leverage in the world operating according to capitalist logic. Transmission of information, which thus constitutes a form of economic exchange, disrupts the clear division between the private and the public, and links characters of different backgrounds. In *The Secret Agent* information is not only a commodity, which can be sold and bought, but also a source of power and thus a stratification device.

WORKS CITED

Bates, Benjamin J. "Information as an Economic Good: A Re-Evaluation of Theoretical Approaches." Paper presented at the 35th Annual Conference of International Communication Association Honolulu, HI. May 1985.

Casper, Cord-Christian. *Against Anarchy: Political Alterity in British Modernism*. De Gruyter, 2020.

Conroy, Mark. "The Panoptical City: The Structure of Suspicion in *The Secret Agent*." *Conradiana* 15 (1983): 203-17.

Glazzard, Andrew. *Conrad's Popular Fictions*. Palgrave Macmillan, 2016.

Hampson, Robert. *Conrad's Secrets*. Palgrave Macmillan, 2012.

Harrington, Ellen Burton. "The Anarchist's Wife: Joseph Conrad's Debt to Sensation Fiction in *The Secret Agent*." *Conradiana* 36 (2004): 51-63.

Juszczyk, Andrzej. "Between Order and Anarchy – Exploring Utopianism in the Political Novels of Joseph Conrad." *Yearbook of Conrad Studies (Poland)* 10 (2015): 35-46.

Lee, Mi Jeong. "The Ugly Politics of (Im)passivity, or Why Conrad's Anarchists are Fat." *Journal of Modern Literature* 44.3 (2021): 1-18.

Lutz, John. "A Rage for Order: Fetishism, Self-Betrayal, and Exploitation in *The Secret Agent*." *Conradiana* 40 (2008): 1-24.

Mallios, Peter Lancelot. "Reading *The Secret Agent* Now: The Press, the Police, the Premonition of Simulation." *Conrad in the Twenty-First Century. Contemporary Approaches and Perspectives*. Ed. Carola Kaplan, Peter Mallios and Andrea White. Routledge, 2004. 155-72.

Marx, Gary T., and Glenn W. Muschert. "Simmel on Secrecy. A Legacy and Inheritance for the Sociology of Information." *Soziologie als Möglichkeit*. Ed. Cécile Rol and Christian Papilloud. VS Verlag für Sozialwissenschaften, 2009. 117-233.

Mathews, Cristina. "'The Manner of Exploding': Joseph Conrad's *The Secret Agent* and Men at Home." *Conradiana* 42 (2010): 17-44.

Mulry, David. *Joseph Conrad Among the Anarchists. Nineteenth Century Terrorism and* The Secret Agent. Palgrave Macmillan, 2016.

Ragnedda, Massimo, and Glenn Muschert. Introduction. *Theorizing Digital Divides*. Ed. Massimo Ragnedda and Glenn W. Muschert. Routledge, 2018. 1-7.

Shaffer, Brian W. "'The Commerce of Shady Wares': Politics and Pornography in Conrad's *The Secret Agent*." *English Literary History* 62 (1995): 443-66.

Simmel, Georg. "The Sociology of Secrecy and of Secret Societies." *The American Journal of Sociology* 11 (1906): 441-98.

Vermeir, Koen, and Dániel Margócsy. "States of Secrecy: An Introduction." *The British Journal for the History of Science* 45 (2012): 153-64.

Nergis Ünal,
Middle East Technical University,
Ankara, Turkey

A Bakhtinian Analysis of the Protagonist's Ethical Dilemmas in Joseph Conrad's *Under Western Eyes*[1]

The starting point of my study is the basis of Joseph Conrad's ethical point of view succinctly stated in his famous quotation in "A Familiar Preface" to *A Personal Record*: "Those who read me know my conviction that the world, the temporal world, rests on a few very simple ideas; so simple that they must be as old as the hills. It rests notably, among others, on the idea of Fidelity" (*PR* xxi). The study of the virtue of fidelity, which Conrad sees as a principal element of life, can span a variety of sources. Jocelyn Baines makes a reference to the partition of Poland by Prussia, Russia, and Austria in the eighteenth century, as a result of which many patriots, including writers, devoted themselves to liberating the country from foreign rule (7). Thus, they expressed fidelity to their country through their works. Zdzisław Najder claims that starting from the early nineteenth century, after the loss of independence, fidelity was a common theme in Polish literature (13, 202-03). In this regard, it was not specific to Conrad to use this concept in his literary works (13). Nevertheless, I believe that there is something special in Conrad's ethical understanding of *fidelity*. Ranging from his disapproval of the political practices of his time to the loss of his family members and to the frustration he felt about religion, Conrad faced many difficulties in his life. A prominent difficulty emerged as a result of his decision to write in a foreign language. Various views were voiced as for Conrad's practice, ranging from Eliza Orzeszkowa's sharp critique that he emigrated and was writing in the language of the "Anglo-Saxons [...] just because they pay better" (188) to the more reflective observation of Przemysław Mroczkowski that

Conrad conveyed "the notion and the reality of the Europe of his time" (87). Although he was widely criticized because of his choice, being accused of infidelity to his own nation (Najder 12, 102, 171), Conrad himself did not feel that he had committed such a misdeed. The English language had a special place for Conrad[2] as he believed it was what made his act of writing feel so natural. In the face of criticism, he wrote *A Personal Record*,[3] in which he defended himself, showing fidelity to his choice. As argued convincingly by Jacques Berthoud, Conrad might have been criticized because "fidelity to his vision was not compatible with fidelity to his community" (19). Depending on the analytical perspective, it would be acceptable to say that Conrad was both faithful and unfaithful in his life; perhaps just like some of the characters he created. It seems obvious that the idea of fidelity haunted him for the rest of his life, and thus, it keeps occurring as a main theme in his works. Yet is it possible to distinguish his characters as faithful or unfaithful as a result of their actions?

This study focuses on how such ethical questions are dealt with in Conrad's *Under Western Eyes* (1911). By looking at the ethical dilemmas presented in the novel, the main character Razumov's conduct is explored through the ethical perspective of the Russian philosopher Mikhail Bakhtin, and it is argued that the novel communicates the truth of the undecidability of a character's moral worth. The reason why *Under Western Eyes* is chosen is that in this particular novel the moral dilemma is dramatized by showing how a character can be faithful and yet unfaithful at the same time, thus providing enough complexity for literary analysis.

Bakhtin's main criterion in his ethical discussion is the idea of responsibility, which he calls "answerability." That concept first appeared in one of his early essays, namely "Art and Answerability." Afterwards, his idea of responsibility was developed, and his ethical views are mainly presented in another early philosophical essay published many years after it was written, *Toward a Philosophy of the Act* (1919–1921), which is used as the main analytical tool in this study.

Bakhtinian ethics differs from the traditional understanding of ethics in the importance he gives to the notion of responsibility. As there is not a pre-set content of what one ought to do at a specific occasion – otherwise this approach would not present much difference from Kantian ethics – the performer of the act is the only one who is responsible for his own deed. The responsibility for the act takes place in "Being-as-event."[4] In fact, Bakhtin endeavours to make "a new definition of the human subject" (Holquist xx). Life given to a person presents alternatives; however, instead of just accepting whatever is given and leading a passive life, one needs to make choices and act upon them. "What makes us whole [...] is a response" to the given (Emerson 412). For Bakhtin, "to *be* in life, to be *actually*, is to *act*, is to be unindifferent" (*Toward a Philosophy* 42). Within this philosophy, one is subject to the ethical consideration of being an active participant in life.

Returning to the novel, Razumov might prove justified in Bakhtinian terms concerning his decision about giving Haldin up to the authorities due to his particular condition; however, he breaches his promise to Haldin at the same time. In addition, he acts under duress in Geneva and keeps deceiving Natalia and the revolutionary circle there. In fact, he commits wrongdoings, yet his acts embody an ethical edge as he bears responsibility for them. In this essay, the protagonist's personal responsibility will be analysed in terms of the character's own uniqueness, in relation to the perspectives of the other characters, and with respect to reader response as necessitated by the Bakhtinian architectonics.[5] Thus, this study provides a phenomenological analysis of the novel by converging the text as the artwork and the reader response as the aesthetic complement to reveal the dynamic nature of the literary work. In terms of an ethical discussion, Razumov will be evaluated as one would evaluate a real person in real life. In fact, this approach is indicative of the Bakhtinian idea that a literary character is a living figure, a "real, actual, thinking human being" (*Toward a Philosophy* 6). Accordingly, outgrowing the narrative frame and declaring his freedom, Razumov makes this analysis more meaningful with his statement: "I am not a young man in a novel" (*UWE* 185-86).

Particularity in Relation to the Protagonist

One of the striking points Bakhtin makes in his *Toward a Philosophy of the Act* is the importance he gives to the uniqueness of the individual. One's own personal differences are the touch of humanity in one's acts and they distinguish one from the others. According to Bakhtin, "[m]an-in-general does not exist; *I* exist and a particular concrete *other* exists" (*Toward a Philosophy* 47). The particulars are what make one act in the way one does. As a result, it is not possible to talk about the universality of the correct way of acting (47-48), and one needs to be evaluated in terms of one's own uniqueness – one's own background, the particulars of one's culture, and one's own point of view. My knowledge of the object is what makes me act in that particular way; it "*answerably obligates me*" (49). I act in my uniqueness as a response to the obligation that is imposed on me by my knowledge of the object. Otherwise, "it is impossible to live in [life], impossible to perform answerable deeds" (9). At the same time, the particularity of a person is exactly what confirms the active participation of the subject in the "Being-as-event."

"Yes, of course, I will go. You must give me precise directions, and for the rest – depend on me" (*UWE* 21). These are the very words after which Razumov's suffering begins. He promises to help Haldin escape without giving it proper thought, in panic and confusion. However, he then decides to report Haldin to the authorities in confusion again. Here what makes the reader question whether his act is betrayal or not does not solely depend on his informing to the police but on the violation of his promise.

According to Bakhtin, as a unique participant in Being, one has to take responsibility for one's actions. Another person or pre-determined criteria cannot be responsible for what one has done. This is called his "non-alibi," which needs to exist constantly (Morson and Emerson 17). Within one's "oughtness," which is "the attitude or position I ought to take" (Bakhtin, *Toward a Philosophy* 18), one needs to choose a stance and enact one's decision. The point of view one takes while doing so is his "emotional-volitional tone" in Bakhtinian terms, which refers to "the experiencing of an experience as *mine*" (36). Being aware of his "non-alibi" and having one's "emotional-volitional tone," the subject is ready to "acknowledge" the event. For Bakhtin, "it is not the content of an obligation that obligates me, but my signature below it" (38).

Thus, with his confession to the authorities, Razumov "signs" his act without an "alibi." He chooses to do so all by himself, and his "emotional-volitional tone" is made up of his self-interest in his future and the confusion he is experiencing at the time. All these aspects make Razumov responsible for his decision, and he indeed suffers for it throughout the rest of the novel. Yet, the question remains to be answered: Can Razumov's act be regarded as betrayal?

In her reading of the question of ethics in the novel, Daphna Erdinast-Vulcan refers to the Bakhtinian perspective to study the question of whether Razumov is a free agent to be held responsible for his act. In addition, she provides a detailed discussion on "*failure* of [narrative] framing" regarding the narrator's unconvincing *alibi* (101-04). However, she does not deal with the question as to whether Razumov's act can be considered "betrayal." More recently, Joshua A. Bernstein has analysed the novel in light of Bernard Williams's concept of "moral luck," focusing on to what extent Razumov can be held ethically responsible for actions outside his control. He argues that due to a lack of moral bond between the two characters, Razumov has "fatally betrayed" Haldin (129), and that Russia's corrupt state makes up the lot that shapes Razumov's moral choices (131-33). In this study, conducted through a Bakhtinian ethical perspective, the two aspects discussed by Bernstein are analysed in the section on "particularity." Together with the following two sections, the Bakhtinian perspective gives a fuller view of the protagonist's conduct by additionally studying the value centres of the other characters and reader response respectively. While the question as to whether Razumov's giving up Haldin to the authorities can be seen as "betrayal" remains unanswered by the major ethical discussions,[6] a reading through the Bakhtinian ethical perspective motivates us to raise this question and reveals that Razumov's act cannot be completely seen as betrayal.

Razumov is devoid of any family ties as his mother is dead, but Prince K—, a Russian nobleman and Razumov's biological father, financially supports him. However, Razumov's connection with the Prince is made even more vague, and the sense of his loneliness and lack of familial support is strengthened through the narrator's deliberate choice of words. For instance, for Prince K—, the narrator prefers to use the expression "[Razumov's] protector" (*UWE* 11), making the limited relation between father and son even more distant. Prince K— calls Razumov "Mr. Razumov." Similarly, the attorney who transmits the Prince's financial support to Razumov is "obscure" (6). His isolation, caused by a lack of family and combined with the illegitimacy of his birth, makes up the Bakhtinian "given" in Razumov's life, and it is this given that makes him vulnerable when decisions must be made: "Others had fathers, mothers, brothers, relations, connections, to move heaven and earth on their behalf – he had no one" (21). How can he "move the heavens" without anyone behind him? The lack underlies his decisions, and he acts toward Haldin the way he does because he knows there is no one to defend him if he is found guilty by the state.

As for Razumov's Russian identity, he tries to make up for his lack of family by sustaining a self-identificatory connection with Russia. His acts might be regarded as resulting from free will; however, he acts mainly in accordance with state policy. That is why he does not reflect "a clear sense of identity or direction" (Hollander 6). Rachel Hollander builds a connection between Razumov and Russia in the way the country is represented in Conrad's essay "Autocracy and War" as an isolated country with a lack of definite history. She asserts that "Razumov reflects Conrad's understanding of Russia itself as rootless and directionless" as the limits of Razumov's character show parallelism to the limits of Russian politics (8). Razumov leads his life within the pre-determined system of autocracy without familial roots in pursuit of certain ideals, which in a way makes it easier for him to proceed without chaos. Rather than acting within the "given" in his life, now he ought to make a decision as Haldin's appearance in his rooms "obligates" him "to act in a certain way" (Bakhtin, *Toward a Philosophy* 49) and enforces responsibility on Razumov.

After his confession to the authorities, Razumov witnesses the true face of autocracy and detests it now as he realizes that they suspect and destroy not only their enemies but also their proponents, just as it is represented via Mikulin's death. This fact is important in order to understand the effect of Razumov's particular situation on his decisions because whatever he does after Haldin's arrival, it is clear that he will be punished by the state. Razumov does not see Haldin as being Russian or as faithful to Russia as he is; therefore, he does not want the state to suspect him because of such a person. However, Haldin has an "organic" connection to Russia (Long 502), confining the Russian spirit within himself, which Razumov has not been able to acquire. Haldin honours Ziemianitch as "[a] bright spirit! A hardy soul! [...] a fellow!" (*UWE* 18) and as "the bright Russian soul" (30), whereas "a drunken brute" (59, 352) is how Razumov describes the sledge driver (Long 502). Haldin's fervent feelings for Russia are what differentiates him from Razumov. He has a tradition of land and, most importantly, of a loving family, which makes it possible for him, unlike Razumov, to storm the heavens against state rule. Therefore, it could be asserted that his particularity of living under Russian autocracy is a kind of mischance for Razumov. As the narrator points out, "[i]t is unthinkable that any young Englishman should find himself in Razumov's situation" (*UWE* 25). Whatever Razumov does, he cannot have a way out. Had he directly told Haldin to leave, he would still have been under suspicion merely because of being approached for help by a revolutionist. Thus, it is not "weakness" (20) not to have told Haldin to go away as Razumov surmises when he questions himself about the validity of his act.

In addition, Razumov's act cannot be seen as betrayal because Haldin and Razumov have "never been intimate" (15). Based on this reasoning, Haldin's request for help challenges "the rational, legalistic notion of responsibility" (Rizzuto 94). Although Razumov learns that Haldin has always spoken highly of him and expressed his appreciation of him to his comrades, confidence "does not require bilateral agreement" (Hepburn 289). Razumov does not have such strong feelings for the fellow student, and he needs to think about his future and about his survival. In this light, Razumov's particulars embodying his lack of family, his Russian identity, and not having a close relationship with Haldin prove a justifiable ground for his act of reporting Haldin.

The Plurality of Value Judgments

"Particularity" in Bakhtin's distinctive world brings along "plurality" with itself as each individual with one's unique being contributes to the plurality within this unitary "Being-as-event." Bakhtin depicts "a relational, participatory understanding of moral personhood" (Juzwik 537); therefore, however much isolated people may try to be, they will eventually need others to sustain their wholeness. Connections made with others keep the process of "Being-as-event" in continuity, and in prospect of further contributions to be made by others, the subject remains unconcluded. Thus, it is important to note that Bakhtinian notion of wholeness is dynamic and unfinalized in its nature.

According to Bakhtin, there are two main value centres: "myself" and "the other."[7] These centres are primarily different from, yet at the same time, indispensable to each other. With respect to the unique position of the subject, other relations gain a value-centre as: "I-for-myself," "the-other-for-me," and "I-for-the-other." Correspondingly, "I-for-myself" refers to what I see and think about myself, "I-for-the-other" is how I am perceived by the other, and "the-other-for-me" is the evaluation of the other through my point of view. It is clear that each value centre is lacking in terms of the field of vision of its own surroundings. Michael Holquist makes a very clear explanation of the phenomenon:

> [T]hat I can see things you cannot, and you can see things that I cannot, is that our excess of seeing is defined by a lack of seeing: my excess is your lack, and vice versa. If we wish to overcome this lack, we try to see what is there *together*. We must share each other's excess in order to overcome our mutual lack. (xxvi)

Each subject needs the other to complete oneself and to contribute to the wholeness of "Being." This process "makes us continually and personally responsible for our actions and for assessing our moral responses" (Morson and Emerson 20), which stresses the dynamic nature of "Being-as-event."

Concerning the aspect of plurality in the novel, Haldin's intrusion into Razumov's laborious life brings along the reality which Razumov is only then able to see: "Life is a public thing" (*UWE* 54). Razumov realizes that he is not alone but is connected to others despite his utmost efforts to stay away from social interactions. Although the novel focuses on the protagonist, one of whose dominant traits is his loneliness, it also emphasizes the importance of social relationships, which is demonstrated through the negative consequences of their absence as a common inclination in Conrad (Pettersson 153). The tragedy Razumov has experienced partly depends on the clash between his own conception of himself and how he is seen by others. This clash between different value centres indicates that the writer maintains an ambivalent attitude toward the protagonist and lets the reader make the final decision about his faithfulness.

The gap between Razumov's and Haldin's value centres illustrates the lack in each one's field of vision. Upon Haldin's request for help, Razumov cannot make sense of what he did to provoke this confidence, yet he does not see the fact that Haldin's one-sided trust in Razumov, his "unsolicited confidence" (Hepburn 290), is enough a reason to choose his fellow student to take refuge. Likewise, when Haldin asserts, as a reason for his choice, that Razumov does not have any family ties, and thus, he has no one to be tortured or interrogated after him, he misses two points: the lack in his own value centre, and the fact that autocracy brings misery to everyone. Razumov does not have a family indeed, but this is the very reason why he cannot undertake a risky action. For Razumov, his silence is his strategy to avoid any danger to his future while for Haldin it is a sign of trustworthiness. In addition, it is when Razumov expresses his disapproval of Haldin's deed, that the latter realizes Razumov has formed a negative opinion of him: "I see now how it is, Razumov – brother. You are a magnanimous soul, but my action is abhorrent to you – alas...," "And even my person, too, is loathsome to you perhaps" (*UWE* 62). Razumov-for-Haldin, which represents Bakhtin's "I-for-others," reveals the fellow student's misconception of Razumov's identity Yet, these moments of revelation justify Razumov's defence that he does not have intimacy with Haldin.

Haldin's opinions of Razumov parallel those of other characters as well. As the university circle believes that Razumov is "always accessible" and holds nothing "secret or reserved in his life" (7), they trust him with forbidden opinions. Thus, from their value centre, it might not be so surprising that a fellow student trusts Razumov with his "forbidden" deed. To this end, the opinions of the university circle present discordance with what Razumov has tried to maintain about himself. This shows the reader that the protagonist is not aware of his existence in its entirety, which is a deficiency in his wholeness in Bakhtinian terms.

Another character to refer to in this regard is Natalia. She has already developed confidence in Razumov based on Haldin's letters even before meeting him. When they meet in Geneva, her previously formed opinion is enhanced by her first impression: "[H]e is a man of deep feeling – it is impossible to doubt it. You should have seen his face. [...] Their friendship must have been the very brotherhood of souls!" (172). Although she tells Razumov, as time passes, that she feels he is hiding something from her, her first impression is in line with the other characters' opinions that Razumov is a trustworthy man.

Razumov-for-the narrator aspect of "plurality" is not easy to deal with as the narrator subverts the credibility of his own narration. Despite the seeming familiarity the narrator tries to create, he does not fully understand Razumov. While on the one hand he seems to express Razumov's despair through his physical appearance and reactions, on the other hand he can also think that Razumov is "deranged" (350). He never, throughout the novel, implies to the reader that Razumov is in much distress due to his particular situation and that we need to interpret his strange reactions in line with that. Thus, the "I-for-others" aspect does not suggest clarity but hesitation in this case. The narrator does not fully condemn Razumov, but he definitely has an ambivalent attitude, which is why the reader cannot fully trust his judgments while evaluating Razumov's ethical dilemma.

From the very beginning, instead of gaining the confidence of the reader, the narrator chooses to build his trustworthiness on shaky ground. He uses words to tell Razumov's story, but he asserts that words are "the great foes of reality" (3), that truth cannot be gracious enough due to "the imperfection of language" (293), and that he has "limitations" in terms of writing (100). The mistrust the unreliable narrator induces is maintained throughout via his going in and out of the story, adding to the account more than the diary tells, creating a "dizzying effect" by switching frequently between his perspective and that of Razumov (Erdinast-Vulcan 102), his ambiguous statements as regards Razumov's character, his pretence of not knowing some of the details of the story and, of course, his feelings for Natalia, which do not let him to remain an objective outsider.

The fact that the narrative setting of the novel changes from St. Petersburg to Geneva and that the narrator functions as the translator of Razumov's diary bring about the question of what language the characters are speaking. We would assume that the Russian characters in both settings speak in Russian among themselves, but there is no clear reference to which language they use when communicating among themselves and with non-Russians, including mainly the narrator. We would still presume they speak in Russian, yet there are interruptions to the text in foreign languages to make things more complicated.[8] Thus, the narrator translates not only the diary but also (at least partially) the dialogues while he is also present and/or when he is a part of them at the intradiegetic narrative level. At this point, the uncertainty about his origins and his linguistic abilities[9] contribute to the unreliability he establishes. The reader cannot be certain about whether the narrator can reflect Razumov's true motives as Razumov-for-the narrator value centre is craftily kept in ambivalence. Christiane Bimberg studies this under loss of narrative distance or "collapse of narrative detachment." As the narrator is gradually involved with the events and characters emotionally, he "falls into the trap of empathy and increasingly loses his narrative distance" (45). Similarly, as another point that contributes to the obscurity of the textual voice and the narrator's value centre, Penn R. Szittya asserts that the narrator "is obsessed with Razumov" and thus fails to keep his distance from the protagonist (819). She calls into question the "narrator-hero doubling" in the novel which "[divides] the reader between two narrators, two stories, two points of view, two chronologies, two styles" (820-21). All these critical observations lead the reader to question the truthfulness of the narrator's account.

All in all, the clash between "I-for-myself" and "I-for-others" reveals itself through different characters in the novel, and the contrast between different value judgments directs the reader to the Bakhtinian idea of plurality. There can be different perspectives on the same subject (in this case Razumov); however, the contradictions do not denote anything negative. They only enrich the subject, leaving him not finalized but open to discussion, which shows parallelism with the author's stance in the novel as for creating an ambiguous attitude toward Razumov and leaving the decision to the reader.

The Place of Empathy and Love in the Assessment of the Protagonist

In this section of the paper, the reader, as the "other" to the protagonist, analyses Razumov through Bakhtin's idea of "active and objective empathizing" and by respecting the value centre and the limits of the character. The approach the reader applies to this practice is "love," "a concentration of attention that enriches" the character (Emerson 408) in the sense that the reader helps the character gain its wholeness. What the reader is doing is to "*linger intently* over an object, to hold and sculpt every detail and particular in it, however minute. Only love is capable of being aesthetically productive" (Bakhtin, *Toward a Philosophy* 64). Eventually, the reader is actualizing this process in an "un-self-interested" (64) way, claiming that Razumov cannot be regarded as totally unfaithful because the reader sympathizes with him due to his particular circumstances, certain narrative devices, his confession to Natalia and the revolutionists, his fulfilment of his answerability, and the perspective of some minor characters.

As for the particular situation of Razumov, while he is a promising student, a man of thought, working his way into academia, he undeservingly lives under an autocratic regime that does not provide freedom of expression. The coexistence of profundity, reason, trustworthiness, and good looks in one person presents him as a heroic figure that would be admired by many people in real life. The fact that he lacks a family discloses the sufferings he has experienced both financially and in terms of loneliness; however, his personal qualities "accorded badly with such humble origin" (*UWE* 6) as if indicating that he does not belong where he is. The revelation of a lacking side in such a character makes the reader feel closer to him.

Following the fatality Razumov experiences with Haldin's totally unexpected intrusion into his rooms, nothing remains the same. After his confession to the state, leading to Haldin's arrest and execution, Razumov is given a position as a state spy in Geneva. However, the reader does not learn about his status until the final chapter of the novel. That the author chooses to delay revealing Razumov's position as a spy also contributes to his being sympathized with by the reader (Hampson 177). Conrad experiments with the chronology and, as a narrative strategy, goes back and forth in time. Until reaching the fourth chapter, the reader does not know the motive behind Razumov's arrival in Geneva although he has spent quite some time among the revolutionist circle there. If it had been revealed as early as the moment of his arrival, it would definitely not have created the same effect.

Another reason why the reader sympathizes with Razumov is his confession to Natalia and the revolutionists even after the letter from a revolutionist student is revealed. The letter inserted into the narrative as a written document states that Ziemianitch was responsible for Haldin's death, and thus Razumov gets cleared of any suspicion. However, Razumov chooses not to maintain his false image and makes a confession. Although the act is belated, Razumov performs Bakhtinian answerability here. After his confession, he confides his grave suffering to his diary and adds: "[P]erdition is my lot" (*UWE* 362). The reader response, in the face of his resolution to take responsibility for his wrongdoings, parallels Sophia Antonovna's response to Razumov's confession expressed to the narrator toward the very end of the novel:

> [H]ow many of them would deliver themselves up deliberately to perdition (as he himself says in that book) rather than go on living, secretly debased in their own eyes? [...] he was safe when he did it. It was just [...] when the possibility of being loved by that admirable girl first dawned upon him, that he discovered that his bitterest railings, the worst wickedness, the devil work of his hate and pride, could never cover up the ignominy of the existence before him. There's character in such a discovery. (380)

Active and objective empathy, which necessitates concentrating attention on a literary character, leads the evaluative process that Bakhtin calls "aesthetic activity," "aesthetic seeing," or "aesthetic contemplation." In real life we might love one due to an advantage or because one shares our point of view so that we can act together. In the world of aesthetics, however, through active and objective empathizing we do not observe any self-interested motive, proving art to be superior to life. Sophia Antonovna echoes the reader's disinterested sympathy for Razumov in the quotation above as she ironically expresses to the narrator Razumov's integrity in a candid manner, which the narrator has never been able to confess to the reader.

Though they are not the main concern of this study, the members of the revolutionist circle in Geneva are also worth mentioning as they function as foils to Razumov in an ethical sense. Peter Ivanovitch, who wears dark blue glasses, is ironically addressed with such titles as "Europe's greatest feminist" (205) or "the noble arch-priest of Revolution" (210). As the revolutionary circle in Geneva represents corruption, narrative-wise the members are treated with sarcasm and disdain. Another revolutionist Madame de S—, also called Eleanor Maximova, is the current partner of Peter Ivanovitch. She is observed to look like a "corpse," an "ancient, painted mummy with unfathomable eyes" (215-16), radiating "ghastly vivacity" (224). Such ghost-like qualities signify the moral hollowness of this character. In addition, these descriptions are made in an equivocal tone, reflecting both the narrator's and Razumov's perspectives. Thus, they further exemplify the ambivalence created by the narrator.[10] Whereas he claims he does not comprehend and does not favour Russian mentality, there are occasions when he provides parallel opinions with the Russian protagonist. While this strategy implemented by the author diminishes the narrator's reliability, it enhances the sympathy the reader feels for Razumov. Although members of the revolutionist circle, except for Sophia Antonovna, are corrupt and Razumov does not feel close to any of them, he is welcomed with respect and admiration even by these characters. Despite abandoning their country and the fact that they "can never live above suspicion, nor can they ever trust one another" (Hepburn 292), the revolutionists confide in Razumov, which might add up to the reader's sympathy for the protagonist.

When the story is considered from the beginning, it is clear that Razumov has been guilty of wrongdoings. Although he is aware that they are not intimate, he promises Haldin to help him. He makes the fellow student Kostia steal his father's money just to give the impression that he is escaping the country. In addition, he deceives Natalia and the revolutionists in Geneva by lying and pretending to have been Haldin's comrade. However, despite these wrongdoings, the reader cannot condemn him because he is not evil intentionally. As Conrad states in Author's Note to *Under Western Eyes*, "Razumov is treated sympathetically. Why should he not be? [...] I don't think that in his distractions he is ever monstrous" (ix). And this idea is further enhanced by the fact that Razumov fulfils his answerability by taking responsibility for his deeds.

The evil nature Razumov lacks is represented through the monstrosity of Nikita who leaves Razumov deaf and successively leads him to be a cripple for the rest of his life. Such conduct is highly disturbing and shocking for the reader as well. The price Razumov has to pay is the loss of his future, the woman he loves, and his health. Although it would not have been surprising if Razumov had been killed, as he himself expected "to be torn to pieces" (336), "[a]llowing Razumov to survive creates a break in the revenge cycle" (Hollander 13), and this contributes to Conrad's purpose of not giving a moral lesson in the story and Bakhtin's theory of not finalizing the character but enriching him in "Being-as-event." For the reader, it is hard to take sides, but there is definitely room for empathy and love. After all, in "aesthetic seeing you love a human being not because he is good, but, rather, a human being is good because you love him" (Bakhtin, *Toward a Philosophy* 62).

To conclude, in this study, it is revealed that Bakhtinian ethics, through its philosophical notions of particularity, plurality, empathy, and love, provides one with the flexibility to analyse a Conradian character who embodies layered moral depth. This theoretical strategy leads one to be engrossed in the inner dynamics of Bakhtin's architectonics and how it organically lets events and characters evolve in an ongoing process. Through this analysis, Razumov is brought to real life, and a bridge between the literary world and real life is built. We do not meet spotless characters in the Conradian canon just as in real life people are not totally moral or totally evil, either. We definitely sympathize with Razumov, and by evaluating him we contribute to his value, helping him gain the dynamic wholeness Bakhtin desires characters to have.

By extension, this analysis brings us to Bakhtin's idea of "great time" as a suggestion for further research. Just as Bakhtin emphasizes the never-ending nature of the contribution different value judgments make to a character, or as he stresses the eventfulness of Being, he also sees the world as everlasting, and he calls the active process of this expansion "great time." In a few pages of *Toward a Philosophy of the Act*, we see Bakhtin implying this concept; however, he does not name it at this point. For Bakhtin, "time is not a line, but a complex form of a rotating body" (Shepherd 49). Like a spiderweb that expands with each silk thread being anchored on radial lines, one gets enriched with the presence of the past, with the dialogues one has over time, and with the potential one has for the future. Everything remains active, and thus unforgotten in this space. As Bakhtin famously observes: "Nothing is absolutely dead: every meaning will have its homecoming festival. The problem of great time" (*Speech* 170). This argument reminds us one more time that novels should not be interpreted for finalization but should attain their dynamic wholeness through their perpetual interpretations. In this way, they will justify Conrad's conviction pointed out in his *A Personal Record*: "The part of the inexplicable should be allowed for in appraising the conduct of men in a world where no explanation is final" (*PR* 35).

Razumov enters into "great time" through the continuous evaluation of his moral profundity, and *Under Western Eyes*, for this reason, achieves the eventual purpose of contributing to the world of literature. "[I]n great time nothing ever loses its significance. [...] [N]othing dies, but everything is renewed. With every new step forward our previous steps acquire a new, additional meaning" (Bakhtin, qtd. in Shepherd 33-34). This is how great works of literature transcend their time, even their writer, and become immortal. To this end, Bakhtinian love will maintain the continuity of the Conrad corpus by making it speak itself to new audiences of different times.

Acknowledgement

I would like to express my thanks to TÜBİTAK (The Scientific and Technological Research Institution of Turkey) for financially supporting me to present an earlier version of this essay in the Seventh International Joseph Conrad Conference held in Lublin, Poland in June 2022.

NOTES

[1] This study is a revised version of my unpublished master's thesis titled, "A Bakhtinian Analysis of the Protagonist's Ethical Dilemma in Joseph Conrad's *Under Western Eyes* and *The End of the Tether*," which was submitted to Middle East Technical University in January 2020.

[2] In Author's Note to *A Personal Record* Conrad claims: "[English] had always been an inherent part of myself. English was for me neither a matter of choice nor adoption" (*PR* vii). He also adds: "if I had not written in English I would not have written at all" (viii). Mary Morzinski studies the mastery of Conrad's English in his narrative style in comparison with his spoken discourse through cognitive, sociological, and psychological factors. She claims that despite the non-native elements of his style such as the "semantic import from Polish," which account for his "[failure] to be native-like," Conrad has a high level of metalingual awareness (131). Of course, she also gives place to biographical reality concerning Conrad's fascination with English. She references Gérard Jean-Aubry's account and traces Conrad's "first taste of the English language" back to when he was eight and one day was "absorbed in the translation of *Two Gentlemen of Verona*" in his father's study (28). Michael A. Lucas mainly focuses on the eccentricities in Conrad's English as a non-native language user. And comparably recently, Ewa Kujawska-Lis has observed that language in Conrad's discursive space does "[not guarantee] mutual understanding" but may transform into a "a tool of inclusion, seclusion and exclusion" (229). Having experienced life in foreign linguistic domains, Conrad was conscious of the isolating potential of linguistic barriers (236), which reveals itself in his works written in a foreign language.

[3] Following Robert Lynd's (a British journalist) review in the nature of an attack on Conrad for not writing in his mother tongue, Conrad wrote *A Personal Record* in reply (Najder 102-04; Ambrosini 42-43).

[4] The Bakhtinian term "Being-as-event" – also referred to as only "Being" – stands for the eventfulness of being. For Bakhtin, act or existence in general terms is seen as an event. It is active, is becoming and is not finished yet.

[5] Bakhtin calls the outline of his ethical philosophy "architectonics" instead of "a set of principles," "a system" or "a structure" that would

usually be used by theoretical philosophies. "Architectonics" refers to "the general aspects of particular acts" (Morson and Emerson 22). It creates a whole, bringing the parts together like architecture, but "architecture suggests the creation of static structures. The matter of architectonics is active in the sense that it is always in process" (Holquist xxiii). There is an "invisible relation" between the parts of Bakhtinian architectonics, and they have "a relation to *other* things" (xxiv). That is the reason why this system is active. As stated earlier, Bakhtin does not prefer to use terms such as "a system," for instance, because of "not only their inaccuracy, their artificiality, and their predictability" but also the fact that they do not "necessarily contain any human beings" (Morson and Emerson 22).

[6] One exception is Nicole Rizzuto's analysis as she puts under scrutiny whether betrayal takes place in the first place, yet she does not incorporate the value centres of the other characters into her discussion. Although she states in her notes that she believes the ethical stance of Conrad's narrative revolves around the "centrality of the subject" (101), Haldin's perception of Razumov plays an important role in the question of "betrayal." Rizzuto maintains that in his response to Haldin's request to help him escape by going to Ziemianitch to pass Haldin's message, Razumov "never clearly promises to do so" (93) and that "the text refuses to verify that this is a promise" because Razumov merely aims to keep Haldin in his place (94). However, Haldin observes that Razumov is "a man of few words" and believes in "the generosity of [Razumov's] sentiments" (*UWE* 15). When Razumov says, "Yes, of course, I will go" (21), there must not be doubt from Haldin's side that this is a promise. When he bids Razumov farewell on his way to Ziemianitch, he calls him "brother" (24) and retestifies his trust in Razumov upon his arrival with the first question he asks him: "Well! And what have you arranged?" (55). The text does not present any hints of hesitation by Haldin, confirming he has confidence that Razumov must have fulfilled his request.

[7] See Nealon for a comparison of Bakhtin and Levinas. In its historical succession, the *self* and *other* relation appears in the studies of Levinas as well. While Bakhtin places the *self* in the centre and regards it as the ever-developing point of reference, Levinas places the *other* in that position. The approaches of both critics show similarities and differences.

[8] See Maisonnat for a detailed analysis.

[9] See Bimberg for a discussion on the identity of the narrator and the quality of his English (45-47).

[10] Bimberg discusses this idea under "double fallacy" (50).

WORKS CITED

Ambrosini, Richard. "A Memoir 'in the shape of a novel': Making the 'still voice' of Conrad's Polish Past Resonate in *A Personal Record*." *Joseph*

Conrad's Authorial Self: Polish and Other. Ed. Wiesław Krajka. Maria Curie-Skłodowska UP, Columbia UP, 2018. 37-55. Vol. 27 of *Conrad: Eastern and Western Perspectives*. Ed. Wiesław Krajka. 32 vols. to date. 1992- .

Baines, Jocelyn. *Joseph Conrad: A Critical Biography*. Hill, 1960.

Bakhtin, Mikhail M. "Art and Answerability." Bakhtin, *Early Philosophical Essays* 1-3.

---. *Art and Answerability: Early Philosophical Essays by M. M. Bakhtin*. Ed. Michael Holquist and Vadim Liapunov. U of Texas P, 1990.

---. *Speech Genres and Other Late Essays*. Trans. Vern W. McGee. Ed. Caryl Emerson and Michael Holquist. U of Texas P, 1986.

---. *Toward a Philosophy of the Act*. Trans. Vadim Liapunov. Ed. Vadim Liapunov and Michael Holquist. U of Texas P, 1993.

Bernstein, Joshua A. "Under Straining Eyes: Joseph Conrad and the Problem of 'Moral Luck'." *Joseph Conrad and Ethics*. Ed. Amar Acheraïou and Laëtitia Crémona. Maria Curie-Skłodowska UP, Columbia UP, 2021. 117-44. Vol. 30 of *Conrad: Eastern and Western Perspectives*. Ed. Wiesław Krajka. 32 vols. to date. 1992- .

Berthoud, Jacques. *Joseph Conrad: The Major Phase*. Cambridge UP, 1978.

Bimberg, Christiane. "Whose are those 'Western Eyes'? On the Identity, the Role and the Functions of the Narrator in Joseph Conrad's *Under Western Eyes*." *Connotations* 20 (2010): 35-79.

Emerson, Caryl. "Bakhtin at 100: Art, Ethics, and the Architectonic Self." *The Centennial Review* 39 (1995): 397-418.

Erdinast-Vulcan, Daphna. "The Conradian Subject-in-Process: The Question of Ethics in *Under Western Eyes*." *The Conradian* 36.2 (2011): 95-105.

Hampson, Robert. *Joseph Conrad: Betrayal and Identity*. St. Martin's P, 1992.

Hepburn, Allan. "Above Suspicion: Audience and Deception in *Under Western Eyes*." *Studies in the Novel* 24 (1992): 282-97.

Hollander, Rachel. "Thinking Otherwise: Ethics and Politics in Joseph Conrad's *Under Western Eyes*." *Journal of Modern Literature* 38.3 (2015): 1-19.

Holquist, Michael. "Introduction: The Architectonics of Answerability." Bakhtin, *Early Philosophical Essays* ix-xlix.

Juzwik, Mary. "Towards an Ethics of Answerability: Reconsidering Dialogism in Sociocultural Literary Research." *College Composition and Communication* 55 (2004): 536-67.

Kujawska-Lis, Ewa. "Language as a Tool of Inclusion, Seclusion and Exclusion in Joseph Conrad's 'Falk'." *Conradiana* 44 (2012): 227-39.

Long, Andrew. "The Secret Policeman's Couch: Informing, Confession, and Interpellation in Conrad's *Under Western Eyes*." *Studies in the Novel* 35 (2003): 490-509.

Lucas, Michael A. *Aspects of Conrad's Literary Language*. East European Monographs, Maria Curie-Skłodowska U, Columbia UP, 2000. Vol. 9

of *Conrad: Eastern and Western Perspectives*. Ed. Wiesław Krajka. 32 vols. to date. 1992- .

Maisonnat, Claude. "The Agency of the Letter and the Function of the Textual Voice in *Under Western Eyes*." *The Conradian* 34.2 (2009): 90-109.

Morson, Gary Saul, and Caryl Emerson. *Rethinking Bakhtin: Extensions and Challenges*. Northwestern UP, 1989.

Morzinski, Mary. *Linguistic Influence of Polish on Joseph Conrad's Style*. East European Monographs, Maria Curie-Skłodowska U, Columbia UP, 1994. Vol. 3 of *Conrad: Eastern and Western Perspectives*. Ed. Wiesław Krajka. 32 vols. to date. 1992- .

Mroczkowski, Przemysław. "Conrad the European." *The Polish Review* 20.2-3 (1975): 87-96.

Najder, Zdzisław. *Conrad in Perspective: Essays on Art and Fidelity*. Cambridge UP, 1997.

Nealon, Jeffrey T. "The Ethics of Dialogue: Bakhtin and Levinas." *College English* 59 (1997): 129-48.

Orzeszkowa, Eliza. "The Emigration of Talent." *Conrad Under Familial Eyes*. Trans. Halina Carroll-Najder. Ed. Zdzisław Najder. Cambridge UP, 1983. 182-92.

Pettersson, Torsten. *Consciousness and Time: A Study in the Philosophy and Narrative Technique of Joseph Conrad*. Åbo Akademi, 1982.

Rizzuto, Nicole. "Ethical Limits and Confession in Conrad's *Under Western Eyes* and 'Poland Revisited'." *Twentieth Century Literature* 59 (2013): 79-103.

Shepherd, David. "A Feeling for History? Bakhtin and 'The Problem of Great Time'." *The Slavonic and East European Review* 84 (2006): 32-51.

Szittya, Penn R. "Metafiction: The Double Narration in *Under Western Eyes*." *English Literary History* 48 (1981): 817-40.

Laurence Davies,
King's College London,
London, UK

Conrad's Fascination with Illicit Bombs and Weaponry

Those Carlists make a great consumption of cartridges. (*AG* 126)

I

Beginning obliquely with one of Conrad's near contemporaries, here is a moment in Robert Louis Stevenson's tale "The Beach of Falesá." After years of trading in remote posts Wiltshire, the narrator, is approaching a larger, more densely populated island in a brigantine. Two disreputable traders and a Polynesian crew row out to meet the brig. Says the captain of the brig: "What'll you bet they ain't after gin? Lay you five to two they take six cases" (Stevenson 4). This is an island whose foreign residents are awash with gin, but there is something better on offer: six cases of guns. A gun, dynamite, and a murder will figure in the final pages.

The term *gunrunning* is surprisingly recent. The online *Oxford English Dictionary* (*OED*) offers the definition: "the practice of illegally conveying firearms and ammunition into a country." The first example dates from 1883 and refers to gunrunning in Pondoland, a politically volatile territory on the wild coast of the Eastern Cape of what is now South Africa. The second example dates from 1899 in a review of *Under the Sjambok: A Tale of the Transvaal*. In between by date, Rudyard Kipling's "The Man Who Would Be King" is rich in references to a score of clandestinely acquired military issue Martini-Henry rifles and a good deal more made by hand in Kafiristan. Of course, the history of smuggling goes back for countless centuries, and pirates went to sea with a whole armoury of weapons, but it was in the middle to late nineteenth century that the traffic in illicit guns and ammunition rapidly increased. The reasons were twofold: political and technological. They were in demand from those resisting the colonial powers and also among rival polities. One can see both at work in Conrad's *The Rescue*, and also in "Karain."[1] The rapid pace of innovation at the time offered more and more accuracy and more ease and speed of firing – for example, in the successive generations of Colt pistols and revolvers. These innovations led to the availability of outdated weapons at knock-down prices. Again *The Rescue* is instructive. On board the *Lightning* Lingard has a well-kept but old-fashioned rack of bayonets and muskets and a goodly supply of gunpowder in the hold. In part V of "The Shore of Refuge" a bloodthirsty arms dealer from New England tries in vain to peddle his stock, both ancient and modern, to the owner of a pearling schooner. Meanwhile, Jörgenson accuses a Dutch salesman of being a spy.[2] The scene is a gathering over cards and drinks:

> "Vat for spy? Vordamte English pedlars!"
> The door slammed. "Is that so?" asked a New England voice. "Why don't you let daylight into him?"
> "Oh, we can't do that here," murmured one of the players. "Your deal, Trench, let us get on."
> "Can't you?" drawled the New England voice. "You law-abiding, get-a-summons, act-of-parliament lot of sons of Belial – can't you? Now, look a-here, these Colt pistols I am selling – " He took the pearler aside and could be heard talking earnestly in the corner. "See – you load – and – see?" There were rapid clicks. "Simple, isn't it? And if any trouble – say with your divers" – *click, click, click* – "Through and through – like a sieve – warranted to cure the worst kind of cussedness [...]." (*Res* 96)

When the pearler shows no interest in shooting his divers with the latest short arms, the salesman offers shot-guns and rifles. The rifles are left-overs from the war with Mexico, fifteen or so years earlier. As an added incentive, the salesman offers to disguise the rifle cases: "Suppose – musical instruments, this side up with care – how's that for your taste?" (98).

Conrad's works abound in guns, bombs, and ammunition. As well as *The Rescue*, among the novels are *Almayer's Folly*

(Almayer and Lakamba purveying gunpowder; their customer Dain Maroola with his plans for rebelling against the Dutch in Bali, while Dutch patrols trying to arrest him); *The Arrow of Gold* (with Monsieur George supporting the Carlist cause); *Under Western Eyes* (the narrator recalls hearing of a revolutionary plot "to dispatch a steamer with a cargo of arms and conspirators to invade the Baltic provinces" [330]); and *Nostromo* (with Martin Decoud returning from overseas in charge of "an improved model of a military rifle. It had just been discarded for something still more deadly by one of the great European powers" [149]). The stories include "Freya of the Seven Isles" (with the unauthorized sale of firearms, thereby enabling Heemskirk's destruction of the *Bonito*), and Karain's acquiring rifles from the English traders; then there is the more or less autobiographical "The Tremolino" from *The Mirror of the Sea*, again with a Carlist connection, and some tantalising allusions in the letters. It is tempting to add bomb-making in *The Secret Agent* and "The Informer" (with its bomb-making anarchists on the top floor of a London house). Furthermore there is the presence in *The Secret Agent* of Michaelis whose name echoes that of Michael Davitt, an Irish revolutionary who on 14 May 1870 was arrested at Paddington Station, London, carrying £153 to spend on 50 pistols from the gunsmiths of Birmingham, a centre of the craft.[3]

Here is an example of Conrad wooing a publisher with an apologia for a romance, the apologia being a combination of explanation and defence, but emphatically not an apology.

> Lingard at an earlier period of his life, when trading on the New Guinea coast, had been helped out of a dangerous scrape by a Malay from the Gulf of Boni, also a trader. You must know that in Malay society it is the aristocracy that trades. This explains why later on that same Malay wronged by his powerful relatives wishes to right himself arms in hand. [...] Lingard out of gratitude, out of spirit of adventure and from that constant desire of his to shape events, engages to help him, with arms, ammunition and also by personal support. The thing is slowly matured. (*CL* 9: 53)

This is an extract from a lengthy letter written on 8 November 1897 but not published until 2007. The recipient is William

Heinemann's partner, Sidney S. Pawling. After many stops and starts, the romance finally appeared in 1920. As it happens, *The Rescue* was one of the author's most fully described books. Further on in the letter, Conrad pictures the "expeditionary force" assembling stealthily in the creeks of the Shore of Refuge and only the arrival of Lingard with the last cargo of arms and powder must arrive before the whole fleet sails for the Gulf of Boni. "Expeditionary force," by the way, is a phrase more often used by colonizers than by the colonized. The depiction of Hassim, the wronged Malay aristocrat, leader of the flotilla and Immada, his sister, is notably sympathetic.[4] In other words, Conrad was already clearing the ground for a fight against their unjust and Dutch-aligned relatives.

Many excellent Conrad scholars have looked into the dynamics of these narratives. I have no intention of covering the whole literary array of guns and explosives in detail. These are speculations about what pulls and pushes might have brought Conrad back again and again to the topic of gunrunning, and how some of these forces might present to readers. But first, there is a chain of riddles to be solved, or if not solved at least to be considered.

II

Bearing Schrödinger's endangered cat in mind, if this section had a title, it would be *Korzeniowski's Cat*.[5] In Conrad's life there may have been at least two adventures with running guns. One was in the Mediterranean, along the coast of Catalonia and perhaps inland, even as far as Euskadi, the Basque heartland. The occasion was the Third Carlist War (1872–1876), in support of the Infante, Count of Molina, who claimed the regal title Carlos VII, King of Spain. His followers were religious enthusiasts who refused to acknowledge the accession of a woman to the throne, and the Basques feared the loss of the *fueros* that gave them some freedom from the central government in Madrid. In *The Mirror of the Sea*, Conrad allots a substantial part to telling the story of four young men, who buy the *Tremolino*, a *balancelle*, a swift traditionally built vessel: "And we were all ardent Royalists of the snow-white Legitimist complexion – Heaven only knows why!" (*MS* 157). Conrad's social acquaintances in Marseille ranged from the far Left to the far Right. I suspect he enjoyed the contrasts.[6] The four purchasers are inspired by the entrancing Doña Rita and guided by the Corsican Captain, Dominic Cervoni, pledge to ship ammunition for the Carlists. On the third sortie they are chased by a Spanish patrol and can only escape capture by scuttling the *Tremolino*. (In many jurisdictions gunrunning was a capital crime, but under Spanish jurisdiction, the crew ran the risk of being sent to the galleys at Ceuta on the north coast of Africa.) A good deal of the essay in *The Mirror of the Sea* also appears in *The Arrow of Gold*, published thirteen years later. Rita and Dominic are there, and the equivalent of the *Tremolino* "had to be killed" (*AG* 290). Monsieur George, the principal narrator, distances himself further from Royalist causes and scorns the "inanities of the religious." Nevertheless he has enabled "a great consumption of cartridges" (126).

The chronology of these and other narratives (especially *The Sisters*) is hard to pin down. For example, when in 1922 Conrad learned that his friend Edmund Candler and his wife were retiring to live in the far South West of France, he wrote:

> Am I right in believing that the summer temperatures are very pleasant where you live? I don't remember now. I hardly remember the features of the land. The last time I stood on Irun bridge (not a railway bridge) was in '76, I think; and when I think of it I am surprised at being still on this revolving stage. (*CL* 7: 444)

Road and rail bridges across the river Bidasoa linked Irún in Spain with Hendaye in France. As the only evidence that Conrad visited the Basque country, this memory is intriguing, especially because the date given is 1876, when the Third Carlist War ended and the defeated claimant to the Spanish throne crossed the road bridge into exile.[7] From 23 December 1875 to 10 July 1876, Conrad was in France between voyages to the Antilles and could possibly have gone to Spain. On the other hand, Zdzisław

Najder and Robert Hampson have argued that the account of Conrad's movements in the period looks like a composite.[8] Maybe Conrad might have been smuggling, but smuggling something other than guns or ammunition. Or again, it is worth bearing in mind that in Catalonia Carlism may not have entirely disappeared after the end of the Third War. In *The Arrow of Gold*, the account of his work that Monsieur George gives Doña Rita suggests further intriguing detail, however shaky the evidence:

> "Freedom!" I protested. I am a slave to my word. There will be a string of carts and mules on a certain part of the coast, and a most ruffianly lot of men, men you understand, men with wives and children and sweethearts, who from the very moment they start on a trip risk a bullet in the head at any moment, but who have a perfect conviction that I will never fail them. (*AG* 223)

The same uncertainties hover over the fragments in Conrad's correspondence about short visits to the coast of Colombia, specifically Cartagena. In order to make the dates match it is necessary to calculate time and the right distances from ports in Haiti and Martinique. In his brilliant reimagination of Conrad's visit to the coasts of Latin American in *The Secret History of Costaguana* Juan Gabriel Vásquez moves the scene to Colón, on the Isthmus of Panamá, with a delivery of Chassepot rifles as used by the French army in the war with Prussia (75-82). A favourite word in Vásquez's critical vocabulary is *distorsión* (distortion: Vásquez, *El arte de la distorsión y otros ensayos*). A more possible scenario would be another and hideously bloody combat between modernists (liberals) and reactionaries (fervent Roman Catholics) in what is known in Colombia as *la guerra de las escuelas* – "the war of the schools" – a war over whom should control the national syllabus.

Earlier on I referred to Korzeniowski's Cat. What might be called Conrad's French years are among the most puzzling in his life. What would happen if we had solid evidence of the cat's condition? I would put it to you that knowing more is saying less. If the hermeneutic net is pulled too tightly, we also stand to lose. Let speculation thrive.

III

Nevertheless, some hard evidence would be welcome. For example, it is only in the last fifteen or so years that scholars have found new information about the *Vidar* and its cargoes. Beside rattan from the forests and city necessities from Singapore, not to mention the occasional pony, it turns out that the ship was also known as a carrier of illegal guns.[9] This information shows the value of interdisciplinary investigations. One of the works in question is Eric Tagliacozzo's *Secret Trades, Porous Borders: Smuggling and States Along a South East Frontier, 1865–1915*, the result of deep searches in official and unofficial archives. Another important work is an essay by J. N. F. M. à Campo concentrating on Berau itself. Recently, that fine scholar of Ford and Conrad Helen Chambers has added to the trove by searching newspapers online. For instance, in "Further evidence" Chambers cites an item from the 8 November 1887 number of the *Straits Times*: "A box containing Winchester repeating rifles and cartridges was on the 4th instant found by the Police in the possession of a native passenger on the point of leaving this port by the steamer *Vidar*, bound for Berouw"(119). The final destination was unknown. Perhaps the weapons were intended to coerce the Dayaks of interior Borneo (now Kalimantan); perhaps Berau was a staging post on the way to other islands.

The smuggler was caught by British colonial police. In Conrad's narratives, the authorities are Spanish or Dutch. Karain, the son of a Ranee from the Celebes (now Sulawesi) is a member of the Bugis diaspora who has founded his own *imperium in imperio* in a remote valley in Mindanao, at the time of the story Spanish, but very soon to be thrust into the fold of the empire-hungry USA. There is a suspicion among the three English traders that naval gunships are stepping up their surveillance, thus disrupting what amounts to a friendly exchange. In payment for the rifles, probably intended for use against the Spanish, the Englishmen accept a case of trade-dollars and make a present of a six-pound cannon. There is no shortage of readings of the other gift, the gilt sixpence. As Cedric

Watts showed in a classic essay ("Fraudulent Signifiers"), the sixpence bearing the image of Queen Victoria could easily be taken for the considerably more valuable half-sovereign, thereby swindling Karain in a material way. Then one could argue in a Joycean sense that this is a case of inverted simony, using, if you'll forgive the pun, a material gift for spiritual effect. Both readings seem to patronise Karain, but one could also claim that laying Matara's ghost is an act of generosity and kindness. (Ironically, his death was caused by a misaimed gun.) In any case, the trio end up in cold, dank London, haunted by the beauty they have left behind. No wonder the secondary title is "A Memory."

"Karain: A Memory" is not the only story that hints at friendships *sub rosa* and not entirely blighted by racial issues. Lingard sticks to his friendship with Hassim and Immada as a matter of affection as well as honour. "When you save people from death you take a share in their life" (*Res* 102). Excepting Almayer with his deluded expectations of finding whole mountains of gold and Heemskirk the predator and sadist, the Dutch characters are shadowy naval officers doing what they are supposed to do, which is to look out for signs of rebellion and track the gun-runners down. For all his determination to drive the Dutch out of Bali, where his father is the Rajah, Dain is good at thinking matters through. Like his creator Joseph Conrad, he is a born chess player:

> As it was he intended to return with half of his men as soon as the brig was clear of the reefs, but the persistent chase given him by the Dutch frigate had forced him to run south and ultimately to wreck and destroy his vessel in order to preserve his liberty or perhaps even his life. Yes, he had come back to Sambir for Nina, although aware that the Dutch would look for him there, but he had also calculated his chances of safety in Lakamba's hands. For all his ferocious talk, the merciful ruler would not kill him, for he had long ago been impressed with the notion that Dain possessed the secret of the white man's treasure; neither would he give him up to the Dutch for fear of some fatal disclosure of complicity in the treasonable trade. (*AF* 82-83)

IV

How is it that gunrunning and the clandestine use of high explosives feature so often in Conrad's oeuvre? One answer might be Conrad's yearning for a wider audience. On 6 January 1902, he brought J. B. Pinker up to date on the progress of what was then called *Seraphina*: "It has been a worry – but I do firmly believe that here at least we hold something with a promise of popular success. There's easy style, plenty of action" (*CL* 2: 366). After completing the revised proofs the following year, Conrad fell into a dark mood at the thought of what the critics might say: "Sneers at collaboration – sneers that those two men who took six years to write this very ordinary tale' – whereas R. L. S. single handed produced his masterpieces etc etc" (3: 59). This was not the first time that Conrad had railed against Stevenson's gift for exciting narrative swiftly written.[10]

Another answer elicits one of Conrad's favourite sayings: *tempi passati* (times gone by). That phrase is relevant both to his own putative exploits and his fiction. Conrad hoped to talk William Blackwood into publishing *Romance* in serial, written as John Kemp's retrospective tale of perils and adventures. Speaking also on behalf of Ford Madox Ford, Conrad told Blackwood: "We try to produce a variation from the usual romance our point of being that the feeling of the romantic in life lies principally in the glamour memory throws over the past" (2: 339).[11] Coupled with nostalgia, this glow of memory is also projected onto the fictional narrator in "Karain" and Conrad as memoirist in the "Tremolino" sections of *The Mirror of the Sea* (*MS* XL-XLV). The result appears to be the contemplation of danger at fluctuating times and distances. The combination is by no means always glamorous, in any sense of the word. The romantic and the violent are offset by grotesquerie and irony. In *Almayer's Folly*, for instance, we have the plotlines of Dain Maroola's search for gunpowder and the love between him and Nina, Almayer's complaints, bigotry, and dreaming futilities, the battered corpse, the activities of the Arabs, the surveillance by the Dutch patrol, Lakamba's and Mrs. Almayer's intrigues, Nina's revolt against the values of "Western" customs, all this and Conrad's memories of Berau. This is a rich mixture, and so the search for gunpowder, the secret waterway, and the pursuit by the Dutch patrols are all integrated into complex patterns that make *Almayer's Folly* a Modernist rather than a Victorian view of the Malay Archipelago.

In Conrad's oeuvre, running guns is neither morally neutral nor morally fixed. Everything depends on who does the running, where, when, and in whose name. Lingard acts in friendship, Blunt and Doña Rita from conviction, Monsieur George for adventure and a stirring cause, the narrator of "Karain: A Memory" for profit and a vein of generosity. In short, the topos brings out in him the dramatist, the ironist, and the moral cartographer. Gunrunning offered Conrad metaphors and metonymies for a cluster of preoccupations – criminality, loyalty, legitimation, the protean faces of colonialism, the making and breaking of nations. All of these concerns raise questions about boundaries and jurisdictions, and gunrunning by its very nature requires crossing lines or taking sides.

Knowing the power of political rhetoric to besmirch or beautify, Conrad also recognised that one person's lawless traitor and destroyer is another's self-denying patriot. The following example is not about gunrunning, but concerns rebellion under arms and a brutal struggle over national identities and loyalties. As an example of Polish heroism surely familiar to Conrad, the officer cadets led by Piotr Wysocki who took possession of the Warsaw Arsenal on the night of 29 November 1830, thus initiating the uprising of 1830–1831, were seen by Tsar Nicholas I as traitors to the Congress Kingdom and his sacred self. Members of the Sejm, who declared the throne of Poland vacant on 25 January 1831 were also denounced as traitors. So were all other rebels in the Kingdom. After the rising, Nicholas gave orders to "gradually remove everything that has historical or national value, and deliver it here," that is to say Saint Petersburg. Among many other restrictions, exactions, and punishments, 100,000 Polish other-rankers were sent off to the Caucasus; ironically, they were to participate in wars of imperial conquest. Having survived forced labour in the mines of Siberia, one of those soldiers was Prince Roman Sanguszko (Davies 234-35, 244, 245; Najder 30).

V

In another example of opposing loyalties, of vilification and veneration, disputed territories, rebellion, and the overweening state, gunrunning to Ireland played a part that touched on Conrad's sensibilities. Sir Roger David Casement was stripped of his knighthood, tried in London in June 1916 on a charge of high treason, found guilty, and executed on 3 August. After resigning from the Foreign Office of the United Kingdom in 1913, "he became even more committed to Irish causes and advocated a fully independent Ireland – which he believed could be achieved with German assistance" (Laffan). Unionists, meanwhile, opposed Home Rule for Ireland, and the militants of the UVF (Ulster Volunteer Force) were snapping up arms and ammunition. In April 1914, its members landed more than 24,000 rifles and a prodigious quantity of ammunition at the ports of Larne, Bangor, and Donaghadee under cover of darkness and with no intervention by the army or police. In response, the pro-Independence Irish Volunteers, among them Casement, who was a member of their provisional committee, sought guns and munitions of their own. On 26 July 1914, from a yawl sailed by Erskine Childers and Molly, his wife,[12] members of the Volunteers landed 900 forty-year-old Mauser rifles and 29,000 rounds of ammunition at Howth, a small fishing port and outer suburb of Dublin.[13] Both sides were breaking the law, but inevitably the Westminster government favoured the Unionists. Casement, on the other hand, would come to be venerated as a martyr in the cause of an independent Ireland.[14]

On 4 August, the United Kingdom declared war on Germany. Casement set out for the USA to raise support for independence among Irish-Americans. In October, he journeyed via Norway to Germany. On reaching Berlin, he wrote in his diary: "If I win all it is national resurrection – a world nation after centuries of slavery. A people lost in the Middle Ages refound and returned to Europe" (qtd. by Mitchell 1). He stayed in Germany till April 1916, looking to acquire weapons and persuade Irish prisoners to join an "Irish Brigade" that would fight for independence. Neither activity had much success: only a small number of captives would sign on,[15] and the German government grudgingly offered 20,000 rifles and ten machine guns without any instructors to train the latter. In the meantime, militant nationalists in Ireland were preparing for an uprising on Easter Day.[16] Disillusioned by the paucity of German aid and a sense that the Germans were exploiting him, Casement tried to head off the would-be insurgents but to no avail. On 21 April 1916, he landed from the dinghy of a German submarine at Banna Strand in County Kerry. Feverish with the malaria he had first acquired in the Congo Basin, Casement was soon arrested and sent off to London for interrogation. The minesweeper HMS *Bluebell* intercepted the vessel carrying rifles and machine guns meant for the insurrection and flying a false Norwegian flag. While under escort, the German captain scuttled his vessel off the coast of County Cork.

Casement had first met Conrad on 13 June 1890 at Matadi in the Congo "Free State," where, for two or three weeks they shared a room at the Company station (*CL* 5: 630). Conrad was impressed. He wrote in his diary: "Made the acquaintance of Mr. Roger Casement, which I should consider as a great pleasure under any circumstances and now it becomes a positive piece of luck. Thinks, speaks well, most intelligent and very sympathetic" ("Congo Diary," *LE* 161). In 1903, Conrad recommended Casement and Cunninghame Graham to each other for their nonchalant bearing and humanitarianism.[17] After returning to the Congo, Casement had now finished his report to the UK Parliament on the shameless cruelty of King Leopold II's regime in the Congo Basin. In a letter to Graham, Conrad compared Casement to Fray Bartolomé de las Casas, the sixteenth-century bishop who defended indigenous rights in the Americas and denounced the methods of the Conquest (*CL* 3: 101-03).

News of Casement's involvement with the foiled attempt to smuggle weapons and ammunition to the Irish rebels would soon have reached Conrad at Capel House. *The Times* of

25 April 1916 (4) carried a report of the captured ship and a long column on Casement's activities in Germany. On the following day, a leader on the "Irish Disturbances" (7) gave the first account of the Easter Rising, and sneered that: "The Casement invasion itself appears to have been the merest *opéra bouffe*" (7), but the consequences were far from comic. High treason was a capital crime.[18] After the sentence of death was pronounced, Sir Arthur Conan Doyle organized a petition for clemency[19]; among the signatories were John Galsworthy, Arnold Bennett, G. K. Chesterton, Sir James Frazer, Sir John Lavery, and the President of the Royal College of Physicians; Bernard Shaw and W. B. Yeats did not sign the petition but wrote eloquently against the verdict, and warned of the likely effect on Irish public opinion of hanging Casement to add to the shooting of fourteen alleged ringleaders of the Rising. Conrad did not sign the petition. Given the fact that his son Borys had joined the army in September 1915 and was now a junior officer in France, supplying a battery of heavy guns, Conrad's choice was hardly surprising. As he put it in a provocative letter to the Irish-American patron of arts and letters John Quinn: "a state grappling for life with such an adversary as German is not likely to meet a stab in the back with a gentle remonstrance" (15 July 1916; *CL* 5: 620).[20] In an earlier letter to Quinn, Conrad revised his first impressions of Casement:

> He was a good companion; but already in Africa I judged that he was a man, properly speaking, of no mind at all. I don't mean stupid. I mean that he was all emotion. By emotional force (Congo report Putomayo – etc) he made his way, and sheer emotionalism has undone him. (24 May 1916; 598)

Meticulously compiling official reports on systematic terror do not thrive on "sheer emotionalism," but evidently Conrad was keeping his distance. The petition drawn up by Conan Doyle and Clement K. Shorter refers to Casement's "abnormal physical and mental state" (Doyle and Shorter).[21]

In a letter to the Irish painter Alice Sarah Kinkead, whom the Conrads had met in Corsica, Conrad writes "As to Ireland

I don't know it at all" (10 Oct. 1921; 7: 351).[22] A letter to Quinn, written shortly before the Armistice on the Western Front, backs up Conrad's admission (16 Oct. 1918; 6: 284-86). Quinn had warned of the effect on Irish public opinion of coerced conscription, just as previously he had warned against executing the ringleaders of the Easter Rising. Conrad's answer is notable for its scanty knowledge of Irish history and politics, and also for a rare use of the first person plural, deployed as if on behalf of the people of England. "I will tell you that we don't think much about Irishmen now.[23] As long as they didn't actually and materially add to the deadly dangers of our situation we were satisfied.[24] [. . .] We had asked the Irish to come to some arrangements among themselves. They couldn't or wouldn't" (284). As the pre-war episodes of smuggling weaponry show, the divisions were already too wide and too many, at Westminster as well as in Ireland, some of it sectarian, some over the ownership of land, some over economics, some over emigration, some over laws, some over armed forces, some over culture, some over class, some over versions of history.

Next, Conrad himself shifts into the first person singular to delve into comparative histories of oppression, Polish and Irish:

> I have seen those things, I, who also spring from an oppressed race, where oppression was not a matter of history but a crushing fact in the daily life of all individuals made still more bitter by declared hatred and contempt. A very different thing from an historical sense of wrong and a blundering administration. (285)

In view of the savage suppression of the Irish uprising in 1798 and *an Gorta mór* (the Great Hunger) of the second half of the 1840s, "an historical sense of wrong" seems inadequate, given the power of commemoration and inherited memory[25] and also given the great complexity of both Irish and Polish history, not least in Conrad's lifetime.

Quinn, who had amassed a considerable collection of Conrad's works, wrote this letter as an Irish-American of moderate views and an influential Democrat alert to public opinion.[26] What had provoked Conrad was the opposition in Ireland to forcible conscription, a move that Quinn predicted "will be a stupendous blunder for England" (5: 284n2). Conrad's long paragraph on the status of Ireland and the temperament of its people rounds off with sceptical remarks about Woodrow Wilson and the League of Nations.

> However the genius of a people will out; and I have an idea that the Angels on the Central Committee running the League of Nations will have their hands full with the pacification of Ireland. It will be the only state that will not be weary of fighting, on the whole round earth. (285-86)[27]

This *reductio ad absurdum* must be at least half in jest, but as prophecy all too horribly wrong, given the state of post-world war hostilities in, for example, Greece, Turkey, Latvia, Lithuania, Estonia, Ukraine – and of course Poland, with the Polish-Ukrainian and then the Polish-Soviet wars. These conflicts involved ethnicity, territory, and national identity; for the Bolsheviks, acquiring new domains and reacquiring old ones clutched hands with Marxist ideology.

Of course, the nineteenth and twentieth centuries were in no way unique in the experience of shifting boundaries, disputed jurisdictions, hideous slaughter and occasional calm, cultures that overlap and cultures that don't, splits and federations (willing or not), dissolution and restoration, submission and rebellion, free and captive nations, secretive and not, binary and multiple. Conrad saw much and imagined more. He also heard and read so much, a whole inheritance of languages and stories: the range is breath-taking. He was secretive about his writing and fascinated by clandestine behaviour and ideas. He explored dangers and situations far from the norm among his colleagues. The range of his knowledge and experience shocked the critics, the academics, and venturesome general readers. Metaphorically, he was himself a literary gunrunner. In short, he was explosive.

NOTES

[1] Conrad refers to "the whole question of improved armaments" in "The Nursery of the Craft." "We are bound to the chariot of progress. There is no going back" (*MS* 150).

[2] Later in the narrative, Jörgenson will destroy both himself and the *Lightning* by jumping into the hold with a lighted cigar.

[3] Davitt was a leading member of the Irish Republican Brotherhood. He was sentenced on 18 July to 15 years penal servitude for treason-felony; unlike high treason, this crime did not carry the death penalty. On 18 December 1877, he was released on a ticket of leave, a form of parole (McLachlan). In *The Secret Agent*, Michaelis is known as "the ticket-of--leave apostle."

[4] For the politics at stake in the struggle against the Dutch, see Hampson 46-51.

[5] As a not entirely serious thought experiment in 1935, the quantum physicist Erwin Schrödinger imagined the plight of a cat locked in a box with a Geiger counter, a flask of poison, and a decaying radioactive sample. If the sample sheds a particle, the counter breaks the flask, thereby killing the cat. Until the box is opened, the cat is assumed to be in a kind of limbo, both alive and dead. A literary known-unknown would involve the hermeneutics of missing evidence. An example would be the question *could Conrad swim?*

[6] For the range of Conrad's acquaintances in Marseilles, see the letter to E. L. Sanderson of 24 August 1895 (*CL* 9: 255-59); Ziejka; and Chambers, "Localities and triangulations."

[7] It is worth noticing, however, that Conrad says he is uncertain of the year.

[8] Hampson 29-30; Najder 60-61.

[9] Guns and slaves: see Hampson 31-33.

[10] See the quarrelsome letter to Pinker of 8 January 1902 (*CL* 2: 371) where among many other complaints, Conrad denounces Stevenson as a literary prostitute. His real offence in Conrad's eye must have been his facility in making up adventure stories.

[11] When Conrad talks of "glamour" it is usually in its ancient sense of a spell or other enchantment.

[12] Nowadays, Childers is remembered as the author of *The Riddle of the Sands* (1903), the novel about a secret German plan to invade Britain. During the Irish Civil War he opposed a peace treaty with the British. Captured by Irish Free State (pro-treaty) forces, he was executed for possession of an automatic pistol.

[13] Despite their age, many of those guns did service during the Easter Rising in 1916.

[14] "Despite his attempts to prevent what he believed would be a doomed insurrection, he was also the last victim of the executions that followed the

Easter rising, and thereby became a nationalist martyr" (Laffan). Casement's remains were brought from Pentonville Prison, London, to Dublin in 1965. After a state funeral, these remains were reburied at Glasnevin Cemetery among the graves of the executed rebels.

[15] Fifty-six recruits out of 2,300 prisoners (Laffan).

[16] The choice of dates was no accident, but planned for Easter Sunday, the day of Resurrection.

[17] Ironically, the first wave of indignation in the UK about conditions in the Congo was in 1895; it concerned not the sufferings and slaughter of enslaved women, men, and children but the summary execution of Charles Stokes, a British subject. Irish born, he was an ivory trader based in German East Africa. While in Belgian territory, he was accused by a Belgian officer of trading guns and hanged without a decent trial. Supposedly, his last words were: "my country will avenge me" (Louis 572). When the news reached the UK, there was great indignation in Parliament and press.

[18] The legal justification for indicting Casement depended on a definition of high treason in a statute dating from 1351, during the reign of Edward III. Casement's counsel, A. M. Sullivan argued that the statute was invalid, since the treasonable actions (the attempts to organize an Irish Brigade and land the weaponry) were not on British (or Irish soil). Sullivan was overruled (Laffan).

[19] He much admired Casement's humanitarian work in the Congo and Peru. Doyle had published *The Crime of the Congo* in 1909.

[20] For a nuanced discussion of Conrad's relations with Casement, see Dodson.

[21] Alison Garden's essay on spectrality in Conrad and Sebald begins with quoting an article in the *New York Evening Post* (11 May 1923: 16) by the pianist and composer John Powell. Powell had known Conrad since 1913 and dedicated to him *Rhapsodic Nègre*, an opus for piano and orchestra said to be inspired by "Heart of Darkness." According to Powell, in a conversation with him during his visit to the USA in 1923 Conrad recalled a Gothic first encounter with Casement as "an unknowable, malevolent figure." From this point, Powell went on to propose Casement as a model for Kurtz. His argument is weakened by the details: Conrad did not spend several months living in a hut with Casement; two or three weeks at the Matadi station would be nearer the mark.

[22] Thus far, there is no evidence of Conrad's having visited Ireland. On his voyage to the USA in 1923 he would have had a glimpse of Lough Foyle when the *Tuscania* moored to pick up mail and passengers. There are two Irish characters in his work: Belfast in *The Nigger of the "Narcissus,"* and Captain MacWhirr in "Typhoon"; both are Ulstermen.

[23] In the sense of "don't have a high opinion of"? By and large, I use "England" rather than "Britain" or "United Kingdom" because here and elsewhere that is Conrad's normal practice.

[24] Probably an allusion to the "stab in the back" of the Easter Rising.

[25] For example, the widely observed but contentious centennial of the 1798 rebellion (Paseta).

[26] In a letter of 1 May 1916, Quinn had called the Easter Rising "sheer lunacy [. . .]. Of all the idiotic asses that ever were these Sinn Feiners are the worst. Before the breaking out of the war I was in favour of Nationalist Ireland arming itself. The war changed everything" (TS carbon New York Public Library; *CL* 5: 596n1).

[27] It is worth noting that in Ireland, responses to Conrad's work were often ambivalent, but came in particular from writers of fiction such as Frank O'Connor, Liam O'Flaherty, and Seán Ó Faoláin, all of whom had taken part in the War of Independence and were well acquainted with clandestine operations (Niland 325-27).

WORKS CITED

Campo, J. N. F. M. à. "A Profound Debt to the Eastern Seas: Documentary History and Literary Representation of Berau's Maritime Trade in Conrad's Malay Novels." *International Journal of Maritime History* 12.2 (2000): 85-125.

Chambers, Helen. "Further evidence for gun-running on the *Vidar*." *The Conradian* 46.1 (2021): 117-21.

---. "Localities and triangulations: topographical footnotes to *The Arrow of Gold*." *The Conradian* 46.1 (2021): 97-116.

Davies, Norman. *God's Playground*. Vol. 2: *1795 to the Present*. Oxford UP, 2005.

Dodson, Sandra. "A Troupe of Mimes: Conrad, Casement and the Politics of Identification." *Conrad in Africa: New Essays on "Heart of Darkness*." Ed. Attie de Lange and Gail Fincham with Wiesław Krajka. East European Monographs, Maria Curie-Skłodowska U, Columbia UP, 2002. 107-28. Vol. 11 of *Conrad: Eastern and Western Perspectives*. Ed. Wiesław Krajka. 32 vols. to date. 1992- .

Doyle, Sir Arthur Conan, and Clement K. Shorter. "A Petition to the Prime Minister on Behalf of Roger Casement." British Library. Stable URL: <https://www.bl.uk/collection-items/arthur-conan-doyle-roger-casement>.

Garden, Alison. "'Leaving Hardly a Sign – and No Memories': Roger Casement and the Metamodernist Archive." *Modernism/modernity*. Accessed 17 Dec. 2017. Stable URL: <https://doi.org/10.26597/mod.0032>.

Hampson, Robert. *Conrad's Secrets*. Palgrave Macmillan, 2012.

Kipling, Rudyard. "The Man Who Would Be King." *The Man Who Would Be King and Other Stories*. By Kipling. Ed. Louie L. Cornell. Oxford World's Classics, 1999. 244-79.

Laffan, Michael. "Sir Roger David Casement." *Irish Dictionary of National Biography*. Accessed March 2021. DOI: <https://doi.org/10.3318/dib.001532.v2>.

Louis, W. Roger. "The Stokes Affair and the Origins of the Anti-Congo Campaign, 1895-1896." *Revue belge de Philogie et d'Histoire* 43 (1965): 572-84.

McLachlan, Noel. "Michael Davitt." *Irish Dictionary of National Biography*. Accessed Jan. 2022. DOI: <https://doi.org/10.3318/dib.002437.v1>.

Mitchell, Angus. "The War Diary of Roger Casement." *Irish Times*. 30 Apr. 2016: 1.

Najder, Zdzisław. *Joseph Conrad: A Life*. Trans. Halina Najder. Camden, 2007.

Niland, Richard. "Conrad's Reception in Ireland." *The Reception of Joseph Conrad in Europe*. Ed. Robert Hampson and Véronique Pauly. Bloomsbury Academic, 2022: 323-31.

Paseta, Senia. "1798 in 1898: The Politics of Commemoration." *Irish Review* (Cork) 22 (1998): 46-53.

Stevenson, Robert Louis. "The Beach of Falesá." *South Sea Tales*. By Stevenson. Ed. Roslyn Jolly. Oxford World's Classics, 2008. 3-71.

Straits Times (Singapore). 8 Nov. 1887. <https://eresources.nlb.gov.sg/newspapers/Digitised/Issue/straitstimes18871108-1>.

Tagliacozzo, Eric. *Secret Trades, Porous Borders: Smuggling and States Along a South East Frontier, 1865-1915*. Yale UP, 2005.

The Times (London) 25 Apr. 1916.

Vásquez, Juan Gabriel. *El arte de la distorsión y otros ensayos*. Alfaguara, 2009.

---. *The Secret History of Costaguana*. Trans. Anne Mclean. Bloomsbury, 2010.

Watts, Cedric. "Fraudulent Signifiers: Saussure and the Sixpence in 'Karain'." *The Conradian* 28.2 (2003): 112-28.

Ziejka, Franciszek "Conrad's Marseilles." Trans. R. E. Pypłacz. *Yearbook of Conrad Studies (Poland)* 7 (2012): 51-67.

Brygida Pudełko,
University of Opole,
Opole, Poland

H. G. Wells and Joseph Conrad: The Art of Fiction and Recurring Themes in Their Works

H. G. Wells and Joseph Conrad first made contact by an exchange of letters in 1896 when Wells reviewed *An Outcast of the Islands* in the *Saturday Review*. Conrad was also grateful for Wells's favourable review of his *Almayer's Folly* (1895). In *Experiment in Autobiography* (1934) Wells wrote: "He had been excited by a review I wrote of his *Almayer's Folly* in the *Saturday Review*; it was his first 'important' recognition and he became anxious to make my acquaintance" (2: 628). In 1898, the Conrads moved to their first Kentish home at Pent Farm. In the same year, Wells moved to Sandgate in Kent, where he was able to add to the literary friendships he had already made with Arnold Bennett and George Gissing those of Henry James and Joseph Conrad, both of whom he had defended as a reviewer and both of whom were now his neighbours. It is no surprise that Wells later became associated with the Bloomsbury Group, but before that influential group of authors, artists, and critics made their impact on literature, Wells was debating the art and purpose of fiction with his Kentish literary circle. That period was characterized by a mutual recognition of the other's talent and a desire for personal acquaintance. The two novelists met frequently and held earnest discussions on each other's work and the craft of fiction, and exchanged letters until at least 1906.

The aim of this essay is to discuss Wells's affinities with Conrad, both writers' approaches to the art of fiction, and to identify certain common themes and motifs which recur throughout Conrad's "Heart of Darkness" (1899) and Wells's *The War of the Worlds* (1897), "When the Sleeper Wakes" (1899), and *Tono-Bungay* (1909).

Jocelyn Baines writes that Conrad admired "Wells's mind and his science fiction such as *The Invisible Man* and *The War of the Worlds*" (231). In 1898, Conrad described Wells to his cousin Aniela Zagórska as "a very original writer with a very individualistic judgement in all things and an astonishing imagination" (Jean-Aubry 1: 264). When "Heart of Darkness" was written in 1899, Conrad may well have been influenced by Wells's *The Island of Doctor Moreau* (1896), a Swiftian fable on the beast in man, which had appeared three years earlier. He dedicated his novel *The Secret Agent* (1907) to Wells: "the Chronicler of Mr. Lewisham's Love, the Biographer of Kipps and the Historian of the Ages to Come" (iv). Although Wells regarded Conrad as "a great writer," he neither fully understood his works nor sympathized with their aims; and "he intensely disliked Conrad's style of expression" (Baines 232):

> But he had set himself to be a great writer, an artist in words, and to achieve all the recognition and distinction that he imagined should go with that ambition, he had gone literary with a singleness and intensity of purpose that made the kindred concentration of Henry James seem lax and large and pale. *The Mirror of the Sea* was his favourite among his own writings, and I think that in that he showed a sound critical judgment. (Wells, *Experiment in Autobiography* 2: 618)

Wells's rather uncomfortable relationship with Conrad is of interest because of what it reveals about both authors' approaches to the art of fiction and the form and purpose of the novel. Upon meeting Conrad, Wells was by no means leaning towards Modernism; he admired the older writer's fresh approach to the novel and short story, but he was still formulating his own techniques. Wells was a novelist whose work implicitly challenges realist conventions. It is precisely because his novels are self-conscious and pessimistic, that they reject the cohesive world view of the Victorians and focus increasingly on the inner lives of their characters, that he can be regarded, like Conrad, as a transitional figure between realism and modernism.

Much of Conrad's writing, covering an era obsessed by a sense of its own fragmentation, the break-up of old structures, old conventions of art, thought and politics, can be seen to continue the nineteenth-century realist tradition. According to Cedric Watts, Conrad, whose writing is a combination of nineteenth-century and twentieth-century preoccupations, was an intermediary between Romantic and Victorian traditions and early Modernism (171). Morally, psychologically, artistically, and philosophically he can be a probing and challenging writer, who, like many great writers, was influenced by and responded to the ideas and ideals of his day as well as to his literary predecessors. Since he began writing under the influence of the nineteenth-century realists, but at a period which is regarded as the first stage of Modernism, and possessed a multi-cultural literary heritage, realist and modernist elements are merged in his fiction.

At the beginning of the twentieth century, Conrad, like Wells, was distancing himself from the form of the Victorian novel. As some of the strains in nineteenth-century realism, such as the importance of individual responsibility, scepticism, a strong sense of doom, continued into the modernist sensibility, it was almost inevitable for a novelist writing in that period to combine the features of both movements. But Conrad opposed many aspects of modernity. His strong reliance on values such as solidarity, authority, and order was in conflict with the modern forms which reflect individuality and the belief that only consciousness can give meaning to the world. The modernist interest in subjectivity and individualism as well as an intense preoccupation with the inner world of the individual exists in Conrad's fiction side by side with an affirmation of the values of human solidarity and fidelity, values which are necessary to escape from existential meaninglessness and for the survival of humanity. The presence of an observing realist's eye persists even when his tendency is to convey the underlying dream effect that destroys the normal solidarity of the world. Moreover, Conrad's concern with ethical choices is in defiance of the modern temper and its relativisation of all truths and values. Conrad's reliance in his fiction on personal responsibility and moments of moral testing followed by an analysis of the underlying causes and effects of the crucial act of decision on the part of an individual, the strong sense of an impersonal destiny and doom and of the individual's responsibility for his fate all emerge from the nineteenth-century tradition. As the realist novel creates the illusion of a shaped and meaningful world, in the Victorian age it required the subordination of the individual to the social. The individual is not displayed acting within the terms given by the represented society, but is rather in conflict with society and socially asserted and approved norms of value and action. What is more, the pessimistic vision of meaningless and often malign nature inevitably brings about an opposition between human consciousness and nature.

For Wells, the modern novel is a medium through which we can discuss the great majority of the problems which are being raised at any given time by contemporary social development. Unlike Conrad, he sees writing as needing "something that pierces always down towards the core of things, something that carries and changes all the activities of the race" (Boon 3). For Wells, "literary form is deliberately fragmented because society is so fragmented" (James 24). Wells's direction had to do with themes of social inequality and deprivation, allied to a need for political reform, often with distinctly scientific themes. His fiction pointed to class divisions and inequalities, to the need for change, both in his more conventional fiction and his scientific romances. Wells, it would seem, counted himself amongst such artists who can enlighten the world, but Conrad felt that this didactic approach to literature and his audience damaged Wells's art and his capacity to reach a wider audience.

Conrad, who was quite familiar with contemporary science, was against establishing close links between natural science and human culture. He also considered scientific methodology limiting. He witnessed the gradual erosion of the certainty of the world of science and the tradition of Western civilization into a world of scepticism and relativity. Hence he noted the impossibility of achieving objective truth. In his fiction there is no objective authorial representation of reality. The mode of presentation is subjected to the consciousness of the protagonists themselves and reality becomes a projection of the hero's perception. The richness of his works lies in his own vacillation between a desire for certainty and a recognition that such certainty is illusory. He rejected the absolute world of realism and insisted upon the relative world of impressionism with individual experience and human subjectivity at its core. It is Conrad's sceptical refusal to accede to any unchangeable truth of things that places him in the Modernist tradition and distinguishes him from most of his nineteenth-century predecessors.

Nevertheless, although literature was vitally important to Wells for shaping the future, despite his imaginative gifts, Baines claims that "Wells proclaimed himself a 'journalist' and his ideals were revolutionary, while Conrad was an artist and profoundly conservative, to whom Wells's intense concern with socialism, democracy, and a world state must have been strongly antipathetic" (232). Conrad systematically avoided all political commitment. He never voted in a British election, in spite of his respect for English institutions; nor would he involve himself in Polish affairs. As Albert Guerard suggests, for Conrad certain "institutions or instruments (notably capitalism, imperialism, revolution, political discourse itself) are regarded as inherently destructive or futile" (177). In his article on Anatole France, written after finishing *Nostromo*, Conrad said: "Political institutions, whether contrived by the wisdom of the few or the ignorance of the many, are incapable of securing the happiness of mankind" (*NLL* 33). Adam Gillon in "Cosmopolitanism in Conrad's Work" observes that Conrad was a "conservative in politics" and "an outspoken critic of socialism" (94-95). According to Conrad, socialism, robbing men of natural incentives to self-government and inner moral restraint, leads to "Caesarism" (*CL* 1: 16-17), and although in his letters and articles we find many pro-democratic statements, democracy also has negative connotations for Conrad because it "elected to pin its faith to the supremacy of material interests" (*NLL* 107), and democracy is tainted with the abstractions that incited the French Revolution. It is a "mounting battle cry for revolutionary forces quickened by hatred for much that is good as well as much that is corrupt in Western civilization" (Knapp Hay 27).

Conrad's stories display an accurate comprehension of the larger operations of public affairs and movements and, even more significantly, of the influence of social instability and tension upon the private or inner life of the individual. Furthermore, Conrad was more sceptical about the possibility for change because of his view of humankind. Within an overall philosophy of sympathy with humanity, Conrad accepted the essential futility of trying to attain perfection in human behaviour. According to Hugh Walpole, at his last meeting with Wells, Conrad outlined the reasons for their estrangement: "The difference between us, Wells, is fundamental. You don't care for humanity but think they are to be improved. I love humanity but know they are not" (Davis 168). Conrad's fiction focuses on the fallibility of humanity; Wells concentrates on achieving social and political ideals that will perfect humanity, or at least the human condition. These are fundamentally opposed views in authors who are both distancing themselves from their Victorian forebears.

Wells claims that while in his own work he was "becoming more and more set upon changing [his] world and making it something entirely different," Conrad was "equally set upon wringing an unprecedented intensity of phrasing out of his" (*Experiment in Autobiography* 2: 627). For Wells, Conrad's style is self-consciously laboured and unnecessarily complex. Wells asserted that Conrad, Ford Madox Ford, and James's search for literary perfection "bothered me, set me interrogating myself, threw me into a heart-searching defensive attitude," and he "revolted" and "refused to play their game," declared himself a "journalist," and declined the role of "artist" (623). Wells found Conrad's style "oppressive, as overwrought as an Indian tracery" ("his incessant endeavour to keep prose bristling up and have it 'vivid' all the time defeats its end"), although even here he conceded that "in chosen passages and some of his short stories" (622-23), Conrad achieves something sublime. This difference in aesthetics is instructive:

> I remember a dispute we had one day as we lay on the Sandgate beach and looked out to sea. How, he demanded, would I describe how that boat out there, sat or rode or danced or quivered on the water? I said that in nineteen cases out of twenty I would just let the boat be there in the commonest phrases possible. Unless I wanted the boat to be important I would not give it an outstanding phrase and if I wanted to make it important then the phrase to use would depend on the angle at which the boat became significant. But it was all against Conrad's over-sensitized receptivity that a boat could ever be just a boat. He wanted to see it with a definite vividness of his own. But I wanted to see it and to see it only in relation to something else – a story, a thesis. And I suppose if I had been pressed about it I would have betrayed a disposition to link that story or thesis to something still more extensive and that to something still more extensive and so ultimately to link it up to my philosophy and my world outlook. (619)

As Conrad argues in his Preface to *The Nigger of the "Narcissus,"* his aim is to make people "see" and "feel" rather than to read, to be educated or to be entertained. The word "*see*" conveys a sense of visceral experience, of instinctive understanding that cannot be contained in a word, a phrase, or even an entire paragraph. It is almost as if seeing supersedes understanding in Conrad's texts. A distinctly impressionist aspect of Conrad's narrative method concerns his approach to visual description. The relation of individual sense impressions to meaning is dealt with by giving direct narrative expression to the way in which the consciousness elicits meaning from its perceptions. One of the devices Conrad used was delayed decoding – a verbal equivalent of the impressionist painter's attempt to render visual sensation directly, a technique to present a sense of impression and to withhold explaining its meaning until later (Watt 175-76). In a truly impressionistic manner, Conrad demonstrates that each person gains knowledge through interaction with objects of consciousness, and one person's knowledge is never exactly the same as another's, not even exactly the same as one's own at a different point in space and time. All phenomena filter through the medium of human consciousness at a particular place and time; therefore, knowledge comes through the medium of human subjectivity

(Peters 3). Conrad also uses impressionist techniques to represent his characters' perception of objects and events, and to demonstrate that each perceptual experience is unique (35). For Conrad, this new direction could take the form of embedded clauses to build the impression of the complexity of experience and perception, but Wells was not convinced.

However, it was their differing approaches to the purpose of fiction and their readerships that set Conrad and Wells at odds. In *Mankind in the Making* (1904), Wells argues that there are artistic individuals who are able to "abstract and express again what they have seen. Such people are artists – a different kind of people from schoolmasters altogether. Into all sorts of places, where people have failed to see, comes the artist like a light" (190).

Wells had certainly read "Heart of Darkness," which, coming so soon after his own allegorical works, must have struck a responsive chord, and despite his differences with Conrad, he was sufficiently impressed with Conrad's novella to assume "that over a hundred years later it would feature in futuristic libraries, as proven by his mention of the story in *When the Sleeper Wakes*" (Dryden, "H. G. Wells and Joseph Conrad" 8). Conrad's story, an intensely felt account of a journey into the Congo jungle which is also a metaphorical description of a journey into the mind, is a deeply pessimistic work which is said to have influenced T. S. Eliot in the writing of *The Waste Land.* Remarkably Wellsian in the density of its symbolism and imaginative power, "Heart of Darkness" embodies a terrifying vision of man's bestiality, a moment of ultimate horror when the depths of human degradation are revealed. The Conradian adventure *Tono-Bungay* which, as Bernard Bergonzi has demonstrated, is among the most directly allusive of Wells's literary imitations, both parodies and reveals what it sees as the shortcomings of Conrad's style of imperial romance in order to account adequately for the machinations of consumer capitalism and scientific innovation driving the quap expedition (13).

In certain passages in "Heart of Darkness," notably in his mention of the Martians, Conrad paid homage to Wells. In Conrad's story Marlow compares his bewildered and incredulous understanding of Kurtz's position in Africa to belief that "there are inhabitants in the planet Mars" ("Heart of Darkness," *YS* 81). As Linda Dryden clearly demonstrates, by invoking an alien planet and its supposed inhabitants, Conrad, through Marlow, "emphasises the very 'otherness' of Africa for his contemporary readers: it was as alien an environment as far off Mars, and Kurtz, squatting at its centre, seems as unknowable as an alien being" ("H. G. Wells and Joseph Conrad" 4).

Conrad's "Heart of Darkness," which is one of Conrad's most ambiguous and difficult stories, tells the story of the cruel treatment of the natives and of Belgian imperialism in the Congo region through the perspective of the main character, Marlow. It is also about death – the death of many men, the death of ethical behaviour, the death of goodness and civility, and the death of our authority as selves. It is an exploration of the nature of evil and how far a man can go towards it when released from the constraints of what can be called civilization. In the story, Conrad takes his deepest look into the human condition and comes to pessimistic conclusions on the various and incompatible pressures that can be imposed on the human spirit. As Daniel Schwarz puts it, Conrad "was also concerned with the dilemma of transforming the 'freedom' of living in a purposeless world from a condition into a value" (52). In Conrad's story, which is based on his own journey to the Congo in 1890 that shattered his health, Marlow enabled him to examine this dilemma. Marlow, who basically retraces Conrad's footsteps, is sent upriver to rescue Kurtz who is seriously ill. Marlow's journey from Europe to the Congo helped prepare him to sympathize with Kurtz. From the outset, Marlow was offended by the standards and perspectives of the European imperialists, and gradually began to sympathize with the natives against the predatory colonists. When he met Kurtz, Marlow understood that he was without the restraint that even the cannibals had: "Mr. Kurtz lacked restraint in the gratification of his various lusts, […] there was something wanting in him – some small matter which, when the pressing need arose, could not be found under his magnificent eloquence" ("Heart of Darkness," *YS* 131).

Marlow's experience in the Congo invalidated his belief that civilization equalled progress. Well before he met Kurtz, he had discovered that conventional standards had not prepared him for understanding of man's potential for evil. Kurtz, the man who seemed to embody all the accomplishments of civilization, has reverted to savagery. He has allowed himself to be regarded as a God. He has murdered and robbed. Kurtz can be described as a self-made evil god, a lawless ivory hunter whose "appetite for more ivory" (130) is associated with the colour of the skeleton heads with which Kurtz adorns his house. Marlow is not so much shocked by the sight of the heads as by what they reveal about the state of mind of Kurtz: "They only showed that Mr. Kurtz lacked restraint in the gratification of his various lusts, that there was something wanting in him – some small matter which, when the pressing need arose, could not be found under his magnificent eloquence" (131). The symbolic association of the ivory with the heads outside Kurtz's house suggests the very essence of Kurtz. Marlow's description of the man combines the two images:

> I could see the cage of his ribs all astir, the bones of his arm waving. It was as though an animated image of death carved out of old ivory had been shaking its hand with menaces at a motionless crowd of men made of dark and glittering bronze. I saw him open his mouth wide – it gave him a weirdly voracious aspect, as though he had wanted to swallow all the air, all the earth, all the men before him. (134)

But we are never to know the secret of Kurtz's degradation, nor the nature of the "abominable satisfactions" (151) in which he has immersed himself. As Grażyna Branny has observed, Kurtz

> achieves a high degree of communication with the natives on all levels except the moral one. [...] His "unsound method" enables him to overcome his verbal, cultural and emotional alienation among the natives, whom he came to reform, but it aggravates his moral alienation both from them and from himself. (18)

It was "great solitude" which allowed Kurtz to be corrupted. Away from the distractions of society, Kurtz was able to be completely alone with his own mind, and it was from this isolation that he lost his principles:

> the wilderness had found him out early, and had taken on him a terrible vengeance for the fantastic invasion. I think it had whispered to him things about himself which he did not know, things of which he had no conception till he took counsel with this great solitude. ("Heart of Darkness," *YS* 131)

When Kurtz dies on the steamer taking him down the Congo, his last words: "The horror! The horror!" impressive and even terrifying as they are, are nevertheless thoroughly ambiguous. They might represent Kurtz's final desire to return to the scene of those "abominable satisfactions" (151), be his judgement on the unworthiness of his end, a comment on the human condition, or a vision of eternal damnation. Marlow, however, is certain of his own interpretation. He sees Kurtz's last words as a confession, a final attempt at self-purification, "a judgment upon the adventures of his soul on this earth" (150). Marlow is sure that Kurtz's final words represent a "supreme moment of complete knowledge [...] an affirmation, a moral victory paid for the innumerable defeats, by abominable terrors, by abominable satisfactions" (151). Kurtz is deeming his own past actions horrible, and this is a "moral victory" (151). Marlow's interpretation of Kurtz's words is the act of a man who needs to believe in conscience, and is determined to see it, even when it is not there. He discovers that the human spirit is stronger than the powers of darkness and this is the ultimate boon which he must carry to the upper world. According to Gillon, Kurtz's fate is "a symbolic warning to Marlow to beware of the danger of extreme isolation" (*Joseph Conrad* 70). Watts has suggested that it is also possible that Kurtz "deems horrible the inner natures of all mankind" (130). "No eloquence could have been so withering to one's belief in mankind as his final burst of sincerity" ("Heart of Darkness," *YS* 145), and his stare could "penetrate all the hearts that beat in the darkness" (151). But, it is also possible to interpret Kurtz's last words as "condemning, loathing all the universe. [...] 'The horror'" (156).

Darkness prevails when Kurtz dies, symbolizing that his actions were evil. "[O]utside it was so beastly, beastly dark" (150) as he was "lying [...] in the dark waiting for death" (149). Marlow, the man whose illusions have been painfully shattered by viewing and participating in Kurtz's tragedy thinks: "Droll thing life is – that mysterious arrangement of merciless logic for a futile purpose. The most you can hope from it is some knowledge of yourself – that comes too late – a crop of unextinguishable regrets" (150). Dryden points out that like Wells's Martians, "Kurtz brutalises those he enslaves, but is corrupted and destroyed by the alien environment in the process" ("H. G. Wells and Joseph Conrad" 5).

Wells's *The War of the Worlds*, which is described by Ignatius F. Clarke as "the perfect nineteenth-century myth of the imaginary war" (84), presents the invasion of peaceful Victorian England by technologically superior, unsympathetic Martians, who wreak havoc in Surrey and London and almost succeed in wiping out the population with their heat rays and black poison gas before they are destroyed by Earth's bacteria. Despite Africa's rich history and culture, the British were able to use their force to invade in a way similar to how the Martians are able to quickly invade England. In the case of the Martians, their advantage rests in their technology, through which they are able to enslave mankind and claim the Earth for themselves.

Contemporary anxieties about decadence, degeneration, class unrest, and reverse colonization are significant, and the Martians function as a defamiliarizing device by which these questions can be objectified. In his story, Wells has given us one of the most enduring images of science fiction: first contact with inhuman and technologically superior aliens who have evil intentions. But, greater than the imagined war between humans and Martians is the actual conflict between ideas of realism and romance. *The War of the Worlds* embodies a battle between forms of writing. On one side, we have realism – the local and everyday – and science; on the other, fantasy and romance. Wells described his novel as "scientific romance." Science fiction tells us more about the society that produces it than about the world it portrays, so Wells's story must be viewed in its *fin de siècle* context. Another label has been supplied by Conrad, who called Wells "a realist of the fantastic" (Batchelor 22).

In *The War of the Worlds*, civilized humanity is displaced by the Martians' superiority which causes that conventional view of evolution which brought Europeans almost to the ultimate point of progress to be radically challenged. Wells uses several images to suggest this: "we men, the creatures who inhabit this earth, must be to them at least as alien and lowly as are the monkeys and lemurs to us" (*The War of the Worlds* 111); the idea of the Martians' injection of the fresh living blood of other creatures into their own veins "is no doubt horribly repulsive to us, but at the same time I think we should remember how repulsive our carnivorous habits would seem to an intelligent rabbit" (133-34); "'It's just men and ants,' says the artilleryman, 'There's the ants build their cities, live their lives, have wars, revolutions, until the men want them out of the way, and then they go out of the way. That's what we are now – just ants. Only [...] [w]e're eatable ants'" (163); "I felt as a rabbit might feel returning to his burrow, [...] I was no longer a master, but an animal among the animals, under the Martian heel. With us it would be as with them, to lurk and watch, to run and hide; the fear and empire of man had passed away" (54).

Like Marlow in "Heart of Darkness," the narrator experiences a vision of the wilderness invading the civilized world. Marlow's belief that European civilization represents a tradition of humane values was shaken when he was observing Kurtz's behaviour in the Congo. When Kurtz – a poet, painter, musician, journalist, and potential political leader – travelled to the Congo, and the wilderness awakened brutal instincts and monstrous passions in him, Marlow began to realize that his version of civilization did not involve an "emissary of light" ("Heart of Darkness," *YS* 59), but was the harbinger of exploitative imperialism at its worst. Marlow, desperate to retain his illusions, wanted to meet a man reputed to be an "emissary of pity, and science, and progress" (79). He "was curious to see whether this man, who had come out equipped with moral ideas of some sort, would climb to the top after all and how he would set about his work when there" (88).

In *The War of the Worlds*, the signs of everyday existence are lost in a moment of metaphysical revelation, and are then suddenly recovered, leaving the narrator with the altered consciousness that affords him a view of his ordinary self and of the eternity of nature that will obliterate him. His altered point of view gives him a dual perspective, which remains with him throughout and beyond the rest of his story. The narrator witnesses the re-emergence of animal behaviour as panic sets into the multitude and he hears of the "savage struggle" (Wells, *The War of the Worlds* 66) for places in the special evacuation trains and of people fighting "savagely" (99) for standing room in the carriages. At the end of the story, the narrator feels a "sense of doubt and insecurity in [his] mind" (192).

In *The War of the Worlds*, Wells applied Darwin's evolutionary theory to the threat, pointing out that what the Martians were doing to mankind was no worse than what the colonial powers had done to other, "inferior" races (11). Wells believed that the violence with which colonial wars were fought supported the Darwinian idea of the survival of the fittest. The Martian war enters every home, it does not discriminate between classes, it does not spare women, children or the clergy, and it offers no quarter. The narrator in *The War of the Worlds* is shocked by such a ruthless enemy: after a near mental breakdown, he realizes that he has to come to terms with this new reality. Mankind has been pushed from its throne: "the fear and empire of man had passed away" (154).

Wells's Martians are all brain and no heart. The narrator believes that they communicate telepathically, but the content of their communications is beyond his comprehension. According to Charles Gannon, their method of reproduction too has complex and crucial implications in that "Wells eliminates a basic reason for, and force in, communal relations, love, compassion, selflessness, and sensuality" (42). Thus, their advanced mental evolution "may entail horrific social, even physiological, alterations" (42). Wells sympathizes with those who resist the Martian monsters, but he prefers an intelligent approach to mindless heroism or wishful boasting. The artilleryman who dreams of surviving underground is a case in point – his talk is cheap – and it is the serious scientists chipping away at the Martian secrets who will ensure that mankind is better prepared if and when the Martians strike again.

What unites Wells and Conrad is their satirical and enlightened approach to the colonial politics of the imperialist powers. Both give a satirical picture of greedy colonial powers that carve up the planet which is in the end turned into a well-organized Martian colony. Wells allows his native England to suffer the fate that it is forcing upon its colonies. At the end of the novel, we know what to expect: we may be wiped out by a ruthless enemy, just like the primitive races that were wiped out by colonial powers.

Wells's novel "When the Sleeper Wakes" was finally published in 1899, but Wells was dissatisfied with it and he rewrote and reissued it in 1910 as *The Sleeper Awakes*. Thus, while Conrad was busy with "Heart of Darkness" in December 1898, Wells was revising his novel for the version that includes references to Conrad's story.

"When the Sleeper Wakes" tells a story of a Victorian hero Graham. After falling into a two-century-long coma, Graham awakes in 2100 and discovers that speculation in his name by others on the stock market has made him owner of half the world and the figurehead of two successive plutocratic regimes. The "White Council," a small group of men who have inherited trustee status for his estate, rule the globe. Since their power depends on the endless deferral of his waking, this Council now plan to kill him, but he is rescued by followers of a revolutionary leader called Ostrog who stages a revolution and overthrows the Council. He pretends to install Graham as ruler, but in fact wants power for himself and manipulates Graham as his puppet. Graham realizes his error, leads a counter-revolution against Ostrog and expels him from London, but Ostrog recruits a police force from Africa, flying them over to act as his enforcers. At the end of the novel Graham takes to the skies in combat against airplanes bringing troops of soldiers from Africa to impose martial law on London and Paris.

When Graham first awakes, he explores his futuristic surroundings. One room is lined with cylinders:

> The lettering on the cylinders puzzled him. At first sight it seemed like Russian. Then he noticed a suggestion of mutilated English about certain of the words. "[o]*i* Man huwdbi Kin," forced itself on him as "The Man who Would be King." "Phonetic spelling," he said. He remembered reading a story with that title, then he recalled the story vividly, one of the best stories in the world. But this thing before him was not a book as he understood it. He puzzled out the titles of two adjacent cylinders. "The Heart of Darkness," he had never heard of before nor "The Madonna of the Future" – no doubt if they were indeed stories, they were by post Victorian authors. (Wells, "When the Sleeper Wakes" 166)

Wells was familiar with James's story "The Madonna of the Future" (1873), and it would seem that Wells also knew about Conrad's story and may have seen the manuscript.

Wells's depictions of African soldiers are also mediated by Conrad's anti-Congo story "Heart of Darkness." In Conrad's story and Wells's novel, racist and anti-colonialist discourses converge in representing the African soldiers as the henchmen of corrupt imperialism. In Conrad's tale, Marlow recounts a sinister close encounter with a Europeanized soldier, one of the reclaimed, driving a gang of enslaved labourers. He moreover pauses his yarn to imagine much the same situation which Wells's novel dramatizes: "a lot of mysterious niggers armed with all kinds of fearful weapons suddenly took to travelling on the road between Deal and Gravesend, catching the yokels right and left to carry heavy loads for them" ("Heart of Darkness," *YS* 70).

In "When the Sleeper Wakes," Graham has not read the post-Victorian "Heart of Darkness," and because of this he is not prepared to tackle the imperialistic society in which he awakes, or to comprehend the dangers – for both himself and his subjects. More important than Graham's ignorance, however, is future society's failure to act upon the warning that "Heart of

Darkness" provides for it. Graham must combat the failings of a society, then, even though those failings are inherited from his own era, of which he is representative. In "Heart of Darkness" criticism of imperialism is compromised by its adherence to racist ideologies which underpinned aggressive colonialism in Central Africa and elsewhere. In Conrad's story, Marlow acknowledges that "[a]ll Europe contributed to the making of Kurtz" (117).

Wells shares his contemporaries' aversion to the prospect of African militancy in his fictional representation of black combatants. He depicts both Ostrog and Graham acting upon deep-seated prejudices against Africans, and Graham admits to his own aversion (an "archaic prejudice," he calls it) to the prospect of blacks ruling over whites (Wells, "When the Sleeper Wakes" 172, 202), and yet despite its suggestion of "atonement" the novel increasingly shares in racialized angst as to what "vicarious" violence African militarism might bring to Europe. The arrival of militant Africans in European cities in Wells's story presents symbolically the consequences of violent colonial rule in Africa. "When the Sleeper Wakes" represents all the fears of the violence of colonialism coming home to roost. By connecting the Congo to Europe, Wells connects imperial wars forged by Europe in Africa to those fought by Africans in Europe.

Tono-Bungay, which is Wells's most ambitious and sweeping indictment of Edwardian England, is fundamentally about how large and ambitious plans come, in the end, to ruin and disaster. In his *Experiment in Autobiography*, Wells writes that the novel was planned on "the Dickens and Thackeray" line (2: 639), but it was not "a concession to Henry James and his conception of an intensified rendering of feelings and characterization as the proper business of the novelist […]. It was planned as a social panorama in the vein of Balzac" (503), which produced novels like *The Forsyte Saga* or *War and Peace* (504). Wells was conscious that the

> vein has produced some physically and mentally great books, and it continues to this day to produce evidences of the nervous endurance of ambitious writers, vast canvasses, too often crude or conventional

> in interpretation, superficial in motivation and smeary and wholesale in treatment. (503)

Its form is that of a Bildungsroman narrated by George Ponderevo, the son of the housekeeper at Bladesover House in Kent which depicts a story of capitalist entrepreneurship.

The story returns to Wells's own autobiography, as *Love and Mr Lewisham* had done. But, instead of following-through one version of his life story, Wells chops up different episodes, characters and even versions of himself. He is, for example, both of the book's two main Ponderevos, mildly modified in each case by the logic of fictionalisation; as well as several minor characters. The reader may compare many incidents in *Tono-Bungay* with the record of Wells's life. George Ponderevo, as a boy, was for some time living with his mother at the great estate called Bladesover House, where she was a housekeeper. Wells had stayed with his mother at Up Park, where she had held a similar position. When Wells became a science student at South Kensington, his existence and his future had for years been worrying his mother. He had been sent to "Uncle Tom" at Windsor, and to "Uncle William" at Wookey. Later, he had been apprenticed to a draper, then to a chemist, and again to a draper; then he had rebelled and had come to Midhurst Grammar School as an assistant master. George had been worrying his mother in a similar way. He, too, had been sent from uncle to uncle, from all of whom he fled back to his mother. Like Wells, he was apprenticed to a chemist; and for this reason, again like his creator, went to a grammar school to learn Latin. Both made their real start in life by the study of Latin, and both escaped from the depressing years of their childhoods to the world of science at South Kensington by winning scholarships. The stories of their early lives are similar in outline. They both studied science, and they both failed in the second year, and, finally, both were divorced men. The form of the novel is autobiographical, and the *I* of the story is always present either as a narrator or commentator, or as a participant in the scenes that are put up.

George Ponderevo recounts his rise from a lower-middle-class, provincial background. After squandering his early promise as a scientist, George is hired by his Uncle Teddy to help produce and market Tono-Bungay, a patent medicine that for a while is hugely successful. Mainly through advertising, George and his uncle quickly become rich, but just as rapidly the bubble bursts and their financial empire collapses. Wells's novel presents various forms of waste (one of the working titles for the book was "Waste"), which are all symptomatic of a rotten society and the wasting away present at the heart of the British Empire. Destruction in all its forms will prove to be the novel's great theme: the destruction of the old aristocracy and its replacement by a rising plutocracy; the destruction of the English countryside, caught in the rising tide of industrialisation; the destruction of all the old orders and divisions and classes.

The chief emblem of waste is the patent medicine Tono-Bungay. For George, the chief ethical dilemma is that he knows from the outset Tono-Bungay is worthless. For Uncle Teddy, however, that is exactly the point: "the quickest way to get wealth," he claims, "is to sell the cheapest thing possible in the dearest bottle" (Wells, *Tono-Bungay* 129). Tono-Bungay produces wealth, leisure, and opportunity. But for George, the fortune and power gained, not just through Tono-Bungay, but through capitalism more generally, "is all one spectacle of forces running to waste, of people who use and do not replace, the story of a country hectic with a wasting aimless fever of trade and money-making and pleasure-seeking" (365-66). The beginning of the end of the Tono-Bungay financial empire lies in Uncle Teddy's final, unfinished architectural project, Crest Hill, a "twentieth-century house" that "grew, and bubbled like a salted snail, and burgeoned and bulged and evermore grew" (256). His commercial expansion and investments become more overreaching and unstable until, inevitably, it all crashes. Having lost their fortune, George and his uncle make a desperate bid to win it back by seizing a quantity of a rare radioactive mineral found on a West African island called "quap" and to convert it into cash. The Ponderevos' trip to Africa can be seen as a distinctly Conradian African sequence. George Ponderevo takes a "Heart of Darkness" kind of trip to West Africa in a boat whose vulgar, cowardly captain with a thick foreign accent sounds like a caricature of Joseph Conrad.

But, unlike Conrad's Kurtz, whose malevolence at least results in the production of ivory, Wells's George Ponderevo kills without actually delivering any quap, this being a parody of the ironic symbolism in "Heart of Darkness," since quap is intended to bring light to England in the form of "Capern's Patent Filament" (Bergonzi 334). Given this pattern of quite deliberate failures, not of imitation but of the representational possibilities of successive fictional models, we should view Wells's *Tono-Bungay* as tending closer to the vein of high Modernism.

Quap, like ivory in Conrad's text, becomes a stimulant of individual needs or desires. On Mordet Island they find vast, stinking, and poisonous heaps of quap. The smell of it is a sickening thing: "we were all ill, every one of us, so soon as we got to sea, poisoned, I firmly believe, by quap" (Wells, *Tono-Bungay* 305). Sailing home with quap, the crew grow sick and the ship sinks. It is a metaphor, of course, to the condition of England: the whole country is sick, feverish, falling apart. What it needs is a cure, good medicine, not a fake pill, a mere stimulant Tono-Bungay that attracts people only temporarily, but in the longer term makes the feverishness and illness worse.

After his uncle's death George wanders through the streets of a Basque village:

> I slammed the door, and went out into the warm, foggy drizzle of the village street lit by blurred specks of light in great voids of darkness, and never a soul abroad. [...] There was no reality except this solitary road, this quite solitary road, along which one went rather puzzled, rather tired. Part of the fog became a big mastiff that came towards me and stopped and slunk round me, growling, barked gruffly, and shortly and presently became fog again. (349-50)

This is surely the novel's "The horror! The horror!" moment. There is a road, but it comes from nowhere and it's going nowhere. There is a mist that becomes a dog that becomes mist again.

On his trip to Africa to steal the lucrative substance George behaves like Kurtz: he encounters and almost immediately kills an inhabitant of Mordet Island. In retrospect, he cites this as a murder without purpose or reason, a senselessly amoral act. "I found out many things about myself and humanity in those weeks of effort behind Mordet Island," George says. However, what he found out and later regrets is his treatment of his crew: "I understand now the heart of the sweater, of the harsh employer, of the nigger-driver" (316). There is neither ethical enlightenment nor repentance for the act of murder he has committed; George's confrontation with the black man suggests, rather, that a series of Othering responses, and their violent outcomes, is seen by him as both appropriate and necessary to the making of meaning in his story.

Tono-Bungay is preoccupied with the Other at every level of text: in its narrative commentary, characterization, plot development, and resolution. In his journey from youth to middle age, George Ponderevo insists upon his status as the only self-identical person in his story; he imagines himself as transcendental signified, to which the other characters, signifiers lacking repletion, gesture. Wells presents a narrating protagonist whose discourse suggests that he alone is a unity; all Others inhabit the space of incompletion outside this centre. In the first moments of his appearance, the negro is a familiar Other whom George easily reduces in a racist presentation of the man as Nigger-Ape: "[h]e wasn't by any means a pretty figure. He was very black and naked, […] his legs were ill-shaped and his toes spread wide. […] His forehead was low, his nose very flat, and his lower lip swollen and purplish red" (317-18).

Contrary to the Other, George appears as a self-proclaimed "elaborately civilized human being." Suddenly, however, his perception shifts: "And each of us was essentially a teeming vivid brain, tensely excited by the encounter, quite unaware of the other's mental content or what to do with him" (318). George then fires his gun to kill him. The significance of the Mordet Island homicide is that George has ensured through his action that the Other signifies again: the flaccid body that has been marked with the self-asserting signature of George's bullet attests to George's humanity and transcendent meaning because a corpse is non-existence.

The presentation of Roumanian captain of the *Maud Mary* in Wells's novel, which sounds like a caricature of Conrad, offers a contrast to George: George is the English citizen of appropriate mannerisms and considered restraint. On the other hand, the convulsive, maddening foreigner, the captain, was "a gentleman of good family and to air a number of views adverse to the English, to English literature, to the English constitution, and the like. He had learnt the sea in the Roumanian navy, and English out of a book" (306). Wells mocks the captain's diction: "he would still at times pronounce the e's at the end of 'there' and 'here'; he was a naturalized Englishman, and he drove me into a reluctant and uncongenial patriotism by his everlasting carping at things English" (306). Robert Hampson notes some similarities in the captain's attitude in this speech "to the attitudes Wells attributes to Conrad in his picture of him" (16) in *Experiment in Autobiography*: "I found [...] something [...] ridiculous in Conrad's *persona* of a romantic adventurous un-mercenary intensely artistic European gentleman carrying an exquisite code of unblemished honour through a universe of baseness" (2: 621).

Wells compounds Conrad's physical foreignness by describing how he used his entire body to dramatic effect: "and the gestures of his hands and arms were from the shoulders and very Oriental indeed. He reminded people of Du Maurier's Svengali and, in the nautical trimness of his costume, of Cutliffe Hyne's Captain Kettle" (628). These accounts of Conrad's behaviour and speech all reveal very clearly that some of his contemporaries and peers regarded him as distinctly Other. Conrad was a foreigner in his adopted country, and despite his extraordinary command of English in his writing, he must have felt keenly what it was like to be an alien in another culture. That sense of being an outsider is threaded through his work with an acute and keenly rendered humanity, work which is made all the more poignant coming from a writer who had experienced at first hand the sense of alienation and otherness born of not quite belonging. Physical and speaking issues aside, Conrad had crossed national boundaries in a number of ways that are clearly reflected in how he presents in his writing the voice of the oppressed and the subjugated.

As a representative Edwardian hero, George is the only one capable of retrieving true meaning in a world depleted of values. He perceives himself as an emblem of humanity and of a universal truth to which all should aspire. He has also a very low opinion of Jewish financiers: "I do not believe in their intelligence or their power – they have nothing new about them at all, nothing creative nor rejuvenescent, no more than a disorderly instinct of acquisition" (Wells, *Tono-Bungay* 58).

Although George repeatedly performs Othering actions for reasons of ethnic background and national origin, his most virulent attacks centre on those whose selfhood has been mutilated by gender and race: whose status as women or negroes constructs them, in his view, as incomplete, irrational, tarnished, and dangerous. He moves through a series of relationships with lovers who are never accorded subjectivity in the text but who appear, rather, as elusive vehicles for George's need. Yet it is precisely because women are seen as agents of relationships that they are most scathingly rejected in George's story. In a dualistic metaphysics, bourgeois culture opposes masculinity and femininity by associating masculinity with individualism and its attendant values – the foremost of which is self-containment.

After the publishing of *Tono-Bungay,* the two novelists' friendship cooled. But in the end the two were politically and temperamentally mismatched. Conrad's last words to Wells pithily sum up their disagreements: "The difference between us Wells is fundamental. You don't care for humanity but think they are to be improved. I love humanity but know they are not" (Hart-Davis 168).[1]

Wells's and Conrad's ultimate break-up was signalled by the interruption of their correspondence in 1911. However, it was followed by Wells's sometimes rather vicious attacks, not only on Conrad, but also on James and Ford during the war, and even during the 1930s and 1940s, when some of the writers concerned were ailing or even long-dead. He lampooned his literary friends as too artistic elite authors and "drama queens," thus rejecting through their parody the too "written," that is, self-consciously experimental modernist art (Dryden, *Joseph Conrad and H. G. Wells* 156).

Nevertheless, Conrad's and Wells's references and allusions to each other, which often appear in their letters and works, indicate that, despite their reservations, each admired the other's talent and commitment to their art and style. They were among the greatest recorders of the problems occupying their generation. Both writers examine the horrors of Western colonialism, depicting it as a phenomenon that tarnishes not only the lands and people it exploits, but also those in the West who advance it. A visible correlation between the analysed stories and colonialism is the stark contrast in development between invaders and their victims. Britain's ability to conquer Africa was due to superiority in military, technological, and economical capabilities. A recurring theme in the discussed works is darkness and mist. It represents everything that is unknown, primitive, evil, and impenetrable. It becomes a symbol of hatred, fear, and symbol of the power of evil. Another aspect of colonialism mirrored by Conrad and Wells is greed. It destroys the moral values of colonists whose thoughts become centred on making a profit without acknowledging the harm they are doing to the natives. The colonialists have selfishly put themselves and their own wealth before the wellness and humanity of the people they desire to profit from.

NOTES

[1] Quoted by Hugh Walpole in his diary for 23 January 1918.

WORKS CITED

Baines, Jocelyn. *Joseph Conrad. A Critical Biography.* Weidenfeld, 1960.

Batchelor, John. *H. G. Wells.* Cambridge UP, 1985.

Bergonzi, Bernard. *The Turn of a Century: Essays on Victorian and Modern English Literature.* Macmillan, 1973.

Branny, Grażyna. *A Conflict of Values: Alienation and Commitment in the Novels of Joseph Conrad and William Faulkner*. Sponsor, 1997.
Clarke, Ignatius F. *Voices Prophesying War. Future Wars 1763-3749*. 2nd ed. Oxford UP, 1992.
Dryden, Linda. "H. G. Wells and Joseph Conrad: A Literary Friendship." *The Wellsian* 28 (2005): 2-13.
---. *Joseph Conrad and H. G. Wells: The Fin-de-Siècle Literary Scene*. Palgrave Macmillan, 2015.
Gannon, Charles E. "'One Swift, Conclusive Smashing and an End': Wells, War and the Collapse of Civilisation." *Foundation* 28.77 (1999): 35-46.
Gillon, Adam. "Cosmopolitanism in Conrad's Work." *Proceedings of the IVth Congress of the International Comparative Literature Association*. Ed. Francois Jost. Moulton, 1966.
---. *Joseph Conrad*. Twayne, 1982.
Guerard, Albert. *Conrad the Novelist*. Harvard UP, 1958.
Hampson, Robert. "The Physical Presence of Conrad in Certain Works by H. G. Wells." *The Conradian* 6.2 (1981): 16-19.
Hart-Davis, Rupert. *Hugh Walpole, a Biography*. Macmillan, 1952.
James, Simon. *Maps of Utopia: H. G. Wells, Modernity and the End of Culture*. Oxford UP, 2012.
Jean-Aubry, G. *Joseph Conrad. Life and Letters*. 2 vols. Heinemann, 1927.
Knapp Hay, Eloise. *The Political Novels of Joseph Conrad*. U of Chicago P, 1963.
Peters, John. *Conrad and Impressionism*. Cambridge UP, 2001.
Schwarz, Daniel. *Conrad.* Almayer's Folly *to* Under Western Eyes. Cornell UP, 1980.
Watt, Ian. *Conrad in the Nineteenth Century*. U of California P, 1979.
Watts, Cedric. *A Preface to Conrad*. Longman, 1982.
Wells, H. G. *Boon. The Mind of the Race, The Wild Asses of the Devil, and the Last Trump: Being a First Selection from the Literary Remains of George Boon, Appropriate to the Times*. Unwin, 1915.
---. *Experiment in Autobiography*. Vol. 2. Gollancz, 1934.
---. *Mankind in the Making*. Chapman, 1903.
---. *Tono-Bungay*. Random, 2003.
---. *The War of the Worlds*. Penguin, 1974.
---. "When the Sleeper Wakes." H. G. Wells. *The Science Fiction*. Vol. 2. Phoenix, 1996.

Grażyna Maria Teresa Branny,
Jesuit University Ignatianum,
Cracow, Poland

Intertextuality and Denegation in Conrad's Earliest Short Story "The Black Mate"

This paper is an attempt at re-reading Conrad's first tale "The Black Mate" (1884–1886) in the context of William Faulkner's *Light in August* (1932) and *Absalom, Absalom!* (1936) as well as *Go Down, Moses* (1942), with a view to revealing Conrad's use in it of the modernist device of denegation (assertion of presence by absence and vice versa) – a narrative method, whose invention has been ascribed to Faulkner.[1] The appearance of denegation in this earliest and largely neglected example of Conrad's writing should enhance the tale's literary reputation, which has heretofore suffered from deprecating remarks about its alleged immaturity.

So far the critical debate on "The Black Mate" has mostly revolved around the circumstances and date of its original composition – whether in 1884 (Watts ix),[2] 1885 (Jean-Aubry 89), or 1886 (Baines 110-11; Graver 4).[3] This factual debate is important for the present essay in so far as it establishes Conrad as a precursor of denegation in his earliest piece of fiction, written well before the turn of the century, and, significantly, on the point of his transition from a seafaring to a writing career, while he was still seriously questioning his predisposition for the latter in 1889, when setting out on the creation of *Almayer's Folly* (1895),[4] which, by his own decree, even so, has officially remained his first literary work.[5] As it appears, however, it is in his allegedly "amateurish" first tale, written a few years before *Almayer's Folly*, that Conrad's use of denegation anticipates the essence of Modernist epistemology, i.e., the relativity of truth. Over a century later, the method of denegation that Conrad applied in both its dramatized and narrative form in "The Black Mate,"[6] as will be demonstrated in the present paper, will be ascribed to Faulkner, and in 1989 defined by François Pitavy in relation to *Absalom, Absalom!* as more than a negation because it actually affirms what it negates.[7]

The poor critical reputation of "The Black Mate" is mostly due to Conrad's own judgement and his belittlement of the story's quality and general significance, although here we are reminded by Andrea White that this was a frequent practice with the writer, also in relation to his highly acclaimed pieces, and, as such, should be taken with a pinch of salt (111). Nevertheless, the critics' own opinions followed suit, and, ever since, the story has been written off as derivative of W. W. Jacobs (Jean-Aubry 1: 89); not serious enough and "a sport in the Conrad canon" (Graver 4); and "trivial" because "told in a breezily colloquial style [...] light-heartedly for a rather low-grade magazine competition or as a potboiler" (Baines 112). Even the semi-Gothic aspect of the tale, as marked by Jacek Mydla, has been largely ignored by critics dealing with the supernatural in Conrad's writings, chiefly on account of the story's "amateurish shortcomings" as his earliest literary piece (88).

Other than that, White sees the tale as largely autobiographical in echoing the later phase of Conrad's career as a sailor (112-13), while Gail Fraser pairs it off with "The Inn of the Two Witches," calling both "formulaic" (35). Keith Carabine and Laurence Davies analyse "The Black Mate" in the context of Conrad's overall literary achievement, while Ted Billy sees it primarily as a story of deception (224). Mydla's recent chapter on the "The Black Mate" discusses it against the background of the spiritualist, utilitarian, and Darwinian theories of the day, hence in an ideological context, and in the context of Conrad's aesthetics in the sense of his "narrativization" of those theories in the tale (89).

The present intertextual and denegative re-reading of "The Black Mate" as an anticipation and ironic dismissal of *otherness* and its criminalization comes the closest to Mydla's combined ideological and artistic approaches, although the kind of ideology and aesthetics identified in Conrad's story in the present paper differs significantly from those discussed in Mydla's.

The ambivalent social perception of and moral judgement on Winston Bunter in Conrad's tale, whether in or out of London Dock – based solely on appearances and a linguistic organization of reality in the Lacanian sense[8] – are clearly evocative of the social and moral response in Faulkner's fictional Yoknapatawpha county to the racial ambivalence of Joe Christmas in *Light in August*. Likewise, unexpectedly enough, "The Black Mate" lays bare Faulkner's indebtedness to this Conrad tale for his famous Shreve's prophecy in *Absalom, Absalom!*, engaging both texts dialogically in the Bakhtinian sense,[9] as is also the case of Faulkner's story "Pantaloon in Black" in his short-story cycle *Go Down, Moses*. Overall, the intertextual reconsideration of "The Black Mate" in the Faulknerian, Bakhtinian, and Lacanian contexts sheds new light on the aesthetic and ideological dimensions of this unjustly ignored Conrad tale.

The narration of "The Black Mate" is structured dramatically rather than narratively around a polyphonic dialogic exchange between the voices of the sympathetic authorial narrator and the scapegoated Winston Bunter – the eponymous black mate – and the confused communal voice of the London Dock, substantiated by the paradoxically combined pragmatic and spiritualistic perspective of Captain Johns of the *Sapphire* – Bunter's own ship. From the very start of the story, Bunter is set by the narrator in opposition to the said lot at the Dock, of an "unromantic-looking set of men [...] with the professional stamp obliterating the personal characteristics," as one who "had a presence" when "he strode down the Jetty to his ship" in front of "a gross lot, who could have no appreciation of the man's dignified bearing" ("The Black Mate," *TH* 85-86). Bunter's distinctiveness from the other seamen is denegatively confirmed towards the close of the story by the appearance at the Dock of the punitive authority of a policeman in search of him after his disappearance, although the police are called in by Johns to look for Bunter's body rather than on account of any criminal act he is thought to have committed. Combined with the nickname given him by the shipmen for his "ravenly" black hair – "the black mate" – all that brands Bunter from the start, placing him permanently in the category of *otherness*, and a criminalized one at that.

The narrator straightens out the facts for the potentially confused reader by asserting that the black mate was "no more black than you or I, and certainly as white as any chief mate of a ship in the whole of the Port of London" and "to call him black was the superficial impressionism of the ignorant" (86). However, as he does so – naturally, above the heads of both Captain Johns and the "gross lot" – the foreman stevedore feels free to express his "ignorant prejudice" against Bunter in the narrator's hearing by saying, "'I bet he's a furriner of some sort'" (86). In this polyphonic exchange, it is the assertion of the narrator – who knows Bunter well enough to be familiar with his secret, which he, however, refuses to divulge to the reader until the story's end – that establishes him as the ultimate authority on Bunter's credibility against the prejudiced opinions of those at the Dock. Hence, the story's internal dialogics works towards dramatized denegation, i.e., an assertion of absence – a *de facto* lack of Bunter's *otherness* – by presence – Bunter's *othering* by those who judge him solely on the basis of his appearance, or follow the opinions of those who let "the world of words [...] create the world of things" for them, after the Lacanian fashion (Lacan, *Écrits* 65).

Dramatized denegation in "The Black Mate" is augmented by verbal denegation in Conrad's description of Bunter, which is evocative of Conrad's denegative description of Heemskirk in "Freya of the Seven Isles" published a quarter of a century later, albeit used there to exactly the opposite effect. Hence, denegation in Conrad's description of the black mate through the polyphony of voices serves to foreshadow the falseness and the absurdity of the allegations of *otherness* directed against him, Conrad thereby implying the protagonist's harmlessness and thus the innocuousness of his deception in dyeing his hair black while keeping everyone around in the dark about it. In contrast, in the case of Heemskirk, denegation foreshadows his unexpected betrayal of Freya and Jasper Allen, despite appearances to the contrary, thus anticipating the revelation of his spiteful and deceptive nature.

As a close reading of two passages from "The Black Mate" makes quite clear, all allegations of *otherness* raised against Bunter are, through denegation, carried by Conrad to absurdity, thus reducing the black mate's *otherness* to his "striking" appearance and bearing, which in itself is neither criminal nor incriminating:

> Bunter's hair was *absolutely black, black as a raven's wing.* [...] and *his eyebrows* were *thick and bushy.* Add to this *steely blue eyes*, which *in a fair-haired man would have been nothing so extraordinary*, but *in that sombre framing* made *a startling contrast*, and you will *easily understand* that Bunter was *noticeable enough. If it had not been* for the *quietness of his movements*, for the general *soberness of his demeanour*, one would have given him credit for a *fiercely passionate nature.* [...]
>
> "Oh, Willy sent him," said Captain Ashton. "He's *a very striking man. If you were to* put a red sash round his waist and a red handkerchief round his head *he would look exactly like* one of them *buccaneering chaps* that *made men walk the plank* and *carried women off into captivity. Look out,* Johns, *he don't cut your throat* for you and *run off with the* Sapphire." (*TH* 86-87, 90; emphasis added)

Incidentally, the Willy who recommends Bunter as a mate, and whose authority Ashton cites above, appears to be quite an authority with the Dock's seamen, many of whom owe their jobs to his intelligence, so if his information in matters of employment is reliable, so too must be his information on the people at the Dock, like Bunter. This in itself negates Bunter's *otherness* and dismisses the criminality implied in Ashton's allegations against him.

In contrast, a close-reading of two denegative descriptions of Heemskirk in the passages from "Freya of the Seven Isles," cited below, reveals the Dutchman's malice, which he takes great pains to camouflage:

> You shall see at once *how unreasonable this dread* of Heemskirk.... *Certainly*, his nature was *malevolent enough*. That was *obvious*, directly you heard him laugh. [...] *But*, bless my soul! *if we were to* start at every *evil guffaw* [...] *we shouldn't be fit for anything but* the solitude of a desert, or the seclusion of a hermitage. And *even there* we should have to put up with *the unavoidable company of the devil.*

> *However, the devil* is *a considerable personage*, who [...] *has moved high up in the hierarchy* of Celestial Host; *but* in the *hierarchy* of mere earthly *Dutchmen*, Heemskirk, whose early days could *not* have been *very splendid,* was *merely* a naval officer [...], of *no particular connections* [...] but there were brains enough in it [his skull] to discover and *take advantage maliciously of poor old Nelson's nervousness* before everything that was invested with the merest shred of *authority.* (*TLS* 159-60; emphasis added)

Conrad, or rather his narrators, put considerable effort into at once being and not being explicit about the harmlessness/ harmfulness of Bunter/Heemskirk, so the ambiguity here is obviously intended, rather than contingent on the narrators' diffidence or the author's inconsistency, a trait that Conrad has not infrequently been accused of in his allegedly "strange" short fiction (Erdinast-Vulcan).

Compared to Faulkner's complex use of denegation in stream-of-consciousness narration – as in Rosa Coldfield's section of *Absalom, Absalom!* cited below – Conrad's application of denegation in the tales cited above is still evidently experimental, limited to the organization of the plot and dialogue combined with third person narration. However, in both passages quoted above, he employs exactly the same array of denegative devices that Faulkner is to do half a century later: qualifiers of certainty (absolutely, certainly, easily, obvious); modal and conditional structures implying a high degree of implausibility (if it had not been for; if you/we were to...), accompanied by Faulkner's favourite reductive qualifier "even"; generalizations to prove the possibility/impossibility of what eventually appears to be false/true; negative analogies or speculative parallels (Bunter vs. buccaneering chaps; the devil vs. Heemskirk); confirming/disproving what has just been cited as falsehood/ fact ("the quietness of [Bunter's] movements" vs. "a fiercely passionate nature"; "no particular connections of Heemskirk" vs. "authority"), etc.

Contrasting the above passages from two of Conrad's short stories with a passage from Rosa Coldfield's narrative section in *Absalom, Absalom!* concerning her love or lack of love for

Charles Bon, it is hard to miss the glaring analogies between Conrad's and Faulkner's use of denegation, with Conrad clearly having blazed the trail:

> (I did not love him; *how could I? I had never even heard his voice,* [...]) [...] *because I who had learned nothing of love, not even parents' love –* [...] *became not mistress, not beloved, but more than even love;* I became all polymath love's androgynous advocate. [...] *I was not spying, though you will say I was. And even if it was spying, it was not jealousy, because* I did not love him. (*How could I have, when I had never seen him?*) And even if I did, *not as women love,* [...]. *If it was love (and I still say, How could it be?)* [...]. *Because I asked nothing of him,* [...]. *And more than that:* I gave him nothing which is the sum of loving [...] *yet who did not do it because I should have had to say* "Don't talk to me of love but let me tell you, who know already more of love than you will ever know or need." (Faulkner, *Absalom, Absalom!* 146-47; deitalicization for emphasis mine as the original passage is enitrely in italics)

As in the passages from Conrad's tales, so also in this Faulkner fragment, what is affirmed is immediately followed by its negation, to become again revoked, and then once more denied in the service of the truth of the matter, which is either obliterated by adverse reality or social milieu, as in Bunter's case, or deliberately kept hidden from public sight, as in Heemskirk's; or else appears downright implausible either to the person directly concerned (Rosa), or the reader: i.e., Rosa's love for Charles Bon, as opposed to her sister Judith's, his actual fiancée's, lack thereof.

Soon after "The Black Mate" opens, in the already mentioned City restaurant scene where the shipmasters meet to eat and gossip, we are confronted with another allegation of criminality coming from Captain Ashton – not just the jocular one involving Bunter's alleged buccaneering, but a quite serious one against his own colleague-in-command, Captain Johns, Bunter's employer and persecutor, whom Ashton accuses of wanting to poison "'every sailor above forty years of age'" (*TH* 87) as not "in their prime" and thus not "equal to modern conditions of push and hurry" (88). This lot includes Bunter, which is why he dyes his hair to keep his "berth." When a storm washes away the bottles with his dyes, he pretends his hair has turned gray from a haunting experience he claims to have had in which he fell off a ladder – a story which both terrifies and exhilarates Captain Johns because it confirms his fascination with and knowledge of spiritualism, but incriminates Bunter, whom Johns suspects of secretly committing a murder for which the alleged ghost – a mere figment of Johns's imagination – keeps haunting the mate. This criminalizes Bunter's *otherness*, but, ironically and denegatively, it also criminalizes Johns's *othering* of Bunter – which occurs for no reason at all as he is unaware of the mate's true age – as well as his *othering* of all sailors over forty – for a very good reason, the way he sees it, i.e., their age.

The narrator's negative depiction of both captains, Captain Johns as "well known without being much respected or liked," suspicious, credulous and mean, and Captain Ashton as "a cynical and teasing sort of man" (87) in contrast to his portrayal of the black mate, whom Johns himself perceives as "irreproachable" and "as near absolute perfection as could be" (98), not only puts things into proportion for the confused reader, but also denegatively invalidates both Johns's *othering* on the grounds of age and his criminalization of *otherness*, asserting the absence of reasons for either by the presence of both in the system of values of a man who, as his sister (who knows him best) asserts, has "got devils on the brain" (120).

What further compromises and denegatively invalidates both *othering* and *otherness* in "The Black Mate" is the narrator's contrasting depictions of the *othered* (Bunter) and the *othering* (Johns) at the close of the tale when the true colour of Bunter's hair is revealed at last:

> Whereas the black mate struck the people as deliberate, and strangely stately in his gait for *a man in the prime of life*, this *white-headed chap seemed the most wonderfully alert of old men.* I don't suppose Bunter was any quicker on his pins than before. *It was the colour of the hair that made all the difference in one's judgment.*
>
> The same with his eyes. *Those eyes*, that looked at you so steely, so fierce, and so fascinating out of a bush of a buccaneer's black hair,

> *now had an innocent almost boyish expression* in their *good-humoured brightness* under those white eyebrows. (116; emphasis added)

The invalidation of Johns's *othering* of Bunter comes denegatively with the elimination of the reasons for that *othering* in Conrad's effacement of the criteria of colour and age and their convergence in Johns's philosophy of employment. Hence, the absurdity of *othering* Bunter is confirmed at the end of the story by the convergence in him of two factors formerly seen as mutually exclusive: age and alertness.

As to the absurd and grotesque figure that the *othering* Captain Johns cuts at the close of the tale in contrast to the *othered* Bunter:

> Bunter said afterwards that nothing could be more *weird* than *this little man, swathed in a sleeping suit three sizes too large for him, shuffling with excitement in the moonlight* near the wheel, and shaking his fist at the serene sea.
>
> *"Photographs! photographs!"* [...]
>
> Nothing could be more *funny* than *this ridiculous little man's conviction – his dogmatic tone* [...] *that grotesquely mean little figure* in striped flannelette alternately *creaking and droning of "personal intercourse beyond the grave."* (100-02; emphasis added)

Johns is denegatively depicted here by both Bunter and the narrator – who validates that perspective for the reader – as his own caricature in the photographic, i.e., denegative sense, of one *othered* in the process of *othering* those around him. His pyjamas, three times his proper size, grotesquely, and denegatively, belittle him as does his *othering* of others, in both the literal and the figurative sense – thus asserting the presence of his *othering* by the absence in those *othered* of the incriminating and criminalizing qualities he ascribes to them, for in ghosting them he ghosts himself, thus downsizing his existence to "personal intercourse beyond the grave."

Conrad's use of denegation for the construction of Bunter's *otherness* reaches beyond narrative technique, and thus aesthetics, into the sphere of ideology, and hence the most destructive consequence of *othering*, i.e., criminalization of the *Other*. This puts Conrad's Bunter on a par with Faulkner's Joe Christmas, both first branded as "furriner[s]" and referred to as "strangers," then *othered* as "black," and later scapegoated as alleged (Christmas) or potential (Bunter) murderers. As underscored by Doreen Fowler in the Lacanian context:

> Faulkner's texts powerfully illustrate the arbitrary relationship between the signifier and the signified. In *Light in August*, Faulkner demonstrates how racial difference is a product of language. Joe Christmas becomes the despised racial other because of a word. [...in that way] language constructs Joe's identity. (168)

As a matter of fact, the same is true of Conrad's hero, whose "ravenly" black hair and stately bearing linguistically brand him as the *Other*, "the black mate," and in consequence bring about Johns's persecution of Bunter all the way to Calcutta:

> He would believe any silly tale, suspect any man of anything, and crawl about with it and ruminate the stuff, and turn it over and over in his mind in the most miserable, inwardly whining perplexity. He would take the meanest possible view in the end, and discover the meanest possible course of action by a sort of natural genius for that sort of thing. ("The Black Mate," *TH* 92)

However, Bunter is denegatively freed of that branding in an ironic ending of the story on a comic note. His dye gone, he turns into his own photographic negative and makes a virtue of necessity both for himself and his persecutor, for the latter, while still kept in the dark about Bunter's truth, is further confirmed in his faith in spiritualism and thus absolutely sure of Bunter's "prime" despite his white hair, which is what Bunter strove for in the first place. Hence, with a simultaneous removal of the reality (black hair as *signifié*) behind his nickname (word as *signifiant*), Bunter becomes denegatively doubly de-*othered* – as now, in Johns's eyes, ideologically, young enough for the position of a mate, and de-criminalized in his new innocent, because white, looks, despite both aspects standing in an obvious, and thus comic, logical opposition to each other.

Not so in the case of Faulkner's white "negro," who, denegatively made by its creator into a Christ figure, although allegedly the murderer of Joanna Burden, in the tragic finale of *Light in August* dies an undeserved death as a result of the workings of the single damning word "nigger," produced off the cuff by Christmas's collaborator Joe Brown to divert the attention of the policeman who suspects him of murdering Joanna. As indicated by Fowler, Faulkner, who constructs Christmas as white,

> is at pains to demonstrate that Joe's racial otherness, like all otherness, depends on what people say. [...] on what Doc Hines says, on what the children in the orphanage say, on what Joe says, on what Brown says, and on what the people of Jefferson say; and inexorably and relentlessly they say "nigger." Like all those who are identified as other, Joe is other by virtue of a word. (170)

Conrad's earliest literary text yields yet another, as puzzling as it is rewarding, discovery pointing to Faulkner's fiction in a passage concerning Bunter's "blackness," possibly a source of and inspiration for Shreve's prophecy in *Absalom, Absalom!*.[10] In "The Black Mate," by appearing at the story's beginning, it functions as a sort of *apologia* for Bunter's alleged *otherness*: "Competent authorities tell us that this earth is to be finally the inheritance of men with dark hair and brown eyes. It seems that already the great majority of mankind is dark-haired in various shades" (*TH* 86). In Faulkner's novel Shreve's words, in closing the book, sound apocalyptic, especially in the context of the fears of the American South, obsessed with miscegnation. Uttered lightly by an outsider to the South and a foreigner (a Canadian student at Harvard, and so in the North of the United States), Shreve's words prophesy a dissemination of miscegenation (in Faulkner's novel tragically embodied in the last scion of the Sutpen line, the mulatto idiot boy Jim Bond) to all corners of the globe, which denegatively implies a de-*othering* of the *Other*:

> in time the Jim Bonds are going to conquer the western hemisphere. Of course it won't quite be in our time and of course as they spread toward the poles they will bleach out again like the rabbits and the

> birds do, so they won't show up so sharp against the snow. But it will still be Jim Bond: and so in a few thousand years, I who regard you will all have sprung from the loins of African kings. (Faulkner, *Absalom, Absalom!* 378)

The intertextual Bakhtinian dialogics of the two passages places them both in the same category as both pertain to *otherness* on the grounds of colouring. By being carried to absurdity in Conrad's text, where the issue of colour refers solely, if not comically, to the dyeing of hair, *otherness* becomes simultaneously invalidated in relation to Faulkner's text where it refers to the colour of skin, and hence racism, with all its tragic consequences in Faulkner's books. In the context of "The Black Mate," with the narrator's words on blackness acquring a universal significance, Shreve's prophecy also acquires a broader meaning, damning all humanity rather than just the Southerners, for *othering* those that differ from them in any way, whether on grounds of race, as in *Absalom, Absalom!*, or age, as in Conrad's tale, or to broaden the issue even further into our times on account of gender, health, nationality, religion, sexual orientation, or, for that matter, social or material status.

Even despite its absurdity and arbitrariness, Bunter's "colouring" threatens to decide about his and his wife's being or not being, which constitutes the best comment on the very nature of *othering* in general. In Faulkner's writing this finds a pertinent reflection – possibly a derivative one to "The Black Mate" – in the title of the story "Pantaloon in Black," which is a part of his short-story cycle *Go Down, Moses* (1942).[11] Interestingly enough, Faulkner does not name the story after the "colouring" of his African American protagonist Rider (i.e., "Black Pantaloon"), but uses the notion of colour in the title to mean an addition to – like Bunter's hair dye – a disguise rather than an inherent and damning attribute of character inseparable from one's very being, thus sharing Conrad's basic premise in "The Black Mate," of the arbitrary nature of *othering*.

Quite apart from indeed implying an article of clothing – for Rider is in mourning following the recent death of his wife –

Faulkner's title serves to offset the notion of criminality and damnation as being connected to blackness in the American South (incidentally, as mentioned before, through Johns's allegations, this notion likewise dogs Conrad's protagonist). Instead, Faulkner enhances the intense humanity and heightened sensitivity of his African American protagonist, in stark contrast to the very denial of those qualities in the callousness of the white sheriff and his wife as well as the murderous instincts of the Birdsongs, who claim the right of control over Rider's fate and life without respecting the acuteness of his suffering, or even marking its existence, because they cannot even imagine that people of colour are human and therefore can suffer and experience pain as does any other human being[12]:

> "Them damn niggers [...]. Because they aint human. They look like a man and they walk on ther hind legs like a man, and they can talk and you can understand them and you think they are understanding you, at least now and then. But when it comes to the normal human feelings and sentiments of human beings, they might just as well be a damn herd of wild buffaloes." (Faulkner, *Go Down, Moses* 113)

Faulkner straightens out the truth of the matter of the distribution of humanity between Rider and the whites for the reader in the closing scene of the story, just as does Conrad by presenting the already cited disparity between the final images of Bunter and Captain Johns to the disadvantage of the latter. In the sheriff's account of the tragi-comic capture of Rider, who has been *othered* for the intensity of his grief over Manny's death because, on account of his skin colour, it is misconstrued as criminal by the insensitive and prejudiced whites, Rider presents the figure of a Pantaloon "laughing, with tears big as glass marbles running across his face [...] like somebody dropping bird eggs, laughing and laughing and saying, 'Hit look lack Ah just cant quit thinking. Look lack Ah just cant quit thinking'." To the sheriff's question, "'And what do you think of that?'," his wife answers callously: "'I think if you eat any supper in this house you'll do it in the next five minutes, [...]. I'm going to clear this table then and I'm going to the picture show'" (116). Both protagonists, Bunter and Rider, are construed denegatively – the blackness of Bunter's hair being the function of its whiteness, and vice versa, each the more present for the absence of its opposite at a given point in time. Similarly, Rider's African American identity as a potential source of *othering* becomes the less conspicuous (absence) for the title of the story which associates blackness with a disguise rather than treating it as an attribute, a fact which casts Rider – in contrast to the corrupt and unfeeling whites – as sensitive, loving, and just (presence), not only because of his devotion to Manny but also through his defence of his ignorant and naïve fellow negroes, who have been cheated by whites in a game of dice.

Just as Conrad's Bunter – like Faulkner's Rider – is described by the narrator as "very sensitive" and "too good for old Johns" ("The Black Mate," *TH* 96-97), so is Johns's fixation on spiritualism potentially as demeaning and destructive for Bunter as is the cynicism of the sheriff for Rider, who is, incidentally, found hanging "at the hands of a person or persons unknown" (Faulkner, *Go Down, Moses* 112) on the day preceding the sheriff's conversation with his wife. Conrad's narrator describes the trauma of the voyage to Calcutta for Bunter under Johns's prying eye, constant nagging, and morbid suspiciousness in this way:

> He knew that on many occasions he was *on the verge of lunacy*, because he could not help indulging *in half-delirious visions* of Captain Johns being picked up by the scruff of the neck and dropped over the taffrail into the ship's wake – the sort of thing *no sane sailorman would think of doing* to a cat or any other animal, anyhow. He *imagined* him bobbing up – a tiny black speck left far astern on the moonlit ocean.
>
> *I don't think* that even at the worst moments Bunter really desired to drown Captain Johns. I fancy that all his *disordered imagination* longed for was merely to stop the ghostly inanity of the skipper's talk.
>
> But, all the same, it was a *dangerous form of self-indulgence.* [...]
>
> It makes me *creepy* all over to think of. And sometimes *the folly of Captain Johns* would appear clothed in a sort of *weird utilitarianism.* ("The Black Mate," *TH* 101-02; emphasis added)

Paradoxically enough, the above passage denegatively confirms the criminality of Bunter, which has been suspected all along by Captain Johns, who believes that he was struck on board by the revengeful spirit of a person he had murdered in the past. However, what denegatively detracts from the black mate's alleged criminality and confirms his innocence is the narrator's stress on his occasional desperate loss of control over reality in consequence of Johns's persecution (*lunacy*) and his letting his *imagination* run away with him as a result (*half-delirious visions*) rather than on any real intention on his part to harm Johns. Conrad's use of denegation here lies in the narrator's reference to *a sane sailorman*, which puts things into proportion for the confused reader, who knows by now that it is Bunter who answers this description despite his moments of occasional *lunacy*, as the insanity on board pertains solely to Johns, who behaves as if "somebody told him [his mate] had a tail and he wanted to find out how [he] managed to conceal it" (91). However, the reader's freshly restored faith in Bunter's innocence here is again undermined by the narrator's diffident *I don't think* even if it is next followed by a return to Bunter's *disordered imagination*. The narrator's comment on the *danger of self-indulgence* seemingly further confirms the plausibility of an accident on board the *Sapphire* but, as the latter part of this passage clarifies (too long to quote here in full), the real danger to the ship is posed by the *folly of the captain* himself, his *weird utilitarianism* potentially leading him to an attempt at "'a personal intercourse beyond the grave'."

The reader's uncertainty as to Bunter's guilt (of whatever sort) is occasionally further teased by the narrator's enigmatic references to some sort of secret that the black mate allegedly harbours in his heart, as in, "I suppose a man with a secret locked up in his breast loses his buoyancy," followed two paragraphs further on by Bunter's own even more teasing words: "'One would think he suspected I had stolen something and tried to see in what pocket I had stowed it away'" (91). Furthermore, the narrator's information about Bunter having lost a ship in the Indian Ocean once and having therefore been deprived of a certificate for a year is preceded barely two pages before by Johns's provocative, insinuating, and malicious admission:

"'*I can't help* thinking. I've seen you before somewhere, Mr. Mate. *If* I heard your name, *perhaps*—'" (94; emphasis added), which, however, features two diffident grammatical structures, *I can't help* and *if*, as well as the speculative *perhaps*, thus denegatively undermining the grounds for Johns's suspicions, and making it difficult if not impossible to establish the truth of the matter, the more so that the sentence is suspended. This again is followed by the narrator's compassionate rumination over Bunter having broken his luck with the loss of his ship "*as it seemed* for good and all, at the same time" (95; emphasis added), the speculative *seemed*, though, leaving a margin of sympathetic disbelief on the part of the narrator because, despite his suspicions of the worst in Bunter, all Johns is confronted with, according to the narrator, is the mate's performance as a man who "was irreproachable, as near absolute perfection as could be." For the doubting reader, the narrator's praises of the black mate are immediately confirmed by a third person statement: "Captain Johns was much annoyed, and at the same time congratulated himself on his chief officer's efficiency" (98).

Notwithstanding, the sympathetic narrator still mentions Bunter's "*remorse* in regard to a certain *secret action* of his life" for which "a man of Bunter's *fine character* would *suffer not a little*" (95; emphasis added). A few pages further on, this seemingly translates into what looks like some sort of threat that Bunter addresses to Johns, when, "being bored *beyond endurance*, and also *exasperated* by the private worry," he "*lost his self-possession*": "'You don't know what a man like me is capable of'" (103). However, Bunter's *remorse* is contingent on the *fineness* of his *character*, and his threat on being driven *beyond endurance* and *exasperation*. When at the end of the story the reader finally discovers Bunter's *secret* of his double deception of Captain Johns, which is meant to save his berth (his dyed hair, broken bottles, and the concocted tale of a supernatural encounter which turned the mate's hair white overnight told to his friend the narrator), Conrad's denegative account is not by any means over. The final denegative narrative twists and meanderings of the story include: Bunter's ouraged confession that Johns harboured "'a notion that at some time or other [he] *had done somebody to death* in some way'" (118; emphasis added); his admission to becoming Johns's trophy as an alleged convert to his spiritualism, and thus *an object of the captain's love and pride*; a confession to being *warned* by Johns in his lunacy *against* "'*tumbl[ing] overboard* perhaps, or something [...] till [they] pacify the spirit-world in some way'" (119; emphasis added); his own admission to *nearly dropping Johns overboard* himself; the story of the captain *summoning the police* to retrieve Bunter's body after his sudden disappearance; and, finally, an account of Johns in his retirement telling others the story of his black mate, "'*a murderous, gentlemanly ruffian*'," a story that his level-headed sister concludes with the telling comment that "'*[h]e's got devils on the brain*'" (120; emphasis added), which denegatively identifies her brother as *the* culprit of the story, thus at last bringing the reader the desired answer as to the truth of the matter. Hence, the final pages of the story are denegatively interspersed with the simultaneous absence and presence of guilt and criminality, which change places between Bunter and Johns, finally landing at the door of the latter, Bunter's sin of deception coming nowhere near Johns's own, because it was the latter's murderous threat to poison every mate over forty that had driven the black mate to resort to deception in the first place, and that only for the upkeep of his family.

The next to impossible process of arriving at the truth of the matter – the greatest challenge of modernist epistemology and Faulkner's writing – is cleverly rendered by Conrad in his earliest text through denegative narrativity, which is applied in "The Black Mate" very consistently from the story's beginning to its very end, in a similar way to that of "The Tale,"[13] which was written thirty-three years later, keeping the tension high for the reader and sustaining the suspense all along. This also runs high because the narrator, evidently the protagonist's confidant, refrains from disclosing to the readers the truth of the matter until the very end of the tale – perhaps to suggest the relativity of truth, or let them form their own opinion when they finally learn about Bunter's secret of dyeing his hair black, his dye bottles all landing in the stormy sea because he neglected to lock the drawers before leaving his berth to fight the storm, and his deception of Johns on board the ship after the accident. Hence the reader is kept in the dark about the reasons for Bunter's behaviour, his actual motives and character – and only slightly less so than is Johns himself – but for the voice of the sympathetic narrator, who, even so, as in the above quoted passages, teases the reader about the protagonist's actual intentions, alleged guilt, and his past. The narrator's denegative account is interspersed with an equally denegative dialogue and veers between absence and presence, one confirming or disproving the other, similarly to what happens in the Rosa Codlfield previously quoted section in *Absalom, Absalom!* albeit in Conrad it is on the level of a more traditional third person narration, rather than the modernist stream-of-consciousness in Faulkner's novel.

To conclude, a denegative and intertextual approach to "The Black Mate," just as to Conrad's other less valued and little discussed short fiction (cf. note 6), when seen in the context of Faulkner's best novels, reveals the precursorship of the former as regards the invention of the modernist technique of denegation, which has to date been mistakenly associated with Faulkner. This signals a sphere of affinities in Conrad and Faulkner studies which could be dubbed systemic because it reaches beyond the heretofore analysed areas of individual, often contingent, analogies of character, scene, phrasing, and imagery, or even similarities of rhetoric, style, and point of view, not to mention those of temperament, background, and systems of values between the two writers.[14]

NOTES

[1] Faulkner never acknowledged this literary debt to Conrad's short fiction (or any other debt, for that matter), evasively stating at University of Nagano (1955) that "a writer never knows where he steals from" (Jelliffe 72). The most glaring example of his unacknowledged derivation from Conrad, if not a downright plagiarizing of a Conrad text, came with his Nobel Prize

Address (1949), for which he had paraphrased fragments of Conrad's essay "Henry James: An Appreciation" (1904) (for a more detailed discussion of the issue see Branny, *A Conflict of Values* 25-27).

[2] Cunnighame Graham, Preface to *Tales of Hearsay* (1925), Conrad's last volume (published posthumously), in which "The Black Mate" followed "The Warrior's Soul," "Prince Roman," and "The Tale" (11). In this way Conrad's oeuvre came full circle, "The Black Mate" marking both the beginning and the end of his literary career.

[3] Following Conrad's own words in a letter to Pinker of January 19, 1922 (*CL*: 7), where he specifically mentions "'86" as the date of the tale's composition "for a prize competition, started [...] by *Tit-Bits*." Jocelyn Baines traces it to the May 1, 1886 magazine competition "Special Prize for Sailors" for an essay on "My experiences as a sailor." Rejected at that time, the story was published in the *London Magazine* 22 years later, in 1908, in a presumably revised form (Baines 110). A subsequent, private edition of "The Black Mate" followed in 1922 (Baines 110n*).

[4] As pinpointed by White (111), in *A Personal Record* Conrad mentions his first novel as composed at the time when he "had written nothing but letters, and not very many of these" (*PR* 68), thus ignoring "The Black Mate," of which he admitted he had rather confused memories, disagreeing with Jessie over the origins of the story itself, which she claimed was hers (Megroz 88).

[5] In his already cited 19th January, 1922 letter to Pinker, Conrad suggested keeping for *Almayer's Folly* the official status of his first work, not to "complicate [his] literary history in a sort of futile way" by "proclaim[ing] [...] the history of the 'Black Mate,' its origin, etc., etc. [...] over the housetops" (Jean-Aubry 2: 264).

[6] Conrad also employs denegative narration in a more advanced way in his later tales "Freya of the Seven Isles" and "A Smile of Fortune" (*'Twixt Land and Sea*, 1912), "The Planter of Malata" (*Within the Tides*, 1914), and "The Tale" (1917) published in *Tales of Hearsay* (1925), along with "The Black Mate." For a detailed discussion of the issue in each, see a series of my articles: "The Unfathomability of Conrad's Shallow Waters," "What 'A Smile of Fortune' Has to Hide," "An Intertextual and Denegative Reassessment," and "An Epistemological and Denegative Reinterpretation." Conrad's use of denegation elsewhere, i.e., beyond his short fiction, remains an unchartered territory yet to be covered by a full scale study, my project having been confined to those Conrad tales that have been deprecated for their "strangeness," incongruity, and/or melodrama, i.e., the qualities that appear to be directly related to the writer's hitherto unrecognized application of denegation.

[7] *Denegation* in Pitavy's understanding of the term as applied to Faulkner's fiction is tantamount to asserting presence by absence, or absence by presence, in the sense of a fact being the more present (absent) for the

absence (presence) of the apparent reasons for that presence (absence). As understood by Pitavy, *denegation* is a psychological term, which refers to the speaker. In calling Sutpen in Faulkner's *Absalom, Absalom!* a "nothusband," Rosa Coldfield does not mean that he did not ever become her spouse but that he was "the more present for being perceived as the negative of a husband" (Pitavy 29).

[8] In "The Insistence of the Letter," Lacan points to the arbitrary relationship within the Saussurian distinction between the signifier and the signified, *signifiant* and *signifié*, the word and the object in the real world that it refers to, stressing the domination of the former over the latter, which surfaces in its uppercasing in the formula *S/s*.

[9] *Intertextuality* is defined here, after Julia Kristeva, in the sense of a work of art being "part of a larger fabric of literary discourse, part of a continuum including the future as well as the past" (Murfin, Ray 249), as well as in the Bakhtinian understanding of dialogic discourse as developed by Kristeva, "a dialogic work" defined as "one that permits numerous voices or discourses to emerge and to engage in dialogue with one another" (Murfin and Ray 111; emphases of entries removed).

[10] In the same novel, without as much as acknowledging the fact, Faulkner paraphrases, almost word for word, the famous Stein passage from *Lord Jim* – "in the destructive element immerse yourself" – in the context of Judith Sutpen leaving the only letter she received from Charles Bon from the Civil War front in the hands of Mrs. Compson as a denegative token of memory, a hard fact and proof of his alleged love for her (for a more detailed discussion, see Branny, *A Conflict of Values* 113-14).

[11] In his 1989 *Conradiana* article "Faulkner's Pantaloon and Conrad's Gaspar Ruiz," W. R. Martin points to a possible derivation of Faulkner's African American protagonist of "Pantaloon in Black" in *Go Down, Moses* (1942) from Conrad's short story "Gaspar Ruiz" (*A Set of Six*), with respect to their analogous representations in both works. However, Martin's comparison of the two characters with regard to their superhuman strength, which translates into their love for their wives, and vice versa, does not reach beyond those similarities into the sphere of interest in the present paper, i.e., narrative techniques and denegation.

[12] In her 1987 essay "The Site of Memory," Toni Morrison delineates one of the purposes of her writing as follows: "to find and expose a truth about the interior life of people [African Americans] who didn't write it (which doesn't mean that they didn't have it)" (47).

[13] For a detailed discussion of Conrad's application of denegative narrativity in "The Tale," see my "An Intertextual and Denegative Reassessment" (cf. note 6).

[14] For an overview of that criticism, see Branny, *A Conflict of Values* 17-32. For another sphere of systemic affinity between the two writers, in analogical patterns of alienation and commitment in their fiction, see also

my *A Conflict of Values*. For Conrad's influence on American modernists, see Mallios, while for an annotated bibliography of Conrad's influence on American literature, see Secor and Moddelmog.

WORKS CITED

Baines, Jocelyn. *Joseph Conrad: A Critical Biography*. 1960. Penguin, 1986.

Billy, Ted. *A Wilderness of Words: Closure and Disclosure in Conrad's Short Fiction*. Texas Tech UP, 1997.

Branny, Grażyna. *A Conflict of Values: Alienation and Commitment in the Novels of Joseph Conrad and William Faulkner*. "Sponsor," 1997.

---. "An Epistemological and Denegative Reinterpretation in the Faulknerian Context of Conrad's Malay Tale 'The Planter of Malata'." *Conrad Without Borders: Transcultural and Transtextual Perspectives*. Ed. Brendan Kavanagh, Grażyna M. T. Branny and Agnieszka Adamowicz-Pośpiech. Bloomsbury, 2023. 53-67.

---. "An Intertextual and Denegative Reassessment of 'The Tale'." *Yearbook of Conrad Studies (Poland)* 15 (2022). Forthcoming.

---. "The Unfathomability of Conrad's Shallow Waters in 'Freya of the Seven Isles': An Intertextual Reading of Conrad's Story." *Yearbook of Conrad Studies (Poland)* 10 (2015): 127-50.

---. "What 'A Smile of Fortune' Has to Hide: An Intertextual and Comparative Reconsideration of the Texture and Theme of Conrad's Tale." *Yearbook of Conrad Studies (Poland)* 14 (2019): 7-33.

Carabine, Keith. "'The Black Mate': June-July 1886 – January 1908." *The Conradian* 13.2 (1988): 128-48.

Davies, Laurence. "Uncanny Conrad: Home, Exile, Memory, and Communication with the Dead." *Hearts of Darkness: Melville, Conrad, and Narratives of Oppression*. Ed. Paweł Jędrzejko, Milton M. Reigelman, and Zuzanna Szatanik. M-Studio, 2010. 227-41.

Erdinast-Vulcan, Daphna. *The Strange Short Fiction of Joseph Conrad: Writing, Culture and Subjectivity*. Oxford UP, 1999.

Faulkner, William. *Absalom, Absalom!* 1936. Random, 1964.

---. *Go Down, Moses*. 1942. Random, 1996.

---. *Light in August*. 1932. Random, 1972.

Fowler, Doreen. *Faulkner: The Return of the Repressed*. U of Virginia P, 1997.

Fraser, Gail. "The Short Fiction." *The Cambridge Companion to Joseph Conrad*. Ed. John Stape. Cambridge UP, 1996. 25-44.

Graham, Cunnighame R. B. Preface. *Tales of Hearsay*. By Conrad. Doubleday, 1926. vii-xv.

Graver, Lawrence. *Conrad's Short Fiction*. U of California P, 1969.

Jean-Aubry, Gérard. *Joseph Conrad: Life and Letters*. 2 vols. Doubleday, 1927.

Jelliffe, Robert A., ed. *Faulkner at Nagano*. Kenkyusha, 1956.

Lacan, Jacques. *Écrits: A Selection*. 1966. Trans. Alan Sheridan. Norton, 1977.

---. "The Insistence of the Letter in the Unconscious." *Yale French Studies* 36/37 (1966): 112-47.

Mallios, Peter Lancelot. *Our Conrad: Constituting American Modernity*. Stanford UP, 2010.

Martin, W. R. "Faulkner's Pantaloon and Conrad's Gaspar Ruiz." *Conradiana* 21 (1989): 47-51.

Megroz, Rodolphe Louis. *Joseph Conrad: Mind and Method*. Faber, 1931.

Morrison, Toni. "The Site of Memory." 1987. *Morrison:* Beloved. Ed. Carl Plasa. Columbia UP, 1998. 43-47.

Murfin, Ross, and Supryia M. Ray. *The Bedford Glossary of Critical and Literary Terms*. Bedford/St. Martin's, 2009.

Mydla, Jacek. "Spiritualism, Utilitarianism and Sympathetic Narration in 'The Black Mate'." *Some Intertextual Chords of Joseph Conrad's Literary Art*. Ed. Wiesław Krajka. Maria Curie-Skłodowska UP, Columbia UP, 2019. 87-102. Vol. 28 of *Conrad: Eastern and Western Perspectives*. Ed. Wiesław Krajka. 32 vols. to date. 1992- .

Pitavy, François L. "Some Remarks on Negation and Denegation in William Faulkner's *Absalom, Absalom!*." *Faulkner's Discourse: An International Symposium*. Ed. Lothar Hönninghausen. Niemeyer, 1989. 25-32.

Secor, Robert, and Debra Moddelmog, eds. *Joseph Conrad and American Writers: A Bibliographical Study of Affinities, Influences and Relations*. Greenwood, 1985.

Watts, Cedric, ed. *Joseph Conrad's Letters to R. B. Cunninghame Graham*. Cambridge UP, 1969.

White, Andrea. *Joseph Conrad and the Adventure Tradition: Constructing and Deconstructing the Imperial Subject*. Cambridge UP, 1993.

David Schauffler,
University of Silesia,
Katowice, Poland

Yanko Goorall and Espen Arnakke: Similarities and Differences between "Amy Foster" and *En sjømann går i land* by Aksel Sandemose

The question of immigration, and the related topics of assimilation and alienation, othering, and identity generally, have in recent decades become objects of earnest, not to say feverish, attention in literary studies, as well as in political debate. Joseph Conrad's short story "Amy Foster" (1901), which has established itself as a classic literary proto-treatment of these concepts, is thus worth re-examining in any way that can shed further light upon them.

In this paper I undertake to compare "Amy Foster" with a semi-autobiographical novel by Aksel Sandemose, which recounts the experience of a Danish sailor who, like Yanko Goorall in "Amy Foster," finds himself alone and *in extremis* in a foreign coastal village. Beyond this basic similarity in their situation, the fate of Sandemose's hero, Espen Arnakke, is so dramatically different from that of Yanko, and Sandemose's style of narration so diametrically opposed to that of Conrad, that juxtaposing the stories may generate some useful ideas about both. It is not possible here to develop comparative analyses of these works on every level, so the discussion will be restricted to a few signal elements of the cultural context of "Amy Foster," and the parallel context of Sandemose's novel, that have, perhaps, received less thorough attention than they warrant. These are: the social structure of a community and the influence of this structure on the reception of the "stranger," the way that the narration situates the stranger in his relation to the community, and the relation between otherness and agency. While "Amy Foster" needs no recounting, a brief summary of Aksel Sandemose's career and the novel I will be discussing follows below. My comparison of the stories' central theme will be articulated by reference to Georg Simmel's seminal essay "The Stranger" (1905), which can supply a theoretical framework for the very different fates of Yanko Goorall and Espen Arnakke.

Aksel Sandemose was born in northern Jutland in 1899, and in his teens served on lumber schooners in Norway and Newfoundland, where he also worked ashore as a lumberjack. After returning to Denmark and publishing several novels and stories in Danish, he moved to Norway in 1930 and, drawing on his childhood and his experiences in Newfoundland, published (in Norwegian) the novel we shall consider here, *En sjømann går i land* (A seaman goes ashore), 1931, and its much better-known prequel, *En flyktning krysser sitt spor* (A fugitive crosses his tracks), 1933.[1] The first of these traces the experiences of a young Danish sailor, Espen Arnakke (usually held to be Sandemose's alter ego), who jumps ship in Newfoundland and later travels to the Canadian prairie, and the second explores the childhood of the young Espen in Denmark (Sandemose's hometown, Nykøbing Mors, appears as Jante in the novels), and its psychological effects on him. This second novel contains the so-called Janteloven (Law of Jante), a village decalogue which has become proverbial throughout Scandinavia and will be discussed briefly at the end of this analysis. Sandemose had success with several later books, fled to Sweden to escape arrest during the German occupation, and died in 1965, with a reputation as one of Norway's most distinctive twentieth-century writers. He is known for his preoccupation with the murky, semiconscious springs of human action (in which he followed Knut Hamsun and Hans E. Kinck, among others) and in particular, for a fascination with the line that can be traced from physical violence back to sexual frustration, humiliation, and competition.[2]

The opening section of *En sjømann går i land*, which provides a parallel to the scenario of "Amy Foster," may be quickly summarized. On board the schooner *Rurik* off the north coast of Newfoundland, deckhand Espen Arnakke finds himself at the bottom of the pecking order: the cook, the helmsman, the captain, and a complacent sailor all patronize him, torment him, and treat him with contempt. It had been to escape just such a life of injustice and impotence that he had fled his native town of Jante and run away to sea, yet here on board the same arbitrary and unappealable order prevails. He resolves on a calm night to jump ship and swim to land, for "half a year longer under the whip on board *Rurik*, and he could never become an honest man" (Sandemose, *En sjømann går i land* 24). The current is running shoreward; he leaves a suicide note, slips over the rail, and swims a few miles through the icy water, chanting to himself: "Espen Arnakke the Dane one night came in from the Atlantic to Deadman's Point.... I am Espen Arnakke, on my way to Deadman's Point, coming out of the endless ocean. I am the Dane Espen Arnakke, who cannot be drowned.... I know where I am, I know who I am, I know everything in the world" (25-26).

Having reached shore, Espen spends a period (not chronicled in the novel) woodcutting in the interior, and then returns "with twenty-five cents" to the coast, to a village called Misery Harbor, where he hopes to find work in a tin mine (29-30). Despite the baleful name, and dreary setting, and his own penury, Espen remains sanguine: "The eternally wet roofs in this place! But it was good to be in Misery Harbor" (30). He finds a job stowing fish on Lunenburg schooners, and takes pride in his freedom and self-sufficiency: "Espen found a cheap billet in a fisherman's house and it seemed to him that this was a wonderful time. His own room! So now he was really a man" (32). Before long he is befriended by Big John Wakefield, a jovial, overbearing local character. Soon, too, he falls in love – rather chastely – with a girl, but one night he witnesses her seduction, or rather assault, by Wakefield. As Wakefield is returning home he runs into Espen and begins boasting of his conquest, and Espen, flying into a rage, knifes his friend and kills him. The Newfoundland episode of *En sjømann går i land* here ends abruptly (Espen is next described arriving in Alberta), but the psychological causes and consequences of the murder are explored for the entire length of the novel's prequel,

En flyktning krysser sitt spor, which, as mentioned, describes in detail the conditions in Espen's hometown of Jante.

In order to articulate the comparison between the accounts of Espen Arnakke and Yanko Goorall, I will first summarize the points made by Simmel in his excursus "The Stranger" ("Exkurs über den Fremden"[3]). This short essay, roughly contemporaneous with the publication of "Amy Foster," provides us with a useful set of traits by which to measure what I will call the "strangerness" of Espen and Yanko in the places they find themselves, and to see how that "strangerness" may be said to have come about.[4] In its brevity and essayistic tenor, "The Stranger" does not lend itself to systematic analysis, and here I would like simply to extrapolate from it four features of the concept of the stranger that Simmel identifies, and add a fifth that can be deduced from these, which singly and in combination may be said to frame the fundamentally adversarial relationship between a stranger and a native community.

The essential quality of the stranger that Simmel identifies is autonomy. This is first described as spatial – that is to say, the stranger "comes from away"; he is not, at least initially, tied to the community in which he appears, and his status as stranger derives most of all from this fact. Simmel distinguishes "the stranger" from "the wanderer." The latter journeys hither and yon, he "comes today and goes tomorrow." But the stranger comes and yet does not go, or, as Simmel puts it, he is "the person who comes today and stays tomorrow" (1),[5] which vividly conjures up that hateful spectre of English society, the guest who will not leave. By staying, the stranger becomes a part of the community, but a self-contradictory one: "The stranger, like the poor and like sundry 'inner enemies,' is an element of the group itself. His position as a full-fledged member involves being both outside it and confronting it" (1). That is to say that the stranger, while being a part of the community, is not made by it, and so his spatial autonomy is duplicated by ontic autonomy. As a member of the group he is, so to speak, inorganic: his place in the group derives not from the group itself, as with the natives, but from him. In these respects, Simmel suggests both directly and obliquely, the stranger *as such* may be an object of resentment, regardless of his personal condition or the circumstances of his coming. He has the freedom to go, yet he does not exercise it, and it is easy to think that his wilful presence might be read by natives as a kind of challenge or taunt. Likewise with his ontic freedom: he owes no allegiance to the creeds and customs of the place, and perhaps pays them none. And even his conformity to them, should he practice any, is optional, and by that fact serves to undercut the edifice of tradition out of which the community and the identity of its members, is made.

The second feature of the stranger that Simmel identifies, closely connected with the foregoing, is his objectivity.[6] This term, Simmel cautions, "does not simply involve passivity and detachment; it is a particular structure composed of distance and nearness, indifference and involvement" (2). Objectivity need not mean neutrality of judgment, but suggests that the stranger's vision is unimpeded by local conditions, and his judgment unimpaired by local habit. The stranger, we might say, looks upon the community as a totality, and not from a position within it. His biases, whatever they might be, come, as he does, from beyond it, and are thus indifferent to its constituent elements. But the objectivity of the stranger is not only epistemic but constitutive; that is, he not only looks upon the community objectively, but is himself seen by it as an object. Because he is unknown to the extent that he does not participate in its inner life, the community can only judge him from the outside, and so he, too, is judged "objectively," that is, in the person of an object or a type.

Allied to the objectivity of the stranger – both in the manner of his seeing and in that of being seen – is a third characteristic, namely a degree of abstraction in all relations to him: "With the stranger one has only certain more general qualities in common, whereas the relation to more organically connected persons is based on the commonness of specific differences from merely general features" (2). Simmel explores the significance of this point by extending it to other human relationships, including intimate ones, but without following him there we can agree that the observation has ramifications for all studies of human otherness, and for our inquiry into the depictions of Yanko and Espen. The abstraction of the stranger, as that which tends toward establishing him on the same human ground with the native, can be conceived in two ways: as that which inspires empathy, and as that which inspires identification. In the first case we bracket out the differences, and focus upon the broad sense of a common feeling that unites people in thought with other humans, with animals, and even with inanimate objects. In the second case we insert ourselves into the position of the stranger, and take our thoughts for his; we universalize not his condition, but our own.

The fourth key feature of the stranger noted by Simmel[7] is his typical role in the community, which Simmel identifies as being in trade, but which we may here describe specifically as outside trade – that is to say, we can call the stranger the one who not only is different, but who trades on his difference and profits from it. Simmel suggests that the stranger occupies this role naturally, because "as long as he is considered a stranger in the eyes of the other, he is not an 'owner of the soil'" (2). It is the role he naturally assumes, Simmel argues, "the sphere indicated for the stranger, who intrudes as a supernumerary, so to speak, into a group in which the economic positions are actually occupied" (2). It is not only his rootlessness that marks the stranger: he brings with him, actually or potentially, different goods, different skills, different views, different ways of doing and being. No doubt the community often sees this, and sees too what benefit it can take from the stranger's presence, from his trade in difference. But this eye to local benefit will not make the stranger popular or accepted; his trade in difference can only underscore the advantage he has over the natives. He knows things they do not know, he has been places they have not been, he may have resources outside of their knowledge or control. And once again, he has a freedom the natives do not have, the freedom to come and go. But he does not go.

The element of conversion, which is implicit in Simmel's description of the social role of the stranger as one who mediates – commercially, culturally, or in other ways – between the community and the outside, leads us to characterize the fifth feature of the stranger "as such" that we should take from Simmel, a feature that needs to be emphasized, although it is not explicitly described by him. This is the role of the stranger as competitor. Any of the traits, skills, tools or materials that the stranger brings from away not only may provide him with grounds for interaction and a source of income; they may also give him a competitive advantage. This advantage might be strictly commercial, it may have social ramifications, and it may also be sexual. All of these spheres of competition are potential sources of conflict between the stranger and the natives, and give them potential reason to view him as a threat, and of them all, the sexual sphere is the most primitive and perhaps the most profound. While the concept of sexual competition is not addressed by Simmel, it ought to be paired not only with the other kinds of competition we have just mentioned, but with the previously discussed traits of the stranger – autonomy, objectivity, and abstraction – to establish that the stranger, regardless of circumstance, is in a structural relationship with the community that is partly, and on some basic level, an antagonistic one.

A curious elision in Simmel's text is one he makes between the concept of *stranger* and that of *foreigner*, for it is not entirely clear to what extent the characteristics he discusses are to be understood as pertaining to strangers who are foreigners, or to all strangers, or whether the conceptual blending is part of his purpose.[8] The question is pertinent to the present case, for in both "Amy Foster" and *En sjømann går i land* we are to find the two concepts rubbing up against each other. In "Amy Foster" we meet a community, I will argue, the constituent elements of which are to a degree strangers to one another, and this situation is both obscured and illuminated by the arrival in their midst of an archetype, a "foreigner." In *En sjømann*, on the other hand, we see a self-declared foreigner arrive in a community where the category of foreigner means almost nothing, yet by the same token everyone is, finally, a stranger to everyone else.

Conrad's characteristic doubling of the narrative voice in "Amy Foster," with the unnamed narrator handing off the tale to the perspicacious Doctor Kennedy, serves also to introduce one of the most notable features of the story, which is its meticulous portrayal of the class structure of a rural English district at the time.[9] In no discernible way are the first narrator and Doctor Kennedy different from one another: they are both gentlemen who are widely travelled and have observant natures. Doctor Kennedy is described, indeed, as having remarkable advantages – he is a well-known amateur scientist with a "penetrating power" of mind, an "unappeasable curiosity," and also "a brisk manner" and "a pair of gray, profoundly attentive eyes" ("Amy Foster," *TS* 106). One reason why Conrad might have split his narrative voice into two in this way is because he wishes to describe the principal narrator in these laudatory terms, and they could not possibly be used by Doctor Kennedy about himself. Conrad apparently wants, in other words, to tell Amy and Yanko's story from the standpoint of a knowledgeable, presumably fair-minded member of the gentry, and in order to establish such a narrator, he must describe him from the standpoint of just another such narrator.

The gentry is thus the class that provides narrative voice and perspective in "Amy Foster," and this perspective does not change, either between the unnamed first narrator and Doctor Kennedy's internal narration, or in response to the shifting emphases of the tale. It is, therefore, interesting to note that in some respects this class (along with the first narrator, Doctor Kennedy is the only member of it to figure in the story, except for "the young ladies from the Rectory" who try to quiz Yanko in German and Italian [126]) exhibits the qualities of "strangerness" for the other inhabitants of Brenzett and Colebrook. Doctor Kennedy's "objectivity" in relation to the community and towards the person and fate of Yanko has been alluded to above as deducible from his stated attributes. He describes the other characters dispassionately, with considerable knowledge of their temperament and antecedents, but from a distance. The appeal of this impartiality also finds a remarkable parallel in Simmel, who says that due to his objectivity, the stranger "often receives the most surprising openness – confidences which sometimes have the character of a confessional and which would be carefully withheld from a more closely related person" (2), while the first "Amy Foster" narrator says of Doctor Kennedy that "[h]e had the talent of making people talk to him freely, and an inexhaustible patience in listening to their tales" ("Amy Foster," *TS* 106). As well as being relatively objective in judgment,[10] Doctor Kennedy is viewed "objectively" by the villagers; his authority is sought out and acknowledged, but we get no sense that they know him personally (that is, in an emotional or psychological relation), nor that they can. In short, he seems to be for them a respected local leader, but beyond that he is essentially a type; he could be anyone who fills that role. A further token of Doctor Kennedy's "strangerness" according to Simmel's criteria is his role as a trader: he trades in knowledge (his specialized knowledge as a doctor, but also his education and experience of the world, all of which, like the skills and goods of Simmel's stranger, and like Doctor Kennedy himself, come from outside the community). This gives him status and power in the district but, very notably, it does not put him in competition with its inhabitants, for none of them have or could have to offer anything similar to what he provides. When we speak of education, skills, and so on in this society we are dealing with mere epiphenomena: the key factor, which both creates the "strangerness" of the gentry in relation to the classes beneath them, and cancels out the possibility of competition, is the class distinctions themselves.

The class next below that of the gentry, also represented in "Amy Foster" by a single figure, or rather, one household, is that of the yeomanry, as I shall call it for want of a less archaic term. This is the class of landholding farmers who, by dint of hard work and natural ability, have over time risen in wealth and local significance to a position of independence, or to recall Simmel, autonomy. It is old Swaffer and his daughters who embody this position in "Amy Foster," and old Swaffer, as described by Doctor Kennedy, also displays in relation to his neighbours some of the characteristics of Simmel's stranger. There is no question of his "coming and going," of course (Doctor Kennedy emphasizes his rootedness in the place: "the Swaffers had owned land between this and Darnford for these three hundred years" [127]). But he is clearly autonomous – "Swaffer would be called eccentric were he not so much respected" (127) – and rejoices in his autonomy, which is shown by his indifference to local opinion, and reflected in his learning and wealth: "Mr. Swaffer sits up as late as ten o'clock at night to read books, and [...] he can write a cheque for two hundred pounds without thinking twice about it" (127). The yeomanry supplied a stream of ambitious young people into the professions, the service, and the universities, and thus into the gentry, and this process is duly noted by Conrad ("Swaffer's younger daughter is married to Willcox, a solicitor and the Town Clerk of Colebrook" [130]), whose portrayal of Swaffer is finely drawn and reveals an appreciation of this class, which did not exist in comparable form on the continent, and so perhaps struck him as a particularly English phenomenon. It is clear that Doctor Kennedy and Swaffer are treated by Conrad differently from the other inhabitants of the district – both are described respectfully and at some length, and both are shown to possess a curiosity and self-confidence that lead them to treat Yanko with humanity.

Beneath the Swaffers in the social scale come *hoi polloi*, the peasants and villagers of the Colebrook district, whom Doctor Kennedy characterizes with a few dismissive epithets: "Preble, the lame wheelwright, and Vincent, the fat blacksmith" (132). These include Smith and his household, tenant farmers who are Amy Foster's employers, and who might be thought to occupy a central role in the story, but are shunted to its margins because Doctor Kennedy takes little interest in them. The casual condescension with which this group is treated by the narrator(s) not only reflects the seamlessness of the class perspective in narration that has been referred to above, but also suggests that Conrad himself viewed this section of the English population with reserve and distance. While there is limited violence directed at Yanko by the locals, and his death cannot be ascribed directly to them, it is clear that Conrad wishes to attach blame for his fate to the hostility he meets with, and that hostility comes chiefly from this class: the natives *ipse*, those who see Yanko as a stranger under all Simmel's categories. These are the inhabitants of the district for whom, because they do not travel often or far, there is an "away" from which the stranger comes, and, unlike him, they lack the freedom to come and go. They are limited in wealth, skills, and experience, and thus vulnerable to competition from a stranger, whatever goods or traits he might bring, and they are the custodians of the customs, manners, and views that define the group, and that might, as observed above, be threatened, diluted or undercut by the stranger's very presence.

The community described in "Amy Foster" includes another class, to which Amy Foster herself belongs, as does, once he becomes settled in the area, Yanko Goorall. This is the class of the landless labourers, herdsmen, servants on farms, and others in the rural population who were born on, or had (like Amy's father) fallen to, the lowest rung on the social ladder.[11] This class was still very numerous in England[12] but would have been socially remote from the gentry (Doctor Kennedy being an exception in this because of his profession), and would not under ordinary circumstances arouse their interest – when the first narrator (and the reader) encounters Amy Foster, even Doctor Kennedy explains his contact with her by her previous connection with Yanko Goorall (107). It transpires that Doctor Kennedy knows Amy's history well, as he seems to know that of everyone in the district, but he speaks of her from start to finish as a lumpen creature, from which it is not difficult to extrapolate his general view of this class. It is, however, emphasized that Amy, its representative, reacts to the appearance of the stranger with spontaneous generosity, unlike those in the class above her, that of the Smiths and other villagers. While it can be assumed that Doctor Kennedy's tribute to her kind heart (109) and later to her affection for Yanko is meant sincerely, it should be evident, as it would have been to Doctor Kennedy himself and to the first narrator to whom he is speaking, that Amy's prospects for a suitable marriage in the district are meagre, and her other prospects even worse – a fact underlined by Kennedy's sardonic allusion to the "well-known frivolousness" of her employer, Mr. Smith (109).

The presentation of social class in Sandemose's novel is a wholly different matter. There are three communities sketched – Espen's hometown of Jante, in northern Denmark, the hierarchy of the crew aboard the schooner *Rurik*, and the coastal settlement of Misery Harbor in Newfoundland. The first, Jante, which receives hundreds of pages of attention in *En flyktning krysser sitt spor*, is only in the background of *En sjømann går i land*, but at every mention there is suggested an absence of class distinction as such, and the same classlessness obtains on the schooner and in Misery Harbor. (It is, indeed, the similarity of these last two environments to that of Jante that sends Espen, as first-person narrator, back to his hometown memories in *En flyktning* to discover how that society had broken him [Sandemose, *En flyktning* 5].) In all these communities there are those who have authority – the captain of the *Rurik*, the parents, teachers and pastors in Jante, the employers in Misery Harbor – but it confers on them no particular respect or status. There are those who are rich, and there are those who, like Big John Wakefield, have physical strength or charisma or some other means for asserting themselves. But there is no inherent social division between the members of these communities; all are in competition with all others, directly or potentially, so those who have acquired high standing are anxious that they may lose it, and those who lack it are anxious to get it. The successful must actively suppress the younger, poorer, and weaker, who represent to them a potential threat, and those who have ambition are subject to continual frustration. Upon arriving in Misery Harbor, Espen coldly summarizes the prevailing social ethos: "When people get power, they get recognition" (*En sjømann går i land* 32). Their class structure, if we were to impose such a thing on these communities, would map just two classes, both unstable and liable to shifts in membership: those who are on top, and those who are beneath them.

We may describe Espen and Yanko, therefore, apart from other differences between them and in their circumstances, as foreign elements introduced into two communities that, *qua* community, run on opposite principles. In Brenzett, there is an elaborate class structure which, though not so rigid that it prevents individuals from moving up or down from one class to another (as has been mentioned, "Amy Foster" refers to several movements of this kind), is categorical in its delineation of the classes themselves and the range of relations between their members. This structure has, I have suggested, the effect of giving members of one class qualities that Simmel ascribes to the stranger in the eyes of members of another class, in particular when these classes are distant from one another. Thus Doctor Kennedy is on terms of confidence and friendship with old Swaffer, whom he views not as an equal but with respect and a certain warmth (he refers to him as "the old chap," which conveys affectionate familiarity ["Amy Foster," *TS* 126]). But his descriptions of the other farmers and villagers, farther from him on the social scale, are, though without malice, cool and perfunctory, as are his interactions with them. These take the character, naturally, of medical calls, and we may think that Kennedy looks on the villagers' lives and personalities much as he looks on their bodies, as mildly interesting natural phenomena. Likewise, as I have suggested, many of the features of Doctor Kennedy, and old Swaffer, too, as they appear to the lower classes, can be mapped onto Simmel's traits of the stranger – autonomy of thought and behaviour, distance from the culture and customs of the natives, sources of wealth or standing that lie outside the community and its control, and, to a degree, the abstractness of a "type." The signal difference between this class-rooted "strangerness" and that which is embodied in the real stranger, the one who comes from afar, is the lack of competition. The "strangerness" of Doctor Kennedy and other members of the gentry for the villagers of Brenzett is not the kind that fosters competition, but that which *eo ipso* forestalls it completely. The villagers pose no threat of any kind to the gentry or their standing, nor do members of the gentry pose a social or psychological threat to the villagers; the social standing of the latter (connected with what we would now call their identity) is a function of their position within their own class, and competition comes from within that class, and from the class directly below it.

In Misery Harbor, by contrast, there is no class structure at all: there are those who possess more or less wealth, influence, respect, or power of another sort within the community, but their interaction is not mediated by difference of kind; they are social equals in the way that John Locke conceived the citizen: differentiated by circumstance but not by essence. Every member of the community is potentially a leader, or potentially a follower, or an outcast, and none of these roles can be considered permanent. Competition in such a society is not suppressed or limited, but dominant and pervasive, although it is mediated by the existing distribution of power (e.g. wealth, legal authority, the force of opinion) and, perhaps more importantly, by the need for cooperation that marks any egalitarian system. Misery Harbor (unlike Jante, ship crews, and the Colebrook district) is, moreover, an open community, where people come and go often, and where, therefore, the category of *stranger* is at least a very general one, and might even be considered universal. And this leads us directly to the difference between the ideas of *stranger* and *foreigner*, as they operate in the stories under discussion.

While the ethnic background of Yanko Goorall has been much discussed (Brzozowska-Krajka; Krajka, "Multiple Identities" 149-61), especially in relation to the Polishness of Conrad,[13] it also plays a constructive role in the story's trajectory, by making his "foreignness" total and, as it were, impenetrable.[14] It is easy to imagine a story strung along the same lines, in which the castaway who turned up in a Kentish village were a German or Scandinavian, a Spaniard, or even a British subject, for example a Scot or an Irishman. In such a story the stranger's treatment by the villagers, and even his eventual fate, might be the same.[15] But in these circumstances his origin would be quickly found out, his language would be accessible to the leaders of the community, and his circumstances would acquire a habitation and a name. Though the plot might proceed in the same way, its emotional tone would likely be quite different, for Yanko would be "located" not only by the gentry, but also by Conrad's readers, who would lay upon him whatever impressions or knowledge – perhaps extensive – they might have of his land of origin and its nature. But as he is presented, a member of "the Sclavonian peasantry in the more remote provinces of Austria" ("Amy Foster," *TS* 121), neither the local worthies of the Colebrook district, nor Conrad's contemporary readers, could be expected to have any acquaintance with his language, his manners, or his world view. He is, not only to the villagers, but to Doctor Kennedy and the first narrator, and also to the reader, a foreigner *tout court*, the essence of foreignness.

Why this is significant can be seen by referring back to the class differences drawn in "Amy Foster" and the prevalence of intramural relations of "strangerness" that follow from them. The common people of late nineteenth-century England would have had a place in their minds for the stranger who exhibits the traits catalogued by Simmel: a person from away, an autonomous person, who comes and remains, who brings his own skills and source of wealth, his own distant engagement and objectifying gaze: this is simply any member of the English upper classes, who is at once both a stranger and completely familiar, and who fits seamlessly into the local community by remaining in a characteristic way above and beyond it. But Yanko Goorall is a stranger of a different kind altogether – an unknown quantity, with eccentric manners that seem almost insolent, and a person, moreover, who possesses, in Pierre Bourdieu's formulation, no social capital (Bourdieu and Wacquant 119) but who seems not to see this, who does not, in the suggestive idiom of the time, "know his place." Doctor Kennedy's account of Yanko describes Simmel's stranger with remarkable exactitude: Yanko is a person of unknown and distant origin, indifferent to local customs and ways of being; he brings with him the freedom of unapologetic difference, and yet he also has the energy that makes him a good employee for old Swaffer, the yeoman farmer, and so makes him a direct competitor to the inhabitants of the district.

As remarked earlier, when Yanko is adopted into the community of Brenzett, it is into its lowest productive class, in accordance with the evidence of his own background, the circumstances of his coming, and his lack of any material or social capital. This is not in consequence of his "foreignness." Depending on his skills and bearing, he might well have been received into the class structure at another level (Conrad himself, when settled in England, lived there as a gentleman, naturally and unselfconsciously, and though he remained a distinct [and often impecunious] foreigner, his class position was never in question). Yanko's class status is signalled immediately by the reactions to him of the members of the community. To Swaffer he is at first a curiosity, "as if [...] a sort of wild animal" or "a bit of a Hindoo" ("Amy Foster," *TS* 126), but later becomes a valued and trusted farmhand, for Swaffer, secure in his land, wealth, and self-assurance, has no deep anxiety about beggars, Hindus, or other strangers: he judges Yanko on his utility and observable character – the "abstract humanity" that Simmel claims we find in the stranger. Doctor Kennedy, from whom Yanko is farther removed socially and economically, approaches nearer to him as an object for investigation and, precisely due to the empirical distance between them, imaginative speculation. This latter interest provides, obviously, the emotional fulcrum of the story; the impermeable foreignness of Yanko, which never abates, is transmuted in Doctor Kennedy's melancholy reflections into a loneliness and solitude that become existential. This shift is identified by Vince Marotta in an essay on Simmel's excursus, when he speaks of

> an existential dimension to Simmel's discussion of the stranger which is sometimes understated [...]. This dimension relates to a sense of dread or existential angst as one comes to the realisation that we are connected to forces beyond our control. There are larger processes working behind the everyday mundane world of individuals in which

> what was thought as unique and individual "is only fulfilling a general human destiny." (680)

Amy Foster, the "dull creature" known chiefly for her tenderness towards animals ("Amy Foster," *TS* 109), spontaneously treats Yanko as an equal, which, from the standpoint of social relations, he is. It is, as has been remarked, only the common people who are frightened or unsettled by Yanko, and later resentful of him. The wagoner cuts at him with his whip, village boys pelt him with stones, and Smith the tenant farmer locks him up in the woodshed (118-21). The absolute strangeness of Yanko on his arrival in the place, which bemuses Swaffer and stimulates Doctor Kennedy's "unappeasable curiosity," and which appeals at once to Amy Foster's forlorn affections, only arouses in the peasantry alarm and hysteria (118-19). It is this class that has something to lose – economically, socially, perhaps physically – from the unwanted appearance of a foreigner in their midst, and that is alive to the threats he may pose to them, by comparison or competition.

Foreignness, like class structure, assumes a very different form in Newfoundland as it is described in *En sjømann går i land*. While Espen Arnakke, as we have noted, has swum ashore at Deadman's Point sustaining himself with his Danishness, this feature remains a purely personal one, for it becomes no more than a matter of idle inquiry for the inhabitants of Misery Harbor, which Espen rebuts with humour:

> He could simply be called Jack the Dane, which sounded good and a bit mysterious. Some kind of German, are you then? No, that's all wrong. I'm from the land of the Vikings, the cradle of England's language and power. From Denmark, a province of that great, warlike Scandinavia, home of Napoleon, Nansen, and Peter the Great! (Sandemose, *En sjømann går i land* 31)

Nationality means little here, except as a moniker. The population of Newfoundland was somewhat mixed and transient, and in coastal settlements ships with diverse crews were a constant presence. It would, therefore, be psychologically and economically difficult to "sort out" local populations on the basis of natives and foreigners, and in Sandemose's narrative there is no hint of this, although these categories, as mentioned above, function as descriptors – Jack the Dane, Gustav the Swede, etc. (8). In Misery Harbor it is with nationality as with class; there is no respect of persons. When he first arrives, as penniless and, *mutatis mutandis*, as bereft of social capital as Yanko on the coast of Kent, Espen accosts a native to enquire about work: "What are you talking about? Work in a tin mine?" asked a man whom Espen had caught hold of. "Now, I've lived here all the forty years of my life, but I've never heard of any sort of tin mine in Misery Harbor" (30). A lifelong resident of the place evinces no surprise at seeing a stranger, or being stopped by him on the street, or being asked questions; he addresses himself only to the burden of the matter. The contrast with Yanko Goorall's initial reception in Brenzett could not be more plain. Even the language barrier, which in Yanko's case is described feelingly by Doctor Kennedy, and assumes an important function in evoking Yanko's ignorance of the world, his social exclusion and at last his mortal isolation, has in the case of Espen a kind of transparency. His practical command of English from the moment he comes ashore is simply taken for granted; it does not impair his interaction with the locals, and his native language, like his nationality, is implicitly given the role of a personal trait or possession, such as an item of clothing. Only once, as will be noted below, does Espen's use of Danish feature critically in the text, in an eerie parallel to Yanko's own last words.

Although the outlines of their stories are broadly similar, we can see that as immigrants – as strangers and foreigners – Yanko Goorall and Espen Arnakke have come to very different places, and meet with very different welcomes. Society in turn-of-the--century rural England is class-ridden and insular; these traits, closely bound up with one another, seem to be essential to it. Newfoundland in the 1920s hosts a society in which there are no recognized classes (though there are varying degrees of wealth, power, and social success), nor is there any clear demarcation between local and stranger, native and foreigner.

Yanko Goorall, therefore, becomes in Brenzett a kind of pawn in the process of negotiation conducted within and between the English social classes: to some in the community he is an object of anthropological interest and cool sympathy; to others, a curiosity but also a ready workman; to still others a source of anxiety and a general repository of "otherness," and to one, a companion in social exclusion and a focus of instinctive feeling. As a foreigner, he represents the one broad category of people to whom almost all lower-class Englishmen can feel superior, so that his "strangerness," however he might have sought to reduce it (which, as Doctor Kennedy often remarks, he does not do) would anyway be constantly reaffirmed by them, as a constituent in the buttressing of their self-esteem. In such a society, where Simmel's markers for the stranger are found, to a degree, in the views of members of one class towards others, the category of *foreigner* is quite distinct, and is organized around that one trait of the stranger that the "native" strangers of different social classes do not have, the trait of being a competitor. Espen Arnakke meets a different challenge in Misery Harbor: he is young, poor, and lacks knowledge of the place. On the one hand, these deficits are his only ones – there is no suggestion that he meets with hostility or even surprise because he is a stranger or foreigner.[16] On the other hand, there is no natural role or definition for him to assume or be fitted into. He is a social atom like everyone else in this raw and chaotic community, forced, as he was on his way to Deadman's Point, to sink or swim, and to compete with everyone for everything, buoyed up only by innate self-assurance and a capacity for aggression. In this community the category of *stranger*, as I have suggested, is extended until it becomes in effect universal, while that of the *foreigner* is stripped of significance. Espen is only (to introduce yet another category) a "newcomer," one who differs not in kind from the locals, but merely in length of stay, and this is a trait that will naturally soon expire.

Two more marked differences between the accounts of Yanko Goorall and Espen Arnakke remain to be examined. One of these is narratological, and shows the ways in which the characters are presented and what we can know of them; the other is narrative, and concerns the outcomes of their unhappy stories. These will be addressed in order.

The situating of the dominant narrative voice in "Amy Foster" in the person of Doctor Kennedy does not only, as remarked above, give it a consistent class tone and, so to speak, personality; it also serves to keep Yanko in character as a strange, largely unreadable figure from a distant and unknown land, the contours of which can only be sketched by Doctor Kennedy's probing of Yanko's recollection. The result of this is that we have an entirely external, and rather clinical, view of Yanko and his time in Brenzett. Doctor Kennedy queries him as to his way of coming thither and his reactions to present circumstances, much as a doctor would query a patient about his history and constitution – a patient who may be ailing, but who can describe his trouble only in vague and uncertain terms, except for some particular, vivid symptoms. Yanko's voice throughout the story has a distinctive quality: it is that of a person whose English is imperfect but highly expressive, who can relate impressions that are both naïve and discerning. In regard both to the language and to the experience it is used to convey, the annotations of Doctor Kennedy are always evident – in describing the English that he actually heard from Yanko ("in his broken English that resembled curiously the speech of a young child" ["Amy Foster," *TS* 112]), in emphasizing his touching ignorance and innocence of spirit ("he did not even know that ships had names – 'like Christian people'" [113]), and in sometimes seeming (implausibly, it might appear) to translate directly from Yanko's language for the sake of narrative colour and poignancy ("There were three [shipping touts], of whom one with a long beard looked venerable; and they had red cloth collars round their necks and gold lace on their sleeves like Government officials" [116]).[17] But the most significant aspect of Doctor Kennedy's narrative voice is the interventions he makes to arouse sympathy for Yanko and to humanize his experience by empathetic suggestion. These interventions are of three kinds. First, there are the numerous epithets ("a poor immigrant," "the poor man," "the poor devil," "our man," etc.) that people of Doctor Kennedy's class would use to refer with bland sympathy to someone who was of a lower station or in unfortunate circumstances. Doctor Kennedy's second significant contribution to our picture of Yanko is his almost uniformly positive description of him (Krajka, "The Alien" 199-200; "Multiple Identities" 154-55); there are repeated paeans to his strength of body and character and to his good nature – he was "of a tougher fibre than he looked" ("Amy Foster," *TS* 112), "a real adventurer at heart," who gave "flashes of white teeth and lively glances of black eyes" (117) that duly impressed Amy Foster, who "had observed that he was good-looking" (124), and he was "lithe, supple and long--limbed, straight like a pine, with something striving upwards in his appearance as though the heart within him had been buoyant" (111). These and more such remarks are made by Doctor Kennedy in his own right, and he attests others made by Swaffer, Yanko's eventual patron: "He did the work which was given him with an intelligence which surprised old Swaffer. By-and-by it was discovered that he could help at the ploughing, could milk the cows, feed the bullocks in the cattle-yard, and was of some use with the sheep" (130). But such praise is juxtaposed with the reaction of the villagers, who on observing what Doctor Kennedy tags as Yanko's good qualities, react with animosity. A single passage may serve as illustration:

> His rapid, skimming walk; his swarthy complexion; his hat cocked on the left ear; his habit, on warm evenings, of wearing his coat over one shoulder, like a hussar's dolman; his manner of leaping over the stiles, not as a feat of agility, but in the ordinary course of progression – all these peculiarities were, as one may say, so many causes of scorn and offense to the inhabitants of the village. (132)

These observations of Yanko's appearance and attributes – both the positive ones that Doctor Kennedy makes himself, and that he reports from the standpoint of Swaffer and Amy Foster, and those (often retailed by him with irony) that reflect the adverse opinions of the villagers – are made entirely from the outside, and so portray Yanko objectively, as we have seen Simmel characterize the natives' conception of the stranger as such, or with what I have called above a clinical gaze: he is a bundle of physical and behavioural traits whose subjective core cannot be penetrated, except by the highest degree of abstraction. And here I believe we see the third function of Doctor Kennedy's depiction of Yanko, which in the narratological view is perhaps the most important. This is performed by the continuous mythologization of Yanko's story and of himself as a person; a process which is heralded by a reference to Greek tragedy and introduced by Doctor Kennedy's first apostrophe to the reader: "There are other tragedies, less scandalous and of a subtler poignancy, arising from irreconcilable differences and from that fear of the Incomprehensible that hangs over all our heads – over all our heads…." (107-08). Yanko's foreignness, the violent circumstances of his arrival in Brenzett, and his irreconcilable position outside the snug-fitting social relations of late Victorian England are all emphasized, but the emphasis in Doctor Kennedy's account is used by him to point up the broadest kind of moral, to abstract from the penniless, inarticulate castaway to man in general, and from his circumstances to the human condition, so that Yanko's little, grotesque history becomes veritably epic, like the "clumsy figure" of the wagon-driver seen against the horizon by the first narrator at the outset, which "projected itself on the background of the Infinite with a heroic uncouthness" (108). This infinite background is re-established by Doctor Kennedy throughout his narration: "there is not one, it seems to me, that ever had to suffer a fate so simply tragic as the man I am speaking of, the most innocent of adventurers cast out by the sea in the bight of this bay, almost within sight from this very window" (113). When describing Yanko's arrival at Smith's farm Doctor Kennedy adds, "From that moment he is plainly in the toils of his obscure and touching destiny" (119); and later, "[h]e was different; innocent of heart, and full of good will, which nobody wanted, this castaway, that, like a man transplanted into another planet, was separated by an immense space from his past and by an immense ignorance from his future" (132). Whether or not this portentous abstraction of his state be justified, it is clear that it comes not from Yanko's own account of himself but is read into him by Doctor Kennedy, precisely because he has no direct access to Yanko's own thoughts. He cannot read Yanko as an individual, and the "type" he presents is, as suggested above, only the type of a foreigner as such, even to such an experienced person as Doctor Kennedy; so the ascription to him of human sentiment will thus operate most naturally on the basis of universality: "the proportion of nearness and remoteness which gives the stranger the character of objectivity, also finds expression in the more abstract nature of the relation to him" (Simmel 2). It is in this way that Kennedy makes of Yanko an object of sympathy and a model of the human experience – for himself, for the first narrator, and for the reader – in a way that Yanko does not, evidently, appear, e.g. to Smith, who to the end thinks him next door to a lunatic ("Amy Foster," *TS* 121), to Isaac Foster, who remarks that his tragic end may be "for the best" (141), and to Amy herself, for whom, of course, he is at last a paralyzing enigma.

The narratological character of *En sjømann går i land* is remarkably different: here the third-person narrator tracks very closely the impressions and outlook of Espen Arnakke; the license of omniscience is used only to establish context and provide some ironic perspective on the immature hero's misadventures. (In *En flyktning krysser sitt spor*, Espen himself takes over as a more mature first-person narrator, and the interiority of the picture he draws of Jante and its inhabitants is intense and claustrophobic.) Thus while "Amy Foster" confronts the reader with a protagonist who is seen essentially from the outside, and as a stranger, by the principal narrator and the surrounding community, and only speculatively, and by abstracting from his outer particulars, from the inside; in Sandemose's novel it is just the reverse: the interior life of Espen Arnakke is depicted in detail and with familiarity, while it is the external, social world that takes on the quality of an impenetrable object, a series of arbitrary "givens" which derive their authority from some distant, unknown place and trade in a foreign currency that puts Espen always at a competitive disadvantage. In short, in Sandemose's narration the protagonist, with his little economy of inner hopes and thoughts, in the native community, and the outer world, the social universe of other people and arbitrary rules, is the stranger. Unavoidably, this scheme puts the reader inside the protagonist rather than amid the community in which he arrives, and further complicates the comparison of Misery Harbor and Brenzett.

The emphasis on Espen's subjective experience in *En sjømann går i land*, and its clear contrast with the inaccessibility in "Amy Foster" – to Amy and the villagers, but also to Doctor Kennedy, and so to the reader – of Yanko's inner life (which is only highlighted by Doctor Kennedy's philosophical generalities about him), provide vivid means for distinguishing the concept of agency in each case. Espen deserts his ship and swims ashore, boisterously claiming, as we have seen, "I know where I am, I know who I am, I know everything in the world" (Sandemose, *En sjømann går i land* 26). Yanko, on the other hand, who has been travelling in the black hold of a vessel to a (for him) unknown and inconceivable destination, is saved by chance from its wreck; he "might have floated ashore on [a] hencoop" ("Amy Foster," *TS* 123), but, however he reached land, he has no idea where he is nor how he came there. It could even be said, given how meagre the information is that he can convey about himself, and how little it means to the locals, that he does not know who he is, either. His lack of knowledge, from the standpoint we have on him, is virtually complete. Both Espen's boastfulness and Yanko's ignorance are hedged with irony; Espen reveals himself to be callow and clueless, while Yanko turns out to be intelligent and capable. But the situation they face in their new environment is nonetheless determined by this initial mental condition. For Espen, Newfoundland is simply an opportunity: for work, for adventure, for love, for autonomy, for a chance "to become a man," and so in just this way does it present itself to him. Buoyed up by his own brash self-regard, he moves hopefully from one settlement to another looking for work, finds it, is accepted into the local population, makes a wage, and falls in love. Yanko, on the other hand, remains somehow incapacitated by ignorance – first, it would seem, by his own, about the place he has come to and his role in it; later, by the ignorance and insularity of the locals; and finally by the gap of ignorance between him and his wife. In the case of Espen, the power of agency dwells in the stranger, the "poor fellow" (*stakkar*) who turns up in Misery Harbor penniless and uninvited; while the community, which is a group of (competing) individuals with no common will, simply absorbs him, until he commits a violent crime. But in "Amy Foster" it is the community of Brenzett – self-assured and self-contained, its social parts articulated like those of a single organism – that holds the initiative, while Yanko, in Doctor Kennedy's account, appears to lack agency, or rather, decisive agency. He does not find Brenzett, but is found there; he does not find work, but it is found for him; he does not choose to stay, but simply will not go; even his emotions seem reactive, for he falls in love with the first young woman in the place to show him affection. It is when he undertakes to marry her that he displays real decision, and it is precisely in this that he sets in motion the engine of his fate.

The last point of comparison that remains to be made concerns the narratives themselves. I have observed that perhaps the most telling role of the stranger in the account given by Simmel, which can be deduced from the traits he discusses, is that of competitor. A stranger who brings from away any goods or skills that are not present within the community has a good chance of improving his standing there, very possibly at the expense of the natives. If the stranger arrives with nothing, he may still impose himself on the local society, and intrude himself into its hierarchy, and displace one or more natives, by physical or psychological force, or by competing with natives on the most fundamental level, namely that of sexual competition. It is, at any rate, in this manner that both Espen Arnakke and Yanko Goorall, who as strangers come from away with almost nothing, enter into open or tacit conflict with their new communities. In both cases the narrative arc of their stories bends towards this conflict, though again the descriptions of the conflict, and its outcome, differ greatly. When Espen comes to Misery Harbor, he sets about establishing himself almost as if he were purposefully scaling Abraham Maslow's pyramid of needs. Having secured work and a room to live in, he takes up with Wakefield, one of the most prominent locals:

> Big John Wakefield was someone Espen wanted for a friend, because the girls liked him. He didn't give a damn about anything and would hug the prettiest girls. He never thought twice when he spoke, as Espen did, and that both drew Espen to him and scared him a bit. (Sandemose, *En sjømann går i land* 32)

Once he has allied himself with the charismatic Wakefield, which affords him social *entrée*, he turns his attention to the local girls who work in the fish-packing sheds (or on the street), but the incipient competition, and conflict, begin in fact when he falls in love with Eva: "One morning a new girl showed up, and that day Espen worked as if he were blind. She was so beautiful that his blood congealed within him; he wanted to cry" (34). There is no social structure to mediate his courtship of the girl, nor is Espen's nationality, his foreignness, an impediment in this sphere, as it is not in any other. But the latter serves as a signal of the psychological tension, the alienation, that he has brought with him to Misery Harbor from his hometown of Jante and the schooner *Rurik*, with their petty tyrannies and insolent exercise of arbitrary control. When Wakefield has raped Eva he then confronts and drunkenly condescends to Espen, who has seen the assault, that he can teach him about sex, "for you probably don't know anything about it, yet, right? You don't know anything." Espen in fury seizes his knife and falls into his own language: "'I don't know anything, what? I don't know anything?' he snarled in Danish [...]. The strange language startled John. '*Fool*,' he said. It was his last word" (47).

The progress of Yanko Goorall from mud-covered tramp to respectable householder (and landowner) with a wife and young son is dogged by feelings just as grim and potent as the inner rage that Espen brings to Misery Harbor, but the narrative logic of "Amy Foster" dictates that these be observed from without, and that they be expressed passively by Yanko, and collectively by the community. The fulcrum of their expression is, in both cases, the entry into direct sexual competition:

> It was only when he declared his purpose to get married that I fully understood [...] how – shall I say odious? – he was to all the countryside. Every old woman in the village was up in arms. Smith, coming upon him near the farm, promised to break his head for him if he found him about again. But he twisted his little black moustache with such a bellicose air and rolled such big, black fierce eyes at Smith that this promise came to nothing. ("Amy Foster," *TS* 134)

The character of this competition is sublimated in "Amy Foster," but not – as the above quote makes clear – because it is unrecognized by the characters, or unacknowledged by the author, but because it is impersonal. Yanko's determination to marry Amy, a young woman for whom he has no competitors, is objectionable to the villagers because it marks his intention to stay, to remain as a foreigner among them, and this objection is reprised in Amy's later revulsion at Yanko's insistence on speaking to their son in his own language (137). The alienation that Doctor Kennedy has already ascribed to him ("His eyes would fill with tears, and, averting them from the immense shimmer of the sea, he would throw himself face down on the grass" [134]) is now codified: he diligently approximates the courtship rituals of his own culture, further exasperating the locals, and his marriage appears to serve not to overcome his loneliness, but to make it deep and inescapable to him, like a fatal illness: "To me he appeared to have grown less springy of step, heavier in body, less keen of eye [...]. [I]t seems to me now as if the net of fate had been drawn closer round him already" (137). It is the sudden eruption of his foreign language during Yanko's illness that drives Amy away in panic and leads to his death, as it is Espen's infuriated outburst in Danish that paralyzes Wakefield before Espen murders him. In both cases the foreign language expresses the "foreignness" of the protagonist at a decisive moment. But the foreignness of Yanko is that of the outcast, the one who is ejected from the community and family as, literally, a foreign object; while the foreignness of Espen is his individuality, his subjective agency, which violently asserts itself in a climax of primitive competition.

The three decades between the publication of "Amy Foster" and that of *En sjømann går i land* saw political, social, artistic, and psychological upheavals; certain effects of all of them can be traced in a comparison of the two works. But a brief consideration of the well-known Janteloven from *En flyktning krysser sitt spor* may help to illuminate some consistent differences in social construct, without needing to make much allowance for the effects of the intervening period, since the bulk of *En flyktning krysser sitt spor* is set in the time of Espen's (and Sandemose's) childhood, that is, contemporaneous with the publication of "Amy Foster." The Janteloven (Law of Jante) is Sandemose's formulation of the code by which an egalitarian, undifferentiated provincial community keeps the peace and suppresses competition, when there exists no recognized social stratification to exercise that function. In paraphrase, the commandments are: that you shall not think you "*are* somebody," nor that you are as great as we are, or cleverer than us, or better than us, or that you know more than we do, or amount to more than us, nor that you're good for anything; you shall not laugh at us, or think anyone cares about you, or that you can teach us anything (Sandemose, *En flyktning krysser sitt spor* 67). Two things about this formula are immediately noteworthy: first, the commandments issue not from any constituted authority but from, seemingly, the community itself, that is to say, from public opinion, in a common effort at self-suppression. As Sandemose writes in introducing the decalogue, "[w]ith these ten commandments Jante keeps Jante down" (67). Second, they could not, even as a thought exercise, issue from the society portrayed in "Amy Foster"; the "us" from whom they might proceed could only be, in such case, the local gentry, and it is hardly conceivable that any Englishman of the time would think in such terms, or countenance them. The Janteloven has become legendary in Scandinavia because of a social structure already prevalent there by the late 19th century, one which was recapitulated, in some essential respects, in North America. The anxiety, insecurity, and mutual mistrust conveyed in the Janteloven are expressive of the social instability that arises from open competition for status, power, and wealth, and when these, as in Victorian England, are already allotted by traditional schemes that allow for very limited fluctuation, even notional commandments urging people to "know their place" are superfluous to the point of absurdity. However, as has been said, the stranger to such a society may indeed enter into competition, or seem to, with some elements of that community, or, as it might seem to them, fail to "know his place" in it, and if the Janteloven finds any application to the social texture evoked in "Amy Foster," it might be to express the feelings of the exasperated villagers of Brenzett toward Yanko Goorall.

I would like to summarize the series of oppositions that we find in the nature of the communities that Conrad and Sandemose describe and the manner in which they describe them. In "Amy Foster" a community of stability and social stratification is portrayed with detached urbanity by a principal narrator who is both in and above it, who portrays the class strata (including his own) and their interactions with detail but without comment, as if they were natural phenomena. A significant aspect of "Amy Foster" from this standpoint, which I have endeavoured to draw attention to, is that the reactions to the advent of Yanko Goorall in the neighbourhood are clearly marked out by class, and that these reactions suggest varying degrees to which an exotic stranger may represent, in turn, a direct competitor and potential threat, a curious foreign object, or a philosophical abstraction, an example of the human condition. Furthermore, these ways of reading the stranger suggest a broad penchant for reading human beings from the outside in, and in some cases for establishing an empathetic connection even – or especially – with those who may exhibit the greatest degree of otherness.

In contrast, the communities depicted by Sandemose in *En sjømann går i land* and *En flyktning krysser sitt spor* are without defined class structure; they are structured, rather, by power relations that are felt by the protagonist to be arbitrary and inimical to freedom and self-fulfilment. There are, thus, no natural human relations either between individuals or classes, but only those that are established competitively; in such a community everyone is, in Simmel's terms, a stranger to everyone else. In this circumstance the mechanisms of social behaviour cannot be understood by reference to type or custom, but only by psychological identification with an individual whose motives, therefore, must be assumed to behave in universal patterns. In effect, the modern, egalitarian, undifferentiated community to which Espen Arnakke comes is one in which everyone, be he a local, a stranger, a newcomer, or a foreigner, is in the end simply a subject, confronted by the objective "strangerness" of the society around him. Since agency is inherently subjective, we observe in "Amy Foster" that it is the community – or rather, that class which defines itself as being such – that identifies and carries to its end that conflict between itself and the other that the term *stranger* implies, and of which Yanko is the tragic victim; in *En sjømann* it is Espen who is the subject, and thus it is he who launches himself into competition, into conflict, and ends up committing murder; but the first cause and meaning of his own action remain as mysterious to him as are, to the speculative Doctor Kennedy, the impersonal workings of fate.

NOTES

[1] References in this paper are to Norwegian editions of *En sjømann går I land* (1979), which has not, as far as I know, been translated into either English or Polish, and *En flyktning krysser sitt spor: fortellingen om en morders barndom* (1996), which appeared in English as *A Fugitive Crosses His Tracks*, translated by Eugene Gay-Tifft (1936), and has recently been reissued in Polish as *Uciekinier przecina swój ślad. Opowieść o dzieciństwie mordercy*, translated by Iwona Zimnicka (2021). All present translations by the author.

[2] There are numerous biographical sketches of Sandemose in Norwegian, most notably a biography by his son, Jørgen Sandemose (*Flyktningen – Aksel Sandemose* 2004)). In English the only biographical monograph of which I am aware is *Aksel Sandemose: Exile in Search of a Home* by Randi Birn (1984).

[3] The German text is available online at <https://romanistik.uni-freiburg.de/raible/Lehre/2006_07/Materialien/1908_Simmel_Haendler.pdf>.

[4] I use the term "*strangerness*" specifically to identify those aspects of a person that may be associated with the characteristics that Simmel attributes to the stranger.

[5] References in this paper are to: "The Stranger," excerpted from *The Sociology of Georg Simmel* (1950).

[6] This is the third trait to be examined in Simmel's essay, but I am taking them here in the order in which they most closely lead one to another and can most clearly inform our present argument (Simmel 1-2). I use the term "*objectivity*" throughout to mean, as it is also used by Simmel, the quality of being or seeming to be an object, that is, something viewed from the outside, or of being unaffected by immediate circumstances or attitudes; and not, as it has come increasingly to mean, being completely neutral in one's description of things or opinion about them. The latter stance seems to be under ordinary circumstances impossible, leading us to wonder why this definition of the term has gained such wide currency.

[7] Though it is the second to be referenced in his essay: see previous footnote.

[8] It is quite possible that Simmel based his reflections on the social patterns of pre-modern continental Europe, when the category of *foreigner* probably overlapped considerably with that of *stranger*, even supposing that *foreigner* had at that time any very distinct meaning. The only categorical comparison of the stranger that Simmel actually makes is not to the foreigner but to the "wanderer" (1).

[9] For a discussion of other critical views on the role of Doctor Kennedy as narrator and the story's narrational layering, see e.g. Schaffer 253-55.

[10] Kennedy's objectivity of judgment has been widely contested, see e.g. Kramer 2003, while Richard Ruppel, on the other hand, writes that "Kennedy's distanced, objective perspective provides 'Amy Foster' with an almost anthropological tone" (128).

[11] The history of Isaac Foster that Doctor Kennedy briefly relates at the outset – "who from a small farmer has sunk into a shepherd; the beginning of his misfortunes dating from his runaway marriage with the cook of his widowed father […] who passionately struck his name off his will" ("Amy Foster," *TS* 107), clearly foreshadows the theme of mésalliance among the labouring classes, and the ostracism it is met with, that will create the crisis of Yanko Goorall's estrangement.

[12] W. Hasbach cites the figure of 733,000 agricultural labourers (i.e. farmhands or seasonal workers without real property) out of a total working male population of just over 10 million in the 1901 census for England and Wales. See: Hasbach 355, and the 1901 National Census, accessed 23 Oct. 22 at <https://www.nationalarchives.gov.uk/pathways/census/events/census1.htm>.

[13] The autobiographical element(s) of "Amy Foster" have been extensively discussed, see e.g. Herndon 1960.

[14] Yanko is described in "Amy Foster" as "a mountaineer of the eastern range of the Carpathians" (*TS* 121), and the words *Pole* and *Polish* do not occur in the story. Aside from the question of the ethnic origin of the character that Conrad had in mind (Brzozowska-Krajka), and the fact that none of the present states of Poland, Ukraine, and Slovakia existed at the time, the vagueness with which Doctor Kennedy describes Yanko's origins only augments the anonymity that his foreignness casts over him. Krajka remarks on this from the standpoint of Yanko: "The spatial distance between the East Carpathians and Kent enhances the unbridgeable gap between the cultures and ethnoses of the protagonist and the English villagers" ("Multiple Identities" 142); cf. Mary Harris: "For Goorall as well as for the villagers there is a lack of understanding about each other's customs and practices" (177).

[15] In the 1867 short story "Malachi's Cove," Anthony Trollope relates the tale of a girl and her grandfather, living at the edge of the sea, who are ostracized by the inhabitants of the Cornish village at the top of the cliffs until the girl rescues a local boy from drowning, as Yanko does Swaffer's granddaughter, and, like him, is thereupon rewarded with social acceptance. There is no overt reference to ethnic difference in this story, but the "strangerness" of the girl, and the antipathy it arouses in the villagers, is made clear.

[16] "People were easy-going and friendly in Newfoundland; it was like a remote Danish village where the people had a strange dialect but otherwise paid no notice to what a poor scrawny fellow Espen really was" (Sandemose, *En sjømann går i land* 31).

[17] The issue is tangential to the present argument, but it is observable that many of Doctor Kennedy's renderings of Yanko's experience are of a kind that can hardly be explained by the supposed state of communication between them. A note of pathos, for example, is struck in the following passage by Doctor Kennedy's translation of Yanko's entreaty to Smith in the stackyard: "As the creature approached him, jabbering in a most discomposing manner, Smith (unaware that he was being addressed as 'gracious lord,' and adjured in God's name to afford food and shelter) kept on speaking firmly but gently to it, and retreating all the time into the other yard" ("Amy Foster," *TS* 120). But it is implausible that Doctor Kennedy could ever have learned that the form of address used by Yanko should have had this meaning in English, or that Yanko might ever have himself acquired the English terms to explain it to him. Here as elsewhere it seems clear that Conrad is letting his intent impose upon the narration – the most noteworthy example of this comes at the end of the story, where Doctor Kennedy reports Yanko's last word: "he pronounced the word 'Merciful!' and expired" (141). It is difficult to believe (especially given the import of

his earlier appeal to Amy in his own language) that Yanko should have at this moment spoken English, and yet it is impossible that Doctor Kennedy should have understood the word otherwise.

WORKS CITED

Birn, Randi. *Aksel Sandemose: Exile in Search of a Home.* Greenwood, 1984.

Bourdieu, Pierre, and Loïc J. D. Wacquant. *An Invitation to Reflexive Sociology.* U of Chicago P, 1992.

Brzozowska-Krajka, "Yanko Goorall: a Waxwork from the Wax Museum of Polish Romanticism." Trans. Wiesław Krajka. Krajka, *Joseph Conrad: East European* 165-82.

Harris, Mary. "'Amy Foster': A Case of 'Colonisation' within Europe." *A Return to the Roots: Conrad, Poland and East-Central Europe.* Ed. Wiesław Krajka. East European Monographs, Maria Curie-Skłodowska U, Columbia UP, 2004. 173-89. Vol. 13 of *Conrad: Eastern and Western Perspectives.* Ed. Wiesław Krajka. 32 vols. to date. 1992- .

Hasbach, W. *A History of the English Agricultural Labourer.* King, 1906.

Herndon, Richard. "The Genesis of Conrad's 'Amy Foster'." *Studies in Philology* 57 (1960): 549-66.

Krajka, Wiesław. "The Alien in Joseph Conrad's 'Amy Foster' and Jerzy Kosiński's *The Painted Bird.*" *Conrad and Poland.* Ed. Alex S. Kurczaba. East European Monographs, Maria Curie-Skłodowska U, Columbia UP, 1996. 195-215. Vol. 5 of *Conrad: Eastern and Western Perspectives.* Ed. Wiesław Krajka. 32 vols. to date. 1992- .

---, ed. *Joseph Conrad: East European, Polish and Worldwide.* East European Monographs, Maria Curie-Skłodowska U, Columbia UP, 1999. Vol. 8 of *Conrad: Eastern and Western Perspectives.* Ed. Wiesław Krajka. 32 vols.to date. 1992- .

---. "The Multiple Identities of Yanko Goorall." Krajka *Joseph Conrad: East European* 131-64.

Kramer, Jürgen. "What the Country Doctor 'did not see': The Limits of the Imagination in 'Amy Foster'." *The Conradian* 28.2 (2003): 1-11.

Marotta, Vince. "Georg Simmel, the Stranger and the Sociology of Knowledge." *Journal of Intercultural Studies* 33 (2012): 675-89.

Ruppel, Richard. "Yanko Goorall in the Heart of Darkness: 'Amy Foster' as Colonialist Text." *Conradiana* 28 (1996): 126-32.

Sandemose, Aksel. *En flyktning krysser sitt spor: fortellingen om en morders barndom.* 1933. Aschehoug, 1996.

---. *A Fugitive Crosses His Tracks.* Trans. Eugene Gay-Tifft. Knopf, 1936.

---. *En sjømann går i land.* 1931. Ascheoug, 1979.

---. *Uciekinier przecina swój ślad. Opowieść o dzieciństwie mordercy.* Trans. Iwona Zimnicka. Czarne, 2021.

Sandemose, Jørgen. *Flyktningen – Aksel Sandemose.* Aschehoug, 2004.

Schaffer, Carl. "'They ain't where they belong to be at': Conrad's and O'Connor's Displaced Poles." *Joseph Conrad's Authorial Self: Polish and Other*. Ed. Wiesław Krajka. Maria Curie-Skłodowska UP, Columbia UP, 2018. 175-203. Vol. 27 of *Conrad: Eastern and Western Perspectives*. Ed. Wiesław Krajka. 32 vols. to date. 1992- .

Simmel, Georg. "The Stranger." *The Sociology of Georg Simmel*. Trans. Kurt Wolff. Free P, 1950. 402-08. Accessed 28 Jan. 2023. <https://www.infoamerica.org/documentos_pdf/simmel01.pdf>.

Trollope, Anthony. *Malachi's Cove and other Stories and Essays*. Tabb, 1985.

Subhadeep Ray,
Bidhan Chandra College, Kazi Nazrul University,
Asansol, West Bengal, India

"Why not tell me a tale?": Dislocating the Genre in Joseph Conrad's "The Tale" and Premendra Mitra's "The Discovery of Telenāpotā"

George Orwell (1903–1950), in an essay entitled "Wells, Hitler and the World State" (1941), humbly acknowledges the contribution of H. G. Wells (1866–1946) in shaping an entire generation of young minds in the 1910s and 1920s: "The minds of all of us, and therefore the physical world, would be perceptibly different if Wells had never existed" (119). However, according to Orwell, Wells belongs to "a non-military nation and class" whose zealous trust in the socialist and liberal humanism makes them incapable of understanding that war-mongers, nationalist fanatics, and religious-bigots can offer "far more powerful forces" than what Wells "would describe as sanity" (119). In Orwell's reservation against the ethical naivety of the art of his predecessors, literary treatments of the external world are directly entangled with the literary form. Wells, in his speculative/science fiction, as Orwell notices, could easily divide the world into two opposing camps: material and intellectual progress and fellowship, on the one hand, and superstitions and totalitarian stupidity, on the other. On the contrary, in the context of the Second-World-War experiences of blurring borders, Orwell decries all sorts of ideological abstractions. Irrespective of Orwell's review of the *fin de siècle*, pre-First-World-War and interwar English literature from a mid-twentieth century perspective, an anti-fundamentalist radicalism is already evident in early-twentieth century English literary modernism. In this connection, Joseph Conrad's later fiction is informed by dual dislocations of the genre and the reality in its affirmation of the unpredictable even in the midst of the most methodical application of a totalitarian scheme. This essay wishes to re-read arguably Conrad's only story on the First-World-War, "The Tale," which is also his final work of fiction, included in *Tales of Hearsay* (1925), along with a Bengali short-story by a chief exponent of the post-Tagore literary experimentalism, Premendra Mitra (1904–1988), "The Discovery of Telenāpotā" (in Bengali vernacular: Telenāpotā ābiskār) (1946). These two tales, representing varying aspects of twentieth-century literary modernism, defy institutionalized norms of fictional genres in favour of an imaginative creation that is both self-critical and non-conformist, as it draws attention to what Jacques Derrida in *Acts of Literature* means by "intangible," that is, "inaccessible to contact, impregnable, and ultimately ungraspable, incomprehensible" (211). The tales by Conrad and Mitra make possible the sudden emergence and the call of the "other" to effect the de-/re-construction of subjectivity through a series of critical moments.

The present study would thus attempt to expand on post-structuralist re-evaluations of textuality, mainly after Derrida and Derridian deconstructionist critic Derek Attridge, in relation to the limit of the "self" and the creation of the "other" in a world that the discussed texts inhabit. Attridge explains in *The Singularity of Literature*,

> The creative writer registers [...] both the possibilities offered by the accepted forms and materials of the time, and their impossibilities, the exclusions and prohibitions that have sustained but also limited them. Out of the former emerge reworkings of existing models, out of the latter emerges the otherness which makes these reworkings new works of literature. (20-21)

In the concerned tales, narratives specifically use a series of guess-works, press at the limits of aesthetic conventions, exploit the discontinuities between the inside and the outside of a fictional world, and both extend and resist the capacity of the "self" to reach out to the "other." These texts renegotiate the existing literary models' relations with the external world of reference. Through this process, to apply Derrida, in "marking itself generically" – or as a tale to be told and attended to – each of the two tales also "unmarks itself," as these tales expose that everything guaranteed by social and literary conventions "remains essentially unstable, as fragile as an artifice" (*Acts of Literature* 230, 185). The Commanding Officer's re-telling of his encounter with the fog and the Northman in "The Tale," and another account of an unfulfilled attraction in the mysterious Telenāpotā, in the hinterland of the British colony of Bengal, followed by disease and forgetfulness, in "The Discovery of Telenāpotā" often blend the image with the object, the dream with the reality, as these tales undermine, in Derrida's words in *Acts of Literature*, "the deciding and decidable *logos*" of the hierarchical discourse (140). The "other" in form of an image in both narratives lurk outside the embrace of the "self," but the "other" offers to be comprehended and held by the "self" only when the latter learns to cross the limit of decidability in art and life. These texts dislocate the generic expectations of the realistic fiction by building narratives of suspicions and ambiguities to question even the identity and integrity of the subject-selves. Subjective dilemmas are inscribed in the narratives of the two stories, and they anticipate the Derridian observations on both requirements and unsettlements of generic laws in establishing literary singularities. The post-structuralist dismantling of the text's unmediated relation to some preconceived and institutionalized truth is of particular relevance here. "The critique of logocentrism" in poststructuralist readings proposed by Derrida and others, "is above all else the search for the 'other' and the 'other of language'" (Derrida, "Deconstruction and the Other" 123), and modernist literature facilitates such readings to a great extent.

Orwell's contemporary modernist theorist, F. R. Leavis (1895–1978), in *The Great Tradition* (1948), distinguishes the fictional narrative from social reporting, and replaces the literary "form" by a deeper enquiry into the moral intensity of characters concerned with reverence for human life. In this sense, modernist scepticism about all socially and aesthetically established norms and modernist search for the "other" seem to seek some lost opportunities to reinvent fictional and living experiences. Interlinked with the generic displacements are the uncertain relationships between subjects and objects, facts and illusions, truths and lies. As suggested before, Orwell's essay detects a Wellsian binary of "[t]raditionalism, stupidity, snobbishness, patriotism, superstition and love of war" (119) on the one hand; and innovation, science, technology, progress, fellowship, and humanity, on the other. Contrary to these ideological binaries, the treatment of explicit and implicit marks in literature is conditioned in the works of modernist authors, like Conrad and Mitra, by the contradictory urges to engage with and escape from a situation accentuating moral and ethical dilemma. In "The Tale" the author revisits many of the narrative strategies of his early writings to engage them in new generic possibilities. The story confirms a basic Conradian preoccupation, i.e., in Wiesław Krajka's words, "a powerful representation of Modernist scepticism about existence of the one and only truth" (6). In Conrad's "The Secret Sharer" (1909), an encounter with the "other" results in the recognition of "otherness" within the subject-self; and, with the captain's "self" conflating two conflicting identities, he learns to accept, as Keith Carabine notices, "his responsibility for another human being" (xxiii). "The Tale" further points out how identities and their representations serve only as cloaks thrown over deeper conditions of change in human relationships. The central narrator of "The Tale" recreates himself as a character, the Commanding Officer, to suggest repetition and difference between multiple narrative frames.

Like "The Tale," "The Discovery of Telenāpotā" establishes its singularity as literary creation by mediating between the available cultural traditions and deviations from those traditions. These two short-stories, written by writers from distinct linguistic, cultural, and literary backgrounds, can be connected by virtue of their narrative affiliations to the strange, erratic, and elusive that cut across the limits of metropolitan modernism.

The present essay is, therefore, an attempt to follow how, from Conrad to Mitra, the short-story as a transnational modernist genre creates a critical uncertainty regarding its constitution, which, as Derrida suggests in *Acts of Literature*, refuses to resolve "whether the unfinished state of the work is a real accident or a pretence" (185). "The Discovery of Telenāpotā," which also includes a tale within a tale, signifies the maturity of Mitra as a leading modernist artist who participates in the literary flight from late-nineteenth and early-twentieth century Bengali historical romance and domestic realism, and engages the reader's interest in the relations of alterity as central to a fictional intervention in a supposedly commonplace world. A continuous discursive shift could be followed in the course of Bengali fiction, which was modelled in the nineteenth century after the Victorian English novel by Bankimchandra Chattopadhyay (1838–1894), and was drawn mainly towards the genre of historical romance, during the final half of the British colonial rule. By the early-twentieth century, the struggle for national self-determination was well advanced, and it was impossible for Rabindranath Tagore (1861–1941), the then chief exponent of the genre, not to be engaged with political upheavals of the first three decades of the twentieth century and various social issues, involving class, religion and gender. It was during the same period that a more popular Bengali novelist, Saratchandra Chattopadhyay (1876–1938), wrote mainly on the rural domestic life in simple, sentimental prose. Against this backdrop Bengali new writings, produced mainly from the late 1920s to the 1940s, account for a definite journey of experimental modernism by "continually infusing foreign influences" of European avant-garde aesthetics, modern psychoanalysis, and radical philosophy of socialism and existentialism, "with the socio-cultural contingencies and uncanny sensibilities of a prolonged colonized subjectivity" (Ray, "Modernism's Footprints" 167). Kris Manjapra associates a major discursive change with this "modernist" turn in Bengali literature: "Bengali intellectual life, framed within a centre-periphery imperial axis in the 1870s, was resolutely reframed within a multipolar international constellation by the 1920s" (327). A cosmopolitan outlook distinguishes the works of a new generation of Bengali authors, like Bibhutibhushan Bandyopadhyay (1894–1950), Tarasankar Bandyopadhyay (1898–1971), Balai Chand Mukhopadhyay (1899–1979), Satinath Bhaduri (1906–1965), Manik Bandyopadhyay (1908–1956), Advaita Mallabarman (1914–1951), and the Kallol group of writers that includes Premendra Mitra, all of whom are found to be participating in the cultural dialogue initiated by the rapidly changing global order of the interwar and postwar period, while remaining sensitive to the heteroglot nature of their native culture beyond the conventional codes of nation, state, and empire. Mitra's immediate literary associations are discussed later in this essay. However, his specific intervention in this cultural turn can be understood in terms of the fact that "[m]odernism and realism are uneasily but powerfully conjoined" in the so-called Bengali "new" fiction (Chaudhuri, "The Bengali Novel" 118). Mitra's own observation that "serious writing cannot afford to be a mere entertainment, as it has to talk about life in the words of life" (cited in Bhattacharya 5; my translation) is rather problematically related to his emergence as perhaps the most prominent author of the speculative fiction in Bengali. Written towards the late nineteen forties, a good part of Mitra's mature fiction tends to challenge and go beyond what is believed to be possible in life. Mitra's first short story in this genre, "Moshā" ("The Mosquito"), was published in 1945, to be followed by "The Discovery of Telenāpotā," which with an apparently more realistic narrative mode pushes realism to the verge of the illusive by creative re-imaginations of cultural materials.

As John G. Peters notes, in "The Tale" "the multiple frame technique reveal[s] Conrad's last foray into formal experimentation and narrative complexity" (117). Simultaneously, after Derrida's *Acts of Literature*, it may be said that with the very opening exchange between the woman listener and the central narrator, the text "gathers together the corpus" of story writing only to keep "it from closing, from identifying itself with itself" (231):

> "Why not tell me a tale?"
> "A tale!" He was really amazed.
> "Yes. Why not?" [...]
> "Why not?" he repeated, with a slightly mocking accent, as though he had been asked to give her the moon. ("The Tale," *TH* 60)

Attridge reminds us that "'the other' [...] is premised on a *relation*. To be 'other' is necessarily to be 'other than' or 'other to'" (*The Singularity* 29). The central narrator's identification of his tale as set in "seas and continents and islands" literally gathers together the Conradian corpus only to unsettle it against a new backdrop of warfront ("The Tale," *TH* 61). That this tale would act along the generic boundary between inclusions and exclusion is suggested by the set of demands to the storyteller: "No. I don't mean that. I mean another – some other – world. In the universe – not in heaven" (61). Therefore, there is an urge to cross the known world with some sort of imaginative non-fulfilment, and the tale needs to situate itself in "another" world. This thus follows Atrridge's suggestion that the "other" – which is discovered as part of a creative process – "does not come from outer space but arises from the possibilities and impossibilities inherent in the culture as embodied in a subject or a group of subjects" (30). It is this invention of the "other" within the objective world that provokes us to read "The Tale" along with Mitra's tale, and also to follow how, as suggested by Derrida in *Acts of Literature*, an "axiom of non-closure or non-fulfillment enfolds within itself the condition for the possibility and the impossibility of taxonomy" (231). The implication requires to be derived from the archaic meaning of *to invent*, that is, *to find*, as in the primary rhetorical term *inventio*, and it becomes a central narrative query in Conrad: "'another world' – who's going to look for it and for the tale that is in it?" ("The Tale," *TH* 61). The "other," which is said to hold the tale in "The Tale," is an atmosphere, a time and place, an event, a feeling, an object and a sight, a voice and a being, whose emergence or re-emergence at a specific narrative moment tests the "self" by offering the latter certain choices of action while confronting a new form of truth. This "other" can never be comprehended for certain as its ineffability points to limitations of a culture, and in this process, the genre, too, declassifies itself. When the storytelling in "The Tale" ends, the woman listener's anxious reaction is thus symptomatic of the dislocation of a value system, which is supposed to have been integrated into humane and aesthetic sensibilities: "She knew his passion for truth, his horror of deceit, his humanity. 'Oh, my poor, poor – ' 'I shall never know,' he repeated, sternly, disengaged himself" (81). What in *Acts of Literature* Derrida terms the "floodgate of genre" has the capacity to generate a "formless form" by unfolding generic possibilities, while systematically destroying any quasi-predictive order, both historical and aesthetic (231). The central narrator of "The Tale" insists that in his tale "[t]here was comedy [...] and slaughter" (*TH* 61). This juxtaposition of these two antithetical forms informs the juxtaposition of two value systems that lie at the heart of the changing subject positions and aesthetic codes. It has been well-analysed that in Conrad's works the ship itself has an authority of a transparent kind, which is exercised through the hierarchy of values and ethical codes held by the sailors. These values and codes are mentioned at the outset of the narrative of "The Tale": "[d]uty," "[s]incerity," and "frankness" (61, 64). Their efficacy is, however, reconsidered during the war under the shadow of absolutely instantaneous but inconceivable death: "some ship in company, blow up all of a sudden and plop under almost before you know what has happened to her. Then you begin to believe" (64). As Catherine Belsey observes in *Culture and the Real*, death, which "itself remains oddly unpresentable" paradoxically constitutes an "absent presence," and "typifies [...] the lost object of immediate experience, subsumed, supplanted, and yet not finally abolished by the signifier," and in death the "absent real anticipates a future absence for the subject itself, marks subjectivity as finite, temporary" (41, 40). The gradually consuming fear of uncanny death in Conrad's early stories, like "The Lagoon" and "An Outpost of Progress" (1896), is replaced in "The Tale" by a deceptive odd emptiness at the heart of an active war-life, what no "delayed decoding"

(Watt 270) would sufficiently explain, or no work-ethics could defend. "The Tale" also reworks the Conradian impressionism by investing the moral and ethical effects "of the visual angle" (*TH* 62) on the momentary experience. With war carried on almost everywhere, there is no certainty beyond the anxiety about some unpredictable danger that may make anyone cease to exist at any moment from any corner. Thus the Commanding Officer of "The Tale" warns that although the "last reported submarined ships were sunk a long way to the westward. [...] There may have been others since then not reported nor seen" (65). Significantly, this study of the war has close similarity with more authentic writings on the First-World-War, as exemplified by Siegfried Sassoon's semi-autobiographical account of the trench-warfare, *Memoirs of an Infantry Officer* (1930):

> Well, here I was, and my incomplete life might end any minute; for although the evening air was as quiet as a cathedral, a canister soon came over quite near enough to shatter my meditations with its unholy crash and cloud of black smoke. A rat scampered across the tin cans and burst sandbags, and trench atmosphere reasserted itself in a smell of chloride of lime. (39)

Having "no choice but between truth and death" ("The Tale," *TH* 64), and any apprehension of truth being dislocated by the physical as well as ethical fog, the Commanding Officer, as the subject-narrator of Conrad's story, finds his own terror materialized by anything that emerges all of a sudden, as first signified in the narrative by the floating barrel; and what may be called an "absent cause" turns him vindictively deceitful. But this fog relates to further ambivalence and unreliability in relation to the work-ethics of the subject: as a soldier he both perpetuates and becomes a victim of the unpredictable death, necessitated by the imperial war; and these two roles seem to be mutually endorsing and exposing. A shift in terms of narrative perspective is, therefore, suggested from the claim of the imperial agent in Conrad's early novella, "Heart of Darkness" (1899). Marlow states, albeit unconfidently: "What saves us is efficiency – the devotion to efficiency" (*YS* 50). As discussed below, the close proximity of death regulates the "self"'s varying approach to the "other" in Mitra's "The Discovery of Telenāpotā," too. Kaoru Yamamoto's study of "The Secret Sharer" points out "[t]he text's emphasis on the priority of presence of the other over the knowledge of the other" (256). In Conrad's late short story, "Because of the Dollars" (1915), Davidson

> displays an unflinching sense of human empathy and responsibility, which is framed within a clear Conradian ethical structure that characterizes sea communities or ship communities. His struggle against a group of European ruffians to save someone else's mistress and her child radically disrupts Victorian bourgeois social compromises. (Ray, "After such knowledge" 270)

On the contrary, meaningful interpersonal communication is restricted in "The Tale." Any contact with an unknown human being is pre-conceived as likely to be menacing by the institutionalization of death by the war.

Simultaneously, the impressionist portrayal of the encounter between two strangers through the fog in "The Tale" differentiates Conrad's tale from the mainstream British war-writings that mainly emphasize comradeship and, therefore, depend on the evocation of "the senses both as a relationship to a world and the senses as in themselves a kind of structuring of space and defining of place," in Paul Rodaway's words (4). In Conrad's narrative, the subject, the Commanding Officer, resists any sympathetic admission of the "other," here the Northman, the captain of a mischievously appearing ship, who being "[a] stranger" becomes an obvious suspect:

> there was another ship in the cove. [...] "'[...] And the strange thing is that we never heard a sound from her. [...]' "'What if she were the very ship which had been feeding some infernal submarine or other?'[...] "'She would get off scot-free. You couldn't prove it, sir.' "'I want to look into it myself.' ("The Tale," *TH* 69-71)

The Commanding Officer, Carabine points out, "attempts to reduce interpretive possibilities," by following the institutional codes of conduct, "only to discover" that "we can 'never know' either the truth about the tales we tell ourselves or the truth in tales others tell us about themselves" (xxiv). Conrad's employment of impressionist technique is of crucial importance here: as a phantom is found to be taking shape of a ship in the most unexpected manner it unsettles the discursive insistence on the object's precedence over its image, and results in a series of ambiguities. Conrad's aesthetics thus establishes what Derrida in a study on Franz Kafka (1883–1924) in *Acts of Literature* calls the "resolution of nonresolution," which "brings the story into being and sustains it" (202). When the Officer's interrogations initiate the Northman's tale of being trapped in the fog, the former hardly listens. No productive discourse, which is "always a combination of what is actually verbalized and what is nonverbalized but assumed by both speaker and addressee" (Clark and Holquist 206), is allowed by the Officer's biased speculations. Carabine points to the possible linguistic gap between these two fellows – a Conradian preoccupation since his early works like *Almayer's Folly* (1895), and "Amy Foster" (1900) – but this provokes the Officer to devise an ambivalent version of the "secret murder plot" on the basis of an unauthenticated suspicion of hostility. In his retelling he admits that "[w]hat he really expected to find there was the atmosphere, the atmosphere of gratuitous treachery, which in his view nothing could excuse" ("The Tale," *TH* 71-72). What is stated in the text as "the atmosphere of murderous complicity" (79) thus acts as what has been referred to as the deciding logos set by the fear and hatred engendered by the totalitarian war to provoke the Officer to deliberately lie to the Northman, a supposed foe, regarding the safe passage. The Officer's narrative, however, seems to be self-deceptive in defending his action that the Northman's ship had probably been well informed of the sea-routes through her illegal actions around that place and the ship might have found the right route, disobeying the Officer's instructions. Conrad's text mirrors the folly of searching for certainty in life and art within the institutional order that spoils the teller, the listener, and the reader. Conrad's use of lying, as a narrative trope both safeguarding and exposing the hypocrisy of imperial institutions, connects the ending of "Heart of Darkness" to that of "The Tale." To refer back to Attridge's understanding in *The Singularity of Literature*, the form of a literary text includes "the mobilization of meanings, or rather of the events of meaning: their sequentiality, interplay, and changing intensity, their patterns of expectation and satisfaction or tension and release, their precision or diffuseness" (109). The Commanding Officer is, therefore, exposed to the self-delusion imposed by the war at the cost of ethical integrity. The Officer can never be sure of the actual effect of his acts, and this epistemological gap, just like what war creates, leads to a more poignant ethical loss. He must remain forever guilty and haunted by his own action. To follow Jennifer Turner's study, if "Falk" "addresses the potential clash between man and sea, exploring the definition and safe limits of masculinity" (147), "The Tale" further shows the helpless and insecure male heroics against the backdrop of the war. The modernist genre's performance thus involves the mobilisation of consciousness towards what remains both outside and inside of the subject to demand relinquishment of official control.

Even in the heyday of Rabindranath Tagore and Saratchandra Chattopadhyay, Premendra Mitra's short-fiction started to reclaim a space for the urban lower-middle class subject to whom the discursive control of traditional Bengali social stratifications ceded. The first short story of Mitra, "Simply a Clerk" ("Sudhu kerāni"), developed on a postcard accidentally found in a mess-hostel in Calcutta, was written and published in the Bengali literary magazine, *Prabāshi*, in 1923. Mitra's work instantiates the hybridity and the global range of what is acknowledged as the "high modernism" of the 1920s. Mitra's writing, which covers a wide range of genres from science/speculative fiction, to bizarre and horror stories, to detective fiction, to naturalist fiction, has a tendency to characterize the most commonplace on the brink of the uncanny. The coming and call of the "other" in a variety of forms in Mitra's tale often mercilessly expose the ethical poverty of the middle and lower middle-class life in Bengal, caught up in the violation of humanity under late and neo-colonial rule, nationalist revivalism and also the challenges of a new world thrown open by socio-economic, political, scientific, and cultural upheavals around the world. These dynamics are entwined with the aesthetic form, because the text participates in a cluster of genres: speculative fiction, romance, domestic fiction, and travelogue; without entirely belonging to any of them, to situate its stake in an unstable modernity. To quote Supriya Chaudhuri: "Bengali literary modernism was experienced as a reaction to Tagore, though Tagore's immediate influence [...] was inescapable. The moment of departure was marked by the foundation of a literary journal, *Kallol* ('The Surge')" ("Modernisms" 12). In a short article on the *Kallol* movement – organized around the literary magazine *Kallol* (1923–1935), and involving a group of young poets and fiction writers like Buddhadeb Bose (1908–1974), Kazi Nazrul Islam (1899–1976), Sailajananda Mukhopadhyay (1901–1976), Premendra Mitra, and Radharani Devi (1903–1989) – Mitra writes: "[this kind of literature] is like a rebel-wave spilling out of a material and ideational vacuum of the post-First-World-War period, and it restlessly experiments with everything feeble and stagnant" (cited in Pathak ix; my translation).

"The Discovery of Telenāpotā" is a much shorter narrative, centred on an event, which is crucial to what has earlier been explained as invention of the "other." While the narrator of "The Tale" seems to set his tale in "once upon a time" (*TH* 61) – a sort of Conradian game with generic conventions of the fairy-tale – Telenāpotā is set as the destination in a hallucinatory travel-guide for the reader. Mitra's narrative performs on the boundary between weird fantasy and realistic fiction, and is set in the future registered by the repeated use of the Bengali register for the English modal verb *may*. This further corresponds to a specifically Bengali sub-genre of speech-acts, known as *addā* – or friendly conversation within a close circle, often imposing the imaginary and chance factors on the factual. Both the fairy-tale beginning of the Commanding

Officer's story in "The Tale" and the use of the modal verb by the unidentified narrator of the "discovery" of Telenāpotā thus suggest a refusal to be specific about what Mikhail Bakhtin defines as literary "chronotope," that is, the way "spatial and temporal indicators are fused into one carefully thought-out, concrete whole" in a literary narrative (Clark and Holquist 280). Speculations and deceit are two themes common to "The Tale" and "The Discovery of Telenāpotā," and these two narratives keep themselves "open to contamination, grafting, accidents, reinterpretation, and recontextualization," to use Atrridge's phrase in *The Singularity of Literature* (63). Significantly, just like the Commanding Officer can never be sure of the outcome of his lie to the Northman, there is no certainty about the repetition of the same sequence of events every time one visits the village of Telenāpotā. Ultimately the indefinite setting and, by implication, unreliability of their narratives seem to waive the burden of ethical responsibility on the two storytellers. The impressionistic narrative of Mitra, like that of Conrad heavily depends upon the "possible" and "accidental" rather than the "actual" and "pre-expected." The Bengali text thus offers a conceivable trip into a rural area, where a young male adventurer, accompanied by two other relatively unromantic male friends, after a sweaty bus journey in the tropical heat of August, may get to ride a small bull-cart through a bumpy, muddy, and dark swamp, bordered by tall trees and visited by wild animals. He may attempt to fish in a pond, come across a mysterious girl, accept, under the false identity of a certain missing fiancé, a marriage proposal from her ill mother in a nearly haunted and crumbling house, where he becomes a target of mosquitoes, and return to catch malaria and forget the whole incident. Fredric Jameson relates the emergence of modernist style in European literature with "the demands and constraints of the spatial perceptions of the individual" created by the "other, vaster, unrepresentable space" of the Empire (158, 160). Although in Jameson's thesis the imperial interaction with and exploitation of the "other" is seen to be forming European modernism, it is possible to find the construction of "otherness" within a native cultural framework of either Western or non-Western fiction. The colonized culture, especially, exposes its internal heterogeneity, and how the modern subject encounters the unrepresentability of "otherness" without crossing the geo-political borders. In this connection, Bengali early-twentieth century fiction is sensitive to the intra-cultural "otherness" in representing a version of what Jameson calls a "bewilderingly varied set of modernisms" (159). The subject-self's discovery of the attractive "other" and their final separation are thus possible even in the setting of the insignificant village of Telenāpotā. His perplexed and bewildered subjectivity dwindles before the "other"'s exteriority that demands the giving of oneself. There is always a threat inscribed in the telling of the story that, in Attridge's words, "otherness may survive to challenge [...] habitual processes of thought and feeling," as like "The Tale," albeit differently, "The Discovery of Telenāpotā" involves what Attridge calls "an encounter with alterity, which is to say the shifting and opening-up of settled modes of thinking and feeling" (27-28).

In his deliberation on the potential of the modernist film, Walter Benjamin (1892–1940) notices that this genre "corresponds to the heightened state of mortal peril that modern man must face" by introducing radical "changes in the apparatus of perception" (49). Benjamin reflects on the applications of cinematic vision in a wide range of literature and art. Perceptual economy plays a crucial role in the narrative of Mitra's tale as it employs "interrupting and isolating" and "stretching and condensing" (Benjamin 30) almost in a cinematic way in respect of the subject's adventure in the mysterious Telenāpotā. Almost in the way the shadowy image of the ship gradually acquires concrete form in Conrad's "The Tale," the unexpected and momentary illumination of some undefined desire in form of a distant image gives way to a series of close-ups to build the concrete details of accidental encounters in "The Discovery of Telenāpotā," although in totally different setting:

> you may see a thin line of light through the window [...]. An enigmatic, shadowy figure may be seen by you. You will wonder who is still

> awake at this hour of the night. [...] [Next morning, when you may be concentrating on fishing in the nearby pond] you will find a young lady pushing aside the hyacinths to fill in her shiny brass pitcher with clear water. She will glance at you directly, and then her eyes may follow your fishing-rod floating on the water [...] she may turn her head to remark, "what are you waiting for? Reel it in." (Mitra 179; all translations from Mitra's text into English are mine)

Such appreciation of the "other" is extremely subjective. But social as well as generic norms of Bengali domestic realism with its specific emphasis on kinship, trust and betrayal are likely to intervene very soon: "Perhaps you will learn that the unreal girl with tragic eyes by the pond is called Yamini, and she is a kin to one of your accompanying friends" (180). The text thus acts as what Gayatri Chakravorty Spivak in *Readings* terms "transactional," that is, it teaches how to read it along with associated literary genres and traditions, and also the world around it (51). Mitra's modernism in "The Discovery of Telenāpotā" relocates a common narrative trope in Bengali fictional treatment of the marriage theme, i.e., a man leaves his betrothed in pursuit of a better life, and the girl finally finds an unknown but responsible groom:

> When Yamini was still a child, her mother had arranged her marriage to a distant nephew of hers, named Niranjan. Four years ago, the fellow had turned up to tell her that he would marry Yamini after returning from abroad. Since then the old mother has been lying there, in this godforsaken house, counting the days of her daughter's marriage. [...] Niranjan basically lied to her because the old woman had been so insistent. (181)

According to the generic conventions of Bengali love-story the "other," or the insecure woman – Yamini – becomes an ethical concern for the male protagonist, who is expected to rescue the woman by marrying her, and, thereby, securing the woman's position within a domestic settlement. This kind of generic form presupposes the domination of "self"'s concern – a sort of masculine work-ethic, sanctioned by the Bengali patriarchal family – and represses the "other"'s separate subjectivity; once this concern wavers, the "other" as the object of both desire and empathy, recedes into some untraceable region:

> Your footsteps will stir the corpselike figure. [...] "Are you Niranjan? You've finally remembered your unlucky aunt [...]. I couldn't even die in peace. You won't run away again, will you?" [...] "No, aunt, I won't run away again." [...] Yamini may come up to you as you are about to leave, raise her wistful eyes to your face and comment: "You've forgotten your fishing-rod." Smiling, you will reply: "Let it be here. I might not be successful this time, but the fish of Telenāpotā cannot elude me next time." (182-83)

The generic form of the speculative fiction itself seems to inhibit the entry of the "other" in the life of the "self," who becomes both the cause and victim of suffering. In his essay on "Amy Foster" Jürgen Kramer points out "why," after all, Yanko "tells his story: he approaches his trauma by making it the elusive topic of a narrative embedded in a conversation" (9). Kramer's observation is applicable to a great extent to the telling of stories by both the Commanding Officer in "The Tale" and the unnamed narrator of "The Discovery of Telenāpotā," but in all these cases the fidelity of the narrators remains questionable, as their empathies are prone to wobble in the face of adversity.

The tale of Telenāpotā thus shares with Conrad's "The Tale" what Ben Hutchinson calls "a fear that secular modernity may have been voided of any meaningful content" (2) in view of the authoritarian appropriation of reality. The intended reader or traveller-turned-lover would come back home to find that he has caught malaria, and once he gets well, the entire episode of Telenāpotā from within the metropolitan restraints becomes only an absurd dream, shattering all the earlier expectations. Attridge, in reading Derrida in *The Singularity of Literature*, makes "a distinction between two kinds of responsibility," which are "responsibility *to* the other and responsibility *for* the other" (123). As Attridge further explains, one can be responsible to the "other" by taking into account the "other"'s call and answering to it, but "this nowhere near as demanding" as one's "responsibility for the other." Because, "[b]eing responsible for the other involves assuming the other's needs [...] affirming it, sustaining it, being prepared to give up" one's "own wants and satisfactions" as well as fears and suspicions "for the sake of the other" (124). Works of Conrad and Mitra allow us to understand that illusion of laws is ethically bankrupt because it suggests the "self"'s failure to be responsible for the "other." Modernist tales "tell of life at the 'actual' micro level performances to disclose the uncensored truths" (Ray, "The Other Within" 46) of the befuddled subjectivity, which undergoes interplay between dream and reality, and between pretence and accident. As the realist narratives dissolve into the speculative ones, the characters and events in both tales within tales emerge only to be eroded to leave an uncertainty about their very existence. As in "The Tale," in the Bengali story self-delusion merges with forgetfulness as the only possible remedy to deceit and resultant guilt. The genre of modernist short stories in a particular turn, exemplified by "The Tale" and "The Discovery of Telenāpotā," exploits the openness of literature that unmakes itself with a wish to see behind the veil of obviously intelligible, and expose the blind spots of totalitarianism and all sorts of sectarianism. Close readings of such textuality, but not closed ones, have to recognize the contingent as well as the strange and new. This is a part of our ethical responsibility *for* the spirit of human liberation from a guilt ridden and internally empty authority.

WORKS CITED

Attridge, Derek. *The Singularity of Literature.* Routledge, 2004.

Belsey, Catherine. *Culture and the Real: Theorizing Cultural Criticism.* Routledge, 2009.

Benjamin, Walter. *The Work of Art in the Age of Mechanical Reproduction.* Trans. J. A. Underwood. Penguin, 2008. Great Ideas Series.

Carabine, Keith. Introduction. *Selected Short Stories.* By Conrad. Ed. Keith Carabine. Wordsworth Classics, 1997. vii-xxvii.

Chaudhuri, Supriya. "The Bengali novel." *The Cambridge Companion to Modern Indian Culture.* Ed. Vasudha Dalmia and Rashmi Sadana. Cambridge UP, 2012. 101-23.

---. "Modernisms in India." *The Oxford Handbook of Modernisms.* Ed. Peter Brooker, Andrzej Gasiorek, Deborah Longworth and Andrew Thacker. Oxford UP, 2010. 942-60.

Clark, Katerina, and Michael Holquist. *Mikhail Bakhtin.* Belknap P of Harvard UP, 1984.

Derrida, Jacques. *Acts of Literature*. Ed. and Introd. Derek Attridge. Routledge, 1992.
---. "Deconstruction and the Other." *Dialogues with Contemporary Continental Thinkers*. Ed. Richard Kearney. Manchester UP, 1984. 105-26.
Erdinast-Vulcan, Daphna, Allan H. Simmons, and J. H. Stape, eds. *Joseph Conrad: The Short Fiction*. Rodopi, 2004.
Hutchinson, Ben. *Modernism and Style*. Palgrave Macmillan, 2011.
Jameson, Fredric. *The Modernist Papers*. ABS and Verso, 2007.
Krajka, Wiesław. Introduction. *"Wine in Old and New Bottles"* 1-12.
---, ed. *"Wine in Old and New Bottles": Critical Paradigms for Joseph Conrad*. Maria Curie-Skłodowska UP and Columbia UP, 2014. Vol. 23 of *Conrad: Eastern and Western Perspectives*. Ed. Wiesław Krajka. 32 vols. to date. 1992- .
Kramer, Jürgen. "What the Country Doctor 'did not see': The Limits of the Imagination in 'Amy Foster'." Erdinast-Vulcan, Simmons and Stape 1-11.
Manjapra, Kris. Abstract. "From Imperial to International Horizons: A Hermeneutic Study of Bengali Modernism." *Modern Intellectual History* 8 (2011): 327-59.
Mitra, Premendra. "Telenāpotā ābiskār" ["The Discovery of Telenāpotā"]. *Shrestha Galpa* [Best stories]. 176-83.
---. *Shrestha Galpa* [Best stories]. Ed. and Introd. Sourin Bhattacharya. Dey's, 2001.
Orwell, George. "Wells, Hitler and the World State." *Selected Essays*. By Orwell. Ed. Stefan Collini. Oxford UP, 2021. 115-20.
Pathak, Ashis. Introduction. *Premendra Mitrer Samasta Galpa* [Complete stories of Premendra Mitra]. Ed. Ashis Pathak. Vol. 1. Dey's, 2015. v-xii.
Peters, John G. *The Cambridge Introduction to Joseph Conrad*. Cambridge UP, 2012.
Ray, Subhadeep. "'After such knowledge what forgiveness?': Nature, Community and Individual Ethics in Joseph Conrad's 'Because of the Dollars' and Adwaita Mallabarman's 'A River Called Titas'." *Joseph Conrad and Ethics*. Ed. Amar Acheraïou and Laëtitia Crémona. Introd. Amar Acheraïou. Maria Curie-Skłodowska UP and Columbia UP, 2021. 261-90. Vol. 30 of *Conrad: Eastern and Western Perspectives*. Ed. Wiesław Krajka. 32 vols. to date. 1992- .
---. "Modernism's Footprints: World, Text and Ideology in Joseph Conrad and Manik Bandyopadhyay." *Some Intertextual Chords of Joseph Conrad's Literary Art*. Ed. Wiesław Krajka. Maria Curie-Skłodowska UP and Columbia UP, 2019. 161-202. Vol. 28 of *Conrad: Eastern and Western Perspectives*. Ed. Wiesław Krajka. 32 vols. to date. 1992- .
---. "The Other Within: Death and Sickness in Selected Short Fictions of Joseph Conrad and Manik Bandyopadhyay." *Jadavpur Journal of Comparative Literature* 57-58 (2022): 29-52.

Rodaway, Paul. *Sensuous Geographies: Body, Sense and Space.* Routledge, 1994.

Sassoon, Siegfried. *Memoirs of An Infantry Officer.* Faber, 1988.

Spivak, Gayatri Chakravorty. *Readings.* Seagull, 2014.

Turner, Jennifer. "'Petticoats' and 'Sea Business': Women Characters in Conrad's Edwardian Short Stories." Erdinast-Vulcan, Simmons and Stape 142-56.

Watt, Ian. *Conrad in the Nineteenth Century.* U of California P, 1979.

Yamamoto, Kaoru. "Hospitality in 'The Secret Sharer'." Krajka, "*Wine in Old and New Bottles*" 253-68.

Balázs Csizmadia,
Independent Scholar,
Budapest, Hungary

Narrated Drama: János Gosztonyi's *Bűvölet* as an Adaptation of Conrad's *Victory*

Of the few creative responses to Conrad's fiction in Hungarian literature, the theatrical adaptation of *Victory* entitled *Bűvölet* (Enchantment, 2002) by playwright, actor and stage director János Gosztonyi (1926–2014) is the most complex and thought-provoking.[1] Perhaps unsurprisingly, Gosztonyi chose to adapt a novel that lends itself particularly well to expression in other media: Basil Macdonald Hastings's *Victory: A Play in Three Acts* (1919), two operas and nearly a dozen film or television versions all attest to its adaptability (Knowles and Moore 437). As Richard J. Hand has pointed out, adaptation of *Victory* into performance is facilitated by its relatively simple narrative and time structure, as well as its "melodramatic sense of action and archetype" (7). It is partly the melodrama that Hastings's adaptation, arguably a shortened and simplified version of Conrad's novel, builds upon and intensifies. The "happy ending" sees Heyst and Lena alive and united in love, which is perhaps the most conspicuous sign that the play was written at least in part with popular success and the tastes of the general public in mind. However, this goal of popular success applies not only to Hastings but also to Conrad himself. In fact, it was Conrad who first suggested giving the story a happy ending. His correspondence with Hastings reveals that he was very much involved in the adaptation, making suggestions with regard to scenery and costumes, as well as drafting several new scenes. It should be noted that the play does have its own points of originality and successful experimentation, but these are more thematic than technical in nature (cf. Hand 13-17; Knowles and Moore 433-34). Unlike the Hastings text, Gosztonyi's *Bűvölet* is highly responsive to the subtleties and characteristic features of the narrative structure of the novel and is altogether more experimental than the earlier adaptation. Indeed, since Gosztonyi was not a Conrad specialist, there is no reason to assume that he was familiar with Hastings's play; it is quite possible that he read *Victory* only in Hungarian translation (published in 1970).

As I have pointed out elsewhere, all of Conrad's major works have been translated into Hungarian, yet they are relatively little known outside academic circles (Csizmadia 309-22). Their true literary value is often masked by the still prevalent and stereotypical image of Conrad as a writer of sea and adventure stories. In addition, the reception of Conrad in Hungary is characterized by an unevenness that largely reflects changes in the political and cultural life of the country in the twentieth century and beyond. Nonetheless, there have been some perceptive critical commentaries on his works and, as noted above, compelling creative responses to them by Hungarian writers and other artists. An interesting example of the latter from the world of popular music is "Angol regény" (English novel, 1994, by János Másik, Géza Bereményi and Tamás Cseh), which was clearly inspired by both "Heart of Darkness" and its film adaptation by Francis Ford Coppola, *Apocalypse Now*. Like both its predecessors, the song is not only about a physical journey but is also about self-discovery, yet with a certain twist on the original stories (Csizmadia 320-21).

Gosztonyi's *Bűvölet* is a play in two parts (a Prologue and Part II) based largely on Conrad's novel, but the author made some modifications to the plot of the source text and changed the name of some of the characters. Thus, Mr. Jones of *Victory* is renamed Mr. James Dodd in the play, Martin Ricardo becomes Albert Ukken, Pedro is called Marmala, Schomberg is known as Stőger, and Mrs. Schomberg's name is modified accordingly (to Stőgerné, meaning Mrs. Stőger). The most conspicuous change to the plot is that, while Mr. Jones dies by drowning, in the play Lena stabs Mr. Dodd to death before she dies from the bullet that hit her. This gives her a more active role in plot development than she has in the novel, one that seems to reflect how the image of women and of female characters in literature has changed since Conrad's time. Another modification to the plot that Gosztonyi introduced concerns the members of the touring ladies' orchestra that performs at Schomberg's hotel. In the novel, Davidson finds out from Mrs. Schomberg that they are of mixed nationality (*V* 40), while in the play, Stőgerné tells Konrad that they are Czechs, Romanians, and Hungarians, with one English girl among them, referring to Lena (Gosztonyi, *Bűvölet* 5). The fact that in Gosztonyi's adaptation some members of the orchestra are Hungarian helps create more sympathy in the Hungarian reader or audience for the plight of these female musicians in general, among them Lena herself.

It is impossible to know with any certainty what kind of audience Gosztonyi had in mind when he wrote the play. I have been unable to locate any reviews of a performance of *Bűvölet* in Hungarian theatres, and indeed it is conceivable that the play has never been put on stage. It was published in a supplement to volume 35 of *Színház* (Theatre), the journal of the Hungarian Theatre Company, and remains little known to date. At some points of the play, as I shall argue, familiarity with Conrad's *Victory* clearly enriches our experience and adds to our understanding. Considering all of the above, one may surmise that Gosztonyi's ideal target audience was an educated readership well versed in modern European literature. The intricate narrative strategies he employed in his adaptation also seem to presuppose readers who are open to unconventional, even experimental forms of literature. In fact, what makes *Bűvölet* a fascinating adaptation is not the part it plays in Conrad's reception in Hungary in the first place, but its use of narrative elements that seem to push the limits of dramatic representation. In this paper, I will argue that the play does this in a way that is entirely consistent with a characteristic feature of Conradian narrative.

Bűvölet opens with a Prologue in which a sea captain named Konrad engages in dialogue with an obscure Voice:

The action takes place in the [Malay] Archipelago, at the beginning of the 1900s

PROLOGUE

KONRAD: Here in the Archipelago, everyone knew who the Swede was…
VOICE: He was something of a traveller, wasn't he?
KONRAD: He was rather mooching around… that doesn't sound very good, but a traveller arrives and departs, goes on somewhere. But he never departed… the Archipelago, like some enchanted circle, held him captive.
VOICE: Were you friends?
KONRAD: I would rather say that I was keeping my eye on him in a friendly way. Everybody was aware of that. I will never forget how, while playing billiards and chalking his cue, he exclaimed suddenly, apropos of nothing: "I am enchanted with these islands!" Because, your Excellency, there are more spells in heaven and on earth than your commonplace magicians ever dreamed of.
VOICE: Captain Konrad! What do you think is the truth behind the Morrison affair?
KONRAD: Have you ever seen a hardened, hopeless tramp trudging around on a road glowing with the heat of the sun, on his way from one prison to another? When the Swede ran into him, Morrison looked like one of these tramps.
Enter AXEL: What a pleasant surprise. Would you like to drink something with me? The sun is really too strong to talk in the street.
MORRISON: All right, thank you, I'd be happy to. (*Bűvölet* 1)[2]

As Konrad answers the Voice's questions about Axel Heyst (who is called simply Axel here), it soon becomes apparent that Konrad is also a narrator: he uses the past tense and even quotes in direct speech what Axel once said about being enchanted with the islands. His narrative of how Axel met Morrison turns into the scene being enacted as the two characters mentioned appear and start talking to each other. Konrad is not heard talking for a while, and he is not part of the scene in the same way that Axel and Morrison are. The implication is that Konrad here is situated on a distinct ontological level, what in narrative theory is called a different *diegetic* level.[3] Clearly, it is Konrad's act of narration that has generated the scene, which – quite surprisingly for drama – makes us think of the play in narrative terms. The immediacy of drama, our sense of being in the present, in the here and now, is undermined right at the outset.

Konrad addresses the Voice as "your Excellency," but beyond that, the reader of the play or the audience in the theatre do not receive any more information about him. Readers familiar with Conrad's novel *Victory*, however, will associate the Voice with the Excellency to whom Davidson relates the final part of the story. Davidson does not feature in the play, but Konrad takes on his narratorial role, and their participation in the action as characters is also comparable. Since Konrad assumes the role of the unnamed narrator of the novel as well, it could be argued that he has a threefold function in the play.

In *Victory* there is an anonymous first-person (or, in Genettean terms, homodiegetic) narrator with limited knowledge of the events who recounts Part I. From Part II onwards, however, the narrator seems to become third-person (or heterodiegetic) since he is now not a character in the events he recounts.[4] He could be regarded as omniscient, considering that he has access to the thoughts of the characters. While many early critics dismissed this shift in the narrative voice as an inconsistency, more recently others have defended Conrad's method as serving his thematic purposes.[5] At the end of the novel, there is a return to homodiegetic narration in Davidson's brief account of the final events, as presented within the omniscient narrative. In what follows, I will compare the narrative structure of *Victory* and that of *Bűvölet* whenever and wherever such a comparison seems relevant to my argument.

In the play, Konrad as narrator retreats into the background after scene 5 of the Prologue, and the Voice even earlier, and both reappear only in the very last scene (Part II, scene 13). This means that there is a narrative frame to the play which foregrounds and dramatizes the circumstances of the telling of the story:

Scene 13 [Part II]

> KONRAD: It was my anxiety that drove me there. One can just sense certain things. But I arrived too late. Not very late, and yet hopelessly so.

> VOICE: Did you return on board immediately?
> KONRAD: I didn't want to intrude on his grief. I thought I would take him away with me the next day.
> [...]
> VOICE: I suppose you are certain that the Baron is dead?
> KONRAD: Yes, he and the girl together. Ashes.[...] That Chinaman I have already mentioned shot the third bandit dead in the boat. "That makes everything safe," he said, and he went over the hill to fetch his woman. And then, your Excellency, I went away too. I will never steam that way again. There is nothing to be done there.
> VOICE: Clearly.
> KONRAD: Nothing in the world. Nothing, nothing. (*Bűvölet* 16)[6]

As the two passages I have cited suggest, the play conflates the opening of the novel told by the anonymous narrator with its final part recounted by Davidson. For instance, at the end of the novel, His Excellency asks Davidson whether he knew the late Baron Heyst well, to which he replies that he was "keeping [his] eye on him in a friendly way" (*V* 408). As the first extract I have cited demonstrates, there is a similar exchange at the beginning of the play.

Traditionally, dramatic representation has been understood as relying on mimetic portrayal (or *showing*) of fictional events, while in narrative texts events are assumed to be *told* diegetically by a narrator (Sommer 122). However, in *Bűvölet* there is clearly a mixture of mimesis and diegesis, of enacting and recounting. Some of the diegetic elements are linked to rhetorical functions such as informing the audience or reader of events that cannot be shown because of temporal, spatial or practical reasons (for example, to provide backstory). But here I would like to focus on the diegetic elements that move beyond such rhetorical functions, and which are an integral part of the play. In doing so, I will rely on Roy Sommer's useful summary of diegetic elements in drama (121-22). In fact, I have already mentioned two key examples of the diegetic mode of representation in *Bűvölet*, the narrative frame and Konrad as narrator figure. Also, I have noted that in much of the play, the narrator is formally absent. Unsurprisingly, it is mainly these passages without Konrad as narrator that correspond to what in *Victory* is told by the omniscient narrator. Representation here is largely mimetic on the face of it as the scenes consist of dialogues between the characters (among them Konrad himself), without narratorial commentary. However, I would argue that because the narrative frame has already been established, it is impossible even here to forget that there is a narrator in the background. Reading these scenes is somewhat reminiscent of reading dialogues that are presented in narrative texts. By way of comparison, one might think of the short story "Hills Like White Elephants" by Ernest Hemingway, which is written mostly in direct speech.

Unusual as Konrad's narratorial role is in drama, there are similar examples in modern and postmodern plays. Brian Richardson, in his paper on "Voice and Narration in Postmodern Drama," discusses several different strategies and examples of narration in dramatic texts. Perhaps the most relevant of these in the present context is the memory play, such as Tennessee Williams's *The Glass Menagerie*. Richardson describes the memory play as "a partially enacted homodiegetic narrative in which the narrator is also a participant in the events he or she recounts and enacts" (682). In *Bűvölet*, Konrad could be described as a homodiegetic narrator as well since he is clearly a character in his own narrative, even though not the main one. However, while at the beginning of *The Glass Menagerie* the narrator draws attention to the fact that what follows is a memory play and thus not realistic, Konrad does not destroy our mimetic illusions to that extent. Another interesting narrative strategy in drama described by Richardson is the use of what he terms a "generative narrator." The name refers to the fact that, by telling their stories, these narrators create or generate a fictional world much like an omniscient narrator in fiction. Generative narrators are heterodiegetic as they are not characters in the stories they tell, residing in a distinct ontological level (685). Examples include the bard or Singer in Bertolt Brecht's *The Caucasian Chalk Circle* and the Stage Manager in Thornton Wilder's *Our Town*. As I have pointed out above, Konrad in *Bűvölet* has a generative function too as his narrative of how Axel met Morrison turns into the scene being enacted. Even though Konrad is also a character in his own narrative and thus homodiegetic, as a narrator he is clearly situated on a different diegetic level than Axel and Morrison. Categorising Konrad strictly as a homodiegetic narrator also raises the problem of narrative authority since he sometimes lays claim to more knowledge than he can possibly have. It would be more accurate to describe his narrative as a mixture of the homodiegetic and the heterodiegetic, a mixture that derives from his threefold function mentioned above.

A further diegetic element in the play is the way in which Konrad as narrator sometimes comments on the events, apparently addressing the audience. For instance, at one point in the Prologue, Stőger makes some derogatory remarks to guests in his hotel on Axel's enterprise, the Tropical Belt Coal Company, implying that it would fail. Konrad then comments as follows, before informing the audience that the company did indeed go into liquidation later: "What was that? Had his idiotic bias turned Stőger into a prophet? Or was he just stupidly clinging to a prejudice?" (*Bűvölet* 2).[7] This direct audience address is at the same time an example of metanarrative comment, a self-reflexive utterance which concerns the act of narration itself. In other words, Konrad here is asking rhetorical questions about how to interpret a certain element in his own story. Interestingly, after he has finished his comments and his summary of some events to follow, the scene continues with Stőger gloating over the Tropical Belt Coal Company's bankruptcy: "You see? Your prophet of an innkeeper! Haven't I told you? A flourishing enterprise? The hell it is! It's gone bankrupt!" (2).[8] In this way, the temporal gap between the two parts of the same scene is foregrounded. All these elements – the direct audience address, the metanarrative comment, the temporal gap within one and the same scene – work against the illusion of mimetic representation.

A similar effect is achieved also by the disembodied Voice and the use of characters who themselves turn into narrators within Konrad's narrative. Both techniques also strengthen our impression that the discussion between Konrad and the

Voice takes place on a different diegetic level than the events described within Konrad's narrative. Perhaps the most intriguing example of a narrating character in the play is Axel telling Lena of his discussion with Mr. Dodd in detail in Part II, scene 7:

> AXEL: The boss is a thin, long person. He's what people would call a gentleman. "I suppose you would like to know who I am?" he began. "I will leave it to you," I replied. Then he said: "I am he who is. I have been ejected from my proper social sphere because I was unable to conform to certain conventions. I am a rebel of some sort who is coming and going up and down the earth." Then he started talking about how he and I pursued the same ends, but that he pursued them with more openness and more simplicity than me. "And what might those ends be?" He evaded the question. When he had finished speaking, he burst into a long and spectral laugh. I didn't join him. (*Bűvölet* 12)[9]

Axel's narrative uses both direct speech and indirect speech to tell Lena (and the audience/reader) what he and Mr. Dodd said to each other. The passage I have quoted shows the beginning of this exchange, but the greater part of the scene continues in a similar fashion. What is particularly interesting about this narrative within a narrative is why Gosztonyi chose to include it at all. *Bűvölet* being a play, he could easily have *shown* this scene mimetically as a dialogue between Axel and Mr. Dodd, instead of having Axel narrate it diegetically to Lena later. It is true that there is a similar passage in *Victory* (Part IV, Chapter V) in which we see Heyst telling Lena about his discussions with Mr. Jones (the play conflates two such conversations into one scene). Yet, in the light of what I have argued above, it seems unlikely that Gosztonyi kept this element from the novel out of unthinking fidelity to the original. I believe the fact that he retained this embedded narrative in spite of adapting the novel for the theatre betrays an acute understanding of Conradian narrative in general. While Conrad used a wide range of narrative strategies,[10] he is noted in particular for his contemplative personified narrators, most of whom produce oral narratives to a listener or a group of listeners. In Conrad's fiction we also often find multiple narrators and framed tales, with the frame narrative and embedded narrative suggesting competing interpretations of the story. Therefore, it is ultimately up to the reader to decide which interpretation is more valid. It should be added that this example of narration by a character in *Bűvölet*, like most others, is found in the part of the play in which Konrad as narrator is formally absent, demonstrating that representation is not entirely mimetic even here.

As a final diegetic element or narrative strategy in the play, I would like to note the use of metalepsis. Metalepsis, the mingling of two different diegetic levels (Prince 50-51), occurs here as Gosztonyi playfully makes the author of *Victory* one of the characters in the play adapted from his own novel. The spelling of the name Konrad, with its initial "*K*," recalls one of Joseph Conrad's three original Polish forenames (Józef Teodor Konrad). Just like Joseph Conrad, the Konrad of the play is both a sea captain and a storyteller, a storyteller whose act of narration has produced the play that we are reading or that the audience sees enacted on stage. More generally, the narrative strategies I have analysed in *Bűvölet* provide further evidence for the range and extent of narration in dramatic texts. In fact, they underline the importance of developing a systematic narratology of drama, work on which has been ongoing.[11]

If *Bűvölet* were an original text unrelated to any novel, its storytelling strategies would perhaps seem even more radical than they are. As it is an adaptation of Conrad's *Victory*, however, these strategies take on a somewhat different meaning. Unusual as they are in drama, they are, I think, perfectly compatible with the way in which many of Conrad's fictions work. As Jeremy Hawthorn remarks, Conrad's use of personified narrators in general, and frame narratives in particular, gives us "that distinctively Conradian sense that we are not perceiving the world and its people in unmediated form, but indirectly, either through one reporting consciousness, or through a chain of linked consciousnesses" (155). Gosztonyi dramatizes this very feature of Conradian narrative by retaining some of the characteristics of the novel adapted and using them in a creative way. The fact that these narrative elements in drama serve to disrupt our mimetic illusions only helps to highlight what is typically Conradian about this play.

NOTES

[1] In "The Reception of Joseph Conrad in Hungary" I wrote very briefly on Gosztonyi's adaptation of *Victory* (319-20). In the present study, I build on some of the points made in the earlier paper to examine the problem of narration in the play in greater detail.

[2] *Történik a Szigetvilágban, a kilencszázas évek elején.*

ELŐJÁTÉK

KONRAD: Itt a Szigetvilágban mindenki tudta, ki a Svéd...
HANG: Olyan utazóféle... nem?
KONRAD: Inkább lődörgő... bár nem hangzik valami jól, mert az utazó, ugye, jön-megy, távozik valamerre... Ő viszont sosem ment el... a Szigetvilág, mint valami bűvös kör, fogva tartotta.
HANG: Barátok voltak?
KONRAD: Inkább azt mondanám: barátságosan rajta tartottam a szemem. Ez köztudomású volt. Sosem felejtem el, ahogy biliárdozás közben, dákóját krétázva, minden előzetes bevezetés nélkül felkiált: "Teljesen elbűvöltek ezek a szigetek!" Mert hát, kegyelmes uram, sokkal többfajta bűvölet van a földön s égen, mintsem köznapi varázslóink álmodni képesek.
HANG: Konrad kapitány! Mi az igazság ön szerint a Morrison históriában?
KONRAD: Látott már afféle megrögzött, reménytelen csavargót, amint egy naptól izzó úton, két letartóztatás közt, bandukol? Amikor a Svéd belebotlott, Morrison ilyen csavargóra emlékeztetett.
AXEL: *(megjelenik)* Micsoda kellemes meglepetés! Nem volna kedve egyet inni velem? Itt, a tűző napon nem lehet beszélgetni.
MORRISON: Jó, köszönöm, megihatunk egy korty valamit.

In my translation of passages from *Bűvölet*, I rely on the text of *Victory* wherever possible. All translations from the play are mine.

[3] *Diegetic level* is defined by Prince as the level "at which an existent, event, or act of recounting is situated with regard to a given DIEGESIS (*diégèse*)" (20). In modern narrative theory, the term *diegesis* is used in two different senses, a distinction that goes back to Gérard Genette: 1. "the universe in which [a] story takes place" – and not the story itself (*diégèse* in French); 2. "pure narrative (without dialogue), in contrast to the *mimésis* of dramatic representation" (*diégésis* in French) (*Narrative Discourse Revisited* 17, 18). In this study, I will use both meanings of diegesis/diegetic, always clarifying which one is intended.

[4] In terms of person, Genette distinguishes between homodiegetic and heterodiegetic narrators. A homodiegetic narrator is one who is present as a character in the story he tells, whilst a heterodiegetic narrator is absent from it (*Narrative Discourse: An Essay* 243-45).

[5] For the latter, see, for instance, Erdinast-Vulcan 182-83.

[6]

13. jelenet

KONRAD: Valami nyugtalanság hajtott arra. Az ember megérez bizonyos dolgokat. Csak hát elkéstem. Nem sokat, de teljesen.
HANG: Rögtön visszatért a hajójára?
KONRAD: Nem akartam őt zavarni bánatában. Gondoltam: másnap elviszem onnan.
[...]
HANG: Biztos hát benne, hogy a báró halott?
KONRAD: Ő és a lány együtt. Igen. Puszta hamu.[...] A kínai, akit már említettem, a csónakban lőtte agyon a harmadik banditát. "Most már nincs veszély" – mondta, s indult a hegyen túlra asszonyáért. És akkor, kegyelmes uram, magam is eljöttem onnan. S többé nem is hajózom arrafelé. Nincs ott már semmi.
HANG: Világos.
KONRAD: Semmi az égvilágon. Semmi, semmi.

[7] "Mi volt ez? A bárgyú elfogultság látnokká tette Stőgert? Vagy csak ostobán ragaszkodott egy előítéletéhez?"

[8] "Mit szólnak? A maguk próféta fogadósa! Ugye megmondta? Virágzó vállalkozás? A fenét, csőd!"

[9] AXEL: A főnök magas sovány, az a fajta, akit a társaság úriembernek nevez. "Gondolom, szeretné tudni, ki vagyok?" – kezdte. "Magára bízom, hogy megmondja-e" – válaszoltam. Mire ő: "Az vagyok, aki vagyok. Kitaszítottak a magam társadalmi köréből, mert képtelen voltam az elfogadott szabályokhoz alkalmazkodni. Afféle lázadó vagyok, aki ide-oda kóborol." Aztán arról beszélt, hogy mi ketten voltaképp azonos célokat követünk, de ő nyíltabban és egyszerűbben tör a célra. "Mi légyen az a cél?" Megkerülte a kérdést. Amikor a mondókáját befejezte, hosszú, kísérteties nevetésre fakadt. Nem nevettem vele.

[10] For a thorough analysis of narrative strategies in Conrad's fiction, see Lothe.

[11] In addition to Richardson's essay mentioned above, see, for instance, Jahn, and Schwanecke.

WORKS CITED

Csizmadia, Balázs. "The Reception of Joseph Conrad in Hungary." *The Reception of Joseph Conrad in Europe*. Ed. Robert Hampson and Véronique Pauly. Bloomsbury Academic, 2022. 309-22. The Reception of British and Irish Authors in Europe.

Erdinast-Vulcan, Daphna. *Joseph Conrad and the Modern Temper.* Clarendon, 1991.

Genette, Gérard. *Narrative Discourse: An Essay in Method.* Trans. Jane E. Lewin. Cornell UP, 1980.

---. *Narrative Discourse Revisited.* Trans. Jane E. Lewin. Cornell UP, 1988.

Gosztonyi, János. "Bűvölet: Játék két részben, Joseph Conrad regénye nyomán." *Színház*, supplement (drámamelléklet) 35.8 (2002): 1-16.

Hand, Richard J. Introduction: "Conrad's *Victory: An Island Tale* (1915) and Basil Macdonald Hastings's *Victory: A Play in Three Acts* (1919)." *Conrad's* Victory: *The Play and Reviews*. Ed. Richard J. Hand. Rodopi, 2009. 1-39. Conrad Studies 4.

Hawthorn, Jeremy. "Joseph Conrad's Half-written Fictions." *The Cambridge Companion to the Modernist Novel.* Ed. Morag Shiach. Cambridge UP, 2007. 151-64.

Jahn, Manfred. "Narrative Voice and Agency in Drama: Aspects of a Narratology of Drama." *New Literary History* 32 (2001): 659-79.

Knowles, Owen, and Gene M. Moore. *Oxford Reader's Companion to Conrad.* Oxford UP, 2000.

Lothe, Jakob. *Conrad's Narrative Method.* Clarendon, 1989.

Prince, Gerald. *A Dictionary of Narratology.* Revised ed. U of Nebraska P, 2003.

Richardson, Brian. "Voice and Narration in Postmodern Drama." *New Literary History* 32 (2001): 681-94.

Schwanecke, Christine. *A Narratology of Drama: Dramatic Storytelling in Theory, History, and Culture from the Renaissance to the Twenty-First Century*. Gruyter, 2022. Narratologia 80.

Sommer, Roy. "Drama and Narrative." *Routledge Encyclopedia of Narrative Theory.* Ed. David Herman, Manfred Jahn, and Marie Laure Ryan. Routledge, 2005. 119-24.

Chris Cairney,
Middle Georgia State University,
Cochran, GA, USA

Conrad in an Age of Social Justice: Teaching *The Secret Agent* in Light of Contemporary Issues

As an English professor at a university in the United States, I must say it's getting easier to teach Conrad to my undergraduate students. It used to be that at the beginning of a course incorporating texts by Joseph Conrad, I felt the need to first justify inclusion of his writing – usually "Heart of Darkness" – in the face of my perception of a generalized – if not specific – postcolonial critique related to Chinua Achebe's idea that, apart from anything else, Conrad was "a thoroughgoing racist" (788). Yet once we had read "The Congo Diary," Conrad's diary of his own time on the Congo River, and discussed Achebe, there was little time to go into other aspects of Conrad. That state of affairs may be changing. For one thing, the preoccupations and concerns one finds in social-justice conversations today might render Conrad's *The Secret Agent* more amenable to classroom study, or at least easier to address in the current classroom, than "Heart of Darkness." That is not to say that "Heart of Darkness" is any less timely or relevant than *The Secret Agent*, but currently resonant issues of personal liberty, social privilege, and equal opportunity can all be addressed (if one so wishes) in the pages of *The Secret Agent*, and, additionally, examining the individual in crisis may give us, as teachers, more chances to talk about Conrad's specific tendencies and contributions, and allows us, in teaching Conrad, to come off the defensive a bit. Why things here may be changing may come down to this: it may have to do with the former preoccupation with overt politics giving way to more ability to relate to the feelings of the individual in the process of soul-searching. Also, reading *The Secret Agent* and thinking about social unrest and violence may make students feel like Conrad knew something about these things. Perhaps these conditions make it easier for them to consider vicariously a character's ethical self-examination, something perhaps related, in Conradian terms, to self-reflection "in a mirror." Conrad is an author I want to share with students, and it may just be easier to do this now by engaging with social-justice issues, beginning with *The Secret Agent* and then moving on, for example, to *Nostromo* and a discussion on the pitfalls of international capitalism or the suffering of the masses. Today's students are ready, and this would be yet another way to "keep Conrad relevant" as we teach younger students.

So, in talking about Conrad in the context of social justice, we might thus consider both our starting place *in* and the implication *of* our title "Conrad in an Age of Social Justice." The title of this paper might imply that the "age of social justice" is temporary. This is an interesting thought for several reasons. For one thing, that would be both historically and sociologically misleading: it could be seen to imply that social justice is only a concern or focus now, and that these issues were not foregrounded before or understood before. But were they foregrounded before? Just two quick examples of earlier movements or practices that touched on or pointed toward social justice as an issue are, arguably, medieval almsgiving (Lepine 1066) and Marxism. There also might be a difference between understanding the importance of (some kind of) social justice and understanding the nature and complexities of social justice itself. I would argue that *The Secret Agent* fits both bills, with Conrad touching on the need for or the importance of social justice generally and also at times digging into the specific practical details of social justice as it applies to the experience of individual characters in *The Secret Agent* such as Stevie. These are all contributing factors, I believe, in the continued relevance of Conrad generally and of *The Secret Agent* in particular.

But first, with the goal of unpacking and discussing the ideology of social justice reflected in *The Secret Agent*, a definition of *social justice* is in order. According to the website of the United Nations, *social justice* "is an underlying principle for peaceful and prosperous coexistence within and among nations" ("World Day"). Further, social justice is "based on the values of fairness, equality, respect for diversity, access to social protection, and the application of human rights in all spheres of life, including in the workplace" ("Message on World Day"). A webpage of Bronx Community College, part of the City University of New York, sees social justice as marked by "justice in terms of the distribution of wealth, opportunities, and privileges within a society" ("Social Justice and Civic Engagement"). Simultaneously economic and social in focus, the active idea of social justice is in many ways an outgrowth of Marxist ideology and requires "a geographical, sociological, political and cultural framework" ("Social Justice in an Open World" 11-12). Loretta Capeheart and Dragan Milovanovic see social justice as related directly to political economy and distribution of wealth, discussing "selectively institutionalized" conceptions of justice (1-2). In contemporary terms, social justice goals usually involve encouraging "a social system where economic and social resources are equitably distributed to guarantee people's active and equal participation in social systems" (Compare and Albanesi). Kathleen Maas Weigert discusses social justice as a subcategory of general justice usually equivalent to "distributive justice" but sometimes equivalent to "contributive justice" (397-400). Nerilee Ceatha et al. see "redistributive" justice as well as "recognitive" justice as distinctions to be drawn when discussing social justice (2).

The history of Western engagement with issues now called *social justice* is long: it can be said to go back to Plato's discussion of justice and class in Book IV of *The Republic* (112-15) and perhaps also to Aristotle's discussion of distributive justice in Book V of *Nicomachean Ethics* (95-104). St. Thomas Aquinas, responding in part to Aristotle, was a major point in the development of the concept, particularly in his discussion of justice in Book V of his *Commentary on Aristotle's Nicomachean Ethics* (293-96). For modern development of the concept there is Thomas Paine's *The Rights of Man* in which he discusses the need for "a fair and universal chance" (228), Luigi Taparelli's mid-nineteenth-century writings in the journal *Civiltà Cattolica* (Behr 100), and John Dewey's writing in the early 20th century, including *Education and Social Change* (416).

Continuing with more immediate implications of the title of this essay, "Conrad in an Age of Social Justice," one might think it is meant to raise a question regarding whether or not we *can* read Conrad in this age of social justice, or is any Conrad text suddenly a "forbidden text" in an American climate, for example, that seems at times to be engaged in "scrubbing" its curriculums of anything remotely – even if unfairly posited as – controversial (Patel). On further examination I do not think this is the case. "Conrad in an Age of Social Justice" takes its nod from somewhere else: from the awareness that it really matters from where within the Conrad oeuvre one begins, fitting texts to current problems. "Heart of Darkness" has for a long time been the text where high school students or undergraduates first "meet" Conrad. But our age is also an age of terrorism, variously defined, and so with less confidence than is perhaps evident in our social-justice statements, we found ourselves in America after 2001 floundering and looking for guidance as a society to help deal with the very real threat and real consequences of terrorist bombs. In looking for one who seemed a "bomb" and terrorist expert, many turned profitably to Conrad, and to *The Secret Agent* in particular. For example, there is David Mulry's 2016 book *Joseph Conrad Among the Anarchists*. Also, there is an article in the *Wall Street Journal* from 2016, "Joseph Conrad's Relevance Today" (Meyers), and another in *The Telegraph* from 2019, "Conrad's *The Secret Agent* Predicted Our Age of Skripal and Cowardly Terrorism" (Self). It can be said, then, that reception of *The Secret Agent* changed dramatically after the 9/11 terrorist attacks of 2001 as people began to suggest a sudden heighted relevance for its terrorist subject matter (Reiss 35; Miller 44-45). Historically, the reception of his great "city" novel had always been generally good among critics (de Vries 83). F. R. Leavis singled it out for particular praise (251). William Alejandro Martin provides an overview of this critical reception (33-34). However, in terms of wider readership prior to 9/11, the public reception of the novel had always been relatively week (Brown). In any case, this recent interest in *The Secret Agent* tends to either place the novel against historical terrorist-related events more-or--less contemporary to the novel (Kilroy) or else directly juxtaposes Conrad's novelistic commentary with contemporary events (Frank).

After noticing such attention being given to *The Secret Agent* regarding terrorism and like concerns, I was curious whether or not *The Secret Agent* could also provide useful information, opinions or guidance on the topic of social justice, especially in America, where the Black Lives Matter movement and the riots in response to the death of George Floyd in 2020 had been associated with both political violence and with heightened soul-searching about social justice seen across society. What I found was that *The Secret Agent* is a veritable smorgasbord of useful and relatable information that can be discussed in class. Along with subjects including terrorism and more specifically the anarchist underground, social-justice issues are covered and discussed.

I am not the first teacher to see the interpretive potential of *The Secret Agent* with regard to issues of social justice, or to sense that the novel carries special relevance for a new generation of readers, particularly American ones. Nóra Wünsch-Nagy examines the potential for the novel to support classroom discussions of terrorism and also discussions of social justice. But these are seen as separate resources. What makes my approach different is that I discuss the two topics in connection with one-another, as part-and-parcel of each other. In this I am true to Conrad's ethical core in the narrative, and I am also engaging with the post 9/11, post George Floyd American experience, applying *The Secret Agent* here in the contemporary American landscape. In the novel, Conrad clearly tries to set the nominal concerns of the anarchists for the common people in the context of their thirst for the "slam dunk" of a violent statement made with a bomb. Conrad quietly juxtaposes this ostensible social concern with Stevie's very real sensitivities regarding the plight of the poor. It is Stevie who shows authentic concern for the plight of poor people by looking first at specific cases of evident human suffering and political vulnerability rather than using platitudes that treat "the poor" as abstract ideological principles.

Stevie is arguably central as a foil given the criticism Conrad levels at others in the novel, providing as he does a moral and ethical counterpoint to the empty posturing and violent desires of the anarchists themselves, albeit with pointed irony, since these statements and real feelings of concern for the poor, and this awareness of the real plight of the poor (Pye 33), are coming from an "idiot" (*SA* 180). Mulry discusses Stevie's ability, unique in the novel, to see the world for what it is, a "[b]ad world for poor people" (*SA* 171). Unlike Stevie, most of the characters in the novel suffer from a "subjective bias" that allows them to operate opportunely within "discourses such as bureaucracy, revolutionary ideologies, justice and progress" (Prickett 54). As Martin points out, "[t]he moral antidote in the novel to Verloc's vindictive selfishness, however, is Stevie's incorruptible morality" which "reflects both his intellectual idiocy and remarkable affective sensibility" (40). Stevie is part of Conrad's attempt to "present an alternative set of humane values distinct from bourgeois ones" (Lutz 1). Unique among the characters in the novel, he is "ethical," possessing "a finely tuned ethical sensibility grounded in compassion. His outrage over human suffering remains uncontaminated by self-interest" (12). As Richard Ambrosini points out, only Stevie seeks to always "go to the bottom of the matter," while Winnie "put her trust in face-values," and thus it is Stevie rather than Winnie "who acts as 'centre of consciousness' in the novel" (85-86).

Therefore, in considering Conrad's engagement with both terrorism on the one hand and social-justice issues on the other, I am encouraging readers to simultaneously engage with both issues just as Western society, and particularly American society, has been forced to do. Another thing is that, in reading *The Secret Agent*, one realizes that Conrad is not promoting here a simple duality of “either-or,” social justice or not, those who want it and those who don’t. Rather, what is presented in the pages of *The Secret Agent* is a kind of *danse macabre* with several participants: the perpetrators of the status quo, the anarchists who ostensibly “fight” them, and then the common sort of folks the anarchists claim to represent, and we may feel that we “see” things from each of their perspectives. But let’s start with more discussion of key terms and issues and then discuss these as they apply to *The Secret Agent*.

First, we should go a bit further with our discussion of social justice: as we have seen, *social justice* is variously defined, but usually that definition conveys the view that everyone deserves equal economic, political, and social rights and opportunities. Its proponents may, however, suggest novel, controversial or contested means of attaining these goals. The four key issues of social justice could be identified as equity, access, participation, and rights. *Social justice* had particularly though not exclusively encompassed *economic justice*, so it seems, again, an idea closely linked to Marxism in terms of the intellectual history of current ideas and suggested practices. Also, some may confuse deep suspicion about suggested ways of attaining social justice for resistance to the social-justice ideas themselves. It should also be said that social justice as pursued in the public sphere often involves the successful or attempted application of “corrective” standards and rules to the speech of others whether it be via court order, via written law, or via social pressure. Finally, *social justice*, it should be said, often appears related to ideas surrounding *political correctness*.

We should also, in this connection, identify Conradian texts that might be useful for finding intersections between Conrad and the topic of social justice (both in terms of understanding Conrad himself and with regard to social-justice issues), and we should also try to locate Conradian texts that might be useful for guiding class discussions to help further an authentic understanding of the goals, contexts, and possible outcomes of a desire for social justice. For example, we can easily place the already mentioned novel *The Secret Agent* of 1907 in the context of the short stories "An Anarchist" and "The Informer," both from 1906 and both eventually published in *A Set of Six* in 1908. To this list we can also add his great political novel *Nostromo* from 1904 and of course "Heart of Darkness" from 1899.

Now, as we consider the novel – any novel – as an avenue for examining social issues, here are the issues that I suggest could be under investigation in *The Secret Agent*:

1. Issues of personal liberty, social privilege, and equal opportunity, including Marxist conceptions of economic, political, and social rights.

2. Social unrest and violence to include anarchistic political revolution or the threat thereof.

3. The individual in crisis or the feelings of the individual in the process of soul-searching – particularly in ways that might impact social-justice ideas or outcomes. To me, this seems ultimately a question of whether the individual in crisis engages in ethical self-examination: this is where we can see Winnie as "the anarchist," as opposed to the anarchists themselves, who could be said to be motivated by perceived gain or political self-interest. Winnie lacks Stevie's inclination to look "deep into things" (*SA* 267), or in other words to see a problem and struggle ethically with it for a good while, with sincere intent.

From what I can see, then, and holding the character of Stevie to the side for a moment, we have three categories Conrad discusses: the anarchists themselves, the actual poor who are relatively helpless and at risk, and Winnie Verloc – I was tempted to call them, from Conrad's narrator's point of view, "the bad, the good, and the ugly"! Certainly, we have definitive and consistent statements Conrad's narrator makes throughout the novel which target the anarchists, revolutionary intent, and potential violence in support of Marxist or Marxist-inspired ideals (Burgoyne 156). We also have these remarkable expressions of deeply felt solidarity on the part of the author with the lower middle class of London and with the working poor of London. What is incredibly striking here is that the places where he speaks directly about anarchists mostly come in areas of the novel and in association with characters in the novel quite apart from the sections and characters involved in issues directly involving the poor – the struggling members of the socioeconomic underclass. The implication by Conrad may be that while social justice should be an issue, Marxist anarchists – while arguably self-appointing themselves to "speak" (via secret meetings and the speech of bombs) for the poor – are not really acting for or even connected with, the poor. The different novelistic real-estate given to discussions of the anarchists and discussions of the plight of the poor in the pages of *The Secret Agent* shows they are both significant issues but are really separate and not actually connected. Therefore, the poor have no one to speak for them, and that's the problem, as Conrad seems to see it. The other issue is Winnie Verloc, the true heroine of this anarchistic story. Martin, like Ellen Harrington ("Anarchist's Wife" 61; "Female Offender" 59), Pouneh Saeedi (316) and others (Oliver 222-25), and indeed, like Conrad himself (*SA* xiv-xv), finds Winnie squarely at the centre of the story and its meaning, but not exclusively so (Martin 40-41). As Ambrosini states, Winnie's tragic story is the "true centre of the tale" (85).

We should also, of course, pay close attention to Conrad's suggestion in his Author's Note to *The Secret Agent* that it was Winnie herself who was the true anarchist in the novel (*SA* xv). In any case, with regard to these three issues, the anarchists, the poor, and Winnie Verloc, we might have expected them to intersect more in the course of the novel, but they really do not, and so from that we can see that Conrad guides us to separate these issues rather than confound them. So, in terms of the question of what Conrad is messaging here, we can turn to Conrad's direct discourse in his Author's Note to *The Secret Agent*: "there had been moments [...] when I was an extreme revolutionist" (xiv). So, Conrad speaks from this point of view, providing a narrative persona imbued with both reason and feeling. This persona claims to feel the plight of the poor while talking about the contemporaneous anarchists of London, who arguably do not (the anarchists, in this narrative line, being more concerned themselves with superficially appropriating the plight of the poor into their own political agendas). In other words, though it was assumed then as now that the anarchists were working for the revolution, for social justice, Conrad saw a need for social justice and felt that anarchists were, in this regard, a scam. We could claim that in reality the anarchists in the novel were not really working, effectively working, or even working at all toward social justice happening – though social justice was, in fact, an actual need acknowledged by Conrad. And given their identity as revolutionists, in the company of each-other, the Professor, Michaelis, Ossipon, and Karl Yundt, Conrad expresses neither respect nor support for their aims or their potency. As the narrator points out: "Mr. Verloc was not devoid of intelligence – and at the notion of a menaced social order he would perhaps have winked to himself if there had not been an effort to make in that sign of scepticism" (12). First of all, regarding the anarchists in the novel, they spend their time not with the poor they claim to support, but with each other or with either the middle class or the rich, police commissioners or the likes of the old lady patroness, of whom the narrator claims: "She was not an exploiting capitalist herself; she was, as it were, above the play of economic conditions" (108).

For the Professor and Ossipon, their toast, "To the destruction of what is" (306), is a vague and general aim, lacking in specifics, while the Professor's attendant statement, "No God! No master," points directly toward a power rivalry and jealousy that does not match with or serve the plight of the masses of poor but pertains rather to the "anarchy" in the anarchists' agonistic struggle with existing authority (306). Again, the aims of the anarchists' bombing and burning is not necessarily matched to the needs of the multitude, as the Professor mocks "the hope of the weak, whose theology has invented hell for the strong" (305). He, for one, would just as soon bomb the poor as bomb the rich. At times, the Professor "lost his high spirits": "The contemplation of the multitudes thronging the pavements extinguished his assurance under a load of doubt" (305). So we see here the activities of a type of anarchist that is more motivated by personal psychological needs than by enlightened desire for social justice for the multitude, to say the least. Verloc is in it for the money, the Professor for pride; neither of them is in it to help specific members of the poor classes or even generally to help the poor – not even vaguely. And "contempt for the weak" really puts the Professor right out of the social-justice equation.

There is little evidence of balanced, reasonable or ethical action here, and their thinking, their action, or indeed their inaction, presents a case of "the end, their victory over the current sovereign government, justifies the means, violence." As Conrad, in his Author's Note, points out regarding the anarchistic mentality of the time: "perverse unreason has its own logical processes" (x). So for Conrad's bombers, or would-be bombers, a lack of rationality is an issue, and anarchistic political revolution seems evidence of personal megalomania on the part of its proponents. Indeed, one sees no actual plan here for "The Future of the Proletariat" (26). As Conrad states in his Author's Note:

> I remember, however, remarking on the criminal futility of the whole thing, doctrine, action, mentality; and on the contemptible aspect of the half-crazy pose as of a brazen cheat exploiting the poignant miseries and passionate credulities of a mankind always so tragically eager for self-destruction. That was what made for me its philosophical pretences so unpardonable. (ix-x)

But then, "life doesn't stand much looking into," if we go with Winnie Verloc's "tragic suspicion" (xiii). She is "a person disinclined to look under the surface of things" (185). We also know that Winnie's philosophy is consistent with "not taking notice of the inside of facts" (154), and we are told that she "always refrained from looking deep into things" (267). Yet, "[s]he had an equable soul" (177). As Conrad states in his Author's Note to *The Secret Agent*: "At last the story of Winnie Verloc stood out complete from the days of her childhood to the end, unproportioned as yet, with everything still on the first plane as it were; but ready now to be dealt with" (xii). So, in a fundamental sense, *The Secret Agent* can be said to be about not anarchists per se, but about this representative and archetypal anarchist, this model anarchist, Winnie Verloc. She becomes the unconventional but essential anarchist standard against which the "anarchists," the Professor, Michaelis, Ossipon, and Karl Yundt, can be measured and shown to be shams. The entire book is really about Winnie in her humanity and what she represents, there in her squalid surroundings, helping us contextualize the fact that she was "confirmed in her instinctive conviction that things don't bear looking into very much" (180). And so *The Secret Agent*, while it certainly covers the anarchists who fall under the disdainful eye of Conrad's narrator, is really meant to be about Winnie, even as it is titled after her husband, the secret agent. As Conrad states in his Author's Note:

> *This* book is *that* story, reduced to manageable proportions, its whole course suggested and centred round the absurd cruelty of the Greenwich Park explosion. I had there a task I will not say arduous but of the most absorbing difficulty. But it had to be done. It was a necessity. The figures grouped about Mrs. Verloc and related directly or indirectly to her tragic suspicion that "life doesn't stand much looking into," are the outcome of that very necessity. Personally I have never had any doubt of the reality of Mrs. Verloc's story; but it had to be disengaged from its obscurity in that immense town, it had to be made credible, I don't mean so much as to her soul but as to her surroundings, not so much as to her psychology but as to her humanity. (xii-xiii)

Beyond Winnie, we might also say that the novel is centred on the struggles of the people, but it also deals definitively with the curiously separate actions and inactions of the self-styled and self-serving "anarchists" in the story, who make so much noise, literally and figuratively. The noise is just noise, and games, and perhaps bombs, but the struggle of the poor people is real. The novel shows us that. And in terms of the necessity to tell Winnie's story, to "deal with that subject" (viii), it is easy to agree with Conrad that "it had to be done" (xii). It certainly allows us to make sincere social-justice observations beyond the platitudes of the anarchists themselves. As Conrad notes: "I do not regret having written it ... still I will submit that telling Winnie Verloc's story to its anarchistic end of utter desolation, madness, and despair, and telling it as I have told it here, I have not intended to commit a gratuitous outrage on the feelings of mankind" (xiv-xv). As for Winnie, "[s]he felt profoundly that things do not stand much looking into" (177). But, as George Panichas points out, "[m]oral responsibility and moral action require effort of attention and decision" (5-6), and so Conrad's story of Winnie can be seen as a criticism of those who, like Mrs. Verloc, casually and habitually avoid "taking notice of the inside of facts" (*SA* 154). In telling the truth to its "bare bones" (xv), Conrad did intend to commit an outrage as he saw it, but it was not gratuitous; rather, it was purposeful: London is also his extended metaphor for the human condition – the human comedy – of fools acting like fools (or rather failing to act). With some irony, Winnie Verloc is the "only" anarchist, the "true" anarchist, and her position of "never look too deeply into things" ends up being shown to be what it is: a recipe for disaster.

And then there is Stevie. Though ironically handicapped in his cognitive abilities, he is arguably the only deep, or undistracted, thinker among the characters in the novel, and therefore he would be the real "social-justice warrior" opposite the anarchists: A social-justice warrior with clenched fists (187). Here we can point to Stevie's sensitivity and anger at the plight of the poor (187-88), generally and as a reaction to specific examples he is presented with, specific examples others seem so used to seeing that they do not react. Stevie hates cruelty (60) and has compassion for the poor (9-10). He reacts with violent anguish to tales of injustice and oppression. He feels a powerless, "pitiless rage" (169) and sees the "bad world" (171). And as for the Professor, Michaelis, Ossipon, and Karl Yundt, their anarchistic but always future fight is about sovereignty, bull against bull, with the poor as muted spectators ostensibly spoken for by anyone, and perhaps everyone, else. Short of something akin to a medieval bread riot, few things speak for the unrepresented poor. But with Stevie, and beyond the "virtue signalling" of the anarchists, Conrad points out that the plight of the poor is real and not entirely of their own making (184-85).

With regard to teaching *The Secret Agent*, this aspect of the novel, this view of the real plight of the poor, proves to be its most universal observation, indicating a social-justice issue as relevant in our own time as it was in 1907, and as students read the novel over several days, class discussion can focus in a rolling way on the political issues presented in the first pages, the domestic drama and our important introduction to Stevie in the middle of the novel, and then can focus on Winnie's end of "utter desolation, madness and despair" (xv). Nodes of particular interest for class discussion include the anarchists, the poor, Winnie as the "true centre of the tale" and Stevie as "centre of consciousness" in the novel (Ambrosini 85-86). The essay that the students write on *The Secret Agent* will come out of their guided reading and class discussion and will test their ability to engage with and relate to the issues in the novel. After first assigning the novel, and while they are reading the initial pages as homework, the students can view and discuss videos about the social-justice movement and also recent as well as historical videos about terrorist activities, particularly in Paris, New York, and London, thus providing the students some context and background knowledge as they prepare to engage with the text of *The Secret Agent*. Eventual discussion of the text itself can focus on statements made by Michaelis, Ossipon, and the Professor. The issues the students can be asked to think about while reading can include the concept of social justice both locally and globally and the political concept of anarchy:

- Where does social justice "end" and terrorism "begin"?
- Is terrorism mistakenly tied up with social-justice movements or is it an integral part of them?
- Is Stevie in the story a kind of unappreciated "court jester" who can speak truth to power, a fool who can instruct the wise?

We might say that Stevie is someone the wise would be wise to listen to if they would gain true insight about and understanding of the thing at hand: the need for social justice at each local level of society. Part of the irony suggested strongly to the reader is that "no one listens" except the narrator, and, hopefully, the reader. Stevie serves as the "centre of consciousness" in the novel, and the narrator affords us, by his commentary on the self-interest and myopia of the other characters, the opportunity to go with Stevie on a kind of guided journey of ethical self-examination, vicariously, and this is exactly in my view the point of the novel, and this is exactly the aspect of the novel where I like to engage students. I begin with a prompt: "Read *The Secret Agent* and think about the issues raised in terms of anarchy on the one hand and social justice as a goal of society on the other. Develop some informed opinions around these issues and use them to generate a thesis regarding the meaning of the novel."

As a result of having shared this experience with my students here at Middle Georgia State University, I would say that *The Secret Agent* should be considered a very important literary text for teaching Conrad at American universities. The success of this method of thus engaging students with social-justice issues germane to the novel is evident in the thoughtful and mature new writing they produce and in the very personal engagement they demonstrate with the issues in the story. I feel that Conrad's approach to the issues in the novel was a key element in each student's own social-justice journey. Reading and then writing about *The Secret Agent* helped my students develop their own ideas about social justice and express them effectively in an essay. It has proven to be an enjoyable as well as an engrossing class activity that encourages deeper engagement with issues and ideas, builds confidence and helps students identify, develop, and express opinions. It can also serve as a great introduction to Conrad as a writer and thinker and as a "jumping off point" for engagement with other works within Conrad's oeuvre.

WORKS CITED

Achebe, Chinua. "An Image of Africa." *The Massachusetts Review* 18 (1977): 782-94.

Ambrosini, Richard. "*The Secret Agent*: An Anti-Classic." *Anglistica Pisana* 12.1-2 (2015): 79-89.

Aquinas, Thomas. *Commentary on Aristotle's Nicomachean Ethics*. Trans. C. I. Litzinger. Dumb Ox/St. Augustine P, 1993.

Aristotle. *The Nicomachean Ethics*. Trans. Robert C. Bartlett and Susan D. Collins. U of Chicago P, 2011.

Behr, Thomas. *Social Justice and Subsidiarity: Luigi Taparelli and the Origins of Modern Catholic Social Thought*. Catholic University of America P, 2019.

Brown, Jonathan. "Conrad, the Literary Outsider Ignored by his Adopted Country." *Independent* 3 Dec. 2007: 18.

Burgoyne, Mary. "Conrad Among the Anarchists: Documents on Martial Bourdin and the Greenwich Bombing." Simmons and Stape 147-85.

Capeheart, Loretta, and Dragan Milovanovic. *Social Justice: Theories, Issues, and Movements*. Rutgers UP, 2020.

Ceatha, Nerilee, Paula Mayock, Jim Campbell, Chris Noone, and Kath Browne. "The Power of Recognition: A Qualitative Study of Social Connectedness and Wellbeing through LGBT Sporting, Creative and Social Groups in Ireland." *Health and Wellbeing in Sexual Orientation and Gender Identity*. Ed. Catherine Meads. MDPI, 2020. 1-18.

Compare, Christian, and Cinzia Albanesi. "Belief, Attitude and Critical Understanding: A Systematic Review of Social Justice in Service-Learning Experiences." *Journal of Community and Applied Social Psychology* 12 July 2022. Accessed 10 Jan. 2023. Stable URL: <https://doi.org/10.1002/casp.2639>.

Dewey, John. "Education and Social Change." *The Later Works of John Dewey*. Vol. 11. Southern Illinois UP, 1987. 408-17.

Frank, Michael C. "Terrorism for the Sake of Counterterrorism: Undercover Policing and the Specter of the Agent Provocateur in Joseph Conrad's *The Secret Agent*." *Conradiana* 46 (2014): 151-77.

Harrington, Ellen Burton. "The Anarchist's Wife: Joseph Conrad's Debt to Sensation Fiction in *The Secret Agent*." *Conradiana* 36 (2004): 51-64.

---. "The Female Offender, the New Woman, and Winnie Verloc in *The Secret Agent*." Simmons and Stape 57-69.

Kilroy, Gerard. "*The Secret Agent*: A Far from Simple Tale." *Yearbook of Conrad Studies (Poland)* 13 (2018): 55-64.

Leavis, F. R. *The Great Tradition*. Penguin, 1977.

Lepine, David. "Cathedrals and Charity: Almsgiving at English Secular Cathedrals in the Later Middle Ages." *The English Historical Review* 126 (2011): 1066-96.

Lutz, John. "A Rage for Order: Fetishism, Self-Betrayal, and Exploitation in *The Secret Agent*." *Conradiana* 40 (2008): 1-24.

Martin, William Alejandro. "'For perverse unreason has its own logical processes': Masochism and Redemption in *The Secret Agent* (1907)." *Conradiana* 36 (2004): 33-50.

"Message on World Day of Social Justice." *Department of Economic and Social Affairs Sustainable Development.* United Nations. Accessed 10 Jan. 2023. Stable URL: <https://sdgs.un.org/statements/message-world-day-social-justice- 10379>.

Meyers, Jeffrey. "Joseph Conrad's Relevance Today." *The Wall Street Journal* 19 July 2016. Accessed 10 Jan. 2023. Stable URL: <https://www.wsj.com/articles/joseph-conrads-relevance-today-1468967215>.

Miller, John J. "Dawn of the Terror Era." *National Review* 68.18. 10 Oct. 2016. Accessed 10 Jan. 2023. StableURL:<https://search.ebscohost.com/login.aspx?direct=true&AuthType=ip,shib&db=rgm&AN=118268192&site=e-host-live&scope=site>.

Mulry, David. "The Anarchist in the House: The Politics of Conrad's *The Secret Agent*." Simmons and Stape 1-12.

---. *Joseph Conrad Among the Anarchists.* Palgrave Macmillan, 2016.

Oliver, Matthew. "Conrad's Grotesque Public: Pornography and the Politics of Reading in *The Secret Agent*." *Twentieth Century Literature* 55 (2009): 209-31.

Paine, Thomas. *The Rights of Man, Common Sense and Other Political Writings.* Oxford UP, 2009.

Panichas, George Andrew. *Joseph Conrad: His Moral Vision.* Mercer UP, 2005.

Patel, Vimal. "A Lecturer Showed a Painting of the Prophet Muhammad. She Lost Her Job." *New York Times* 8 Jan. 2022. Accessed 10 Jan. 2023. Stable URL: <https://www.proquest.com/blogs-podcasts-websites/lecturer-showed-painting-prophet-muhammad-she/docview/2761616088/se-2?accountid=12418>.

Plato. *The Republic.* Trans. Desmond Lee. 2nd ed. Penguin, 2007.

Prickett, David. "No Escape: Liberation and the Ethics of Self-Governance in *The Secret Agent*." Simmons and Stape 49-56.

Pye, Patricia. "A City that 'disliked to be disturbed': London's Soundscape in *The Secret Agent*." Simmons and Stape 21-35.

Reiss, Tom. "The True Classic of Terrorism." *New York Times* 11 Sept. 2005. Accessed 10 Jan. 2023. Stable URL: <https://www.proquest.com/magazines/true-classic-terrorism/docview/217318469/se-2>.

Saeedi, Pouneh. "Winnie Verloc: A Case of 'Female Malady' in *The Secret Agent*." *Canadian Review of Comparative Literature* 45 (2018): 315-27.

Self, Will. "Conrad's *The Secret Agent* Predicted Our Age of Skripal and Cowardly Terrorism." *The Telegraph* 21 Apr. 2019. Accessed 10 Jan. 2023. Stable URL: <https://www.telegraph.co.uk/books/authors/conrads-secret-agent-predicted-age-skripal-cowardly-terrorism/>.

Simmons, Allan, and J. H. Stape, eds. The Secret Agent: *Centennial Essays.* Rodopi, 2007.

"Social Justice and Civic Engagement." *Campus Life.* Bronx Community College. Accessed 10 Jan. 2023. Stable URL: <http://www.bcc.cuny.edu/campus-life/student-life/campus-diversity/social-justice-civic-engagement/>.

"Social Justice in an Open World." *UN-iLibrary*. United Nations, 2006. 1-146. Accessed 10 Jan. 2023. Stable URL: <https://doi.org/10.18356/56bfb5b6-en>.

Taparelli, Luigi. "Analisi critica dei primi concetti dell'Economia sociale." *Civiltà Cattolica* series III, 8 (1857): 546–59.

Vries, Jetty de, and J. A. Verleun. *Conrad's* The Secret Agent *and the Critics, 1965-1980*. Bouma's Boekhuis, 1984.

Weigert, Kathleen Maas. "Social Justice: Historical and Theoretical Considerations." *International Encyclopedia of the Social and Behavioral Sciences*. Ed. James D. Wright. 2nd ed. Vol 22. Elsevier, 2015. 397-400.

"World Day of Social Justice 2017." *Department of Economic and Social Affairs, Social Inclusion*. United Nations. Accessed 10 Jan. 2023. Stable URL: <https://www.un.org/development/desa/dspd/international-days/world- day-of-social-justice/world-day-of-social-justice-2017.html>.

Wünsch-Nagy, Nóra. "*The Secret Agent* in the English Classroom." *Helbling Readers Blog*. 11 Apr. 2018. Accessed 10 Jan. 2023. Stable URL: <https://www.helbling.com/int/en/blog/the-secret-agent-in-the-english-classroom>.

Published volumes of the series
Conrad: Eastern and Western Perspectives
Editor: Wiesław Krajka

I 1992 Carabine, Keith, Owen Knowles, and Wiesław Krajka, eds. *Conrad's Literary Career*

II 1993 Carabine, Keith, Owen Knowles, and Wiesław Krajka, eds. *Contexts for Conrad*

III 1994 Morzinski, Mary. *Linguistic Influence of Polish on Joseph Conrad's Style*

IV 1995 Lothe, Jakob, ed. *Conrad in Scandinavia*

V 1996 Kurczaba, Alex S., ed. *Conrad and Poland*

VI 1998 Carabine, Keith, Owen Knowles, with Paul Armstrong, eds. *Conrad, James and Other Relations*

VII 1998 Davis, Laura L., ed. *Conrad's Century: The Past and Future Splendour*

VIII 1999 Krajka, Wiesław, ed. *Joseph Conrad: East European, Polish and Worldwide*

IX 2000 Lucas, Michael, A. *Aspects of Conrad's Literary Language*

X 2001 Fincham, Gail, Attie de Lange, with Wiesław Krajka, eds. *Conrad at the Millennium: Modernism, Postmodernism, Postcolonialism*

XI 2002 Lange, Attie de, Gail Fincham, with Wiesław Krajka, eds. *Conrad in Africa: New Essays on "Heart of Darkness"*

XII 2003 Carabine, Keith, and Max Saunders, eds. *Inter-Relations: Conrad, James, Ford and Others*

XIII 2004 Krajka, Wiesław, ed. *A Return to the Roots: Conrad, Poland and East-Central Europe*

XIV 2005 Krajka, Wiesław, ed. *Beyond the Roots: The Evolution of Conrad's Ideology and Art*

XV 2006 Paccaud-Huguet, Josiane, ed. *Conrad in France*

XVI 2007 Gőbel, Walter, Hans Ulrich Seeber, and Martin Windisch, eds. *Conrad in Germany*

XVII 2008 Bobrowski, Tadeusz. *A Memoir of My Life*. Trans. and ed. Addison Bross

XVIII 2009 Krajka, Wiesław, ed. *Joseph Conrad: Between Literary Techniques and Their Messages*

XIX 2010 Krajka, Wiesław, ed. *In the Realms of Biography, Literature, Politics and Reception: Polish and East-Central European Joseph Conrad*

XX 2011 Sokołowska, Katarzyna. *Conrad and Turgenev: Towards the Real*

XXI 2012 Acheraïou, Amar, and Nursel Içőz, eds. *Joseph Conrad and the Orient*

XXII 2013 Krajka, Wiesław, ed. *From Szlachta Culture to the 21st Century, Between East and West. New Essays on Joseph Conrad's Polishness*

XXIII 2014 Krajka, Wiesław, ed. *"Wine in Old and New Bottles": Critical Paradigms for Joseph Conrad*

XXIV 2015 Curreli, Mario, ed. *Conrad in Italy*

XXV 2016 Brodsky, G. W. Stephen. *Joseph Conrad's Polish Soul. Realms of Memory and Self.* Ed. George Z. Gasyna

XXVI 2017 Maisonnat, Claude. *Joseph Conrad and the Voicing of Textuality*

XXVII 2018 Krajka, Wiesław, ed. *Joseph Conrad's Authorial Self: Polish and Other*

XXVIII 2019 Krajka, Wiesław, ed. *Some Intertextual Chords of Joseph Conrad's Literary Art*

XXIX 2020 Krajka, Wiesław, ed. *Various Dimensions of the Other in Joseph Conrad's Fiction*

XXX 2021 Acheraïou, Amar, and Laëtitia Crémona, eds. *Joseph Conrad and Ethics*

XXXI 2022 Pawlowski, Merry M. *Joseph Conrad and Material Culture: From the Rise of the Commodity Transcendent to the Scramble for Africa*

XXXII 2023 Kujawska-Lis, Ewa, ed. *Joseph Conrad's Texts and Intertexts. In Honour of Professor Wiesław Krajka*